DATE DUE

S0-ABZ-869

DATE DUE

JAN 10 1991			
	DEC 19 1990		

Demco, Inc. 38-293

75
76
77
141-143
166-167
320-326

The Demand for Money

This book is part of the
WORLD SERIES IN ECONOMICS
E. E. Liebhafsky, *Consulting Editor*

Other books in this series

The Demand for Money

WILLIAM J. FRAZER, JR.
University of Florida

THE WORLD PUBLISHING COMPANY
CLEVELAND AND NEW YORK

To Will

PREFACE

The subject—the demand for money—came to the forefront of monetary economics in the late 1950's and early and mid-1960's. References to the subject, as a somewhat distinct area of study, appear in earlier monetary literature, but recent work is particularly distinguished by references to "the demand for money," by emphasis upon the possible identification of empirical demand functions for money, by the desire to advance economics as an empirical science, by the stability of elasticity coefficients, and by the intensive utilization of the computer in analyses of masses of data, including time-series, cross-section, aggregative, and sectoral data. All of this has meant that various aspects of monetary theory were being tested, evaluated, and pinned down empirically, rather than that monetary theory was being negated. The empirical developments have been particularly interesting in view of the explicit introduction of monetary analysis (theory) and of prospects such as (a) that of exercising some indirect control over the economy generally through control of the factors found to impinge upon the demand for money in the aggregate, by sectors, and by businesses and other units, and (b) that of focusing upon broad aspects of the performance of the entire economy through emphasis upon the demand for money.

Articles and essays by both academic and Federal Reserve economists on the demand for money continue to proliferate, even as this preface is written. Furthermore, additional literature has evolved on the supply side of the market for money. Doubtless, these developments will stimulate further interest in our subject and add to its quality. I have, nevertheless, been motivated to prepare this book for publication at this time, in part with the view to bringing the demand-for-money work to date into perspective, and in part with the view to recording my own assessment of the developments to date concerning the literature on the demand for money.

The material in this book was originally presented in summary form to a group of economists in November 1965 at the Deauville Hotel, Miami Beach, Florida. The summary paper was entitled "Multiple Regression Analyses of the Demand for Money in the United States," but aspects of the demand for money other than the multiple regression results were dealt with. The initial paper was an outgrowth of the summer portion of my study as a science faculty fellow (NSF), the University of Pennsylvania in 1964–65. The final writing of the book was facilitated by a research appointment for the summer of 1966 by the Graduate School, University of Florida.

A number of individuals contributed to the development of the book: Professor J. W. Wilson of North Carolina State University served as a most helpful reader on the manuscript in its preliminary stages; Professor Montgomery D. Anderson of the University of Florida collaborated in the preparation of the appendix to Chapter 2 and the glossary of statistical terms at the end of the book; Professor William P. Yohe of Duke University read the proofs for Chapter 8; Professor Allan H. Meltzer of Carnegie Institute of Technology made available some prepublication copies of manuscripts, and read the galley proofs on Appendix to Chapter 6; and Prof./Dr. H. G. Bieri, editor of *Schweizerische Zeitschrift für Volkswirtschaft und Statistik*, gave permission for the use of parts of one of my articles, "The Demand for Money, Statistical Results and Monetary Policy." Messrs. John A. Doukas and Larry R. Mote, colleagues at the Federal Reserve Bank of Chicago, were also helpful—Mr. Doukas discussed and reviewed portions of the literature involving topics in Chapters 9 and 10, and Mr. Mote read entire sets of proofs.

I wish, in particular, to express my appreciation to all of the individuals and institutions who are mentioned above. I wish, further, to absolve them from any responsibility for commissions and omissions.

Chicago, Illinois
May 1967

WILLIAM J. FRAZER, JR.

CONTENTS

ix

Chapter 1

INTRODUCTION

This book is about the demand for money—monetary analysis (theory), and results from analyses of time-series, cross-section, aggregative, and sectoral data. The data are for the most part those for the United States economy. Although various aspects of the demand for money are dealt with, the emphasis is on the vast output from statistical analyses in the late 1950's and early and mid-1960's. The empirical studies mainly have been by American economists, doubtless as a continuing reflection of the empirical tradition in American economics generally, beginning with Thorstein Veblen (1857–1929) and continuing on through Wesley C. Mitchell (1874–1948) and the National Bureau of Economic Research (1918–   ). It is more than coincidence that the parent of the recent outpouring of empirical literature on the demand for money—namely, Milton Friedman—had early ties with the empirical tradition in the United States, and that the National Bureau of Economic Research published his monumental work (with Anna Jacobson Schwartz)[1] as well as some of his other works.[2]

The present book is more than a survey of analysis (theory) and statistical results concerning the demand for money. It is a survey with a point of view involving several elements. These include the following: (1) statistical analyses (mainly, regression

---

[1] Milton Friedman and Anna Jacobson Schwartz, *A Monetary History of the United States, 1867–1960* (Princeton University Press, for the National Bureau of Economic Research, 1963).

[2] See, e.g., Milton Friedman, "The Demand for Money: Some Theoretical and Empirical Results," *Journal of Political Economy*, August 1959. This article was approved for publication as a report of the National Bureau of Economic Research.

and correlation analyses) alone are inadequate for dealing with questions concerning the determinants of the demand for money and causation (such as whether changes in the demand for money in relation to assets or income cause interest rates to change or vice versa), at least as evidenced by the present state of statistical work in monetary economics; (2) the consistency of a theory with the empirical evidence and the evidence concerning the test of a theory or hypothesis against alternatives are of importance in establishing the economic relevance of particular theories or hypotheses; and (3) effort is called for to identify the more consistent sets of hypotheses and statistical results, and to assess, finally, the over-all meaning and the significance of the statistical results for monetary policy and for monetary economics.

In Chapter 2 we review antecedents to the more contemporary monetary studies dealing with demand functions for money. We also introduce some regression results and notions concerning statistical demand functions, and then review measures of the velocity of money and some facts about the behavior of the velocity of money in the United States. These include some facts about velocity for the economy as a whole and sectoral velocities. A portion of Selden's work on sectoral velocities[3] is introduced, mainly as a means of dealing with the method for relating sectoral velocities to the over-all measures.

Chapter 3 consists of an outline of the evolutionary strands of monetary analysis concerning the demand for money. The emphasis is upon the testable hypotheses implicit in the mainstream of monetary theory. Other relevant aspects of monetary theory, which have not yet found widespread acceptability in the textbook literature, are introduced in subsequent chapters, as appropriate occasions arise.

In Chapter 4 we reintroduce liquidity-preference analysis of the demand for money, review the empirical evidence concerning the liquidity-preference function, the liquidity trap, and all that. This review involves a modified statement of the liquidity-preference

---

[3] Richard T. Selden, "The Postwar Rise in the Velocity of Money: A Sectoral Analysis," *Journal of Finance*, December 1961. This article was approved for publication by the National Bureau of Economic Research.

model, and anticipates the immediately succeeding Chapter 5 on the velocity-interest rate association and some alternative explanations for the association. In Chapter 6 we review elements of theory and statistical results concerning stable demand relations. An appendix to Chapter 6 deals with some measurement procedures and other special aspects of this latter study, including a review of Allan Meltzer's statement of the monetary theory implicit in Milton Friedman's monetary history.

Chapters 7, 8, and 9 deal with analyses and statistical results most closely aligned with specific sectors of the economy—including, in particular, the corporate manufacturing and household sectors. The analyses and statistical results concerning these sectors have implications for selected aspects of monetary theory and the latter's application to the respective sectors. In Chapter 8, the widely cited works by Baumol and Tobin on the transactions demand for cash[4] are treated in connection with the business sector, in part because writers dealing empirically with the notions attributed to Baumol and Tobin view the notions as being primarily related to business firms, particularly firms dealing in government securities and related investments. The hypotheses attributed to Baumol and Tobin are tested against alternatives.

Portions of Chapters 6, 9, and 10 introduce some notions about lagged relations between time series for the money stock, income, interest rates, and so on. Chapter 10, in fact, deals almost exclusively with the notion of adjustment lags between "desired" and actual holdings of money balances in response to changes in such variables as the rate of interest.

Chapters 11 and 12 are in large part reviews. In Chapter 11, in particular, we review some statistical results and seek to do the following: pull together certain notions about monetary policy and the effects of changes in monetary policy; to assess the relevance of certain notions about monetary policy; recognize the need for explicit, analytically useful, and, hopefully, operational

---

[4] William J. Baumol, "The Transactions Demand for Cash: An Inventory Theoretic Approach," *Quarterly Journal of Economics,* November 1952; and James Tobin, "The Interest-Elasticity of Transactions Demand for Cash," *Review of Economics and Statistics,* August 1956.

definitions of monetary policy; suggest some indicators of changes in monetary policy; and evaluate some significant aspects of the selection of certain indicators.

Some of the questions dealt with in this book are as follows: (1) whether the elasticity coefficients for the demand for money with respect to interest rates, income, and wealth are greater than, equal to, or less than one; (2) whether the liquidity trap exists or whether such a trap was evidenced in the 1930's in the United States; (3) whether changes in the stock of money as a proportion of income (assets or other substitute measures) occur in response to interest-rate changes or vice versa; (4) whether a ceiling on the velocity of money exists; (5) whether the stock of money broadly defined to include time deposits (as well as currency and demand deposits) provides a more stable demand relation; (6) whether the relationship between money variously defined and its determinants is stable; (7) whether the empirical definition of money should be broadened to include time deposits, as indicated by the results from regressing the money stock defined narrowly, and then broadly, on given sets of variables; (8) whether regression results indicate a form of switching between money narrowly defined and time or savings-type deposits; (9) whether there are economies of size or wealth or "luxury" effects on the demand for money; (10) whether changes in the rate of interest contribute to switching between cash and bonds or reflect switching between broader classes of assets, including assets with a residual claim against future income such as plant and equipment; (11) whether changes in noncash sources of liquidity relative to income (or substitute measures) affect the demand for money relative to income, and so on; (12) whether differences in manufacturing industries' demands for cash can be explained by differences in firm sizes; (13) whether lagged relations between time series for the money stock, interest rates, and so on reflect lags in the adjustment in holdings of money balances to changes in interest rates and so on; (14) whether increasing the money stock at a relatively faster rate during a period of rising interest rates will contribute to a reduction in interest rates; (15) whether changes in monetary policy as revealed by changes in the rate of interest will exert a direct causal effect upon holdings of money balances in relation to income; (16) whether the rate of interest may properly be included as a determinant of the velocity of money along with such determinants as the rate of change in prices; and (17) whether over-all statistical results are consistent with the broad underlying foundations of monetary economics.

Chapter 2

SOME ANTECEDENTS TO EMPIRICAL
STUDIES OF THE EARLY AND MID-1960's

Regression analyses concerning the demand for money began to appear in the late 1930's and mid-1940's. There were others in the mid-1950's, and the outpouring of regression results accelerated sharply in the early 1960's, as the computer became involved as a means of handling masses of data. There also evolved in these later years additional tests, methods, and clarifications to help in the evaluation of the significance of regression results based on time-series data in particular. There were, however, antecedents to these more contemporary analyses of the demand for money, both in monetary theory and in the organization of data and in the reporting of basic facts about changes in income in relation to the stock of money.

On the monetary-theory side, the quantity-theory approach to the study of the demand for money was predominant. Prior to the 1930's this approach emphasized the relation between the average of prices and the money stock rather than the causes governing changes in the velocity of money, as indicated by changes in the ratio of income to the stock of money (i.e., $V = Y/M$), and as implicitly defined by such equations as $PQ = MV$, where income (Y) is a flow variable, defined in one way or another, the money stock (M) is a stock variable, also defined in one way or another, and money income is the product of the average of the prices (P) being considered and the real income or output (Q). In referring to this change in emphasis in the quantity-theory approach, a former Federal Reserve Bank president and later United States Senator commented as follows, on the occasion of some 1957 Congressional hearings:

> I am glad to see now that they have come around to recording velocity, and I am interested to see the significance that you [W.

Randolph Burgess, former Undersecretary of the Treasury] have given it in your testimony to date, since I am a velocity fan.

It seems to me that too little attention has been given to the question of why money moves fast at some times and moves slowly at others. And it is the element of the *MV* side of the equation that is more or less mysterious. We find it, but so far as I have been able to observe, we do not endeavor to predict it or to know what to do about it or whether we want to do anything about it, as we do about the *M*, we focus on the amount of money and then watch the *V*.

We deal with these evolutionary aspects of monetary theory since the early 1930's in the next chapter, with emphasis on the demand for money. In the present chapter, we introduce some of the immediate antecedents of more contemporary analyses of the demand for money. We also mention the more prominent econometric problems and regression criteria involved in the interpretation of regression results in subsequent chapters, and introduce some basic facts and some possible explanations of changes in the velocity of money. The various topics of the present chapter—particularly the antecedents, the methods and problems, the basic facts about changes in the velocity of money, and possible explanations of the facts—are, for the most part, rather lightly treated, mainly in anticipation of future chapters.

2.1 ANTECEDENTS

In the late 1930's A. J. Brown, a Britisher, published the regression results he derived concerning the demand for money.[1] In 1945 Kisselgoff presented his results,[2] and in 1954 those of Latané[3]

---

[1] See, e.g., A. J. Brown, "Interest, Prices, and the Demand Schedule for Idle Money," *Oxford Economic Papers*, No. 2, May 1939, reprinted in T. Wilson and P. W. S. Andrews, eds., *Oxford Studies in the Price Mechanism* (London: Oxford University Press, 1951), pp. 31–51.

[2] Avram Kisselgoff, "Liquidity Preference of Large Manufacturing Corporations," *Econometrica*, October 1945, pp. 334–344.

[3] Henry Allen Latané, "Cash Balances and the Interest Rate—A Pragmatic Approach," *Review of Economics and Statistics*, November 1954, pp. 456–460.

were published; both were subsequently widely quoted. In 1956 a host of results due to the workshop in money and banking at the University of Chicago appeared in a volume edited by Friedman.[4] The Brown and Kisselgoff studies were in large measure motivated by Keynesian liquidity-preference analysis, as outlined in Secs. 3.3 and 4.1 of this book. Both Brown and Kisselgoff dealt with an arbitrary distinction between so-called idle and active balances, as outlined in Sec. 4.1, and both found a relationship between the velocity of money and the rate of interest, as implied by the orthodox Keynesian analysis. Brown, in particular, also introduced other possible determinants of the demand for money, including the preceding year's change in the average of prices as a measure of expectations of appreciation or depreciation in the purchasing power of money, but many later analysts ignored this prospect (Sec. 4.1). Latané, in his initial work, also found a covariation in the velocity of money and the rate of interest, and later he attempted to explain this in terms of a form of switching from cash into bonds as the transactions demand for cash declined in response to increases in the rate of interest (Sec. 5.1).

In the work edited by Friedman, many variables were dealt with, e.g.,

$$V = f\left(r_b, r_e, \frac{1}{P}\frac{dP}{dt}, w, Y/P, u\right)$$

where r_b is the rate of interest on bonds,

r_e is the rate of interest on equities,

$\frac{1}{P}\frac{dP}{dt}$ is the rate of change in prices[5] and is interpreted as the expected rate of price rise,

w is the ratio of total income from nonhuman wealth to total income from human wealth,

Y/P is real income (Y alone serving as an index of wealth), and

---

[4] Milton Friedman, ed., *Studies in the Quantity Theory of Money* (Chicago: University of Chicago Press, 1956).

[5] Here prices are viewed as a function of time, $P(t)$, and $\frac{d[\ln P(t)]}{dt} = \frac{1}{P}\frac{dP}{dt}$ by logarithmic differentiation and the composite function rule.

u stands for any variable that can be expected to affect tastes and preferences.[6]

The over-all findings, however, supported mainly the inclusion of Y/P, the interest rate(s), and, with some exceptions, the rate of change in prices.

2.2 METHODS AND PROBLEMS

On the methodological side, these early studies involved correlation coefficients, coefficients of determination, regression coefficients, *t*-tests, standard errors of the regression coefficients, total correlations in multiple regressions, partial correlation coefficients, partial regression coefficients, and a test for autocorrelation in the residual error terms, all as defined in the glossary of statistical terms in this book. Brown, in particular, made special effort to deal with the problem of correlation due to the trend in the variables, and both Brown and Kisselgoff suggested that they had identified liquidity-preference schedules (Sec. 4.1).

The problem of identification of an actual schedule (or function) looms large in the literature on demand functions for money, though certainly not so large as in econometrics generally. The problem, as dealt with in somewhat greater detail in the appendix to this chapter, concerns simultaneous-equations bias and the identification of a supply and/or a demand relation from empirical observations in a time series. In the case of the analysis of cross-section data—i.e., data for a given period of time or at a given moment in time—the supply conditions may be taken as given, and observed points may be designated by the stock of money $\overline{M}_d$ held in relation to wealth $\overline{W}$ (or total assets), such as $(\overline{M}_d, \overline{W})_1$, $(\overline{M}_d, \overline{W})_2, \ldots, (\overline{M}_d, \overline{W})_n$. These points, further, may be taken as raw data for a demand relation, and cross-section estimates may approximate long-run parameter values.[7] In the case of changes over time and the analysis of time-series data, however,

[6] Friedman, "The Quantity Theory of Money—A Restatement," *Studies in the Quantity Theory of Money* (Chicago: University of Chicago Press, 1956), p. 11.

[7] See Allan H. Meltzer, "Reply," *Quarterly Journal of Economics*, February 1965, p. 164.

the supply conditions are not given as constant, and an effort must be made to specify whether the observations reflect some sort of mongrel set of supply and demand relationships or whether the relationships can be separated. In the case of the demand for money, in particular, there is a set of prospects:[8] namely, that the demand function is a reasonably stable function of some set of variables such as income (Y) and the rate of interest (r); that changes in credit conditions and monetary policy are reflected in changes in the rate of interest as a first approximation (and perhaps the velocity of money, too, since changes in velocity reflect disproportionate changes in the money stock and income); and that over time the money-supply function moves so as to trace out a set of coordinates that constitute a demand function $f(Y, r)$, $r = $ constant, and/or a function $f(Y, r)$, $Y = $ constant. The supply may or may not always vary at the same rate as income or wealth, but any such imbalances may be reflected in the rate of interest, another determinant of demand, so that a demand function is still identified.

To support the use of the velocity of money (V_1) as a substitute variable for the rate of interest (r) and as an indicator of changes in monetary policy, after allowance for effect of currency and time deposit drains on the money supply, regression results such as the following have been reported:

(all series seasonally adjusted)

1952–65
$$\ln \widehat{V_1} = \quad 0.25 + 0.71 \ln r, \qquad \text{coefficient of determination} = 0.86$$
$$(0.04)$$

1948–65
$$\ln \widehat{V_1} = \quad 0.11 + 0.81 \ln r, \qquad \text{coefficient of determination} = 0.89$$
$$(0.03)$$

1952–65
$$\ln \widehat{r} \ = -0.12 + 1.21 \ln V_1, \qquad \text{coefficient of determination} = 0.86$$
$$(0.07)$$

---

[8] See William J. Frazer, Jr., "The Demand for Money, Statistical Results and Monetary Policy," *Schweizerische Zeitschrift für Volkswirtschaft und Statistik,* March 1967.

1948–65

$$\ln \widehat{r} \;=\; 0.02 + 1.09 \ln V_1, \qquad \text{coefficient of determination} = 0.89$$
$$(0.05)$$

These results are from analyses of data such as are shown in Table 2–1, and in Table 2A–1 in the appendix to this chapter. As the results from analyses following logarithmic transformations of the data indicate, percentage changes in the rate of interest are associated with almost equal percentage changes in velocity (e.g., $d \ln r / d \ln V_1 = 1.09$, in the last equation above), and the logarithmically linear regression line fits the data very well (e.g., coefficient of determination $= 0.89$, in the last equation above). There is, of course, a good bit more to the rationale of the use of the velocity of money as an indicator of changes in monetary policy, but this subject is postponed until much later.

Another way of dealing with the identification problem—and, incidentally, one somewhat similar to that above—appears to be suggested by Friedman's use of the real or deflated stock of money vis-à-vis the nominal stock of money.[9] As he points out, "the nominal stock of money is determined in the first instance by the monetary authorities or institutions and cannot be altered by the non-bank holders of money." In contrast, "the real stock of money is determined in the first instance by the holders of money," since they can adjust the real stock of money as they like. They can do this by increasing expenditures so as to effect a rise in the average of prices and/or income and the velocity of money, or they may effect the adjustment via the demand for balances by effecting a decline in the average of prices. Friedman also suggests that given the level of deflated income, the income velocity of money is uniquely determined by the real stock of money, and consequently the above comments apply to velocity as well as to the stock of deflated money balances. Income velocity, too, "is determined by the holders of money," or, in other words, "it is a reflection of their decisions about the real quantity of money they desire to hold."

---

[9] See Milton Friedman, "The Demand for Money: Some Theoretical and Empirical Results," *Journal of Political Economy*, August 1959, pp. 330–331.

The above methods of dealing with the identification problem assume rapid adjustments to imbalances between "desired" and "actual" levels of money balances. Allais, in an analysis dealing with these, says that the former "is a psychological concept and of course no statistical data to measure it are available." Continuing, however, he notes that economic agents are in a position to adjust their money towards desired levels by spending more or less. Allais assumes "that the discrepancy between the actual and desired value of money holdings is always relatively small." He justifies the assumption by its consequences.[10]

Of course, on the supply side, the monetary officials may not always be on target in giving effects to the money supply, and there may be substantial lags in the market adjustments to the desired amount of balances. Hence, other approaches have been taken to facilitate the identification of demand schedules. Teigen, e.g., proceeds to treat the money supply as an endogenously rather than exogenously determined variable, and he deals with a structural model as a "distinct improvement over the single-equation analysis of the demand for money" He has taken the approach that the single-equation estimates of regression coefficients or elasticities of the demand for money are biased, and that his method involving a structural model with the money supply endogenously determined results in less biased estimates of elasticities. He says that a logical way to eliminate the simultaneous-equations bias is to demonstrate the existence of a supply function for money, and then to estimate the coefficients for the two functions jointly, "thus taking account of the interdependence of the functions." He notes further, however, the presence of the problem of specifying the functions correctly, and his own estimates are said to be biased on such an account.[11] Others, too, have been

---

[10] Maurice Allais, "A Restatement of the Quantity Theory of Money," *American Economic Review*, December 1966, pp. 1137–1138, pp. 1150–1151, and p. 1154.

[11] Ronald L. Teigen, "Demand and Supply Functions for Money in the United States: Some Structural Estimates," *Econometrica*, October 1964, pp. 476–509; and Ronald L. Teigen, "The Demand for Money and the Supply of Money," *Readings in Money, National Income, and Stabilization Policy,*

dealing with supply equations for money, and related problems.[12] These efforts will undoubtedly contribute to improvements in our subject in one way or another.

Bias in the sampling variance of estimates of regression parameters is another of the problems arising in connection with analyses of time series. This problem must be dealt with and/or allowed for in some uses of regression results, but, as indicated in the appendix to this chapter, unbiased estimators of regression coefficients may be obtained even in the presence of autocorrelation in residual error terms.

In addition to the previously mentioned statistical criteria and problems such as those of identification and autocorrelation in the error terms, other criteria or methods have come to be used in more contemporary empirical studies. Among the criteria or methods used in later studies are the following: the Durbin-Watson statistic,[13] Chow tests, F-ratios,[14] coefficients of determination for multiple regressions (adjusted for degrees of freedom),[15] and three-pass least squares.[16] (The above problems and some of the frequently recurring criteria or methods are dealt with in the appendix to this chapter.)

Warren L. Smith, and Ronald L. Teigen, eds. (Homewood, Illinois: Richard D. Irwin, Inc., 1965), p. 59.

[12] See, e.g., Phillip Cagan, *Determinants and Effects of Changes in the Stock of Money, 1875–1960* (New York: Columbia University Press for the the National Bureau of Economic Research, 1965); Leonall C. Andersen, "A Study of Factors Affecting the Money Stock: Phase One," *Staff Economic Studies,* Board of Governors of the Federal Reserve System, 1965; and Allan H. Meltzer, "Money Supply Revisited: A Review Article," *Journal of Political Economy,* April 1967.

[13] T. J. Courchene and H. T. Shapiro, "The Demand for Money: A Note from the Time Series," *Journal of Political Economy,* October 1964, pp. 498–503.

[14] G. S. Maddala and Robert C. Vogel, " 'The Demand for Money: A Cross-Section Study of Business Firms': Comment," *Quarterly Journal of Economics,* February 1965, pp. 153–159.

[15] Allan H. Meltzer, "A Little More Evidence from the Time Series," *Journal of Political Economy,* October 1964, pp. 504–508.

[16] Frank de Leeuw, "The Demand for Money: Speed of Adjustment, Interest Rates and Wealth," *Monetary Process and Policy: A Symposium,* George Horwich, ed. (Homewood, Illinois: Richard D. Irwin, Inc., 1967).

As matters have evolved to date, regression analyses have centered about an association between the velocity of money (Y/M) and the rate of interest (r), and/or the demand function $M = f(Y, r)$ or the linear relation in the logarithms between the stock of money (M), the rate of interest (r), and income $(Y = rW)$ or wealth (W). The relationships (or at least the predominant portion) posited between the variables, however, are implicit in the standard liquidity-preference model or in a version of the standard model with modifications to accommodate switching between broad classes of assets, such as fixed-claim assets and others with a residual claim against future income. Multitudinous results, in fact, suggest the following single-equation models as first approximations to the aggregate relations:

(1) $\qquad \ln M = \ln k + \alpha \ln r + \beta \ln Y, \qquad \alpha < 0, \beta \approx 1$

(2) $\quad \ln (Y/M) = \ln k + \alpha \ln r, \qquad \alpha > 0$

Equation (2) is actually of the same form as Eq. (1)—i.e., $\ln Y - \ln M = \ln k - \alpha \ln r$, and Eq. (1) follows, after rearranging terms. Equation (1) itself may serve as a loglinear approximation to a relationship implied by the elementary liquidity-preference model, as set forth later.

Interesting questions raised in the present context include the following: whether changes in interest rates cause changes in velocity, or vice versa, or whether both sets of changes are due to some other factor; whether regression results to date suggest the prospect of exercising control over expenditures (and, therefore, the levels of employment and prices) directly by manipulating an independent variable such as the rate of interest. An absence of the prospect of control over expenditures generally and the stock of money entering into exchange via the manipulation of independent variables need not suggest, of course, the absence of some possible monetary-policy effect on aggregate expenditures and related variables. The absence of such an effect, nevertheless, may suggest that many of the empirical demand relations being presented are misleading, with respect both to the effects of possible policy changes and to the role of policy-making officials. We propose to deal with these questions later—much later, in fact.

2.3 AGGREGATE AND SECTOR VELOCITIES: MEASURES AND BASIC FACTS

The velocity ratio, as previously noted, includes a flow variable for income and a stock variable. The number of different income and money-stock series for the numerator and denominator, respectively, gives rise to a wide variety of different velocity ratios. In this section, we review some of the more common velocity ratios, repetitive and nonrepetitive facts about changes in velocity, the method of relating velocity measures for individual units or sectors to aggregate velocity, and the role of studies of sectoral velocities. Some possible explanations for the facts reported in this section are mentioned as a means of anticipating their fuller development in subsequent chapters.

The development of satisfactory measures for velocity and the stock of money, together with the evolution of a certain amount of agreement as to the meaning of these measures, seemingly had to precede the sophisticated analyses characteristic of some of the more contemporary literature on the demand for money. Here we review some of the measures in a relatively developed state.[17]

ALTERNATIVE MEASURES OF VELOCITY

In reference to the numerator of the definition of velocity, it is common to encounter such measures as Gross National Product (GNP), permanent income (Y_p), the money value of sales (S), the value of total transactions (PT), and total debits against bank deposits—where GNP $(= Y)$ is the nominal dollar value of the current output of goods and services; Y_p is defined in a variety of ways (Sec. 6.1) as well as the average value of income (Y) over a National Bureau of Economic Research reference cycle; S is the dollar value of sales, usually by some segment of the business sector; and PT is the value of the current output of goods and serv-

---

[17] Selden's early work provides a detailed statement of alternative terminologies, concepts, and the multiplicity of early estimates of the income velocity for the United States. See Richard T. Selden, "Monetary Velocity in the United States," in Friedman, ed., *Studies in the Quantity Theory of Money, op. cit.*, pp. 179–195.

ices and the value of other items entering into exchange. In all of these instances the flow quantities may be expressed for a period such as a year or a quarter, or as an annual rate during a given quarter. In reference to the denominator in the velocity ratio, several measures are often encountered: the sum of currency plus demand deposits, the sum of currency plus demand deposits plus time deposits at commercial banks, the latter sum plus savings deposits, and the stock of cash balances held by business firms. Sometimes the stock of money balances held by business firms involves both demand and some business time deposits, as an empirical matter, since balance sheets serve as sources of data. In these instances one might work with a stock of balances at a given date or with some average such as that for totals at monthly dates within a quarter.

With the above numerators and denominators, at least twelve different measures of velocity for the economy as a whole could be worked out. We denote only a few for the economy as a whole and one for the business sector. First, the ratio of income per annum to the stock of money (i.e., Y/M) is *income velocity* (V_y), often expressed on a quarterly basis. Second, the ratio of permanent income to the money stock (i.e., Y_p/M) is *permanent velocity* (V_p). Third, the ratio of sales to the cash balances of firms is used as a substitute measure for that portion of income velocity arising in the business sector, since sales by these firms concern current output. The value added to current output in GNP terms in the latter instance, however, has not been isolated, and in some respects the measure for sales is a component of the current value of all transactions. Fourth, the ratio of the total value of current transactions to the money stock (i.e., PT/M) is *transactions velocity* (V_t). Finally, the ratio of total debits against bank deposits to the stock of bank deposits is *deposit turnover*.

The numerators and denominators for all of the measures for income velocity could be expressed in so-called real or constant price terms. This is accomplished by dividing the various flow and stock variables by the most appropriate index for the level of prices (P) in question. For instance, Y/P is aggregate income in real terms, M/P is real money balances, and the ratio of the latter two deflated measures yields the turnover of real balances (or money balances in constant prices) with respect to the value of the current output of goods and services in constant prices.

Since one of the repetitive and frequently recorded facts about the behavior of velocity, whether utilizing measures in current or constant-price terms, is that velocity rises in the expansion phase of the reference cycle and declines in the contraction phase, an important feature of using permanent income in measures of velocity may be noted. Namely, permanent velocity is more stable than income velocity, sometimes distinguished as "measured velocity" (Secs. 6.1 and 6A.1). Clearly, if $\frac{\Delta M/M}{\Delta Y/Y} < 1$ in the expansion phases of the reference cycles, if $\frac{\Delta M/M}{\Delta Y/Y} > 1$ in the contraction phases, and since velocity varies inversely with these inequalities, we would expect an averaging of the numerator of the velocity measure (Y/M) to modify the measured swings in velocity over the cycles. As Professor Friedman notes, "Permanent income need not itself be stable over a cycle. It may well rise during expansions and fall during contractions. Presumably, however, it will rise less than measured income during expansions and fall less during contractions."[18]

The averaging of income over reference cycles is supposed to serve as a measure of income expected in the future. It permits one to establish a relationship between the demand for money and expected future income or permanent income. At the same time, however, the use of the average aids in isolating the residual fluctuations in the demand for money, as indicated by the difference between income velocity and permanent income velocity. These residuals may be due to some special factor operating in the short run, as we note later (Secs. 6.1 and 6A.1).

From among the various measures of velocity, those relating most directly to GNP or income are of greatest interest to economists. This is because changes in GNP or income are, in turn, related rather directly to national economic goals confronted by the monetary officials, such as maximum employment, production,

---

[18] Friedman, "The Demand for Money," *op. cit.*, pp. 333–334.

and purchasing power.[19] It is also likely due to the "absence of reliable estimates of V_t for the total money stock" and the "paucity of data on the volume of currency transactions."[20]

THE REPETITIVE FACTS

The repetitive facts of the behavior of velocity concern the seasons of the year and cycles such as those reported by the National Bureau of Economic Research. With respect to the seasonal patterns, Selden reports from observations of raw data for some years following 1946 that low velocity values occur in the first quarter of the year and then rise successively throughout the year.[21]

With respect to the cycle, velocity varies positively. Using the ratio of Net National Product (i.e., GNP less depreciation) to the money stock (including time deposits), Friedman and Schwartz note that this "means that income varies more widely than money." They have noted, also, "that the standard deviation of year-to-year percentage changes in income tends to be roughly double the standard deviation of year-to-year changes in the stock of money."[22]

The Friedman-Schwartz results are illustrated in Figure 2–1. They state several reasons, moreover, for their use of the money stock as including time deposits: (1) "The distinction between commercial bank demand and time deposits did not acquire its current significance—or indeed have much significance at all—until after 1914," and (2) there is some evidence that banks managed to classify some demand deposits as time deposits in the 1920's. The incentive for doing this was the lower reserve requirement for time deposits.

The same cyclical pattern—an increase in velocity in the ex-

---

[19] William J. Frazer, Jr. and William P. Yohe, *Introduction to the Analytics and Institutions of Money and Banking* (Princeton, N.J.: D. Van Nostrand Company, Inc., 1965), Sec. 8.1 and Sec. 25.1.

[20] Selden, "Monetary Velocity in the United States," *op. cit.*, p. 181.

[21] *Ibid*, p. 195.

[22] See Milton Friedman and Anna J. Schwartz, "Money and Business Cycles," *Review of Economics and Statistics*, 1963 Supplement, *The State of Monetary Economics*, p. 56.

pansion phase and a decrease in the contraction phase—is also shown in Table 2–1 for the postwar years, using the ratio of GNP per annum to an average money stock and using the ratio of GNP per annum to an average money stock plus time deposits. Also, as shown in Table 2–1, the addition of time deposits to the money stock reduces the velocity ratio considerably. Regressing the velocity of money plus time deposits (denoted V_2), as in Table 2–1, on the long-term rate of interest results in the following equations and coefficients of determination:

(all series seasonally adjusted)

1952–65
$$\ln V_2 = 0.52 + 0.21 \ln r, \qquad \text{coefficient of determination} = 0.70$$
$$(0.09)$$

1948–65
$$\ln V_2 = 0.29 + 0.37 \ln r, \qquad \text{coefficient of determination} = 0.66$$
$$(0.03)$$

As contrasted with the initial set of results from regressing the ratio of GNP to the money stock on the rate of interest (Sec. 2.2), the immediately preceding coefficients of regression are considerably smaller and the coefficients of determination are smaller too.

A number of determinants of the above cyclical changes in velocity as well as others are subsequently mentioned, inluding the rate of interest. Covariations in velocity and various rates of interest are subsequently reported (Secs. 4.2 and 5.1), and several classes of explanations are offered for these. Conventional liquidity-preference analysis, e.g., leads to the prospect of an activation of "idle" balances and an increase in velocity in response to an increase in the rate of interest (Sec. 4.1). Analyses identified with William Baumol, James Tobin, and Henry Latané lead to a similar prospect of increases in both velocity and interest rates, only the emphasis is on the inducement to effect a decline in transactions balances in the form of cash relative to government securities (Secs. 5.1, 8.1, and 8.2). The latter inducement occurs as the rate of interest rises above the transactions costs, or as economies occur in transactions costs. Another explanation of the covariation in velocity and the rate of interest involves switching between broader classes of assets—including cash and bonds, on the one hand, and assets, such as plant and equipment, with a residual claim against future income, on the other (Secs. 4.2, 5.2, and 8.3).

Table 2–1.   Money Supply, Money Supply Plus Time Deposits, and Velocity Series, 1947–65
(seasonally adjusted dollar amounts in billions)

Year	Quarter	Col. (1) Money stock (M_1)*	Col. (2) Money stock plus time deposits (M_2)†	Col. (3) Gross National Product (GNP)‡	Col. (4) Income velocity of money Col. (3) ÷ Col. (1) (V_y or V_1)	Col. (5) Income velocity of money plus time deposits Col. (3) ÷ Col. (2) (V_2)
1947	1	109.8	143.3	223.6	2.03	1.56
	2	111.6	145.4	227.6	2.03	1.56
	3	112.6	146.9	231.8	2.05	1.57
	4	113.1	148.3	242.1	2.14	1.63
1948	1	113.0	148.6	248.0	2.19	1.66
	2	112.1	147.8	255.6	2.27	1.72
	3	112.2	148.1	265.2	2.36	1.79
	§4 (Peak)	111.8	147.7	263.9	2.36	1.78
1949	1	111.2	147.3	258.5	2.32	1.75
	2	111.3	147.6	255.2	2.29	1.72
	3	111.0	147.4	257.1	2.31	1.74
	4 (Trough)	111.0	147.4	255.0	2.29	1.72
1950	1	112.0	148.5	266.0	2.37	1.79
	2	113.6	150.4	275.4	2.42	1.82
	3	114.9	151.6	293.1	2.55	1.93
	4	115.9	152.5	304.5	2.62	1.99
1951	1	117.1	153.7	318.0	2.71	2.06
	2	118.2	155.0	325.8	2.75	2.10
	3	119.7	157.1	332.8	2.78	2.11
	4	121.9	159.9	336.9	2.76	2.10
1952	1	123.5	162.1	339.5	2.74	2.09
	2	124.5	163.8	339.1	2.72	2.06
	3	125.8	165.8	345.6	2.74	2.08
	4	127.0	167.8	357.7	2.81	2.13
1953	1	127.5	169.1	364.2	2.85	2.15
	2	128.4	170.8	367.5	2.86	2.15
	3 (Peak)	128.6	171.8	365.8	2.84	2.12
	4	128.7	172.9	360.8	2.80	2.08

Table 2–1 (Continued)

Year	Quarter	Col. (1) Money stock (M_1)*	Col. (2) Money stock plus time deposits (M_2)†	Col. (3) Gross National Product (GNP)‡	Col. (4) Income velocity of money Col. (3) ÷ Col. (1) (V_y or V_1)	Col. (5) Income velocity of money plus time deposits Col. (3) ÷ Col. (2) (V_2)
1954	1	129.1	174.3	360.7	2.79	2.06
	2	129.4	175.8	360.4	2.78	2.04
	3 (Trough)	130.6	178.3	364.7	2.79	2.04
	4	131.9	180.1	373.4	2.82	2.07
1955	1	133.5	182.1	386.2	2.89	2.12
	2	134.3	183.3	394.4	2.93	2.15
	3	134.8	184.2	402.5	2.98	2.18
	4	135.1	184.9	408.8	3.02	2.21
1956	1	135.5	185.5	410.6	3.02	2.21
	2	135.9	186.4	416.2	3.06	2.23
	3	135.9	187.1	420.6	3.09	2.24
	4	136.6	188.3	429.5	3.14	2.28
1957	1	136.8	189.9	436.9	3.19	2.29
	2	136.9	191.3	439.9	3.21	2.29
	3 (Peak)	136.9	192.6	446.3	3.25	2.31
	4	136.2	193.2	441.5	3.24	2.28
1958	1	136.0	195.1	434.7	3.19	2.22
	2 (Trough)	137.6	199.9	438.3	3.18	2.19
	3	139.0	203.4	451.4	3.24	2.21
	4	140.7	205.8	464.4	3.30	2.25
1959	1	142.0	208.0	474.0	3.33	2.27
	2	143.1	209.8	486.9	3.40	2.32
	3	143.6	210.8	484.0	3.36	2.29
	4	142.6	209.9	490.5	3.43	2.33
1960	1	141.2	208.2	503.0	3.56	2.41
	2 (Peak)	140.4	207.9	504.7	3.59	2.42
	3	140.8	210.4	504.2	3.58	2.39
	4	141.0	213.1	503.3	3.56	2.36
1961	1 (Trough)	141.6	216.3	503.6	3.55	2.32
	2	142.6	219.8	514.9	3.60	2.34
	3	143.4	223.3	524.2	3.65	2.34
	4	144.9	227.0	537.7	3.70	2.36
1962	1	149.1	235.0	547.8	3.67	2.33
	2	146.2	235.8	557.2	3.80	2.36
	3	145.9	238.6	564.4	3.86	2.36
	4	146.9	243.2	572.0	3.89	2.35

Table 2–1 (Continued)

Year	Quarter	Col. (1) Money stock (M_1)*	Col. (2) Money stock plus time deposits (M_2)†	Col. (3) Gross National Product (GNP)‡	Col. (4) Income velocity of money Col. (3) ÷ Col. (1) $(V_y$ or $V_1)$	Col. (5) Income velocity of money plus time deposits Col. (3) ÷ Col. (2) (V_2)
1963	1	148.4	248.7	577.0	3.88	2.31
	2	149.7	253.3	583.1	3.89	2.30
	3	151.3	258.4	593.1	3.92	2.29
	4	152.8	263.8	603.6	3.94	2.28
1964	1	153.8	268.2	614.0	3.99	2.28
	2	154.8	272.1	624.2	4.03	2.29
	3	157.3	278.1	634.8	4.03	2.28
	4	159.2	284.2	641.1	4.02	2.25
1965	1	160.0	290.6	657.6	4.11	2.26
	2	160.9	295.6	668.8	4.15	2.26
	3	163.1	302.9	681.5	4.17	2.24
	4	166.2	311.5	697.2	4.19	2.23

* The quarterly amounts for the money supply series are averages of daily figures. The money supply consists of the following: (1) demand deposits at all commercial banks other than those due to domestic commercial banks and the U. S. Government, less cash items in the process of collection and Federal Reserve float; (2) foreign demand balances at F. R. Banks; and (3) currency outside the Treasury, the F. R. Banks, and the vaults of all commercial banks.
† Time deposits are adjusted. They are time deposits at all commercial banks other than those due to domestic commercial banks and the U. S. Government.
‡ GNP is at an annual rate. The series includes changes in definitions of components reflected in the August 1965 revision by the Department of Commerce.
§ Peaks and troughs are turning points as reported by the National Bureau of Economic Research.
Source of data: Board of Governors of the Federal Reserve System.

Possibly the comparison of the results from regressing, first, the velocity of money on the rate of interest and, then, the velocity of money plus time deposits on the rate of interest reflects a form of switching between demand and time deposits as interest rates rise. Some analysts present such an explanation (Secs. 5.1 and 6.3). On the other hand, the lower coefficients following from the use of the money stock plus time deposits in the regression analyses may simply reflect the prospect that time deposits are less susceptible to cyclical movements and more susceptible to

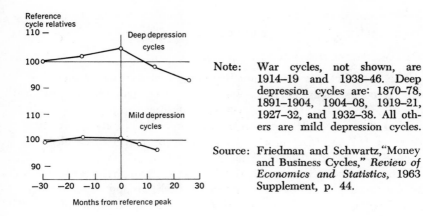

Note: War cycles, not shown, are 1914–19 and 1938–46. Deep depression cycles are: 1870–78, 1891–1904, 1904–08, 1919–21, 1927–32, and 1932–38. All others are mild depression cycles.

Source: Friedman and Schwartz,"Money and Business Cycles," *Review of Economics and Statistics*, 1963 Supplement, p. 44.

Figure 2–1. Income Velocity: Average Reference Cycle Patterns for Mild and Deep Depression Cycles, 1870–1958.

Source: Milton Friedman and Anna J. Schwartz, *A Monetary History of the United States* (Princeton, N. J.: Princeton University Press, 1963), p. 640.

Figure 2–2. Two Measures of Velocity, Annually, 1869–1960.

some nonrepetitive factors, such as changes in the ceiling of interest rates payable on time deposits.

THE NONREPETITIVE FACTS

The nonrepetitive facts may be thought of as those concerning special occurrences, such as wars, and those concerning secular trends. Reviewing the war years, including both world wars, Selden notes that "V_y apparently rose initially, [and] fell during years of full military effort."[23] This pattern is also discernible in Figure 2–3 for the World War II years, 1941–45. In explaining a decline in velocity during the World War II years, Selden mentions an increased precautionary demand for cash, among other factors, and Friedman and Schwartz introduce special factors affecting expectations. Selden refers, in particular, to "the extensive movement of people about the country" and to "uncertainty about jobs" as providing needs for contingency balances.[24] Friedman and Schwartz mention the "obvious necessity for much reshuffling of economic activity in the course of reconversion to peacetime pursuits" and "the extensive talk—a legacy of depression—of the dangers of a postwar collapse."[25]

Observing a variety of data, Selden reports the following facts for secular trends: "(1) There was a marked decline in V_y from 1839 to 1939; (2) a decline also shows up in V_y series covering the period 1899–1938 and 1909–46; (3) there was little net change in V_y from 1929 to 1951, although regression lines for this period have slight positive slopes; and (4) a single linear trend line fits the entire data poorly."[26]

A secular decline in the velocity of money balances including time deposits from 1880 to World War I, and in the velocity of currency plus demand deposits during the interwar period are also clearly evidenced in Figure 2–2. These observations are roughly

---

[23] Selden, "Monetary Velocity in the United States," *op. cit.*, p. 192.

[24] *Ibid.*, p. 229.

[25] See Milton Friedman and Anna J. Schwartz, *A Monetary History of the United States, 1867–1960* (Princeton, New Jersey: Princeton University Press for the National Bureau of Economic Research, 1963), p. 674.

[26] Selden, "Monetary Velocity in the United States," *op. cit.*, p. 190.

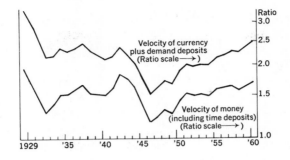

Source: Milton Friedman and Anna J. Schwartz, *A Monetary History of the United States* (Princeton, N. J.: Princeton University Press, 1963), p. 647.

Figure 2–3. Two Measures of Velocity, Annually, 1929–1960.

in accord with Selden's conclusions (1) and (2), immediately above. In addition, a decline in the velocity of currency plus demand deposits in the 1930's is shown in Figure 2–3, and this, too, is in accord with Selden's statements (1) and (2). Figure 2–3, however, shows a rise in the velocity of money balances including time deposits in the 1932–1940 periods, and this trend moves in the opposite direction from the trend for currency plus demand deposits during those years.

The series in the latter figure for the velocity of both sets of balances clearly reflect the post-World War II rise in velocity. Such a rise, as reported in a variety of sources,[27] is reflected in in Table 2–1. Moreover, an analysis of data in Table 2–1 to determine linear trend provides results such as the following:

---

[27] See Richard T. Selden, "The Postwar Rise in the Velocity of Money: A Sectoral Analysis," *Journal of Finance*, December 1961, pp. 483–545; and Friedman and Schwartz, *A Monetary History, op. cit.*, Chapter 12, "The Postwar Rise in Velocity," pp. 639–675; and William J. Frazer, Jr., "Monetary Analysis and the Postwar Rise in the Velocity of Money in the United States," *Schweizerische Zeitschrift für Volkswirtschaft und Statistik*, December 1964, pp. 584–596.

1947–65 $M_1 = 107.9 + 0.67t,$ $r^2 = 0.96$
                (0.01)

standard error of the estimate = 2.82 billion dollars

1947–65 $T_D = 14.9 + 1.25t,$ $r^2 = 0.84$
                (0.06)

standard error of the estimate = 12.18 billion dollars

1947–65 $M_2 = 122.8 + 1.91t,$ $r^2 = 0.91$
                (0.07)

standard error of the estimate = 13.10 billion dollars

where in addition to the variables defined in Table 2–1, T_D is time deposits, t is time ($t = 1, 2, \ldots, 76$, for the seventy-six observations in Table 2–1), and r^2 is the coefficient of determination. As the regression coefficients in the above equations reveal, the upward linear trend in time deposits has been much stronger than that for the money stock exclusive of time deposits in the post-World War II years. We may note, too, that a linear regression line fits very closely the observations for the money stock and time (i.e., $r^2 = 0.96$), and such a line fits somewhat less closely the sets of observations for time deposits and time, and the money stock plus time deposits and time, respectively.[28] Indeed, the standard error of the estimate is 2.82 billion dollars for the money stock and 12.18 billion for the stock of time deposits. The average annual growth rates for the narrow and broad definitions of money, respectively, also reflect the large differences in the logarithmically linear trends for the 1947–65 period. For example,

---

[28] The latter differences in the trend, the fit of the regression line, and the standard error of the estimate are also reflected in the differences in the results from regressing the velocity of money on time ($t = 1, 2, \ldots 76$) and the velocity of money plus time deposits on time—namely,

$$V_1 = 2.194 + 0.0276t, \qquad r^2 = 0.98$$
$$(0.0004)$$
standard error of the estimate = 0.076

$$V_2 = 1.869 + 0.0079t, \qquad r^2 = 0.70$$
$$(0.0006)$$
standard error of the estimate = 0.107

Period:

1947–65 $\widehat{M}_1 = (107.8)(1.020)^t, \qquad r^2 = 0.96$

average growth rate (per annum) = 2.0 percent

1947–65 $\widehat{M}_2 = (129.5)(1.039)^t, \qquad r^2 = 0.96$

average growth rate (per annum) = 3.9 percent

where $(1.020 - 1.00) \times 100 = 2.0$ percent, $(1.039 - 1.00) \times 100 =$ 3.9 percent, and t is time ($t = 1.00, 1.25, 1.50, \ldots, 19.50, 19.75$, for the seventy-six observations in Table 2–1).

In attempting to explain the above secular changes in velocity, analysts have usually invoked special explanations or exercised a good bit of imagination. Dealing with cyclical changes in velocity and the secular decline in the velocity of money (defined to include time deposits) in the pre-World War II years, Milton Friedman presents an explanation involving his "luxury goods" hypothesis (Sec. 3.5).

According to the hypothesis, as dealt with on subsequent occasions, the stock of money demanded rises more than in proportion to income (or wealth).[29] In the explanation, the quantity of money demanded is adjusted, from the holder's point of view, to the anticipated longer-term levels of income and prices, as indicated by "permanent" income and "permanent" prices. The latter measures, however, are averages over the "whole reference cycles," and they consequently rise and fall with the series being averaged, but they rise and fall less than the "measured" income and prices. Thus, adjusting to the permanent measures, the stock of money demanded varies less than in proportion to income and prices (or the product of real income and the average of individual prices at a given time) over the cycle, as required by the cyclical changes in velocity as usually measured. In this case, furthermore, money

---

[29] See Milton Friedman, "The Demand for Money: Some Theoretical and Empirical Results," *American Economic Review*, May 1959, pp. 525–526. This paper is a summary of the Friedman article by the same title in the August 1956 issue of the *Journal of Political Economy*. See also Milton Friedman and Anna Jacobson Schwartz, *A Monetary History, op. cit.,* pp. 642–643 and Milton Friedman, "The Quantity Theory of Money—A Restatement," *Studies in the Quantity Theory of Money*, Milton Friedman, ed. (Chicago: University of Chicago Press, 1957), pp. 18–19.

holdings may rise more than in proportion to "permanent" income and prices as a secular matter, and this would be consistent with the luxury goods hypothesis. The post-World War II rise in velocity, of course, has been a source of difficulty for Friedman's hypothesis. His attempts to deal with it, as outlined later (Sec. 6A.2), have added to the *ad hoc* character of portions of the theory implicit in his work.

AGGREGATE VELOCITY AND SECTOR VELOCITIES

The method of relating the velocities of the various spending units or sectors to the aggregate velocity, and, in fact, the sectoral approach to velocity analysis is set forth by Selden.[30] According to the relatively simple method, "aggregate velocity is a weighted average of payments—money ratios for individual spending units [or sectors], the weights being the fraction of the total money stock held by each spending unit [or sector]." The weights for the *n* different sectors or units are

$$\frac{m_1}{M}, \frac{m_2}{M}, \ldots, \frac{m_n}{M}$$

where M is the total money stock, and $m_1, m_2, \ldots, m_n$ are the stocks held by the respective sectors. These weights, of course, indicate the relative importance of velocity for each of the *n* different units. The sector velocities for the *n* different sectors, then, are

$$\frac{s_1}{m_1}, \frac{s_2}{m_2}, \ldots, \frac{s_n}{m_n}$$

and upon combining the sector weights and the corresponding velocities,

$$V = \frac{m_1}{M}\frac{s_1}{m_1} + \frac{m_2}{M}\frac{s_2}{m_2} + \ldots + \frac{m_n}{M}\frac{s_n}{m_n}$$

or

$$V = \frac{s_1}{M} + \frac{s_2}{M} + \ldots + \frac{s_n}{M}$$

[30] Richard T. Selden, "The Postwar Rise in the Velocity of Money: A Sectoral Analysis," *Journal of Finance*, December 1961, pp. 483–534. For Selden's reference to the earlier proponents of velocity analysis by sector, see note 5 in Selden's latter work.

where V is aggregate velocity. In accord with this approach, one may wish to study changes in the velocity of money in the various sectors to better understand the respective sector contributions to changes in aggregate velocity, or one may wish simply to analyze changes in aggregate velocity resulting from changes in the weights.[31] Indeed, as an examination of the combination of sector weights and velocities would indicate, and as Selden demonstrated, changes in the weights may result in changes in aggregate velocity, even with constant sector velocities.

In his study of sector velocities, Selden reported some interesting observations. According to his methods of measurement and data, for instance, he found for 1956 that "corporate velocity was 1.34 times federal velocity, 1.44 times non-corporate velocity, 1.87 times insurance velocity, 2.88 times consumer velocity (excluding withheld taxes), 3.86 times state and local velocity, and 6.89 times velocities in the other investors sectors." Also, he found for the two recessions covered by his study (i.e., the 1948–49 and 1953–54 recessions) that "the decline in aggregate velocity during these recession years resulted solely from sharply falling velocity in the corporate sector." And, continuing, Selden noted that the increase in the corporate sector's share of money balances tended to contribute to the postwar increase in aggregate velocity.[32] These are, indeed, interesting observations, and they emphasize the importance of dealing at times with the determinants of velocity for separate sectors as a means of explaining and identifying the source of changes in aggregate velocity or changes in the aggregate demand for money relative to expenditures (income, or other substitute measures). In the present book, apart from the review of studies dealing with the aggregate demand for money, we deal mainly with two of the major sectors comprising the economy, the nonfinancial corporate and consumer sectors.

---

[31] Selden employs this method by taking velocity measures at some base time, and then comparing aggregate velocity at one time with that at another after the weights have changed. Any change in aggregative velocity revealed by changing the weights would be that portion of a change in aggregate velocity resulting from the change in weights over the period in question.

[32] See Selden, "The Postwar Rise in the Velocity of Money," *op. cit.*, p. 494.

2.4 SUMMARY

Regression analyses pertaining to the demand for money began to appear in the late 1930's and the mid-1940's. These involved aggregate and sector velocities, respectively, as well as liquidity-preference analysis, and an arbitrary distinction between so-called idle and active balances. The earliest of the studies, made by A. J. Brown, also dealt with the preceding year's change in the average of prices as a measure of expectations of appreciation in the purchasing power of money, but many later analysts ignored this prospect. The early studies revealed a relationship between the velocity of money and the rate of interest, and Latané in his regression analyses dealt further with such a relationship. In a 1956 publication edited by Milton Friedman, velocity was emphasized as a possible function of a wide variety of variables—the rate of interest on bonds, the rate on equities, the rate of change in prices, real income (as an index of wealth), the ratio of income from nonhuman wealth to the income from human wealth, and a variable representing possible effects on tastes and preferences. The over-all results from the studies reported in the volume edited by Friedman, with some exceptions, tended mainly to support the inclusion of real income and the interest rate(s) as determinants of velocity.

Relationships between the stock of money, income (or wealth), and the rate of interest appear to stand out in a variety of analyses. They, in turn, suggest relationships implicit in various aspects of liquidity-preference analysis. In fact, coefficients resulting from regressing velocity on the rate of interest and vice versa, following logarithmic transformations of the data, reflect such relationships.

Analyses of data concerning the demand for money involve a wide variety of statistical criteria and concepts. The analyses of time-series data, in particular, encounter two common problems—that concerning the presence of simultaneous-equations bias and that concerning the presence of autocorrelation in the error terms. Simultaneous-equations bias in the regression coefficients results when the coefficients reflect observations (or equilibrium points) possibly resulting from shifts in both a supply schedule and a demand schedule, rather than, say, from a smooth movement of a supply schedule along a demand schedule. To deal with the need to assure the proper identification of the demand schedule, several approaches are suggested. There is the prospect, in one instance, of viewing the demand for money as a function of income or wealth and some additional variable such as the rate of interest (or a substitute measure for monetary policy). If these variables can account for most of the variation in the stock of money demanded, and if the supply schedule may properly be treated as an exogenously determined variable, then the demand schedule can be said to be properly identified. These assumptions seem to require a great deal—monetary policy's being on target and a nominal lag in adjustments to the desired amount of balances. Even so, the approach may have merit, and alternatives may not do as well or better.

Teigen proceeds to treat the money supply as endogenously rather than exogenously determined. He proposes to demonstrate the existence of a supply function for money and then to establish jointly the coefficients for the two functions. In his attempt to demonstrate the approach, he notes that his own estimates are biased by an inadequate specification of the functions. Other analysts have been working on money-supply functions, too, and monetary analysis should benefit from these efforts.

The possibility of autocorrelation in the error terms in regression analyses of time-series data must be recognized as being of importance in tests of some hypotheses. Measures and tests to determine its presence may involve the Durbin-Watson statistic and/or other measures. Mainly, the presence of autocorrelation introduces bias in the sampling variance of estimates for regression coefficients rather than in the regression coefficients themselves.

In the present context of monetary analysis and statistical analyses of data for the money stock, income, and interest rates, a number of questions may be raised: (1) Do changes in the rate of interest cause changes in velocity or vice versa? (2) Do changes in both the rate of interest and velocity simply reflect responses to identical forces? (3) Do regression results suggest the prospect of exercising control over expenditures (and, therefore, the level of employment and the level of prices) by manipulating some independent variable such as the rate of interest?

Answers to such questions concern monetary policy and the role of the policy-making officials.

The velocity of money is the ratio of income to the stock of money but, in fact, there are a variety of ratios depending on the definitions for income and the stock of money. A common definition in which the economist is interested—in view of its direct tie to national economic goals of maximum employment, production, and purchasing power—is the ratio of GNP to demand deposits plus currency. Sometimes time deposits are added to the money supply and a smaller, additional ratio is obtained. The ratio of permanent income to the stock of money yields still another velocity measure—permanent velocity, which is a more stable measure.

A number of basic facts have been recorded about changes in velocity, including both repetitive and nonrepetitive changes. The repetitive changes pertain to the seasons of the year and cyclical changes. With respect to the seasons, low velocity values occur in the first quarter of the year and then velocity values rise throughout the succeeding quarters. With respect to the cyclical changes, velocity varies positively with the cycle, rising in the expansion phase and declining in the contraction phase.

Possible explanations of cyclical as well as some other changes involve conventional liquidity-preference analysis, analyses identified with James Tobin and others, and an alternative analysis dealing with a form of switching between broad classes of assets. The first of these explanations pertains to changes in velocity as a result of forms of switching between money balances and bonds in response to interest-rate changes. Such an explanation has also been applied to the differential results from regressing, first, the velocity of money on the rate of interest, and, then, the velocity of money plus time deposits on the rate of interest. The latter results include lower coefficients, and several writers have suggested that these occur because the velocity of money plus time deposits conceals switching between demand and time deposits. There are complications. Time deposits may simply be less susceptible to cyclical movements for other reasons.

The basic facts about nonrepetitive changes mainly pertain to special occurrences such as wars and secular trends. The latter include the following: a secular decline in velocity from 1880 to World War I; a decline in the velocity of money in the 1930's; a rise in the velocity of money plus time deposits in the 1930's; and post-World War II rises in both the velocity of money and the velocity of money plus time deposits. One hypothesis offered as an explanation for the secular decline in the velocity of money in the pre-World War II years has been Milton Friedman's "luxury goods" hypothesis. The explanation of the secular decline in combination with cyclical changes also involves notions about permanent income. The "luxury goods" hypothesis has stood up less well over time, however, as we will see and as the post-World War II rise in velocity suggests.

Major portions of the literature on the demand for money deal with aggregative measures for the money stock, income, and so on. The predominant portion of monetary analysis as it relates to monetary policy, too, has been at this level. Selden, however, has introduced a method for relating sector velocities to aggregate velocity, and others have studied sector velocities, usually with the view to testing theories or dealing with the impact of sector velocities on the aggregates. Some sectors hold more money balances than others; some sectors, such as the nonfinancial business sector, have relatively more active balances; and Selden's sectoral analysis reveals that changes in aggregate velocity could come about by a simple redistribution of balances. The study of sector velocities may throw light on the behavior of aggregate velocity and related measures.

Appendix to Chapter 2

SOME ECONOMETRIC PROBLEMS
AND CONCEPTS[1]

As a means of introducing some econometric problems and concepts concerning the substantive area, the demand for money, this appendix deals with several somewhat interrelated topics—the regression line, simultaneous-equations bias, analysis of variance, autocorrelation, and multicollinearity. These topics pertain to basic econometric problems or concepts that appear and reappear in various portions of the demand-for-money literature. This appendix and, more especially, the glossary of statistical terms and criteria at the end of the book are included as a partial source of ready reference for the nonspecialist. The present appendix, however, utilizes results from analyses of data and anticipates in some respects subsequent treatments of some aspects of the applied study of the demand for money.

In many instances the meaning of terms is illustrated—both in this appendix and in the glossary at the end of the book—by the utilization of a single equation model from the text: $\ln V_y = \alpha + \beta \ln r$, where $\ln V_y$ is the logarithmically transformed velocity of money, and $\ln r$ is the logarithmically transformed rate of interest (i.e., yield on high-grade corporate bonds). This simple model, with logarithmically transformed variables, is used because of the importance of such transformed variables in the literature concerning the demand for money. Indeed, the broad framework of aggregative analysis (Sec. 3.3) leads us to postulate equal per-

---

[1] This appendix was prepared with the collaboration of Montgomery D. Anderson, Professor of Economics and Statistics, University of Florida.

centage changes in a number of selected variables, and the transformed variables permit us to deal readily with percentage changes, since changes in natural logarithmic transformations are proportional changes (times 100, percentage changes) in the original data. The transformed variables are, of course, themselves variables—i.e., ln V_y and ln r are variables in the above equations, and α and β are parameters. The data used in the present instance are for the 72 quarters, 1948 through 1965, as shown in Table 2A–1. There they are shown both before and after the natural logarithmic transformation.[2]

Table 2A–1. Income Velocity and High-Grade Corporate Bond Yields, 1948–65 (seasonally adjusted data)

Year	Quarter	Income velocity of money (V_y)*†	Aaa bond yields (r)‡	Income velocity of money (ln transformation)	Aaa bond yields (ln transformation)
1948	1	2.19	2.86	0.78	1.05
	2	2.27	2.77	0.81	1.01
	3	2.36	2.81	0.85	1.03
	4 (Peak)§	2.36	2.81	0.85	1.03
1949	1	2.32	2.72	0.84	1.00
	2	2.29	2.69	0.82	0.98
	3	2.31	2.62	0.83	0.96
	4 (Trough)§	2.29	2.59	0.82	0.95
1950	1	2.37	2.60	0.86	0.95
	2	2.42	2.59	0.88	0.95
	3	2.55	2.62	0.93	0.96
	4	2.62	2.66	0.96	0.97
1951	1	2.71	2.72	0.99	1.00
	2	2.75	2.86	1.01	1.05

[2] The notation "ln" denotes the natural logarithm. Sometimes, however, as in the many sources dealt with in the book, writers use the notation "log" and "ln" without specifying the use of common or natural logarithms. The distinction is not particularly important for present purposes, except we attempt to make the distinction between the use of the common logarithm (i.e., $\log_{10}$) and the natural logarithm (i.e., $\log_e$). In particular, 100 d $\log_{10}$ $\neq$ percentage rate of change, and 100 d $\ln$ = percentage rate of change, but if $d \log_{10} x = d \log_{10} y$, then percentage change in x = percentage change in y.

Table 2A–1. (Continued)

Year	Quarter	Income velocity of money $(V_y)^{*\dagger}$	Aaa bond yields $(r)\ddagger$	Income velocity of money (ln transformation)	Aaa bond yields (ln transformation)
	3	2.78	2.88	1.02	1.05
	4	2.76	2.95	1.01	1.08
1952	1	2.74	2.98	1.00	1.09
	2	2.72	2.90	1.00	1.06
	3	2.74	2.93	1.00	1.07
	4	2.81	2.99	1.03	1.09
1953	1	2.85	3.10	1.04	1.13
	2	2.86	3.29	1.05	1.19
	3 (Peak)	2.84	3.25	1.04	1.17
	4	2.80	3.14	1.02	1.14
1954	1	2.79	2.98	1.02	1.09
	2	2.78	2.86	1.02	1.05
	3 (Trough)	2.79	2.86	1.02	1.05
	4	2.82	2.88	1.03	1.05
1955	1	2.89	3.01	1.06	1.10
	2	2.93	3.04	1.07	1.11
	3	2.98	3.07	1.09	1.12
	4	3.02	3.08	1.10	1.12
1956	1	3.02	3.14	1.10	1.14
	2	3.06	3.30	1.11	1.19
	3	3.09	3.38	1.12	1.21
	4	3.14	3.61	1.14	1.28
1957	1	3.19	3.77	1.16	1.32
	2	3.21	3.83	1.16	1.34
	3 (Peak)	3.25	4.01	1.17	1.38
	4	3.24	3.91	1.17	1.36
1958	1	3.19	3.67	1.16	1.30
	2 (Trough)	3.18	3.63	1.15	1.28
	3	3.24	3.81	1.17	1.33
	4	3.30	4.00	1.19	1.38
1959	1	3.33	4.18	1.20	1.43
	2	3.40	4.40	1.22	1.48
	3	3.36	4.43	1.21	1.48
	4	3.43	4.49	1.23	1.50
1960	1	3.56	4.58	1.26	1.52
	2 (Peak)	3.59	4.49	1.27	1.50
	3	3.58	4.28	1.27	1.45
	4	3.56	4.27	1.26	1.45

Table 2A–1. (Continued)

Year	Quarter	Income velocity of money (V_y)*†	Aaa bond yields (r)‡	Income velocity of money (ln transfor- mation)	Aaa bond yields (ln transfor- mation)
1961	1 (Trough)	3.55	4.27	1.26	1.45
	2	3.60	4.32	1.28	1.46
	3	3.65	4.40	1.29	1.48
	4	3.70	4.39	1.30	1.47
1962	1	3.67	4.40	1.30	1.48
	2	3.80	4.34	1.33	1.46
	3	3.86	4.29	1.35	1.45
	4	3.89	4.25	1.35	1.44
1963	1	3.88	4.05	1.35	1.39
	2	3.89	4.30	1.35	1.45
	3	3.92	4.48	1.36	1.49
	4	3.94	4.27	1.37	1.43
1964	1	3.99	4.55	1.38	1.51
	2	4.03	4.52	1.39	1.50
	3	4.03	4.83	1.39	1.57
	4	4.02	4.32	1.39	1.46
1965	1	4.11	5.39	1.41	1.68
	2	4.15	4.59	1.42	1.52
	3	4.17	5.14	1.42	1.63
	4	4.19	4.53	1.43	1.51

* GNP, the numerator of the velocity ratio, is at an annual rate (in billions of dollars). The series includes changes in definitions of components reflected in the August 1965 revision by the Department of Commerce.

† The quarterly amounts for the money supply, the denominator of the velocity ratio, are averages of daily figures. The money supply (in billions of dollars) consists of the following: (1) demand deposits at all commercial banks other than those due to domestic commercial banks and the U. S. Government, less cash items in the process of collection and Federal Reserve float; (2) foreign demand balances at F. R. Banks; and (3) currency outside the Treasury, the F. R. Banks, and the vaults of all commercial banks.

‡ Bond yields are averages of daily figures expressed as a per cent per annum.

§ Peaks and troughs are turning points as reported by the National Bureau of Economic Research.

Source of data: Board of Governors of the Federal Reserve System.

2A.1 THE REGRESSION LINE (SURFACE)

The regression line is the line resulting from the application of ordinary least-squares regression analysis. It is the line fitted to a set of observations such that the sum of the squares of the vertical distances between the line and the observed points is a minimum, in the case of the analysis of the relationship between two variables. As additional variables are added for analysis, the line becomes a surface, again fit to observations so as to minimize the squared differences between real values of some "dependent" variable and estimated values comprising the regression surface. In the two-dimensional case, as would concern the analysis of data from Table 2A–1, two ordinary least-squares regression lines may be shown—one, as defined by Eq. (1) in Figure 2A–1, is for the

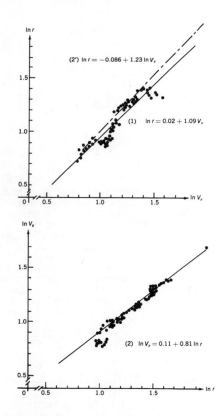

Figure 2A–1. Scatter Diagrams for Logarithms of the Velocity of Money and Logarithms of the Rate of Interest.

relationship between ln r and ln V_y; and the other, as defined by Eq. (2), is for the relationship between ln V_y and ln r.[3]

2A.2 SIMULTANEOUS-EQUATIONS BIAS

Simultaneous-equations bias concerns false estimates from time-series data of slope parameters (or elasticity coefficients) for demand or supply schedules of the common type occurring in economics. The false estimates or bias in the estimates arise from inadequate identification of the demand or supply relationships. The bias, in fact, is said to arise under the following circumstances: (1) two or more variables are actually determined jointly by the intersection of a supply and a demand schedule or by the intersection of two or more functional relationships, and yet (2) coefficients of regression are estimated statistically with the use of only one equation.

Teigen illustrates simultaneous-equations bias by the use of a

---

[3] Still another least-squares regression line is possible for the ln r and ln V_y relation in the classical theory of regression. It is the line resulting from the minimization of the square of the horizontal distances involving the scatter of observations in the upper part of Figure 2A–1.

This alternative to regression line (1) may be obtained in several steps. First, its slope is $(0.81)^{-1}$, which is obtained by *implicit* differentiation of ln r with respect to ln V_y in equation (2). Next, the intercept parameter is equal to the arithmetic mean of ln r less the product of the slope $(0.81)^{-1}$ and the arithmetic mean for ln V_y, i.e.,

$$\ln r = \text{intercept} + 1.23 \ln V_y$$
$$\text{intercept} = \overline{\ln} r - 1.23 \overline{\ln} V_y$$

$\overline{\ln} r = 0.126$, the mean of ln r, and
$\overline{\ln} V_y = 0.114$, the mean of ln V_y.

The resulting equation, then, becomes

(2′) $$\ln r = -0.086 + 1.23 \ln V_y$$

The alternative line defined by this equation is shown by the broken line in the upper part of Figure 2A–1.

The two classical lines defined by Eqs. (1) and (2′) may be virtually the same as shown in the upper part of Figure 2A–1, or they may be widely different. In any event, the likely "true" relation between ln r and ln V_y is probably somewhere between the lines defined by Eqs. (1) and (2′).

simple supply-demand model, similar in type to the following:[4]

Demand for Money (M_d): $M_d = \beta Y + \alpha$
Supply of Money (M_s): $M_s = \gamma$
Equilibrium: $M_d = M_s$

where Y is GNP and β and α are parameters. Demand and supply schedules of the type defined by this model are shown in Figure 2A–2.[5] The schedules in this model, however, are subject to shifts, as shown in Figure 2A–2. These are possibly random and possibly due to unexplained factors or inadequate specification of the model. In any event, the schedules interact to determine equilibrium points and, in the particular figure, these points are given by the coordinates for GNP and the money supply for the 76 quarters, 1947–56, shown in Table 2–1, and reflected in the data for income velocity in Table 2A–1. Since the first-quarter-1947 function and the fourth-quarter-1965 function shown in the figure are virtually extremes for the 1947–65 period, the other equilibrium points tend to lie in the parallelogram $ABCD$. Thus, if a least-squares regression line is fitted to all the coordinate points, the line will tend to pass through the points A and C and, as Teigen notes, "its slope will not be the slope of the demand curve—that is, the estimate of the slope is biased."

We could say that the regression line in Figure 2A–2 was a true demand line (or that we had identified such a line), if we could

---

[4] Teigen also attempts to demonstrate that a supply function for money exists, and then to estimate the coefficients of the demand-for-money function and the money-supply function jointly, thus taking account of the interdependence of the functions. He attempts such an estimation, noting the availability of techniques for such an estimation. He notes, further, that his own econometric model involves the problem of the inadequate specification of the variables appearing in the relationship(s). See Ronald L. Teigen, "The Demand for and Supply of Money," *Readings in Money, National Income, and Stabilization Policy*, Warren L. Smith and Ronald L. Teigen, eds. (Homewood, Illinois: Richard D. Irwin, Inc. 1965), p. 59.

[5] For a review of the method of calculating the slope of intercept parameters in the elementary simultaneous-equations model, see William J. Frazer and William P. Yohe, *Introduction to the Analytics and Institutions of Money and Banking* (Princeton, New Jersey: D. Van Nostrand Company, 1966), pp. 9–11.

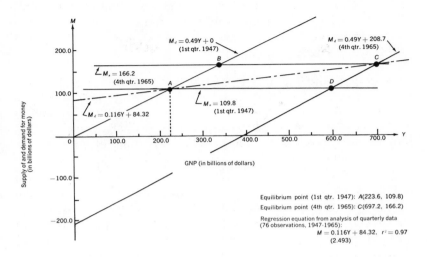

Figure 2A–2. The Demand for Money as a Function of Income.

view the locus of points comprising the line as simply a set of coordinates resulting from movements of the supply schedule. On the other hand, we may view all of the shifts in the demand function $f(Y)$ as due to a monetary policy variable (call it r)[6] and then write the function $f(Y, r)$ noting a small random-error term. This latter function, then, would be fully identified as the supply function shifting and tracing out points on a surface in three-space. Of course, as the coefficient of determination of 0.97 for the regression equation in Figure 2A–2 indicates, a good bit of the variation in the money balances is accounted for by changes in income. Even so, there is more variation in the money balances to be accounted for, and the policy variable helps account for it, although such a variable introduces problems of multicollinearity due to its effect on income.

The method of treating one function as exogenously determined

---

[6] For such a definition of monetary policy, see William J. Frazer, Jr., "The Demand for Money, Statistical Results and Monetary Policy," *Schweizerische Zeitschrift für Volkswirtschaft und Statistik*, March 1967.

and the other as fully specified, so that the former traces out points comprising the latter, is probably the simplest solution to the identification problem. The identification problem was dealt with in this way in early econometric studies.

2A.3 ANALYSIS OF VARIANCE

Analysis of variance concerns mainly the analysis of variations in some sample observations about their arithmetic mean. This form of analysis has been used in selected portions of the demand-for-money literature, as illustrated below. The analysis of variance may also be concerned with (1) the proportion of the variance in the "dependent" variable that is "accounted for" by a regression line (or surface), and (2) the proportion of the variation in a dependent variable that is due to the scatter "within classes" as opposed to the proportion due to variation between the means of classes.[7]

At the heart of the variance-analysis procedure, in some simple cases, lies the comparison of two measures of variation such as two squared standard deviations (or variances). Here two sample variances are compared to determine whether they may be regarded as independent estimates of the same "normal" parent population. We have to deal with F-ratios, wherein

$$F = \frac{\text{sampling variance} + \text{variance due to common factor(s)}}{\text{sampling variance}}$$

or

$$F = \frac{s_1^2}{s_2^2}$$

where s_1^2 and s_2^2 are two sample estimates of the variance from some parent population or populations. If the two sampling variances in the F-ratio are in fact independent estimates of the same

---

[7] The essential difference between (1) and (2) is that (2) is a more general test of relationship (or its absence) than (1). The technique in (2) allows for an *unspecified* relationship, whereas in (1) the probability structure between variables must be explicitly stated. Method (2) may also be applied to *qualitative* differences between classes.

normal population variance (or squared standard deviation), then the F-ratio is one, or differs from one only by some chance factor. To test whether the F-ratio is significantly different from one, critical F-values are selected from F-tables based on probability calculations.[8] The values commonly appear for 1 and 5 per cent significance levels (called 1 per cent and 5 per cent points, respectively), and a given value is located according to the 1 or 5 per cent points and according to the degrees of freedom in the sample value of the variance in the numerator and the sample value of the variance in the denominator.

An analysis of the demand for money by Maddala and Vogel provides one example of the use of variance analysis of the type mentioned under (2) above.[9] They were concerned with Allan Meltzer's estimate (Sec. 7.3) of a unitary sales elasticity of the demand for money by manufacturing corporations, and they dealt with the matter by analyzing variances for the cash-to-sales ratio between years and between size groups. It would appear that they calculated s_1^2's and s_2^2's, such that[10]

$$s_1^2 = \frac{\text{sum of squares of deviations of class means from over-all mean}}{\text{degrees of freedom for variation between classes}}$$

$$s_2^2 = \frac{\text{sum of the sums of squares of respective deviations from class means}}{\text{sum of degrees of freedom for variations within each class}}$$

where the denominator for s_1^2 is number of classes minus one, and the denominator for s_2^2 is the number of observations involved in s_2^2 less the number of classes.[11] The computed F-value, $F = s_1^2/s_2^2$, was

---

[8] For such tables, see e.g., Robert Ferber and P. J. Verdoorn, *Research Methods in Economics and Business* (New York: The Macmillan Company, 1962), pp. 552–555; and Frederick C. Mills, *Statistical Methods*, 3rd Edition (New York: Henry Holt and Company, 1955), pp. 774–777.

[9] G. S. Maddala and Robert C. Vogel, " 'The Demand for Money: A Cross-Section Study of Business Firms': Comment," *Quarterly Journal of Economics*, February 1965, p. 157.

[10] For such formulas see Mills, *op. cit.*, p. 549.

[11] When s_1^2 is divided by "degrees of freedom" instead of number of items (e.g., cash ratios) in the Maddala-Vogel study, the numerator of the F-ratio is, in effect, converted into the variance of a line of relationship running through the means of classes. The F-ratio thus becomes the *reciprocal* of a

then compared with the critical F-value for the 1 or 5 per cent point from the F-table for the given degrees of freedom. If the computed value were greater than the critical value, the difference between the two values would be significant—i.e., too great to be attributed to chance at the per cent level in question, using a one-tail test.

Maddala and Vogel concluded in their study that "an analysis of variance test reveals significant variation in the cash/sales ratio between years and between size groups." This suggested to them that the elasticity coefficient in the equation log $M = a + b$ log S was not consistent when b was estimated for different industry groups and for different years for all industry groups.

Courchene and Shapiro[12] also use F-values, but they use them in the application of a test developed by G. C. Chow.[13] Chow, in general, was interested in the use of a linear regression to represent an economic relationship and the question of "whether the relationship remains stable in two periods of time, or whether the same relationship holds for two different groups of economic units." Continuing, he says, "We are asking whether subsets of coefficients in two regressions are equal." Courchene and Shapiro, on the other hand, were interested in the specific question of whether the demand function for money was stable—i.e., whether regression results showed that the coefficients for the demand function from two different periods were drawn from the same population. To deal with this question, they note that "merely looking at the estimated regression coefficients and their standard errors is not a reliable method of determining the consistency of the underlying 'behavioral' mechanism which generates the data." They proceed to apply Chow's procedure for testing the hypothesis "that $B_1 = B_2 = B$ where B_1 and B_2 represent the estimated regression coefficients of a specified function from two nonoverlapping subperiods, and B

---

squared index of *alienation*, i.e., a kind of measure of functional relationship between cash ratios and size of industry. It is just an index of determination in disguise.

[12] T. J. Courchene and H. T. Shapiro, "The Demand for Money: A Note from the Time Series," *Journal of Political Economy*, October 1964, pp. 500–501.

[13] Gregory C. Chow, "Tests of Equality Between Sets of Coefficients in Two Linear Regressions," *Econometrica*, July 1960, pp. 591–606.

represents the estimated regression coefficients for the entire period."

The Courchene-Shapiro results from the use of *F*-values in carrying out the Chow test are shown in Table 2A–2. In the table, the subperiods for which annual data were originally analyzed are shown. In their table

M_1/P is deflated money balances,

M_2/P is deflated money balances plus time deposits at commercial banks,

(W, i) specifies the function with nonhuman wealth and a long-term rate of interest as independent variables, and

(Y, i) specifies the function with GNP and a long-term rate of interest as independent variables.

Table 2A–2. Chow Test*

Period and Subperiods	Definition of Money	Specification	F-Value	1	5
		Computed F-Value		Critical F-Value Significance Level (Per Cent)	
1900–58:					
1900–29	M_1/P	(W, i)	12.80		
		(Y, i)	5.13	4.20	2.79
1930–58	M_2/P	(W, i)	7.24		
		(Y, i)	16.20		
1920–58:					
1920–39	M_1/P	(W, i)	16.00		
		(Y, i)	8.61	4.46	2.90
1940–58	M_2/P	(W, i)	2.93		
		(Y, i)	1.72		

* Reject hypothesis (that $B_1 = B_2 = B$) if computed *F*-value > critical *F*-value. Source of Table: T. J. Courchene and H. T. Shapiro: "The Demand for Money: A Note from the Time Series," *Journal of Political Economy*, October 1964, p. 499.

After applying the Chow test to the subperiods 1900–29 and 1930–58, Courchene and Shapiro concluded "that under either specification of the demand function for money balances, we must *reject* (at the 1 per cent level) the hypothesis that the same model generated the data in both periods."

Finally, in regression analysis, the total variation displayed by a set of observations may be separated into components that are associated with definite sources. For example,

$$\text{Variance in } \ln r = \text{Variance in } \ln r \text{ explained by } \ln V_y + \text{Variance in } \ln r \text{ not explained by } \ln V_y$$

In the case of the equation, $\ln r = 0.02 + 1.09 \ln V_y$, obtained by minimizing the squared deviations in $\ln r$, the coefficient of determination is 0.89. This suggests that 89 per cent of the variation in $\ln r$ is accounted for by the variation in $\ln V_y$, provided the relationship between $\ln r$ and $\ln V_y$ is linear, as assumed by the use of this particular kind of estimate of regression. The remaining portion of 11 per cent must be explained by some other factor or factors disregarding sampling errors.

2A.4   AUTOCORRELATION

The total variance, as indicated in the section above, includes the variance explained in some special sense by a given factor or factors, and unexplained variance. The latter portion is determined by the deviations from a regression line (or surface) due to errors or other factors, and the deviations are assumed to be independent of the estimated or explained values in ordinary least-squares regression analyses. Autocorrelation, however, refers to the self-correlation of error terms over time, and it may or may not be present in economic time series. Its presence and tests of its presence, nevertheless, are of special importance in the demand-for-money literature, because its presence leads to an understatement of the sampling variance in estimates of elasticity coefficients in money-demand relationships. Johnston, for example, says that "if one applies simple least squares unwittingly to estimate the parameters of a relationship with autocorrelated errors, then one will obtain unbiased estimators, but one is likely to obtain a serious understatement of their sampling variance."[14] In view of the relevance of this hazard of autocorrelation to monetary analyses, this section will define "autocorrelation" more specifically, illustrate the presence of autocorrelation in some regression equations, note the use

---

[14] J. Johnston, *Econometric Methods* (New York: McGraw-Hill Book Company, Inc., 1963), pp. 187–188. See also, p. 179.

of procedures for adjusting the error term for autocorrelation and for reducing autocorrelation, and review two tests for the presence of autocorrelation.

As subsequently noted, one of the tests for dealing with the presence of autocorrelation is the Durbin-Watson test. It involves the Durbin-Watson statistic that frequently appeared in the demand-for-money literature of the mid-1960's. In the present section, consequently, the test is applied to results from analyses of the relation between the rate of interest and the velocity of money. Results from an application of the Durbin-Watson test, next, are reviewed, after taking first differences to try to remove some of the autocorrelation between the series. In the latter instance, a hypothesis of positive autocorrelation is rejected but, after taking first differences, there is not much left in the data to analyze, as far as the monetary theory goes. Some monetary analysis in Chapter 2 and in subsequent chapters, indeed, leads us to expect both cyclical and secular serial correlation in the interest rate and velocity series, possibly as a result of the series responding to identical forces. Thus, some complications may arise in the use of first differencing as a means of meeting the Durbin-Watson test for an absence of autocorrelation, in the sense that the demands of the test are too severe in the particular analysis.

In a regression analysis with equations of the form

$$y_t = \alpha + \beta x_t + u_t, \qquad t = 1, 2, \ldots, n$$

where t is the time of the observation, we have the condition of autocorrelation in the error terms (i.e., the u's) when u_t may be correlated with $u_{t-1}, t = 1, 2, \ldots, n$. This autocorrelation may arise from the presence of serial or intracorrelation in the series y_t and x_t, t $= 1, 2, \ldots, n$. Serial correlation itself is sometimes defined as the correlation between members of a time series and the leading (or lagging) members of the series, and two such series moving more or less in phase cyclically and with monotonic secular trends may give rise to the presence of autocorrelation in the residual error terms. In any event, a problem in the presence of autocorrelation is that ordinary least-squares estimates of the parameters in a regression equation will result in a serious understatement of sampling variances.

Table 2A–3. Comparison of Estimation Procedures

Line	Time Period*	$\ln M_1/P = \ln a + b \ln i + c \ln W/P + u$ b-Value Standard Error	c-Value Standard Error	Durbin-Watson Statistic†	R^2 r‡	$\ln M_2/P = \ln a + b \ln i + c \ln W/P + u$ b-Value Standard Error	c-Value Standard Error	Durbin-Watson Statistic†	R^2 r‡
1a	1900–58	−1.001 (0.061)	1.150 (0.032)	0.70	0.98 / −0.46	−0.579 (0.057)	1.329 (0.030)	0.50	0.98 / −0.46
1b	1902–58	−0.784 (0.109)	1.183 (0.076)	1.48	0.89 / −0.41	−0.534 (0.097)	1.270 (0.071)	1.48	0.90 / −0.38
2a	1900–49	−1.01 (0.067)	1.17 (0.043)	0.65	0.97 / −0.37	−0.574 (0.049)	1.439 (0.032)	0.81	0.98 / −0.37
2b	1902–49	−8.809 (0.125)	1.231 (0.113)	1.42	0.86 / −0.44	−0.559 (0.084)	1.418 (0.069)	1.42	0.94 / −0.45
3a	1900–29	−0.317 (0.161)	0.876§ (0.081)	0.66	0.90 / +0.82	−0.454 (0.171)	1.420 (0.086)	0.66	0.96 / 0.82
3b	1902–29	−0.232 (0.204)	0.803 (0.110)	1.34	0.75 / 0.66	−0.203 (0.206)	1.281 (0.168)	1.34	0.70 / 0.35
4a	1920–58	−1.001 (0.079)	1.161 (0.074)	0.42	0.97 / −0.60	−0.696 (0.058)	1.106 (0.055)	0.66	0.97 / −0.60
4b	1922–58	−0.731 (0.162)	1.166 (0.162)	1.39	0.69 / 0.03	−0.608 (0.103)	1.100 (0.098)	1.39	0.86 / −0.24
5a	1930–58	−1.214 (0.087)	1.260 (0.067)	0.96	0.96 / −0.23	−0.794 (0.080)	1.147 (0.062)	0.82	0.96 / −0.23
5b	1932–58	−0.888 (0.164)	1.205 (0.131)	1.33	0.82 / 0.10	−0.777 (0.130)	1.165 (0.094)	1.33	0.89 / 0.02

* The time periods cannot be the same in estimates (a) and (b) because the Durbin procedure involves the loss of at least one observation. Since we found that a first difference transformation rendered the disturbance term random, we used a first order autoregressive system for the Durbin procedures.

† The first figure in this column is the Durbin-Watson statistic; the second is the critical value below which we must reject the hypothesis of a random disturbance term at the 1 per cent level (see H. Theil and A. L. Nagar, "Testing the Independence of Regression Disturbances," Journal of the American Statistical Association, LVI [1961], 793–897).

‡ The first number in this column is the coefficient of determination; the second is the correlation coefficient between the independent variables [see Meltzer, op. cit.].

§ On p. 229 of Meltzer's article the wealth coefficient for his equation (3) for M_1 for the period 1900–29 is listed as 1.84. From our equation (3a) and Meltzer's general argument, it is obvious that this coefficient should have been 0.84.

Source: T. J. Courchene and H. T. Shapiro, "The Demand for Money: A Note from the Times Series," Journal of Political Economy, October 1964, p. 499.

To deal with the question of the presence of autocorrelation in regression analyses made by Meltzer,[15] Courchene and Shapiro analyzed results concerning two of Meltzer's equations,[16]

$$\ln (M_1/P) = \ln a + b \ln i + c \ln (W/P) + u$$

$$\ln (M_2/P) = \ln a + b \ln i + c \ln (W/P) + u$$

where M_1/P is deflated money balances (i.e., currency plus demand deposits adjusted), M_2/P is deflated money balances plus deflated time deposits at commercial banks, i is a long-term rate of interest on corporate bonds, and W/P is deflated nonhuman wealth. In this instance, Meltzer was interested in showing that the wealth elasticity for M_2 balances was significantly greater than the wealth elasticity for M_1 balances. The Courchene-Shapiro results for the two equations are presently shown in Table 2A–3. The results in the rows designated $1a, 2a, \ldots, 5a$ are estimates by Courchene and Shapiro that correspond to Meltzer's earlier estimates, and the results in the rows designated $1b, 2b, \ldots, 5b$ are estimates obtained by applying a Durbin procedure[17] as a means of providing "asymptotically true estimates of the sampling variance in an autoregressive system." In comparing the respective $1a, 2a, \ldots, 5a$ and $1b, 2b, \ldots, 5b$ sets of results, we are interested in what happens to the standard errors of the coefficients, as shown in parentheses in Table 2A–3. In particular, we note that the standard errors are much larger for the estimates obtained by applying the Durbin procedure. Since the larger standard errors imply smaller empirical t-values (see t-test), Courchene and Shapiro conclude that Meltzer failed to present sufficient evidence to establish his conclusion—namely, "the real M_2 wealth elasticity is 'significantly' greater than the corresponding elasticity for real M_1 balances." "The high t-values (low standard errors) of Meltzer's estimates," they say, "are to a large extent merely a function

---

[15] See Allan H. Meltzer, "The Demand for Money: The Evidence from the Time Series," *Journal of Political Economy*, June 1963, pp. 219–246.

[16] Courchene and Shapiro, *op. cit.*, p. 499.

[17] See J. Durbin, "Estimation of Parameters in Time Series Regression Models," *Journal of the Royal Statistical Society*, XXII, Series B, No. 1, (1960), 139–153.

of the autocorrelation in the disturbance term, probably arising from the serial correlation present in the time series."[18]

The question of the presence of autocorrelation in a regression analysis reduces to the question of whether the residual error terms, as defined in the glossary at the end of the book, are random with respect to time. To help deal with the question, statistical measures due to von Neumann and, more recently, Durbin and Watson have appeared in the monetary literature.[19] These involve the von Neumann ratio of the mean square successive difference to the variance for the error terms, and the Durbin-Watson statistic (d),[20]

$$d = \frac{\sum\limits_{t=2}^{n} (\widehat{\epsilon}_t - \widehat{\epsilon}_{t-1})^2}{\sum\limits_{t=1}^{n} \widehat{\epsilon}_t^2}$$

where n is the number of observations, and $\widehat{\epsilon}_t$ and $\widehat{\epsilon}_{t-1}$, $t = 1, 2, 3, \ldots, n$, are the residual error terms from the classical regression model. As a comparison of the ratio and the statistic reveals, the two are approximately the same except for division by $n - 1$ in the numerator of the ratio, and even this difference is of no special consequence for n over thirty. A difference to be emphasized, however, lies in the test involved in the significance of the

---

[18] See Courchene and Shapiro, *op. cit.*, p. 499.

[19] See, e.g., Philip Cagen, "The Monetary Dynamics of Hyperinflation," *Studies in the Quantity Theory of Money*, ed. Milton Friedman (Chicago: University of Chicago Press, 1956), p. 58; Ronald L. Teigen, "Demand and Supply Functions for Money in the United States: Some Structural Estimates," *Econometrica*, October 1964, pp. 487–494; and Courchene and Shapiro, *op. cit.*, October 1964, p. 499.

[20] On the von Neumann ratio and background material on the analysis of time series, see Mordecai Ezekiel and Karl A. Fox, *Methods of Correlation and Regression Analysis* (New York: John Wiley and Sons, Inc., 1959), pp. 325–340. See also, J. von Neumann, "Distribution of the Ratio of the Mean Square Successive Difference to the Variance," *Annals of Mathematical Statistics*, December 1941, pp. 367–395.

On the Durbin-Watson statistic see Johnston, *op. cit.*, pp. 243–244; and J. Durbin and G. S. Watson, "Testing for Serial Correlation in Least Squares Regression, I," *Biometrika*, December 1950, pp. 409–428.

computed values for the ratio and the statistic—namely, the table of critical values for the d-statistic shows values that vary for the number of "independent" or "explanatory" variables.[21]

Durbin and Watson have, in particular, tabulated critical d-values for values of n and k (i.e., the number of explanatory variables.) Hence—after computing d and locating the appropriate critical value—a one-sided test for positive autocorrelation may be carried out. According to the test positive autocorrelation exists if the computed d-value is below the critical value or lower limit (d_L), i.e., $d < d_L$. As indicated by the test just outlined and as suggested by the test applied by Courchene and Shapiro in Table 2A–3,[22] significantly high positive autocorrelation is present in all of the relationships dealt with in Table 2A–3.

When autocorrelation exists, it is perhaps desirable to explain its presence in terms of, say, monetary theory, or to adopt an alternative estimating procedure, or to adjust the standard errors to allow for its presence, as in Courchene's and Shapiro's Table 2A–3. The use of first differences is a commonly employed means of reducing autocorrelation. In other words, applying regression analysis to series resulting from first differences—such as $r_{t+1} - r_t$, $t = 1, 2, \ldots, n$, and $V_{y, t+1} - V_{y, t}$, $t = 1, 2, \ldots, n$—will still reflect a possible relationship and typically reduce autocorrelation. Thus, to illustrate the effect of first differencing, as well as to illustrate an application of the Durbin-Watson test, the following operations have been carried out: the rate of interest is regressed on velocity, and vice versa; first differences in the rate of interest are regressed on first differences in velocity, and vice versa;

---

[21] For the table for von Neumann's ratio, see B. I. Hart and J. von Neumann, "Tabulation of the Probabilities for the Ratio of the Mean Square Successive Difference to the Variance," *Annals of Mathematical Statistics,* June 1942, pp. 207–214; and, for a short version, see Ezekiel and Fox, *op. cit.,* p. 341.

For the table for the Durbin-Watson statistic, see J. Durbin and G. S. Watson, "Testing for Serial Correlation in Least Squares Regression, II," *Biometrika,* June 1951, pp. 172–175.

[22] Courchene and Shapiro apply an alternative to the test of the computed d as just outlined. As the footnote (†) in Table 2A-3 indicates, they apply an alternative due to H. Theil and A. L. Nagar.

residual error terms are computed for the series before the first differencing and after the first differencing; and the Durbin-Watson test for autocorrelation is applied for the regression results, both before and after first differencing.

Regression results from the analysis of data in Table 2A–1, both before and after first differencing are as follows:

(1)
$$\hat{r} = 1.26\,V_y - 0.38, \qquad \text{coefficient of determination} = 0.88$$
$$(0.55)$$

   t-test for slope of one[23]:   empirical $t = 4.73 > 1.645$

(2)
$$\Delta\hat{r} = 1.46\,\Delta V_y - 0.01, \qquad \text{coefficient of determination} = 0.08$$
$$(0.62)$$

   t-test for slope of one: empirical $t = 0.74 < 1.645$

(3)
$$\hat{V}_y = 0.70\,\hat{r} + 0.63, \qquad \text{coefficient of determination} = 0.88$$
$$(0.04)$$

   t-test for slope of one: empirical $t = 9.74 > 1.645$

(4)
$$\Delta\hat{V}_y = 0.05\,\Delta\hat{r} + 0.03, \qquad \text{coefficient of determination} = 0.08$$
$$(0.03)$$

   t-test for slope of one: empirical $t = 45.34 > 1.645$

From these results we note the following: the coefficients of determination are high before the first differencing; the regression coefficient resulting from regressing r on V_y is 1.26 and significantly greater than one; first differencing increases the standard error of the regression coefficient for the r-V_y association, and decreases it for the V_y-r association; and, after first differencing, with the increased standard error in Eq. (2), the slope parameter is not significantly different from one, but the coefficient of determination is too small to be of much value.

The Durbin-Watson d-statistic may be computed for each of the following sets of error terms:

---

[23] The one-tail test is at the 5 per cent level of significance.

$$r_t - \widehat{r}_t = \epsilon_t, \qquad t = 1, 2, \ldots, 72$$
$$\Delta r_t - \Delta\widehat{r}_t = \epsilon_t, \qquad t = 1, 2, \ldots, 71$$
$$V_{y,t} - \widehat{V}_{y,t} = \epsilon_t, \qquad t = 1, 2, \ldots, 72$$
$$\Delta V_{y,t} - \Delta\widehat{V}_{y,t} = \epsilon_t, \qquad t = 1, 2, \ldots, 71$$

The d-statistics corresponding to Eqs. (1), (2), (3), and (4), respectively, are as follows:

(1′) $d = 0.72 < 1.58$, indicating significant positive auto-correlation

(2′) $d = 3.00 > (4.00 - 1.58 = 2.42)$, indicating significant negative autocorrelation

(3′) $d = 0.64 < 1.58$, indicating significant positive auto-correlation

(4′) $d = 1.45 < 1.58$, indicating significant positive auto-correlation.

where the empirical d is followed in each case by the critical value. The critical d from the Durbin-Watson table[24] for 70 observations, one independent variable and positive autocorrelation, at the 5 per cent level is $d_L = 1.58$. Since d may possibly vary between zero and four, a critical value for d above which negative autocorrelation exists is $4.00 - d_L$. Hence, relatively low and relatively high d-values signify the presence of autocorrelation, either positive or negative autocorrelation as the case may be. In view of the Durbin-Watson criteria, significant autocorrelation is present in the residual error term for all four equations, both before and after first differencing. The first differencing increases the standard error term in the case of equation (2), but autocorrelation of the opposite sign still exists. After first differencing, furthermore, there is not much absolute variation remaining in the dependent variable to be explained by changes in the independent variable, so the coefficient of determination drops catastrophically following the differencing.

As stated, the presence of autocorrelation results in an understatement of calculated standard error for the estimated slope

---

[24] See Durbin and Watson, "Testing for Serial Correlation in Least Squares Regression, II," *op. cit.*, p. 173.

parameter. Its presence is important, consequently, in studies of monetary phenomena that rely on the standard error of a slope parameter. In some instances, as in Chapter 2 and elsewhere, on the other hand, analyses of monetary phenomena may lead to the hypothesis of cyclical and secular variation in both velocity and the rate of interest as a result of the prospect of responses in both variables to identical underlying forces. These responses, furthermore, may be of a type giving rise to autocorrelation in the residual error term, and in this instance one would not wish to remove all intracorrelation in the observed series as a means of preparing data for the test of hypotheses calling for the presence of such correlation. What is needed rather is a non-classical formula for the standard error which allows for autocorrelation.

2A.5   MULTICOLLINEARITY

Multicollinearity exists in a linear (or logarithmically linear) regression analysis when some or all of the so-called independent variables in such an analysis are correlated. It becomes difficult, in its presence, to disentangle the separate influences of the "explanatory" variables and to obtain reasonably precise estimates of their influence. The presence of multicollinearity is illustrated in the following least-squares, partial-regression results from annual data:[25]

1900–58
$$\ln (M/P) = \ln a - 0.674 \ln i + 0.971 \ln (Y/P) + u, \qquad R^2 = 0.98$$
$$ (0.064) \qquad (0.027)$$

−0.51, coefficient of correlation between independent variables

1900–49
$$\ln (M/P) = \ln a - 0.665 \ln i + 0.987 \ln (Y/P) + u, \qquad R^2 = 0.97$$
$$ (0.072) \qquad (0.036)$$

−0.52, coefficient of correlation between the independent variables

---

[25] These results are from Courchene and Shapiro. See Courchene and Shapiro, *op. cit.*, Table 2, p. 500.

1900–29
$$\ln (M/P) = \ln a - 0.233 \ln i + 0.739 \ln (Y/P) + u, \qquad R^2 = 0.90$$
$$\quad\quad\quad\quad\;\; (0.159) \quad\;\; (0.070)$$

−0.80, coefficient of correlation between the independent variables

1920–58
$$\ln (M/P) = \ln a - 0.664 \ln i + 0.934 \ln (Y/P) + u, \qquad R^2 = 0.97$$
$$\quad\quad\quad\quad\;\; (0.086) \quad\;\; (0.054)$$

−0.73, coefficient of correlation between the independent variables

1930–58
$$\ln (M/P) = \ln a - 0.544 \ln i + 0.940 \ln (Y/P) + u, \qquad R^2 = 0.96$$
$$\quad\quad\quad\quad\;\; (0.112) \quad\;\; (0.056)$$

−0.55, coefficient of correlation between the independent variables

where M/P is the deflated stock of currency plus demand deposits adjusted, i is the rate of interest on long-term corporate bonds, Y/P is deflated gross national product, and R^2 is the coefficient of total determination. From these results, we note that the independent variables were not highly correlated except in the case of 1900–29, and that this is also the only period in which there is a *great* disturbance in the values of the estimated partial regression coefficients.

The standard error of 0.159 in the equation for 1900–29 gives a warning of instability in the first partial regression (−0.233), but the error of (0.070) does not give a similar warning for the second partial regression based on 1900–29. The big potential damage which may be done by multicollinearity, however, lies in the fact that the operative efficiency of the partial-regression coefficients may be completely nullified in the sense that, in the event of high intercorrelations, the operational effect of one independent variable cannot be determined in isolation from the effect of another independent variable by ordinary least squares techniques. In technical terms, the big problem is one where the restraints upon the apparent effect of the "independent" variables on the "dependent" variable may completely destroy the operational domain of the partial-regression coefficients.

In considering multicollinearity, Johnston finds it convenient to consider several distinct cases.[26] In one extreme case with an exact linear relation between two independent variables, the estimating procedure for the regression coefficients is shown to break down because the partial regression coefficients become indeterminate. In a less extreme case, with only "high" correlation between the two independent variables, he outlines two arguments: one in which the standard errors of the estimated slope parameters increase as the correlation between the independent varibles increases; and another, due to F.R.W. Stone, whereby the coefficient of multiple correlation increases (i.e., $R_{1.23}$ increases) as the intercorrelation of the explanatory variables increases. Johnston, however, finds Stone's argument implausible on a priori grounds and unconfirmed by a numerical example. He cites the example as bearing witness to the greater indeterminacy of estimates as multicollinearity becomes more serious. In still another case, labeled the Frisch case, there are again several possibilities: one in which high but imperfect correlation between two independent variables in a three variable equation results in estimates being dominated by the error terms; another, called the pure-error case, in which different determinations "give radically different values for any given coefficient;" and still another in which the various determinations give relatively closer values for any given coefficient. Finally, in a fourth case, multicollinearity is said to be "serious in the sense that estimated parameters give an unsatisfactorily low degree of precision," and the remedy is said to lie in such directions as using some estimates from cross-section data in combination with time-series analysis.

Over-all, the difficulty in the presense of multicollinearity is primarily one of obtaining operational estimates. "Intercorrelation of explanatory variables may not be too serious," as Johnston points out, "if forecasting is a primary objective" and if the intercorrelation "may reasonably be expected to continue in the future."

---

[26] Johnston, *op. cit.*, pp. 201–207. For an article that attempts to place the multicollinearity problem in perspective, see Donald E. Farrar and Robert R. Glauber, "Multicollinearity in Regression Analysis: The Problem Revisited," *Review of Economics and Statistics*, February 1967, pp. 92–107.

Chapter 3

MONETARY ANALYSIS AND THE DEMAND FOR MONEY

Since the publication in 1936 of John Maynard Keynes's *The General Theory of Employment, Interest, and Money* the analysis of the demand for money has evolved as a part of liquidity-preference theory. This evolutionary strand is related, also, to developments concerning the theory of consumer choice and the study of empirical demand functions and to the integration of various aspects of general-equilibrium analysis and the theory of money. Keynes, in the *General Theory*, dealt with the demand for money primarily as a part of liquidity-preference theory, introduced the motives for holding money, and related the demand for money to the demand for the current output of goods and services. In the 1930's and 40's, following the advent of the *General Theory*, the study of money in the older, pre-1930's tradition took a secondary position, and continued mainly as only a part of an oral tradition at the University of Chicago. In the Chicago school, nevertheless, the demand for money was studied as a part of the general theory of consumer choice; money was treated as an asset, and elements of consumer tastes and preferences were involved. As matters further evolved, the demand for money came to be studied as other demand functions in the theory of consumer choice, and there were other efforts at integrating the theory of relative prices and output to monetary analysis.

To deal with the above matters and the way they have come to involve the empirical study of the demand for money, this chapter introduces some evolutionary aspects of monetary analysis and a variety of other topics: some matters of procedure in the study of the demand for money (Sec. 3.2), elementary models involving the demand for money (Sec. 3.3), the motives for holding money (Sec. 3.4), and some aspects of general equilibrium analysis and the theory of choice (Sec. 3.5). Throughout the chapter the emphasis will be upon the demand for money and certain notions in monetary analysis about the homogeneity (or unitary elasticity) of the demand for money with respect to certain variables. These variables appear and reappear in the empirical studies of the demand for money. The procedural matters taken up in the second section concern the treatment of the supply function and the notion of a homogeneous demand function for money. In the next section, analysis is introduced concerning the Cambridge cash-balance approach to the quantity theory, an elementary model involving a form of switching between money and assets with a residual claim (as contrasted with a fixed claim) against future income, such as plant and equipment, and two formulations of the liquidity-preference model. The models are presented with a minimum of embellishments, since they are expanded in later chapters.

3.1 SOME EVOLUTIONARY ASPECTS OF MONETARY ANALYSIS

In the evolution of economic analysis before Keynes's *General Theory* (1936), the theory of money and absolute prices and the theory of output and relative prices were treated separately. On the theory-of-money side, there was the general approach to analysis that has been labeled the "quantity theory of money," and, on the theory-of-output side, there was Say's law of markets lurking in the background. In the quantity-theory tradition before Keynes's *General Theory*, there were various approaches that received emphasis—the equation of exchange approach in the United States, and the Cambridge cash-balance approach in England, for example. The former of these approaches was symbolized by a rather mechanical statement in the form of the equation of exchange, and the latter symbolized by a somewhat less mechanical treatment of money balances as a proportion of income. There was, in the Cambridge approach, the factor of proportionality k that introduced the notion of a preference for money in relation to expenditures for real capital goods, although the factor k came to be treated as a constant in everyday use by the Cambridge school.

As matters evolved, perhaps in part as anticipated by the treatment of k in the Cambridge tradition, Keynes introduced motives for holding money, and emphasized the liquidity-preference demand for money, along with other building blocks in his *General Theory of Employment, Interest, and Money*—namely, the investment-demand model, and the aggregate supply-demand model symbolized by the consumption function. In the *General Theory*, Keynes attacked Say's law of markets, among other things, and related[1] the theory of money to the theory of output. Via shifts in the demand for money to satisfy a form of the speculative motive, the rate of interest, investment in capital goods, and income would change. The theory of money was related to the theory of output and the demand for money was shown to be related to the existence of equilibrium at the less than full-employment level of income (or output). In the liquidity-preference model the choice of assets giving rise to the rate of interest involved mainly money and bonds.

With the advent of the *General Theory*, in the 1930's and 1940's the quantity-theory approach fell into disrepute, except perhaps at the University of Chicago. There the quantity-theory approach was integrated with the general analysis of choice, with a constraint in the form of wealth. In 1956, a work by the Chicago school appeared to indicate this integration, and another more recent work summarizes some restatements of the quantity theory.[2] The 1966 work in question emphasizes the approximate equality of "desired" and "actual" money balances (M) and the relevance of such statements as $PQ \approx (1/k)M$, $(1/k) = V$, $P = (1/k)(M/Q)$, where P and Q are the product of the average of prices and output, and k is the Cambridge k, the recoprocal of velocity (V), all as

---

[1] For a review of traditional theory and Keynes's indictment of orthodox economics, see Robert Clower, "The Keynesian Counterrevolution: A Theoretical Appraisal," *The Theory of Interest Rates*, F. H. Hahn and F. P. R. Brechling, eds. (London: Macmillan and Co., Ltd., 1965), pp. 103–110; and, at an introductory level, Robert Lekachman, ed., *Keynes and the Classics* (Boston: D. C. Heath and Company, 1964).

[2] See Milton Friedman, "A Quantity Theory of Money—A Restatement," *Studies in the Quantity Theory of Money*, Milton Friedman, ed. (Chicago, Illinois: University of Chicago Press, 1956), pp. 3–21; and Maurice Allais, "A Restatement of the Quantity Theory of Money," *American Economic Review*, December 1966, pp. 1123–1157.

mentioned below. The economist responsible for this work, Maurice Allais, recognizes a proportional relationship between the price level and the quantity of money, and the variable nature of the constant k. He views the quantity theory as fundamentally correct, provided that it is redefined on the basis of certain formulations. Going back earlier, other works were appearing that dealt with various aspects of the integration of classical and monetary economics.[3] Today there is little doubt about the role and importance of the demand for money in the economic analysis of the demand for the output of goods and services and of the level of employment and prices. Questions remain about whether the integration of monetary and general equilibrium analyses have been successfully worked out, but, apart from the remaining questions: money has come to be treated as an asset from the demand point of view; money demand functions have come to be treated in a form similar to the market demand functions for other goods; and statistical methods have come to be applied to them.

3.2   SOME PROCEDURAL MATTERS

The present emphasis is on the demand for money. On the supply side, following established procedure, the quantity of money (M) is usually specified as an "exogenous" variable $(M_s = \gamma)$ because of the control exerted by the monetary authorities. The procedure may be questioned, however, "as a gross oversimplification," where, according to Lawrence Klein, "authorities . . . make direct decisions about the discount rates, open-market operations, reserve requirements and a host of minor credit conditions."[4] But there is, too, the view that the monetary authorities

---

[3] See, e.g., Don Patinkin, "The Indeterminacy of Absolute Prices in Classical Economic Theory," *Econometrica*, January 1949, pp. 1–27; Gary S. Becker and William J. Baumol, "The Classical Monetary Theory: The Outcome of the Discussion," *Econometrica*, November 1952, pp. 355–357; Don Patinkin, *Money, Interest, and Prices: An Integration of Monetary and Value Theory*, second edition (New York: Harper & Row, 1965); and Robert Clower, *op. cit.*, pp. 103–125.

[4] See L. R. Klein, "Stocks and Flows in the Theory of Interest," *The Theory of Interest Rates*, F. H. Hahn and F. P. R. Brechling, eds. (London: Macmillan and Co. Ltd., 1965), p. 149.

make decisions about changes in credit conditions and leave the use, say, of open-market operations to achieve them to the manager of the open-market account. Here the other instruments of credit policy—discount rates and changes in reserve requirements—tend simply to get brought in line with the conditions.[5] By such an approach the relevance of the practice of treating the money supply as exogenously determined may be viewed differently.

James Tobin says, "No doubt a skillful central bank can generally manipulate its control to keep M on target," but, continuing, he notes, "part of the job of monetary theory is to explain how."[6] Indeed, a good bit of empirical study is being devoted to the supply function for money,[7] and in time there should be fruitful results. Nevertheless, the work on the supply side is still rather rudimentary, and a good bit can be said about the broad outline of monetary analysis and the results from statistical analyses of data concerning the demand for money. Indeed, as noted earlier (Secs. 2.1 and 2A.2), it is possible to facilitate the identification of a demand function for money by invoking the appropriate definition of monetary policy.

3.3 SOME ELEMENTARY ANALYSIS

The main objective, in this section, is to introduce some elementary analysis and deduce some notions about the homogeneity of the demand for money with respect to a variety of factors. The notions deduced are said to appear and reappear in the study of empirical demand functions for money.

---

[5] William J. Frazer, Jr., and William P. Yohe, *Introduction to the Analytics and Institutions of Money and Banking* (Princeton, New Jersey: D. Van Nostrand Company, Inc., 1966), Secs. 10.2 and 24.2.

[6] James Tobin, "Money, Capital, and Other Stores of Value," *American Economic Review*, May 1961, p. 30.

[7] See Karl Brunner, "A Scheme for the Supply Theory of Money," *International Economic Review*, January 1961, pp. 79–109; Ronald L. Teigen, "Demand and Supply Functions for Money in the United States: Some Structural Estimates," *Econometrica*, October 1964, pp. 476–509; and Philip Cagan, *Determinants and Effects of Changes in the Stock of Money, 1875–1960* (New York: Columbia University Press for the National Bureau of Economic Research, 1965).

THE CAMBRIDGE CASH-BALANCE APPROACH

The Cambridge cash-balance approach to the quantity theory has been symbolized by expressions such as:

(1) $M = k(PQ)$ or, in real balance terms, $M/P = kQ$

where M is the money stock, P is the average of prices on the current output (Q) of goods and services, $Y(= PQ)$ is income, or the current output of goods and services in current prices, k is money balances as a proportion of income (i.e., $k = M/Y$) or the reciprocal of the income velocity of money (i.e., $V_y = Y/M$, $k = 1/V_y$)
We may also write the expression (1) as:

(1.1) $PQ = (1/k)M$, $PQ = Y$

(1.2) $P = (V/Q)M$

and note, in the respective instances, that as income changes (or prices, $Q =$ constant), the demand for money changes by the same proportion ($k =$ constant), and that as the stock of money changes ($k =$ constant), income (or the average of prices, $Q =$ constant) changes in the same proportion.

The Cambridge cash-balance approach to the quantity theory, as with other contemporary approaches in the pre-*General Theory* years, was characterized by a number of things: (1) an attempt to deal with the determinants of the price level, or absolute prices, and (2) an emphasis on the use of money as a medium of exchange or as a means of effecting transactions.

In the Cambridge formulation, however, the k depended upon the convenience obtained and the risk avoided by holding money instead of increasing expenditures on real capital, and it anticipates some of Keynes's emphasis on the motives for holding money in the liquidity-preference model of the *General Theory*, although the latter model dealt mainly with the choice between holding money and bonds.[8]

---

[8] For a review of the Cambridge version of the quantity theory and some aspects of liquidity-preference theory see James Tobin, "Money, Capital and Other Stores of Value," *American Economic Association*, May 1961, reprinted in Edwin Dean, ed., *The Controversy Over the Quantity Theory of Money* (Boston: D. C. Heath and Company, 1965), pp. 107–120.

AN ELEMENTARY MODEL

We could denote a very elementary model concerning the demand and supply of money, concerning notions of the type outlined with respect to the cash-balance approach, and enlarging upon the notions—namely:

(2)   Demand: $M_d = \alpha Y + \beta$, $\beta = 0$ at time zero.

   Supply: $M_s = \gamma$

   Equilibrium: $M_d = M_s$

where, in addition to the variables defined above, α is the reciprocal of the velocity of money at some basis time (e.g., time zero) from which changes are being considered, $\Delta\beta$ (i.e., changes in β) are associated with changes in the demand for money as a means of realizing gains (or avoiding losses) by a form of switching between some portion of money balances and assets such as plant and equipment with a residual claim against future income.

In the elementary model

(2.1) $Y = (\gamma - \beta)/\alpha$

changes in the money stock (γ) parallel equal percentage changes in income ($\beta = 0$), and on other occasions the following conditions hold: a decline in the speculative demand for money (i.e., $-\Delta\beta$) gives rise to an increase in income and the income velocity of money since actual balances tend to exceed the desired balances, and an increase in the rate of change in the money stock under these conditions causes velocity to rise faster; and an increase in the speculative demand for money (i.e., $\Delta\beta$) gives rise to a decline in velocity, since desired balances tend to be above actual balances, and an increase in the rate of change in the money stock under such conditions helps satiate the desire for actual balances, and mitigates or reverses the decline in velocity. Such changes in the speculative demand for money could come about in anticipation of price-level changes—a prospective increase reducing the purchasing power of cash balances and increasing the value of assets such as plant and equipment, and so on—and for other presently unstated reasons.

THE LIQUIDITY-PREFERENCE MODEL

The liquidity-preference model[9] most commonly dealt with over the first two decades of the *General Theory* may be denoted, as follows:

(3)   Demand for money (M_d): $M_d = a + \dfrac{b}{r}$, $a = cY,\ b > 0$

Supply (M_s): $M_s = \gamma$

Equilibrium: $M_s = M_d$

(3.1) Rate of interest (r): $r = \dfrac{b}{\gamma - a}$

where a is the demand for money to satisfy the transactions and precautionary motives as denoted by some proportion (c) of income (Y); b/r is the demand for money to satisfy the speculative motive; and γ is the stock of money exogenously determined by the monetary authorities.

In some instances, the balances a have been called transactions balances to emphasize their relation to expenditures (or income), and the remaining balances have been called speculative balances to emphasize the motive for holding them,[10] all as defined in greater detail below (Sec. 3.3). Hicks, in citing Keynes and dealing with the general form of the liquidity-preference demand functions, says: "In the first place there is a demand for money to finance current transactions, and in the second place there is a demand for money to act as a liquidity reserve." Continuing, he

---

[9] See, e.g., J. R. Hicks, *A Contribution to the Theory of the Trade Cycle* (London: Oxford University Press, 1950), pp. 140–141; Harry G. Johnson, *Money, Trade and Economic Growth* (Cambridge: Harvard University Press, 1962), pp. 114–115; Ronald L. Teigen, "The Demand for and Supply of Money", *Readings in Money, National Income, and Stabilization Policy,* Warren L. Smith and Ronald L. Teigen, eds. (Homewood, Illinois: Richard D. Irwin, Inc., 1965); and Frazer and Yohe, *op. cit.,* pp. 64–73, 441–445.

[10] See, e.g., Teigen, *op. cit.,* pp. 48–49; and John Maynard Keynes, *The General Theory of Employment, Interest, and Money* (New York: Harcourt, Brace and Company, 1936), pp. 165–174, 194–209.

says, "The amount of money required for the first purpose will depend, in the main, upon the volume of transactions in money terms, and this will vary with money income. . . . The amount of money required for the second purpose will be a matter of the relative advantage, at the margin, of holding money"—as against the holding of an interest-yielding asset.[11]

A common emphasis in explaining the shape of the liquidity-preference curve, defined by equation (3.1), is on holding bonds or money balances, and a rise in the rate of interest, usually above the "normal" or safe rate, provides the inducement for holding more bonds, since there is a greater likelihood of a future rise in bond prices and the prospect of a capital gain.[12] The converse set of changes also holds, in explaining the shape of the curve at a given time, given expectations about the future. The underlying expectations also change, however, and the demand for speculative balances increases (decreases) in response to an expected rise (decline) in the rate of interest and therefore, an expected decline (rise) in the price of bonds being traded in the market. In terms of this rather plausible explanation for changes in the demand for money, we may also note that a change in expectations leads to transactions in bonds that tend to bring about the interest-rate (or bond-price) changes expected.[13]

The liquidity-preference model could also be formulated as follows:[14]

---

[11] See Hicks, *op. cit.*, pp. 140–141.

[12] For discussions of the "normal" or "safe" rate see Keynes, *op. cit.*, pp. 201–202; and Teigen, *op. cit.*, p. 48.

For an assignment of probabilities of changes in the price of bonds to some points on the liquidity-preference function and for a rationale of the shape of the function in terms of these probabilities see William J. Frazer, Jr., "Some Comments on Professor Ritter's Interpretations of Keynes and Changes in Income Velocity," *Schweizerische Zeitschrift für Volkswirtschaft und Statistik*, March 1963, pp. 70–73; and Frazer and Yohe, *op. cit.*, pp. 64–66.

[13] For a more detailed statement of these matters see Frazer and Yohe, *op. cit.*, Chapter 4.

[14] William J. Frazer, Jr., "The Demand for Money, Statistical Results and Monetary Policy," *Schweizerische Zeitschrift für Volkswirtschaft und Statistik*, March 1967.

(4)   Demand: $M_d = cY + \dfrac{bY}{r}$

             Supply: $M_s = \gamma$

             Equilibrium: $M_d = M_s$

(4.1)   Rate of interest (r): $r = \dfrac{bY}{\gamma - cY}$

Here we may view the quantity of money balances sought to satisfy all of the motives for holding money as varying proportionally with income, including those held to satisfy the speculative demand (i.e., bY/r) as it concerns the bond market and changes in the rate of interest. But—as we note, in subsequently dealing with regression results, analysis, and the effects of changes in monetary policy—the monetary authorities do not exercise control over the money stock independently of influence on expenditures (and, therefore, income) via such factors as prospective price-level changes (Sec. 11.2 and 11.3). Indeed, already we have suggested the prospect of using both the rate of interest and income velocity of money (i.e., Y/γ) as indicators of monetary policy (Sec. 2.1).

HOMOGENEITY AND THE DEMAND FOR MONEY

Now with reference to the various elementary formulations of the demand for money, we may illustrate some very basic hypotheses that lend themselves to empirical investigation. These concern the elasticity of the demand for money with respect to income, prices, and so on. In fact, if we take logarithms of both sides of Eqs. (1), (1.1), and (1.2) we find that all the coefficients are one (and, therefore, the elasticities of the demand for money with respect to the reciprocal of velocity, prices, output, and so on, respectively, are one). Also, linear approximations to the relationships implicit in Eqs. (2), (3), and (4)—after effecting a logarithmic transformation of the variables—would yield an income elasticity coefficient of one for the demand for money and an interest rate coefficient with a negative sign. This means, in the context of the introductory analysis (Sec. 3.1), that the functions defined by equations such as (1), (1.1), and (1.2) are homogeneous,[15] and that the various elasticities of the untransformed variables in those instances are unity.

3.4 THE MOTIVES FOR HOLDING MONEY

The motives for holding money—the transactions, the precautionary, and the speculative motives—have been briefly noted above. They are now defined more fully, as they were introduced by Keynes, and as they have been modified since his time. Keynes said, in developing in detail the motives to liquidity preference, that the subject was "substantially the same as that which has

---

[15] Money-demand functions in much of monetary analysis are homogeneous of degree one. A function is homogeneous of degree one where each of the variables can be replaced by t times each of the variables, and where t can be completely factored out after taking on the power of the respective variables. The degree of the function is the power of t when factored out. For example, suppose we view the demand for money (M) as equal to some proportion (k) of the product of prices (P) and output (Q) and view k and P as constant—namely,

(1) $$M = kPQ, \qquad kP = \text{const.}$$

In this case,

$$kP(tQ) = t(kPQ) = tM$$

and the demand for money is homogeneous of degree one with respect to real output, and the exercise may be repeated with respect to k and P, respectively. On the other hand, if all three of the terms in the right-hand member of equation (1) vary simultaneously, and the demand is homogeneous of degree one with respect to each, $M = k^\delta P^\sigma Q^\rho$, $\delta + \sigma + \rho = 3$, and $(tk)^\delta (tP)^\sigma (tQ)^\rho = t^{\delta+\sigma+\rho} (kPQ) = t^{\delta+\sigma+\rho} (M)$. The function $f(k,PQ)$, then, is homogeneous of the third degree. (Note: the exponent δ may have been given a sign and the degree of the function reduced to the second degree.)

The property whereby proportional changes in one variable (or set of variables) calls forth equal proportional changes in another is dealt with in monetary analysis and in empirical study in economics in two ways, each of which amounts to the same thing. In the case of economics generally, one may refer to the elasticity of demand with reference to the percentage change in one variable called forth by a percentage change in another. In the case of empirical study, the variables (or variable constants) may be dealt with in a linear regression analysis, after a logarithmic transformation of the variables (M transformed into $\ln M$, k to $\ln k$, and so on), and, in such been sometimes discussed under the heading of the Demand for Money." Continuing, he may be quoted as follows:

> It [the analysis of the motives to liquidity preference] is also closely connected with what is called the income-velocity of money—for the income-velocity of money merely measures what proportion of their incomes the public chooses to hold in cash, so that an increased income-velocity of money may be a symptom of a decreased liquidity preference. It is not the same thing [as the analysis of the motives to liquidity preference], however, since it is in respect to his stock of accumulated savings rather than his income, that the individual can exercise the choice between liquidity and illiquidity.[16]

THE TRANSACTIONS MOTIVE

The transactions motive concerns the demand for money balances as a medium of exchange, as a means of bridging the gap between the receipt of payments and the disbursement of such proceeds, or as a means of bridging the interval between purchase and realization. Keynes, in dealing with the transactions motive recognized both an income and a business motive. In the first instance, the motive was "to bridge the interval between the receipt of income and its disbursement." In the second, it was "to bridge the interval between purchase and realization" as in "the receipt of sale-proceeds." One of the more elaborate post-Keynesian definitions of transactions balances is given as follows by James Tobin:

> No economic unit—firm or household or government—enjoys perfect synchronization between the seasonal patterns of its flow of receipts and its flow of expenditures. The discrepancies give rise to balances which accumulate temporarily, and are used up later in the year when expenditures catch up. Or, to put the same phenomenon the other way, the discrepancies give rise to the need

---

a case, the coefficients of the transformed variables become measures of elasticity for the dependent variable with respect to the independent variable in question. For example, $\ln M = \delta \ln k + \sigma \ln P + \rho \ln Q$, and the coefficients δ, σ, ρ become measures of elasticity.

The logarithmic transformation, of course, is more than an algebraic exercise. In some instances, it facilitates the transformation of an essentially nonlinear relationship to a more manageable logarithmically linear relationship.

[16] John Maynard Keynes, op. cit., p. 194.

for balances to meet seasonal excesses of expenditures over receipts. These balances are *transactions balances*. The aggregate requirement of the economy for such balances depends on the institutional arrangements that determine the degree of synchronization between individual receipts and expenditures. Given these institutions, the need for transactions balances is roughly proportionate to the aggregate volume of transactions.[17]

THE PRECAUTIONARY MOTIVE

The precautionary motive according to Keynes concerns the two aspects of the demand for balances:

(Type 1)   the demand for cash as a proportion of assets (or income) "to provide for contingencies requiring sudden expenditure and for unforeseen opportunities of advantageous purchases. . . ."

(Type 2)   the demand for an asset whose "value is fixed in terms of money to meet a subsequent liability (e.g., bank indebtedness) fixed in terms of money. . . ."[18]

A form of the precautionary demand appears to have been dealt with by Friedman and Schwartz:

After all, the major virtue of cash as an asset is its versatility. It involves a minimum of commitment and provides a maximum of flexibility to meet emergencies and to take advantage of opportunities. The more uncertain the future, the greater the value of such flexibility and hence the greater the demand for money is likely to be.[19]

THE SPECULATIVE MOTIVE

The speculative motive is at times related to the store-of-value property of money. It concerns an increase in the demand for balances (or the acceleration of the turnover of balances) as a means of avoiding a loss (or realizing a gain)—possibly in antici-

---

[17] See J. Tobin, "Liquidity Preference as Behavior Towards Risk," *Review of Economic Studies*, February 1958, p. 65.

[18] *Op. cit.*, pp. 170–171, and pp. 195–197.

[19] Friedman and Schwartz, *A Monetary History of the United States, 1867–1960* (Princeton, New Jersey: Princeton University Press for the National Bureau of Economic Research, 1963), pp. 673–675.

pation of likely changes in the value of bonds, but also, most generally, in anticipation of changes in the value of a variety of assets, including money, as well as assets with a residual claim against future income, as in the Cambridge cash-balance approach to the quantity theory. Keynes himself emphasized the choice between money and bonds in dealing with liquidity preference, as have others in the post-Keynesian era. Keynes said, "The aggregate demand for money to satisfy the speculative motive usually shows a continuous response to gradual changes in the rate of interest, i.e., there is a continuous curve relating changes in the demand for money to satisfy the speculative motive and changes in the rate of interest as given by changes in the price of bonds and debts of various maturities." And, continuing, he said, it is "important to distinguish between changes in the rate of interest . . . due to changes in the supply of money . . . and those which are primarily due to changes in expectations affecting the liquidity function itself."[20]

3.5 SOME ASPECTS OF EQUILIBRIUM ANALYSIS AND THE THEORY OF CHOICE

Since Keynes, there has been work on the integration of the classical theory of prices (or value) and monetary theory, and there has been a tendency to view money as an asset and to view the demand for money as a part of the theory of choice. In the first instance, general-equilibrium analysis has been involved quite generally, and, in the second, the theory of choice has been involved as it would concern budget constraints and equilibrium asset conditions, equilibrating adjustments, and wealth effects.

We deal, then, with some selected aspects of the integration of value and monetary theory, and proceed with brief subsections on equilibrium asset conditions, equilibrating adjustments, and wealth effects. There are also references to sources of the importance of the asset approach. In the review of equilibrium analysis and the use of income (asset or wealth) constraints, some

---

[20] Keynes, *op. cit.*, p. 197.

matters arise concerning the use of stock versus flow, or stock and flow variables.[21]

MONETARY THEORY, VALUE THEORY, AND THE REAL-BALANCE EFFECT

Some of the efforts to integrate value and monetary theory extend beyond the scope of the present work, but a few features of the specialized work devoted to the integration of value and monetary theory should be mentioned. For one, some issues centering about the existence of a total integration of contemporary price and monetary theory are unsettled.[22] For another, the effort toward integration, as carried forward by Don Patinkin[23] and other general-equilibrium theorists, has resulted in the "real-balance effect." This effect is summarized by Dean:

> Suppose that a person holds a given amount of money and that these money assets are larger than his total debt. . . . If the price level falls, the real value of these money balances rises. This person will have a larger stock of money than previously, in real terms, though not in nominal units. If his demand for money balances in real terms is constant, then, when the price level falls, his demand for nominal money balances will fall. He is likely to spend part of his money balances, since he no longer wishes to hold as much money as previously.
>
> The same reasoning may apply to a community as to an individual. If the private sector, taken as a whole, has money balances larger than its net debts (that is, if the government is a net debtor), then a fall in the price level will lead to increased spending.[24]

---

21 "Stock and flow analyses are not trivially equivalent," as Professor Klein has said, in inquiring "whether interest theory ought to be stated in terms of relevant stocks or flows or both." Klein, *op. cit.*, pp. 136–151.

22 Clower, *op. cit.*, pp. 103–125.

23 For a summary of the differences between Patinkin's theory (as a classical theory) and Keynes's theory see G. L. S. Shackle, "Recent Theories Concerning the Nature and Role of Interest," *The Economic Journal*, June 1961, pp. 211–222, also reprinted in *Survey of Economic Theory*, Vol. I (London: Macmillan and Co. Ltd., 1965).

24 See Dean, *op. cit.*, p. 85.

Note here that the effect of price-level changes on spending is just the reverse from that expected when price-level changes operate on expectations, as in the earlier analysis (Sec. 2.3). Via the "real-balance effect," a decline in prices leads to a rise in velocity whereas a rise in prices operating on expectations leads to an expected loss of purchasing power and a rise in velocity via a form of switching between money and assets, such as real property with a residual claim against income.

AN EQUILIBRIUM FRAMEWORK

One may think of business, household and governmental units adjusting their assets to suit their satisfaction, all subject to a budget constraint, and in accordance with changes in the rates of return from the various classes of assets.[25] The units may also be viewed as attempting to make some sort of simultaneous adjustment on the liabilities side, subject to the same sort of budget constraint, and with the view to minimizing the loss of satisfaction due to the costs, usually expressed as rates of interest or return on net worth. On the asset side, the equilibrium is in terms of the equality of the rates of return from additions to the various classes of assets, after allowing for the various risks (or liquidity) and other elements entering into the rates of return, and where the return in the case of money is primarily in terms of convenience, flexibility to take advantage of unforeseen opportunities, and a temporary store of value.

For the business sector the constraint is quite simply total assets in the balance-sheet sense, although there may be reasons for using sales as a substitute constraint, where asset size and sales are highly correlated. For the household and government sectors, the constraint need not be thought of as essentially different, but there are empirical problems in selecting the constraints, in part because of the role of human capital. For the over-all economy, the wealth constraint (W), a stock variable, may be simply viewed as the discounted value of the flow variable income (i.e., $W = Y/r$, where Y is income and r is the rate of interest).[26] A value, in the latter instance, is implicitly attributed to human capital, according

---

[25] See, for example, Frazer and Yohe, *op. cit.*, Sec. 4.1, and Chapter 17.
[26] See Friedman, *op. cit.*, p. 1.

to the usage and salary portion of income received for the services of the labor force.

EQUILIBRATING ADJUSTMENTS

Equilibrating adjustments take place within the above framework. The constraints concern stock variables—total assets, human capital, nonhuman capital, and so on. They are constantly subject to change at the margin, and adjustments in the allocation of funds to the various assets or expenditures may be thought of as occurring first in relation to the flow of returns (i.e., income) from assets and then possibly being extended to alterations in the various assets as proportions of the total, through the net disposal of some assets such as cash, liquid securities, housing, and so on.

Usually the asset type of constraint will be changing in response to the flow of income in the form of sales, interest, dividends, rent, salaries, and wages or in the flow of funds from increases in such liabilities as bank loans, but the equilibrating changes in income will be larger in relation to income than in relation to the accumulated stock of assets. Klein makes the analogy to an iceberg in which the flow quantity is similar to the part above the water and the stock quantity is similar to the part below the water,[27] and the matter comes up in a review by Lydall of Professor Hansen's statement of Marshall's theory of the demand for money. In Lydall's review,[28] Professor Hansen expresses the theory in terms of the equation $M = kY + k^*A$, where M is total demand for money, Y is money income, A is total value of assets, k is the proportion of income people desire to hold in the form of money, and k^* is the proportion of assets people will desire to hold in the form of money. As Lydall notes, Hansen concludes that the demand for money is, "particularly in the short run, mainly a function of income and the rate of interest" since "in short-run analyses, A may be neglected on the grounds that it can be changed only by a small amount compared to the total stock." According to Lydall, however, "It is conceivable that Marshall felt that in his historical study it would be impossible to identify

27 Klein, *op. cit.*, pp. 136–139.
28 See H. F. Lydall, "Income, Assets, and the Demand for Money," *Review of Economics and Statistics*, February 1958, pp. 2–3.

separately the income demand for money and the asset demand for money, since the changes in aggregate income and aggregate capital over time are closely associated—so that, for practical purposes, to make the demand for money dependent on income alone was equivalent to making it dependent on income and capital separately."

The above details touch on the likely equivalence of making the demand for money dependent on income or on wealth (given the rate of interest), and the importance of changes in income and the rate of interest in effecting equilibrating adjustments in assets. General equilibrium analysis has often been viewed as a statement of equilibrium conditions that may be attained in the long run, but the process of adjustment—the groping, searching, feeling-in-the-dark process—toward equilibrium is applicable to the analysis of shorter run developments.[29]

WEALTH EFFECTS

In the context of various aspects of equilibrium analysis as it applies to the demand for money, and as it involves simple changes in scale, a number of propositions follow. As introduced earlier (Sec. 3.3), these concern the homogeneity of the demand for money—namely, the demand for money is homogeneous of degree one with respect to prices and assets (changing the latter calls for an increase in the money stock by the same proportions), and the rate of interest is homogeneous of degree zero with respect to changes in all the stock and flow variables in the same proportions. In the analyses of actual changes in asset size or wealth (as contrasted with simple analytical changes of a scale nature), however, some assets or other accounts may vary slightly more or less than in proportion to total assets or wealth. At the sector level, some demands for money may vary more or less than in proportion to total assets or wealth, and still over-all analyses of

---

[29] Commenting on such a point, Kuenne notes the following: "Walras' models were not 'long-run models in the Marshallian sense, but rather were short-run models in which extreme mobility of factor services allowed long-run characteristics such as the equality of price and average cost to emerge.'" See Robert E. Kuenne, "Say's Law and Walras' Law Once More: Comment," *Quarterly Journal of Economics*, August 1964, pp. 482–483.

aggregate data may reflect equal proportional changes, or more or less than equal proportional changes. Some such prospects and studies involving empirical data have led some economists to deal with "wealth effects" on the demand for money. One such widely studied hypothesis is, in the language of consumption theory, the "luxury goods" hypothesis. It says *the demand for money balances rises more than in proportion to the stock of wealth.* We will deal with some of the matters concerning this widely studied hypothesis and other wealth-effect hypotheses.

SOURCES OF THE IMPORTANCE OF THE ASSET APPROACH

The wealth or asset approach to the demand for money gains its importance from several sources: For one, it introduces a form of analysis that readily permits the consideration of a narrower choice situation involving money and bonds or a situation involving broader classes of assets, including those with a residual claim against future income such as plant and equipment. For another, notions about subjective elements—tastes and preferences —in the theory of consumer choice carry over to a consideration of the demand for money. Friedman emphasizes this,[30] and Lydall writes about it in connection with liquidity-preference analysis.[31] Lydall—in introducing Keynes's liquidity-preference theory and surveying the antecedents of the asset-demand theory—says, in effect, that "since the demand for the stock of money was thought to be related solely to income," the Cambridge real-balance equation (Sec. 3.3) failed to treat the role of money as a store of value. He then notes that "Keynes's liquidity-preference theory was the first great departure from the income or transactions approach," since it introduced the notion of money as an "asset," or store of value, and since in this store-of-value context appeared the speculative motive and the precautionary motive.

3.6 SUMMARY

Before Keynes's *General Theory* (1936), the theory of money and absolute prices was separate from the theory of output. The

---

[30] Friedman, *op. cit.*
[31] Lydall, *op. cit.*, pp. 1–3.

one was symbolized by the quantity theory of money and a demand for money for effecting transactions. The other was symbolized by Say's law of markets. The latter implied a full-employ-
ment-equilibrium level of output. J. M. Keynes, however, introduced
the motives for preferring liquidity in the form of money—including the speculative motive for holding money as an asset or
store of value—and related these to the demand for money and
the prospect of equilibrium at less than full employment. A
change in the speculative demand for money could give rise to a
change in the rate of interest and reduced expenditures for the
current output of goods and services. The approach had elements
of an analysis of the demand for money as an asset rather than
simply as a means of effecting transactions. It became of increasing importance following the publication of Keynes's major
work in 1936.

The quantity-theory approach to the demand for money, on the
other hand, was relegated to a secondary role in monetary analysis
in the 1930's and 1940's. Interest in the approach continued mainly
at the University of Chicago, as a part of an oral tradition. The
demand for money in this tradition at Chicago came to be studied
as a part of the theory of consumer choice with emphasis on
tastes and preferences, subject to a budget constraint. As matters
evolved, this study led to consideration of demand functions for
money, similar to demand functions for other goods and services.
There were, also, other developments in the period leading to
the integration of various aspects of general-equilibrium analysis
and the theory of money. These have been symbolized by the
work of Don Patinkin and others.

Some matters remain to be worked out in the integration of
general-equilibrium analysis and the theory of money, but the
notion of the possible existence of an interrelationship between the
demand for money and the demand for other goods and services
is widely accepted, and various aspects of equilibrium analysis
have affected our approach to the study of the demand for money.
Wealth, or some substitute stock variable, becomes a constraint on
the demand for money, and wealth may be defined as the discounted value of income, a flow variable. The more general analysis,
also, accommodates a number of other notions: the notion of a wide

range of adjustments in the various classes of assets, with adjustments taking place at the margin or primarily in the flow variables; the notion of a form of switching between money and bonds, as well as a form of switching between broader classes of assets, including real capital; and notions about the homogeneity of the demand for money. In an over-all stock-flow or equilibrium framework simple changes in scale, as in a doubling of wealth and income, led to several conclusions: that the demand for money is homogeneous of degree one in prices and assets; that the rate of interest is homogeneous of degree zero with respect to scale changes in the stock and flow variables.

Given wealth as income discounted by the appropriate rate of interest, and given various elementary models emphasizing the rate of interest, income, and the motives affecting the demand for money, in the asset approach to the demand for money—a number of important possible determinants of the demand for money may be considered, including income and the rate of interest. The general form of the elementary demand functions for money appearing in this chapter, and the monetary analysis appearing in (or assumed in the discussion of homogeneity) lead us to expect the following: that the demand for money is unit elastic with respect to income, assets, the level of prices, and the level of real income or output, respectively; that the demand for money is unit elastic (but of a negative sign) with respect to the rate of interest; and that the income velocity of money is unit elastic with respect to the rate of interest.

All the prospective elasticities are not necessarily unitary. There is the prospect that asset size or wealth changes in the real world give rise to more or less than equal proportional changes in the demand for money. One such widely considered "wealth effect," or "luxury goods" hypothesis in the language of consumption theory, is that the demand for money changes more than in proportion to wealth. There is also the possibility of speculative shifts in the demand for money and a form of switching between broad classes of assets in anticipation of changes in the price level and in response to other factors. These lead to the prospect of including changes in prices or the rate of change in prices as a determinant of the demand for money. This latter prospect, however, is somewhat in contrast to the effect of price-level changes on the demand for money that follows from the "real-balance effect." This latter effect concerns an increase in spending as a result of a decline in prices and the increased purchasing power of money balances.

All the variables introduced as determinants of the demand for money in this review of monetary analysis appear and reappear in subsequent chapters. A wide variety of results from analyses of empirical data involve the variables in question.

Chapter 4

LIQUIDITY PREFERENCE, THE TRAP,
AND ALL THAT

The demand for money is frequently treated in elementary models in economics as a function of income (or assets or wealth) and/or the rate of interest. One such model containing the function and the rate of interest as a variable—with selected balances, a constant proportion of income—is the liquidity-preference model. In a formulation of the demand for money, as it evolved from Keynes's *General Theory*, those balances related to income specifically are called "transactions" or "transactions and precautionary balances." They are implicitly a linear function of income with an elasticity coefficient of one. The balances related most directly to the rate of interest are called "speculative balances."

The liquidity-preference demand for money has most commonly been thought of as involving a choice between holding money and bonds in some varying combination, usually, but not always, with only incidental or no references to a choice between other classes of assets, including real capital such as equipment. There is the view that a movement of interest rates away from the more normally prevailing rates puts a premium on holding relatively more or less cash balances—depending on whether bond prices are expected to fall [and yields (as rates) rise] or on whether bond prices are expected to rise (and yields fall). This rationale about the demand for balances in relation to the rate of interest, moreover, suggests a relationship between the ratio of money balances and income (or the reciprocal of the income velocity of money)—namely, a rise in the rate of interest (and a decline in bond prices) results in a form of switching in favor of the bonds and gives rise to an increase in the turnover or velocity of cash balances, and a decline in the rate has a reverse set of effects.

The views of the liquidity-preference model up to about the early 1960's, in most instances, led to its being used to explain possibly nothing more than co-movements in two variables— velocity and the rate of interest. They also involved efforts to isolate specific types of balances—"transactions" and "idle" or "speculative" balances. There has been discussion, too, about whether short- or long-term rates of interest should be most appropriately considered in dealing with the effect of the rate of interest on the demand for money, and there has been the prospect of a very low rate of interest calling forth an almost insatiable demand for cash, such that there would be almost no turnover of balances and such that monetary officials could not increase spending by lowering the rate of interest. Such prospects as these and the explanation of movements in velocity and the rate of interest implicit in the formulations of the liquidity-preference demand for money have led to numerous empirical studies. Some have attempted to identify empirically the liquidity-preference function; a number of others have attempted to deal with the possible existence of a situation in which low rates of interest called forth an excessive preference for money balances; and others have attempted to present elasticity coefficients for the changes in velocity and the rate of interest.

The choice of assets pertaining to the demand for money and the velocity of money has on other occasions been more broadly considered, and the demands for balances to satisfy the various motives have been treated as homogeneous of degree one with respect to income. In particular, analysis of a broader choice situation has been shown to provide an alternative to the explanation of the velocity-interest rate association implicit in earlier formulations of the liquidity-preference demand for money. This alternative explanation is shown to be more consistent with statistical results from analyses of time-series data. A minor modification in the formulation of the elementary liquidity-preference model also is presented.

The subjects, as introduced above, are considered in this chapter in two sections—(Sec. 4.1.) The Liquidity-Preference Model:

Velocity, the Trap, and the Velocity-Interest Rate Association; (Sec. 4.2.) Liquidity Preference and an Alternative Explanation: The Velocity-Interest Rate Association.

4.1 THE LIQUIDITY-PREFERENCE MODEL: VELOCITY, THE TRAP, AND THE VELOCITY–INTEREST RATE ASSOCIATION

The topics contained in this section include the liquidity-preference model, the liquidity trap concerning the liquidity-preference demand for money, short rates versus long rates, methods of defining and considering idle balances, and the trap and the velocity-interest rate association.

THE LIQUIDITY-PREFERENCE MODELS AN EARLY FORMULATION

The liquidity-preference model most frequently implied[1] may be denoted as follows:

Demand: $\qquad M_d = a + \dfrac{b}{r}, \qquad a = cY, b > 0$

Supply: $\qquad M_s = \gamma$

Equilibrium: $\quad M_s = M_d$

where M is the money stock, r is the rate of interest, a is the demand for money to satisfy the transactions and precautionary motives (Sec. 3.4) as denoted by some proportion (c) of income (Y), b/r is the demand for money to satisfy the speculative motive (Sec. 3.4), and γ is the stock of money exogenously determined by the monetary authorities. A sketch of this model is shown in Figure 4–1.

---

[1] See, e.g., J. R. Hicks, *A Contribution to the Theory of the Trade Cycle* (London: Oxford University Press, 1950), pp. 140–141; Harry G. Johnson, *Money, Trade and Economic Growth* (Cambridge: Harvard University Press, 1962), pp. 114–115; Ronald L. Teigen, "The Demand for and Supply of Money," *Readings in Money, National Income, and Stabilization Policy,* Warren L. Smith and Ronald L. Teigen, eds. (Homewood, Illinois: Richard D. Irwin, Inc., 1965); and William J. Frazer, Jr., and William P. Yohe, *Introduction to the Analytics and Institutions of Money and Banking* (Princeton, New Jersey: D. Van Nostrand Company, Inc., 1966), pp. 64–73, 441–445.

Figure 4–1. The Liquidity-Preference Demand for Money Balances.

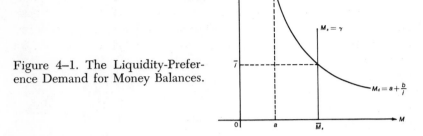

In some instances, the balances a have been called transactions balances to emphasize their relation to expenditures (Sec. 3.4), and the remaining balances have been called speculative balances to emphasize the motive for holding them.[2] Hicks, in citing Keynes and dealing with the general form of the liquidity-preference demand function, says, "In the first place there is a demand for money to finance current transactions, and in the second place there is a demand for money to act as a liquidity reserve." Continuing, he says, "The amount of money required for the first purpose will depend, in the main, upon the volume of transactions in money terms, and this will vary with money income. . . . The amount of money required for the second purpose will be a matter of the relative advantage, at the margin, of holding money"—as against the holding of an interest-yielding asset.[3] Professor Johnson proceeds along this same line. He distinguishes between "the demand for speculative balances . . . as a function of the rate of interest" and "transactions demand for money" as a fraction k of national income.[4]

It is also common to relate changes in the income velocity of money to the liquidity-preference model, to refer to "active" and

---

[2] See, e.g., Teigen, *op. cit.*, pp. 48–49; and John Maynard Keynes, *The General Theory of Employment, Interest, and Money* (New York: Harcourt, Brace and World, 1936), pp. 165–174, 194–209.

[3] See Hicks, *op. cit.*, pp. 140–141.

[4] See Johnson, *op. cit.*, pp. 114–115.

"idle" balances,[5] and to discuss the relationship between "safe" or "normal" rates of interest and abnormally high or low rates. Professor Ritter says, "It is generally assumed that, with a given money supply, the Keynesian system requires that interest rates and velocity vary directly. . . . This is usually explained in terms of the Keynesian demand for idle or speculative balances, in which the amount of idle balances demanded varies inversely with the rate of interest."[6]

A common emphasis is on holding bonds or money balances, and a rise in the rate of interest, usually above the normal rate, provides the inducement for holding a larger portion of bonds, since there is a greater likelihood of a future rise in bond prices and the prospect of a capital gain.[7] The result of actions to acquire a larger volume of bonds in lieu of money balances is, according to the usual analysis, a rise in the income velocity of money or the level of income relative to the stock of money. The converse set of changes also holds. These changes, moreover, help explain the shape of the curve since the inducement to hold money becomes less and less or stronger and stronger, depending on a rise or decline, as the rate of interest departs from the "normal" or "safe" rate.

The emphasis in liquidity-preference analysis on holding bonds or money is frequently to the exclusion of the consideration of assets with a residual claim against future income, such as plant,

---

[5] See, e.g., Avram Kisselgoff, "Liquidity Preference of Large Manufacturing Corporations," *Econometrica*, October 1945, pp. 334–344; and Lawrence S. Ritter, "The Structure of Financial Markets, Income Velocity, and the Effectiveness of Monetary Policy," *Schweizerische Zeitschrift für Volkswirtschaft und Statistik*, March 1963, pp. 70–79.

[6] See Ritter, *op. cit.*, p. 280.

[7] For discussions of the "normal" or "safe" rate, see Keynes, *op. cit.*, pp. 201–202; and Teigen, *op. cit.*, p. 48.

For an assignment of probabilities of changes in the price of bonds to some points on the liquidity-preference function and for a rationale of the shape of the function in terms of these probabilities, see William J. Frazer, Jr., "Some Comments on Professor Ritter's Interpretations of Keynes and Changes in Income Velocity," *Schweizerische Zeitschrift für Volkswirtschaft und Statistik*, March 1963, pp. 70–73; and Frazer and Yohe, *op. cit.*, pp. 64–66.

equipment, and inventories.[8] On some occasions this emphasis is retained, but references are made to real wealth. In an early paper on liquidity preference, Kisselgoff says the holding of cash under conditions of declining economic activity "is profitable in terms of real wealth because of the general fall in prices."[9] On

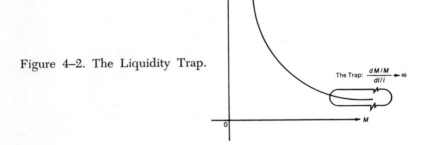

Figure 4–2. The Liquidity Trap.

more recent occasions, as discussed below (Sec. 4.3), the analysis of liquidity preference is related to broad classes of assets including "real wealth" or assets with a residual claim against future income. In fact, as we will note, the liquidity trap concerning the liquidity-preference demand for money may be defined in terms of either the liquidity-preference demand for money or in terms of the Keynesian investment-demand model.

THE LIQUIDITY TRAP

The liquidity trap may be defined as the set of points on the liquidity-preference curve where the percentage change in the demand for money, i.e., $\Delta M/M$, in response to a percentage change in the rate of interest, i.e., $\Delta r/r$, approaches infinity or a large number.[10] The reader will recognize this as the set of points involving a highly interest-elastic demand for money, denoted as

---

[8] See, e.g., Teigen, *op. cit.*, pp. 48–49; Martin Bronfenbrenner and Thomas Mayer, "Liquidity Functions in the American Economy," *Econometrica*, October 1960, pp. 810–834; and Robert Eisner, "Another Look at Liquidity Preference," *Econometrica*, July 1963, pp. 532–533.

[9] Kisselgoff, *op. cit.*, p. 335.

[10] See Frazer and Yohe, *op. cit.*, p. 383.

$$\eta_{r \cdot M} = \frac{dM}{dr} \frac{r}{M} \quad \text{or} \quad \eta_{r \cdot M} = \frac{d \ln M}{d \ln r}$$

In the latter case of the logarithmically transformed variables, the liquidity-preference curve (Figure 4–1) may be defined as $\ln M_d = \alpha + \beta \ln r$, where the coefficient β is the elasticity coefficient. Sometimes the trap is discussed in terms of the slope of the tangent to the liquidity-preference curve (or simply the slope of the curve),[11] and the trap is said to be located in the curve as the slope with respect to the vertical axis becomes horizontal, usually at a low rate of interest or when the yield on long-term bonds reaches zero or some institutional floor. At other times, the trap in question has been discussed in terms of an extremely interest-inelastic investment demand for real capital, plant and equipment, and so on.[12]

In the first instance, the existence of the trap in the real world

---

[11] See Eisner, *op. cit.*, p. 532; and M. Bronfenbrenner and Thomas Mayer, "Rejoinder to Professor Eisner," *Econometrica*, July 1963, pp. 539–542.

[12] See Milton Friedman and Anna J. Schwartz, "Money and Business Cycles," *Review of Economics and Statistics*, 1963 Supplement on "The State of Monetary Economics," p. 46; and Frazer and Yohe, *op. cit.*, pp. 383–384.

Additional types of liquidity traps too have actually been set forth and studied empirically, as discussions have emanated from the considerations of the liquidity trap in the context of the liquidity-preference model.

(See Karl Brunner and Allan H. Meltzer, "Liquidity Traps for Money, Bank Credit and Interest Rates," a paper delivered at the annual meeting of the Econometric Society, December 1965.) Types of traps, for example, are introduced in connection with the responses of the money supply and bank credit to changes in bank reserves in excess of borrowings. In such instances one recognizes the differential responses in the stock of credit and the stock of money (Frazer and Yohe, *op. cit.*, pp. 39–48, 564–566), and one may deal with a demand function for banks somewhat like the liquidity-preference function in connection with the willingness of banks to expand loans in response to an increase in excess reserves (Frazer and Yohe, *op. cit.*, pp. 566–572). In the present context, however, we confine ourselves mainly to "the liquidity trap" as defined in connection with the Keynesian type liquidity-preference demand for money. Where the several types of traps have been studied jointly by Brunner and Meltzer, nevertheless, the study supports conclusions denying the existence of liquidity traps, even in the 1930's when a liquidity trap is often said to have occurred. (See Brunner and Meltzer, *op. cit.*)

would be characterized by a situation at a moment in time when large increases in the money stock would simply be absorbed as speculative balances in anticipation of a future rise in the rate of interest. Such changes would have little or no effect on the rate of interest, or a small decline in the rate of interest would have the effect of increasing considerably the speculative demand for money balances. In the instance involving real capital, a decline in the rate of interest would have little or no effect on investment in real capital. The portion of assets comprising cash in relation to the portion comprising plant and equipment, for example, would increase.

In discussing empirical evidence in support of the existence of a liquidity trap of the demand-for-money type, Eisner notes that by effecting a linear approximation to logarithmically transformed data for the money stock and the rate of interest as a means of obtaining a measure $\eta_{r.M}$, one assumes a constant elasticity. Continuing, he says,

> Evidence that the elasticity goes to infinity or even gets larger at lower interest rates is quite unnecessary for the proposition that the money demanded goes to infinity as the rate of interest is lowered. Findings that the elasticity does not get smaller in absolute amount as the interest rate gets smaller would be sufficient—but not necessary—evidence for the liquidity trap.
>
> In view of the implication of a floor or bottom stop from any constant interest elasticity, information bearing on the liquidity trap might better be got from estimates of arithmetic (as opposed to logarithmic) slopes. For the Keynesian theory would require the slope of the demand curve to be closer to horizontal for low interest rates or high amounts of idle balances.[13]

In commenting on slopes versus measures of elasticity, Bronfenbrenner and Mayer make some additional points about the Keynesian hypothesis of "absolute liquidity preference" (which has since been called the "liquidity trap"). They note that the phenomenon called the "liquidity trap is mentioned incidentally in terms of elasticity." They say, "It makes little difference whether Keynes

---

[13] See Eisner, op. cit., p. 532.

(or anyone else) defines the liquidity trap in terms of an infinite elasticity or a zero slope of a liquidity function."[14]

SHORT RATES VERSUS LONG RATES

In a 1960 study of liquidity functions, Bronfenbrenner and Mayer[15] use a short-term rather than a long-term rate of interest, such as more customarily appears in the context of a liquidity-preference analysis. Further, in a later use of liquidity-preference analysis, Ritter notes,[16] "The orthodox Keynesian model is formulated almost exclusively in terms of behavior responses to *long-term* interest rates, and to long-term interest rates only." Continuing, he says, "It visualizes a world in which the only financial assets in existence are cash and long-term bonds: in a sense the orthodox Keynesian system may be said to have a capital market, but not a money market." In both instances—the Bronfenbrenner-Mayer study and the Ritter analysis—a number of defensible and consistent comments by the latter authors and others on long- and short-term rates follow and relate to matters of Keynesian liquidity-preference analysis.

Eisner says, in commenting on the Bronfenbrenner-Mayer study, "It must be recognized that the Keynesian theory about the demand for money tending to become 'absolute' at low rates of interest, applies to long-term rates. For that theory," he says, "states that because of the 'speculative motive' with regard to capital gains and losses which are peculiar to long-term securities, the rate of interest cannot get indefinitely low without the market becoming dominated by those who prefer to hold cash in expectation of a fall in prices of long-terms." Continuing, Eisner relates the question of the short versus the long rate to real capital investment, as others have done in recognizing a broader range of assets to choose among rather than simply cash and bonds. He says with reference to the liquidity trap rather than the rationale of the shape of the liquidity-preference function: "The peculiar

---

[14] Bronfenbrenner and Mayer, "Rejoinder to Professor Eisner," *op. cit.*, p. 539.

[15] See Bronfenbrenner and Mayer, "Liquidity Functions in the American Economy," *op. cit.*, pp. 810–834.

[16] Ritter, *op. cit.*, p. 283.

Keynesian issue is that of getting down the long-term rate (which is most relevant to investment)."[17] As noted earlier, the liquidity trap can be stated in terms of Keynes's investment-demand model.

In rebutting Eisner's points about the long-term rate, Bronfenbrenner and Mayer comment as follows:

> When using Keynes' speculative motive to explain people's reluctance to buy long-term securities, one should refer specifically to . . . the return from that viewpoint. . . . But the absolute liquidity preference doctrine, as we understand it, does not only assert that at low rates people refused to buy long-term securities; rather, it asserts that at low rates they refuse to buy long-term securities *and hold money instead.* Short-term securities are complementary with long-term securities against money. For the decision to hold money, it is the short rate which is relevant. If, for example, I expect the long rate to rise, I will buy bills instead of bonds (ignoring transactions costs). Only if I expect the bill rate to rise as well will I hold cash.

> One should ideally use no interest rate alone, but a vector of all interest rates jointly, which we are able to do only in the trivial case where relative rates are constant. Eisner does not show that this ideal measure is approached more closely by the bond rate than the bill rate, and two considerations suggest that the bill rate is the better measure. The first is a major theory of the interest rate structure: given the bill rate, the level of other rates can be explained by anticipations *cum* liquidity preference. The second consideration involves less theoretical elegance, but more practicality. Eisner may be correct that the long-term rate is more important than the short for investment as a whole, but this does not make the short rate irrelevant. . . .[18]

In commenting on the Ritter position cited above, the view was set forth that a broader range of financial markets could be dealt with in terms of analysis growing out of *General Theory.* In particular, it was noted that the rationale concerned with the shape and the assignment of probabilities to the liquidity-preference function was applicable to the choice between short-term securities

---

[17] Eisner, *op. cit.,* pp. 532–533.

[18] Bronfenbrenner and Mayer, "Rejoinder to Professor Eisner," *op. cit.,* pp. 540–541.

and money as well as the choice between long-term securities and money.[19] There was also the view that by a change in "the rate of interest" a change in the entire structure was implied.[20] This structure would be analogous to the Bronfenbrenner-Mayer "vector of all interest rates." Ritter's subsequent reference to a basic proposition is quite acceptable, too. Namely, a given increase (decrease) in the rate of interest causes the value of a marketable bond to decline (rise) more, the longer the time to maturity.

METHODS OF DEFINING (AND CONSIDERING) IDLE BALANCES, AND OTHER PROBLEMS

A number of studies have attempted to identify empirically the liquidity-preference function of the above (Figure 4–1) equilateral-hyperbola form, with distinct transactions balances a ($= cY$) and speculative balances b/r.[21] "Following Keynes's original formulation," as Klein notes, "they tried to separate the stock of transactions cash from the stock of idle cash by using the velocity ratio calculated on a stock basis at a time when turnover of cash was at a historical peak."[22]

In the Bronfenbrenner-Mayer study, idle balances were derived in several steps: (1) by dividing private money holdings (i.e., "currency outside of banks plus demand deposits other than government or interbank deposits") into private GNP (i.e., "total

---

[19] Frazer, *op. cit.*, pp. 70–78.

[20] *Ibid;* and see Ritter's reply, *op. cit.*, pp. 80–82.

[21] See, e.g., Kisselgoff, *op. cit.;* Bronfenbrenner and Mayer, "Liquidity Functions in the American Economy," *op. cit.;* and James Tobin, "Liquidity Preference and Monetary Policy," *Review of Economic Statistics,* February 1947, pp. 124–131, reprinted in Arthur Smithies and J. Keith Butlers, eds., *Readings in Fiscal Policy* (Homewood, Illinois: Richard D. Irwin, Inc., 1955), pp. 233–247.

See also A. J. Brown, "Interest, Prices, and the Demand Schedule for Idle Money," *Oxford Economic Papers,* No. 2, May 1939, pp. 46–69, reprinted in T. Wilson and P. W. S. Andrews, eds., *Oxford Studies in the Price Mechanism* (Oxford: Oxford University Press, 1951), pp. 31–51.

[22] See L. R. Klein, "Stocks and Flows in the Theory of Interest," F. H. Hahn and F. P. R. Brechling, eds., *The Theory of Interest Rates* (London: Macmillan & Co., Ltd., 1965), p. 148. See also reference in Teigen, *op. cit.,* n. 13, p. 49.

GNP minus government purchases of goods and services"); (2) by dividing the maximum velocity values thus obtained into GNP for each year, and by subtracting these active balances from total balances an estimate of idle balances was obtained.[23] Roughly, where M is the money holdings in question, Y is the GNP measure in question, and V is velocity,

$$\frac{Y}{M} = V$$

$$\frac{Y}{(V)_{max}} = \text{active balances}$$

and *total balances* less *active balances* yields *idle* or *speculative balances*. Bronfenbrenner and Mayer then proceed to regress their measure of idle balances on a short-term rate of interest and other variables with the view to presenting an empirically derived liquidity-preference function.

As Bronfenbrenner and Mayer and others agree, these methods involve an arbitrary definition of so-called idle balances. Bronfenbrenner and Mayer say, "We define idle balances as the residual monetary stock after subtracting balances with a velocity equal to that of 1926. This is an arbitrary definition . . . but all definitions of idle balances are arbitrary. Whether balances are idle or not depends upon the period one uses, which period itself is arbitrary."[24]

Another formulation of this velocity-speculative balances relation, in an introductory text,[25] however, avoids some elements of the arbitrariness in dealing with speculative balances. Here we invoke the notion of a homogeneous demand (Sec. 3.3) for all classes of balances as being of degree one with respect to income. We then view shifts in the simple linear relationship $M = f(Y)$, at any given time, as resulting from speculative changes in the demand for money and as giving rise to changes in the velocity of

---

[23] Bronfenbrenner and Mayer, "Liquidity Functions in the American Economy," *op. cit.*, pp. 813–814; and Eisner, *op. cit.*, p. 533.

[24] Bronfenbrenner and Mayer, "Rejoinder to Professor Eisner," *op. cit.*, p. 542.

[25] See Frazer and Yohe, *op. cit.*, pp. 4–12, 83–102.

money. The speculative shifts in question arise in a form of switching between broader classes of assets with the view to realizing gains or avoiding losses from holding some portion of the respective classes of assets. This explanation of changes in velocity, we continue below (Sec. 4.2), but, by assuming that changes in the speculative demand for money balances give rise to velocity changes (or by assuming that transactions balances, in particular, are a more stable function of income over time) we can identify changes in income due to changes in the stock of speculative balances as distinct from those changes in income due to changes in the stock of money. Quite simply, the reciprocal of the velocity of money, i.e., $1/V = \alpha$, at any time one wishes to view the analysis of changes, becomes the coefficient relating the demand for money to income (i.e., $M_d = \alpha Y + \beta$, $\beta = 0$). In this approach, changes in the stock of money contribute to changes in income, the extent of such changes being the product of the changes in the stock of balances and the factor $1/\alpha$. Other changes in income are due to a form of speculation or switching between broad classes of assets and the change in speculative balances needed to generate these other changes equals the product of the change in income due to speculation and the factor $-1/\alpha$.

Problems in the empirical identification of a liquidity-preference function—other than those concerning the role of a distinct class of speculative or idle balances—include the identification problem itself and the related problem of simultaneous-equations bias (Sec. 2A.2), although these problems do not arise in the simple arithmetic approach to the demand relationship just outlined. As Eisner points out in dealing with the Bronfenbrenner-Mayer study and their method of isolating idle balances. "The identification problem can be met if it can be assumed that the demand function remained fixed throughout the relevant period while the supply function shifted." Continuing, he notes, "Observations of actual quantities of money and interest rates would then trace out the demand function."[26]

Bronfenbrenner and Mayer react to the point about identification as follows:

---

[26] Eisner, *op. cit.*, p. 533.

Neither we nor Eisner fitted liquidity functions as parts of complete econometric models. We use single-equation models instead, and we must bear the burden of explaining why we believe the particular single equations we fit represent demand functions for money, rather than supply functions or hybrids. There is no dispute between us as to the interpretation of the data for our later period. . . . Our dispute relates to the earlier period, prior to approximately 1934. Monetary supply functions in this period approximated vertical lines [envision the supply line in Figure 4–1] under the influence of "needs of trade" banking theory,[27] but whereas we envisage these vertical lines as shifting with cycles and growth, Eisner envisages "these vertical lines" as shifting hardly at all. We suggest that the more obvious and simple interpretations of the "needs of trade" theory of bank credit involves shifts with the growth of the economy, and likewise . . . shifts with the business cycle.[28]

Lawrence Klein discusses the latter shifting supply line. He says: "The theory of liquidity preference is usually developed in a model that assumes strict and direct control over the supply of cash by monetary authorities." Continuing, he says, "It is a gross oversimplification to assume that the authorities fix supply as they like."[29] His view, whereby "authorities . . . made direct decisions about the discount rates, open-market operations, reserve requirements, and a host of minor credit conditions," is likely not any more acceptable. Truly, these matters affect the money supply in a complicated way. Some may even note that *"changes in bank reserves and possibly in the tone of the market, or the cost and availability of credit, are not necessarily the result of action on the part of the monetary authorities"* (Frazer and Yohe). The notion, at least, of the monetary authorities achieving long-run goals for the money stock and, possibly, even short-run goals[30] is probably no cruder

---

[27] Think of the money supply and credit as varying with output or income under this theory. See Frazer and Yohe, *op. cit.*, pp. 142–159.

[28] Bronfenbrenner and Mayer, "Rejoinder to Professor Eisner," *op. cit.*, pp. 542–543.

[29] Klein, *op. cit.*, pp. 147–148.

[30] For some discussions of monetary policy along this line, see Frazer and Yohe, *op. cit.*, pp. 157–159, 207–224, 563–672.

than the efforts at deriving empirically identifiable supply functions to date.

There is also reason for expecting that the speculative portion of the liquidity-preference demand for money itself may be unstable in its relation to the interest rate over time (Sec. 4.2). In any event, as Meltzer notes, "The substantive issues [in the Bronfenbrenner-Mayer and similar studies] are whether the interest elasticity of money demand varies with interest rates and/or whether the function 'kinks' at low interest rates."[31]

Meltzer deals empirically with this substantive issue, but he does not attempt to identify a liquidity-preference function as such. Below we present some of Meltzer's statistical results concerning the substantive issue and an association between velocity and the rate of interest. Subsequently, we recall that liquidity-preference analysis, as set forth above, predicts a velocity-interest rate association as a result of a form of switching between cash and bonds. Viewing an alternative explanation of the association, and testing the usual liquidity-preference explanation against the alternative, however, we find that the liquidity-preference explanation fails the tests, at least as it applies to evidence from the important corporate manufacturing sector. This shortcoming of the liquidity-preference explanation of the tendency for velocity and interest rates to vary together is further evidence that studies to date have not succeeded in identifying empirically a stable and simple relationship between the demand for speculative balances and the rate of interest. The alternative explanation involves a modification of the simple liquidity-preference model as set forth earlier.

THE TRAP AND THE VELOCITY-INTEREST RATE ASSOCIATION: SOME MELTZER RESULTS

In dealing with the question of whether a liquidity trap exists, Meltzer[32] introduces statistical evidence from an analysis of annual data that supports his own long-run money-demand function and

---

[31] See Allan H. Meltzer, "Yet Another Look at the Low Level Liquidity Trap," *Econometrica*, July 1963, pp. 545–549.
[32] *Ibid.*

the existence of a constant interest elasticity of the demand for money. He also shows that the reciprocal of velocity (i.e., $1/V$) is associated with the rate of interest such that a percentage increase in velocity is associated with an equal percentage increase in the rate of interest. Here he is not identifying a liquidity-preference function of the type sketched earlier (Figures 4–1 and 4–2). Instead he is relating his results to the controversy over the prospect of a liquidity trap by drawing upon a prediction

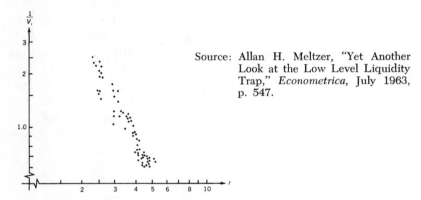

Source: Allan H. Meltzer, "Yet Another Look at the Low Level Liquidity Trap," *Econometrica*, July 1963, p. 547.

Figure 4–3.   Inverse Permanent Velocity $(1/V_1)$ and the Rate of Interest (r), 1900–1958: Logarithmic Scales.

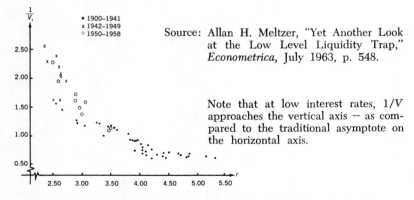

• 1900–1941
x 1942–1949
○ 1950–1958

Source: Allan H. Meltzer, "Yet Another Look at the Low Level Liquidity Trap," *Econometrica*, July 1963, p. 548.

Note that at low interest rates, $1/V$ approaches the vertical axis — as compared to the traditional asymptote on the horizontal axis.

Figure 4–4.   Inverse Permanent Velocity $(1/V_1)$ and the Rate of Interest (r), 1900–1958: Arithmetic Scales.

implicit in the usual liquidity-preference analysis—namely, an increase in the rate of interest gives rise to switching from cash to bonds such that velocity increases. As we note subsequently (Sec. 4.2), this explanation of the velocity-interest rate association is inadequate when tested against an alternative explanation involving a form of switching between a broader range of assets. Nevertheless, Meltzer's results and conclusions are of interest, particularly those concerning the substantive issue of whether analysis of time-series data reveals a constant elasticity of the demand for money with respect to the rate of interest.

Meltzer uses annual data. His regression results concern the period 1900–49, and his scatter diagrams (Figures 4–3 and 4–4) include observations for the period 1900–49, as well as for the years 1949–58. Meltzer proceeds in his analysis by presenting an equation used in his work on business firms, as discussed later (Sec. 7.2). The equation has the form

(1) $$M = kr^\alpha A^\beta$$

where, upon taking logs of both sides,

(2) $$\ln M = \ln k + \alpha \ln r + \beta \ln A$$

and "where M is total real money balances (the sum of currency and demand deposits), r is a long-term interest rate, A is a measure of real assets . . . and k, α, and β are parameters."[33]

---

[33] "Specifically, the series on M is series X 267 from *Historical Statistics of the U.S.*, Washington, 1960. Interest rates are measured by the Durand basic yields for twenty year maturities published as series X 346 in *Historical Statistics*. The data on total assets are based on R. W. Goldsmith, *A Study of Saving in the United States* (Princeton: Princeton University Press, 1956), Vol. III. Tables W-9 through W-16 were available for eight benchmark dates from 1900–49. The series used was obtained by taking the ratio of total assets A to Goldsmith wealth G (from Table W-1) for the eight base years. G was available in all years 1900–49 and A_t was obtained by interpolating according to the following formula:

$$A_t = \left[\frac{(n-i)}{n} b_0 + \frac{i}{n} b_n \right] G_t$$

where b_0 is the beginning base year ratio, b_n is the next base year ratio and $i = 0, 1, \ldots, n$ is an index of the years between base year dates inclusive of the

Upon regressing data for ln M on data for the other variables in Eq. (2) for the period 1900–49, Meltzer obtains the results

$$\alpha = -0.89 \qquad \text{and} \qquad \beta = 1.15$$
$$(0.08) \qquad\qquad\qquad (0.06)$$

(Standard errors are shown in parentheses.)

Using data for the period, 1930–39, Meltzer finds $\alpha = -0.88$ and $\beta = 0.78$. He notes that for his measure of the money stock, the interest elasticity of the demand for money for the 1930's did not fall.

Proceeding, by dividing Eq. (1) by permanent real income, defined as rA, we get

(3) $$\frac{M}{rA} = kr^{\alpha-1} A^{\beta-1}$$

(4) $$\ln \frac{M}{rA} = \ln k + (\alpha - 1) \ln r + (\beta - 1) \ln A$$

where M/rA is the reciprocal of permanent velocity $(1/V_1)$. These measures of permanent income and an inverse permanent velocity, of course, tend to add elements of stability. Wealth, as noted earlier (Sec. 3.5), is less volatile than income, in part since income, along with changes in interest rates, is a source of changes in wealth, and in part since the changes in interest rates and wealth vary directly in the short run. Next, since the regression coefficient for ln A in Eq. (2) is approximately one (i.e., $\beta = 1.15$), the coefficient $\beta - 1$ in Eq. (4) is small and one may simply consider $\ln (M/rA) = \ln k + (\alpha - 1) \ln r$, and show permanent velocity (or its inverse) as a function of the rate of interest in two scatter diagrams—one logarithmic, the other arithmetic. These diagrams, as produced by Meltzer, are shown in Figures 4–3 and 4–4, respectively.

From the regression results and the scatter diagrams, Meltzer arrives at a number of conclusions bearing on the substantive

end points. Preliminary estimates of data for the years 1950–58 were kindly furnished by Goldsmith and Lipsey and were used to increase the number of observations shown in the scatter diagrams below." (See Meltzer, *op. cit.,* n. 5, p. 546.)

issue concerning the liquidity trap, as he sees it. For one, he concludes "that the money demand and velocity functions are stable," independent of any arbitrary separation of "active" and "idle" balances. For another, the elasticity coefficient emanating from the velocity-interest rate association appears to be stable. In other words, percentage changes in velocity in relation to percentage changes in the rate of interest appear about the same for either a high or low rate of interest. This would suggest a straight line as a fit to the scatter in Figure 4–3, and an equilateral hyperbola as in Figure 4–1 for the scatter of points in Figure 4–4. For still another conclusion, the evidence for the United States does not support the notion of a liquidity trap.

Finally, in dealing with the association between velocity and the rate of interest as Meltzer deals with it and as Latané does in another context (Sec. 5.1), Teigen points out that it implies a unitary income elasticity.[34] To demonstrate this, Teigen[35] considers a general expression (M/Y) for the reciprocal of velocity, using M/Y as the dependent variable and r as the rate of interest. Thus

$$\frac{M}{Y} = f(r) \quad \text{or} \quad M = Y \cdot f(r) \quad \text{or} \quad \Delta M = \Delta Y \cdot f(r)$$

Since

$$\eta_{M \cdot Y} = \frac{\Delta M/M}{\Delta Y/Y} = \frac{\Delta M}{\Delta Y}\frac{Y}{M} \quad \text{and} \quad \frac{\Delta M}{\Delta Y} = f(r)$$

then

$$\eta_{M \cdot Y} = f(r)\frac{Y}{M} \quad \text{or} \quad \eta_{M \cdot Y} = \frac{f(r)}{f(r)} = 1$$

Given a high or perfect correlation between wealth and income,

---

[34] Presumably it would imply a slope parameter such as in the simple money demand equation $M_d = \alpha Y + \beta$ and method of dealing with changes in the speculative demand for money balances in the preceding subsection. Moreover, the earlier arithmetic method—that of calculating the slope parameter for money in relation to income and then attributing changes in the demand for money, other than those due to income, to a weakening of the speculative motive—is analogous to the procedures used by Meltzer in his empirical consideration of the velocity-interest rate association.

[35] See Teigen, *op. cit.*, p. 54.

this "unitary income elasticity" was implicit in Meltzer's dropping the last term in Eq. (4) in his consideration of the velocity-interest rate association.

4.2 LIQUIDITY PREFERENCE AND AN ALTERNATIVE EXPLANATION: THE VELOCITY–INTEREST RATE ASSOCIATION

An alternative explanation of the velocity-interest rate association involves a broader range of assets than the cash and bonds dealt with in the more common liquidity-preference explanation. In this section, we summarize the alternative explanation as it applies to the manufacturing sector, present a modified statement of the elementary liquidity-preference model, and present statistical results from analysis of data concerning the two contrasting explanations of the velocity-interest rate association.

AN ALTERNATIVE EXPLANATION OF THE VELOCITY–INTEREST RATE ASSOCIATION

The alternative explanation of the velocity-interest rate association involves a choice among two broad classes of assets—those such as cash and bonds with a fixed claim against future income, and those such as inventories, plant and equipment with a residual claim against income. The choice among alternatives is subject to a constraint in the form of total assets; such a formulation results in equilibrium when the rates of return from additional assets in the various classes are equal, after allowance for risk and liquidity elements, and a decrease in bank loans, or a rise less than in proportion to an increase in asset size, is a substitute for government-security holdings.[36]

In this alternative explanation, adjustments in asset holdings take place at the margin (i.e., in the flow quantities) in response to changes in the rates of return on the additions to the respective

---

[36] Such analysis is developed in several sources: see, mainly, William J. Frazer, Jr., "The Demand for Money, Statistical Results and Monetary Policy," *Schweizerische Zeitschrift für Volkswirtschaft und Statistik*, March 1967, pp. 11–27; and Frazer and Yohe, *op. cit.*, pp. 4–11, 19–21, 50–78, 88–104, 157–159, 215–221, 353–388, 636–638.

classes of assets. The rates on bonds are in part exogenously determined by the monetary authorities, and the rates for assets with residual claims against future income are in part exogenously determined by tax factors, economies in automation, prospective price changes, uncertainty about the future, and so on. Proceeding with a rise in the latter rates, for example, the following changes occur: the flow of expenditures on inventories, plant and equipment, etc., increases faster than the flows on assets with a fixed claim against future income; total assets (or wealth) increase and the flow of income increases, with the result that velocity increases; and the assets with a fixed claim against future income increase absolutely, but they decrease as a proportion of total assets or income. The converse set of changes also holds. One is led to hypothesize that velocity and the rate of interest vary directly; that the ratio of government securities to bank loans declines in response to a rise in the rate of interest, rather than rises as would happen if governments were acquired at high interest rates as in the earlier liquidity-preference analysis; and that the ratio of cash to governments fails to decline significantly as the usual liquidity-preference explanation suggests.

The process involving the form of switching outlined above works itself out over time intervals such as post-World War II business cycles rather than in the very short run usually implied by liquidity-preference analysis. The above analysis, therefore, leads one to suggest a modified statement of the very elementary liquidity-preference model.

A MODIFIED STATEMENT OF THE ELEMENTARY
LIQUIDITY-PREFERENCE MODEL

To accommodate the above explanation of the velocity–interest rate association, the elementary liquidity-preference model has been restated:

Money demand (M_d): $M_d = aY + bY/r$

Money supply (M_s): $M_s = c$

Equilibrium: $M_d = M_s$

The rate of interest (r): $r = \dfrac{b}{(c/Y) - a}$

According to the restatement, "As income (Y) rises the rate of interest (r) rises, but the monetary officials control c, and in the very long run they may cause c to vary proportionately with Y, in which case

$$r = b/(k - a), \qquad c/Y = k = \text{constant}"$$

Moreover, as we emphasize later (Sec. 11.2), an increase in the rate of change in the money stock, when interest rates are rising, may cause both income and interest rates to rise. This, as may be noted, "results via an expectations effect—such as the effect of price level changes on expenditures—so that velocity rises further . . . and so does the rate of interest. . . ."[37] Even so, in the present analysis, a homogeneity postulate of monetary analysis is satisfied. Namely, the rate of interest remains constant as one changes all stock and flow variables by the same proportion,[38] as may be seen by changing the variables in the elementary model and noting that $r = b/(k - a)$.

SOME EMPIRICAL RESULTS

In presenting results for testing the usual liquidity-preference explanation for the velocity–interest rate association against the present explanation of the velocity–interest rate association in the corporate manufacturing sector, we note several things: The liquidity-preference model has been interpreted as applying to business firms in an earlier study by Kisselgoff, as well as in the more recent Bronfenbrenner-Mayer study of liquidity functions;[39] following a Meltzer study, and relying on regression results supporting the substitution, the ratio of sales to cash is substituted as a measure for the velocity of money; the yield on high-grade corporate bonds is used for the rate of interest, and other time-series data for firms with assets over 10 million dollars for the forty-eight quarters, 1952–64, are from corporate accounting state-

---

[37] Frazer, "The Demand for Money," *op. cit.*

[38] See Frazer and Yohe, *op. cit.*, p. 445.

[39] See Kisselgoff, *op. cit.*; and Bronfenbrenner and Mayer, "Liquidity Functions in the American Economy," *op. cit.*

ments as reported by the Federal Trade Commission and the Securities and Exchange Commission.

Analyses of the data give the following results using seasonally adjusted data:

ln (sales at annual rate/cash)
$$= \text{const.} + 1.01 \ln (\text{Aaa bond yields}), \qquad r^2 = 0.85$$

ln (government securities/bank loans)
$$= \text{const.} - 1.12 \ln (\text{Aaa bond yields}), \qquad r^2 = 0.49$$

ln (cash/government securities)
$$= \text{const.} + 0.04 \ln (\text{Aaa bond yields}), \qquad r^2 = 0.01$$

Similar results may be shown using yields on 90-day Treasury bills, although a larger variance in their yields weakens the velocity–interest rate association somewhat (Sec. 2A.3). Here, the regression coefficient is consistent with other findings concerning the velocity–interest rate association. The coefficients resulting from regressing the ratio of government securities to bank loans on the Aaa-bond yields and from regressing the ratio of cash to governments on this yield, on the other hand, do not conform to the time-series changes predicted by the usual liquidity-preference analysis. In contrast, all of the above results are consistent with the velocity–interest rate association anticipated by the alternative explanation in terms of a form of switching between broad classes of assets, including those with a residual claim against future income.

4.3 SUMMARY

In its traditional formulation the liquidity-preference demand for money balances involves a choice of assets, primarily including money and bonds, and the demand for money as a function of the rate of interest, given selected balances as a constant proportion of income. In the formulation of the function through most of the post-war years, the money balances relating to the rate of interest were called "speculative" balances, and those relating most directly to income were called "transaction" or "transactions and precautionary" balances. The choice between assets, in the more popular formulations of the situation, favored an increasing portion of cash over bonds as the rate of interest declined in relation to the normal rate of interest, and a decreasing portion of cash as the rate of interest rose in relation to the normal rate of interest.

The rationale for the variations in the quantity of money demand in response to interest-rate changes, in fact, provides the basis for the shape of the liquidity-preference curve in its common two-dimensional form. The reasoning in question has also provided explanations for variations in the velocity of money and the rate of interest and for the possible existence of a liquidity trap. In the case of the frequently observed tendency for the velocity of money balances and the rate of interest to vary directly, the explanation commonly stated or implied is, for example, that a rise in the rate decreases the relative demand for money as an asset and gives rise to an increase in the velocity of money balances, given the demand for transactions balances as a constant proportion of income.

In the case of the liquidity trap, there is the possibility that at sufficiently low rates of interest, the demand for money balances becomes effectively insatiable in response to small decreases in the rate of interest. This situation is, indeed, the liquidity trap. It is important, in part, since it is thought to concern situations in which the monetary officials lose control over investment in real capital goods via the rate of interest. In this case there is an implicit broadening of the choice of assets to include assets other than money and bonds.

The explanations concerning the tendency for velocity and the rate of interest to vary directly and concerning the liquidity trap have led to much statistical analysis of empirical data. Prominent among the analyses are those of Bronfenbrenner and Mayer, and Meltzer. In the Bronfenbrenner-Mayer study of liquidity functions in the United States idle balances were arbitrarily derived and said to vary inversely with the rate of interest so as to give rise to changes in velocity. There was the view that they had identified a liquidity-preference function. Meltzer, on the other hand, recognized the prospect of changes in velocity and interest rates as simply a co-movement of two variables and he raised the substantive issue of whether the elasticity of the demand for money with respect to the rate of interest varies with the rate of interest. Meltzer avoided the arbitrary distinctions between "idle" and "active" balances. Nevertheless, his approach at least implied that changes in the speculative demand for balances relative to the over-all demand were varying inversely with the rate of interest, and using a special definition (the inverse of permanent velocity) he found the inverse to have an elasticity of about one with respect to the rate of interest. His observations were also presented in scatter diagrams, using both logarithmic and arithmetic scales. The regression results and the scatter diagrams supported the notion of a constant elasticity. The scatter diagram for the inverse velocity and the rate of interest, using arithmetic scales, moreover, suggests a hyperbolic curve of the type characterizing the liquidity-preference function in the common two-dimensional sketches. Meltzer's empirical evidence for the United States fails to support the liquidity-trap hypothesis.

As Teigen shows, Meltzer's analysis of the co-movement in velocity and interest rates implies an income elasticity of the demand for money of unity. This elasticity is also implied in a simple arithmetic method for viewing the demand for money as a simple linear function of income with a slope parameter consisting of the inverse of velocity at any given time. The broader framework involving this function suggests homogeneous demands of degree one for balances to satisfy the various motives. As income increases, and as implied in the Meltzer analysis, changes in velocity are associated with shifts in the speculative demand for money balances.

The evidence concerning the liquidity-preference demand for money and the liquidity trap does not suggest that a liquidity-preference function has actually been identified. Instead, it more strongly supports the notion of a simple co-movement in velocity and the rate of interest. Moreover, the liquidity-preference explanation of the velocity–interest rate association does not hold up well, at least as applied to the important sector of manufacturing firms, when tested against an alternative explanation. The evidence from the time series for forty-eight quarters, 1952–64, indicates that the ratio of government securities to bank loans declines in response to a rise in the rate of interest and the ratio of cash to governments fails to decline (or decline significantly) as interest rates rise. The alternative explanation for the velocity–interest rate association, as exhibited for manufacturing firms, consists of viewing two broad classes of assets—those with fixed claims against future income, such as money and bonds, and those with a residual claim, such as plant and equipment. In this explanation, there is a form of switching between the broader classes of assets that gives rise to the co-movement of velocity and interest rates. For example, as the returns on instrumental capital increase relative to the returns on cash and bonds, after allowance for risk and liquidity elements, the flow of outlays on instrumental capital increases relative to the flow for cash and governments (and their substitutes). A net result here is a decline in cash as a proportion of assets, although the absolute cash holdings are increasing in response to a parallel increase in assets and sales (or income or expenditures). These sets of changes give rise to an increase in the velocity of cash. Changes involving a reverse switching process may be shown to give rise to a decline in velocity.

In the latter explanation of the co-movement in velocity and interest rates, the demands for money to satisfy the various motives are homogeneous of degree one with respect to assets, and so on. The switching of assets is said to involve a form of speculation— the acquisition of one set of assets at a faster rate than another with the view to realizing a gain or avoiding a loss and with the view to maximizing the flow of income.

The elementary liquidity-preference model may be modified to allow for phenomena of the type just described. In the modified liquidity-preference function, balances to satisfy all motives are a constant proportion of income, and balances to satisfy the speculative motive as it concerns the rate of interest in particular are the quotient of a proportion of income and the rate of interest. Here, both the rate of interest and the proportion may change, but in particular the proportion declines as asset size, and so on, increases, although the absolute amount of speculative balances will increase with asset size, and so on.

Another question involved in liquidity-preference analysis is whether the demand for money should be treated as a function of a short- or long-term rate of interest. The long-term rate is said to be more directly involved with investment demand and therefore the liquidity-trap hypothesis. The long rate is more appropriate in considering the liquidity-preference demand for money and a wider range of assets than just money and bonds. The short rate, however, is appropriate in considering the liquidity-preference demand for money in relation to short-term securities. And, in any event, short rates and long rates tend to move together, although the short rates show a larger variance than long rates.

Chapter 5

THE VELOCITY–INTEREST RATE
ASSOCIATION AND OTHER MATTERS

Changes in the velocity of money were introduced earlier as possibly reflecting a number of things: changes in the stock of money effectively demanded relative to changes in the numerator in question; changes in monetary policy; and changes in the stock of money effectively demanded that are due to an income size (or wealth) effect and/or to some factor or set of factors other than the measure of income in question. It has been said, too, that as a consequence of the interrelationship between changes in velocity and the demand for money, some analysts interested in the determinants of the demand for money have dealt with velocity relative to its determinants, rather than with the stock of money per se. One of these, whose work has been widely cited and discussed in economics journals,[1] is Henry Latané. This chap-

---

[1] For references to the Latané articles in question and for discussions of his findings see, for example, Milton Friedman and Anna Jacobson Schwartz, *A Monetary History of the United States, 1867–1960* (Princeton, N.J.: Princeton University Press, 1963), pp. 646–654; Milton Friedman and Anna Jacobson Schwartz, "Money and Business Cycles," *Review of Economics and Statistics*, 1963, Supplement on the State of Monetary Economics, pp. 44–45; Allan H. Meltzer, "The Demand for Money: The Evidence from the Time Series," *Journal of Political Economy*, June 1963, p. 221 and pp. 238–239; T. J. Courchene and H. T. Shapiro, "The Demand for Money: A Note from the Time Series," *Journal of Political Economy*, October 1964, p. 502; Carl F. Christ, "Interest Rates and 'Portfolio Selection' Among Liquid Assets in the U.S.," in *Measurement in Economics* (Stanford, California: Stanford University Press, 1963), p. 201–217; L. R. Klein, "Stocks and Flows in the Theory of Interest," in *The Theory of Interest Rates*, eds., F. H. Hahn and F. P. R. Brechling (London: Macmillan and Company, Ltd., 1965), pp. 147–151; William J. Frazer, Jr., "The Demand for Money, Statistical Results, and Monetary Policy," *Schweizerische Zeitschrift für Volkswirtschaft und Statistik*, March 1967.

ter then, in view of the widespread interest shown in Latané's work on velocity, proceeds with a review of Latané's results from simple regression analyses of time-series data and with a review of the Latané (or Latané-Tobin) explanation for the recurring association of velocity and the rate of interest. It also deals with other results, explanations, and doctrines concerning the velocity–interest rate association, especially as these have concerned simple regression results, and the work and results due to Latané. These include an alternative to the Latané-Tobin explanation for the velocity–interest rate association, the availability doctrine, the notion of a ceiling on velocity, some views of Selden and Friedman, and Meltzer on Friedman's demand function.

Some of the matters dealt with in this chapter have come up earlier in one form or another, and some will come up again. In considering the more common liquidity-preference function in the previous chapter, for example, we noted among others the following tendencies: a tendency to attempt to identify the liquidity-preference function (or test some aspect of liquidity-preference theory) by regressing the reciprocal of velocity on the rate of interest, following a practice of separating transactions of stocks and speculative balances by using a velocity ratio for some historical peak; and the tendency to draw upon early post-Keynesian liquidity-preference analysis for an explanation of the velocity–interest rate association. Also, some demand functions and results due to Friedman and Meltzer are the special subject of the next chapter, although some aspects of their functions and results are introduced in this chapter; and an explanation for the velocity–interest rate association in terms of the transactions demand for money is related to an analysis due to James Tobin, although the Tobin model (and the somewhat related Baumol model) for the transactions demand for money appear in later chapters.

A number of themes appearing and reappearing in the works and topics reviewed in this chapter provide some unity for the otherwise possibly unrelated topics. These themes concern the following: the special emphasis upon the close and the recurring association between the velocity of money and the rate of interest; the stability of the results from the regression of the velocity of money (or its inverse) on the rate of interest (or its inverse); and attempts to explain the velocity–interest rate association and/or to introduce ideas about the effects of changes in the rate of interest (possibly by the monetary officials) on income or the velocity of money. There are also some special matters that arise—the possible existence of a ceiling on the velocity of money; the effects from broadening the definition of money to include time deposits, when dealing with the demand for money as a function of the rate of interest and other variables; and the relationship between the various explanations for the velocity–interest rate association and the possible effect of changes in the rate of interest, possibly by the monetary officials.

In reviewing statistical results reported in this chapter, and in comparing results due to various analysts, as on some subsequent occasions, one should keep in mind that some of the results were obtained prior to the widespread use of the modern computer in analyses of data. This becomes a matter of some importance when one realizes the magnitude of the reduction in the labor required to analyze additional data, effect logarithmic transformations of masses of data, and so on.

5.1   LATANÉ ON VELOCITY

One of the most unencumbered theses about velocity and the rate of interest is that of Henry A. Latané, a professor and former stockbroker. He develops the thesis in two papers—one appearing in 1954 and one in 1960.[2]

Latané's results support a major conclusion. The second paper offers additional empirical support for the conclusion; and it presents an explanation for the velocity–interest rate association in which Latané draws on analysis due to Tobin. His conclusion is as follows:

---

[2] Henry A. Latané, "Cash Balances and the Interest Rate—A Pragmatic Approach," *Review of Economics and Statistics,* November 1954, pp. 456–460; and "Income Velocity and Interest Rates: A Pragmatic Approach," *Review of Economics and Statistics,* November 1960, pp. 445–449.

A high rate tends to be associated with a speed-up in the turn-over of money. Conversely, a decline in rates has been associated with an increased demand for cash balances at a given level of income.[3]

In this section we review the following: analyses supporting the latter conclusion, Carl Christ on his and Latané's results, Meltzer on Latané's results, some results due to Lawrence Klein, the Latané (or Latané-Tobin) explanation for the velocity–interest rate association, the Latané-Christ results and monetary policy, Friedman and Schwartz on the Latané results and explanation, and Friedman and Schwartz on the velocity–interest rate association with respect to the postwar rise in velocity. "A study by Latané," Friedman and Schwartz say, "is the only one we know that not only attributes the postwar movement in velocity to interest-rate changes but also presents empirical evidence to support the conclusion that the postwar relation is the same as the prewar."[4]

LATANÉ'S EARLIER RESULTS

Latané deals with time series, annual data, and familiar variables: demand deposits plus currency in circulation (denoted M) as reported by the Board of Governors of the Federal Reserve System,[5] GNP (denoted Y),[6] and yields as rates (denoted r) on high-grade, long-term corporate obligations.[7] The (M/Y)-r asso-

---

[3] Latané, "Cash Balances and the Interest Rate," *op. cit.*, p. 460.

[4] See *A Monetary History of the United States, 1867–1960, op. cit.*, p. 649.

[5] The money supply data are those reported at the mid-year call date.

[6] The Department of Commerce series runs from 1929. It is supplemented by Federal Reserve estimates for 1929–58, and estimates by Simon Kuznets for earlier dates. See Simon Kuznets, *National Product Since 1869*, National Bureau of Economic Research, Publications, No. 46 (New York: National Bureau of Economic Research, 1946).

[7] The series for yields since 1936 is that reported in the *Federal Reserve Bulletin*. For earlier dates, Latané uses annual averages of Macaulay's high-grade railroad bond yields. See Frederick R. Macaulay, *Some Theoretical Problems Suggested by the Movements of Interest Rates, Bond Yields and Stock Prices in the United States since 1856*, National Bureau of Economic Research Publications, No. 33 (New York: National Bureau of Economic Research, 1938).

ciation for which Latané has particular concern[8] may be denoted in a modified quantity theory form $M = f(r)Y$, when money balances as a proportion of income vary with the rate of interest. He chooses to define this (M/Y)-r association with an equation of the form

(1) $$M/Y = c(1/r) + d$$

whereby he regresses M/Y on $1/r$ as if M/Y were dependent on $1/r$. He then uses the form

(2) $$1/r = g(M/Y) + h$$

and regresses $1/r$ on M/Y as if $1/r$ were dependent on M/Y. The results of these regressions after excluding data for unrepresentative years (1932, 1933, 1942, 1946, and 1947) are such that the results are about the same. Since equations of the forms (1) and (2) yield about the same results, a satisfactory approximation to a "joint estimating equation" becomes

(3) $$M/Y = 0.008 \ (1/r) + 0.09$$

From this little exercise involving the two regressions, an important conclusion can be drawn: The variable $1/r$ does not explain M/Y any better than the latter variable explains the former. "It is impossible to tell which is the independent and which the dependent variable," but "the correlation is high considering the number of observations." This is strong evidence in support of a later conclusion to the effect that movements in the rate of interest and velocity largely reflect the same changes in the setting or some exogenous factor impinging on the rate of return

---

[8] Latané also deals with a crude version of the quantity theory of money $(M/Y = k)$, an early formulation of the Keynesian liquidity-preference demand for money as stated by Franco Modigliani ("Liquidity Preference and the Theory of Interest and Money," *Econometrica*, January 1944, pp. 45–48), and an early money-demand equation presented by Lawrence Klein [*Economic Fluctuations in the United States, 1921–1941* (Cowles Commission, 1950), p. 109]. He gives good reasons for rejecting all of the notions in question. (See Latané, "Cash Balances and the Interest Rate," *op. cit.*, pp. 456–458.)

on additional capital expenditures. Latané concluded his 1954 paper with a simple statement of the (M/Y)-r association: As r changes, the demand for money relative to income varies inversely —i.e., r and V_y vary directly over time.

LATANÉ'S LATER RESULTS

In his 1960 paper, Latané was able to extend the above results from the period 1919–52 to cover the period 1909–58, because the Department of Commerce released additional estimates for income. In his latter study, two regression lines were fitted, as in the earlier study. This time, they were fitted to data for the logarithms of proportionate cash balances (i.e., log M/Y) and the logarithms of corporate bond yields (i.e., log r), with a resulting correlation coefficient of 0.88. The lines had slopes of -0.77 and -1.01, as shown in Figure 5–1. It was then noted that a linear relationship between the logs M/Y and r with a slope of about -1 was consistent with a linear relationship between income velocity V_y (i.e., the reciprocal of M/Y) and r. Thus, Latané states that the crosses in Figure 5–1 all represent the logarithms of points from the following single equation, expressed in two forms:

$$r = 1.3V - 0.5$$
$$V = 0.77r + 0.38$$

Once again the rate of interest and the income velocity of money are shown to vary directly over time.

THE LATANÉ-CHRIST RESULTS

Carl Christ[9] also has presented results. These show a direct variation between the rate of interest and income velocity, and expand somewhat on Latané's original results. Implying an equation of exchange, GNP $= MV_y$ or $1/V_y = M/$GNP, Christ refers to the reciprocal of velocity as the Cambridge k and, among other things, he regresses k on the inverse of a long-term rate of interest analogous to the rate used by Latané. His data are for the 1919–52 period initially studied by Latané, and for a longer period,

---

[9] See Christ, *op. cit.*, pp. 201–218.

1892–1959. In addition, he presents results for proportionate cash balances including time deposits (k') as well as for proportionate cash balances defined as currency and demand deposits (k). (In proceeding, Christ notes that "if the Cambridge k and the inverse of the rate of interest are linearly and positively related," as Latané originally indicated, "then k and the interest rate itself are related by a hyperbola that looks much like the Keynesian liquidity-preference curve.")

Note: Log (M/Y) + 1.0 is used rather than log M/Y, since the logarithm of a number between zero and 1 is negative.

Source: Henery A. Latané, "Income Velocity and Interest Rates: A Pragmatic Approach," *Review of Economics and Statistics*, November 1960, p. 445.

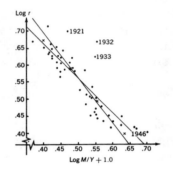

Figure 5–1. Proportionate Cash Balances (M/Y) and the Rate of Interest (r): the Variables in Log Form.

Christ found that even without excluding unrepresentative years for the period 1919–52, the inverse of the rate of interest explained 76 per cent of the variation in k. He says, "As the years went by, I plotted the new data on Latané's graph, and something happened that is very remarkable in the brief history of econometric equations: the new points were closer to the regression line than the points of the sample period!" He then fitted the same regression equation by least squares to data for a longer period, 1892–1959, and found

$$k = \frac{M}{\text{GNP}} = 0.131 + 0.716 \, \frac{1}{r}$$

The slope of 0.72 in this equation was almost the same as Latané's 0.80, when expressing the ratios as percentages, and "again the inverted interest rate explained 76 per cent of the variation of k." The results further showed that the inverted interest rate did very poorly as an explanation of the ratio of currency plus demand and time deposits to GNP. Christ noted that there may be shifts from demand deposits to time deposits when interest rates are high. A portion of Christ's results appear as follows:

Period	Dependent variable	Regression coefficient	Coefficient of determination
1919–1952	k	0.795	0.76
1892–1959	k	0.716	0.76
1892–1959	k'	0.676	0.26

Christ concluded, among other things, that the result from regressing k on the inverse rate of interest "appears quite constant."

MELTZER ON LATANÉ'S RESULTS

Meltzer also recognizes that Latané's high correlations "suggest a stable relationship between velocity and interest rates over long periods, which is linear in the logarithms," and he recognizes, as well, that Latané's Eq. (1) implies a demand function for money with an income constraint such that $M = f^*(r, Y)$, and that Latané implicitly assumes a homogeneous demand function of degree one in prices and real income in working with the velocity equation $M/Y = f(r)$. Since Meltzer's own findings reveal a real income elasticity of unity in the demand for money, e.g.,

$$\frac{\partial \ln (M/p)}{\partial \ln (Y/p)} = 1.05$$

for the period 1900–58, he finds the latter assumption reasonable.[10]

However, for real money balances (M/p) and the rate of interest (r), Meltzer's results[11] reveal the following elasticities:

---

[10] Meltzer, "The Evidence from the Time Series," *op. cit.*, Table 2 (p. 232) and p. 238.

[11] See Table 2, Meltzer, "The Evidence from the Time Series," *op. cit.*, p. 232.

$$\frac{\partial \ln (M/p)}{\partial \ln r} = -0.79 \text{ for the period } 1900\text{-}58$$

$$\frac{\partial \ln (M/p)}{\partial \ln r} = -0.05 \text{ for the period } 1900\text{-}29$$

$$\frac{\partial \ln (M/p)}{\partial \ln r} = -0.69 \text{ for the period } 1930\text{-}58$$

where the lower-case p is the implicit deflator for Net National Product. Thus, he concludes that Latané's result for the period 1909–58 is "spurious since it combines the significant results of the latter period [i.e., 1930–58] with nonsignificant results of the first two or three decades" as revealed by the above elasticity for the period 1900–29. Nevertheless, Meltzer deals with Latané's notion of an association between velocity and the rate of interest by working with the function

$$\frac{M}{rW} \equiv \frac{1}{V} = f(r, W)$$

where rW is a measure of "permanent" income from nonhuman assets. His results for the period 1900–58 reveal

$$\frac{\partial \ln (1/V)}{\partial \ln r} = -1.78$$

and a negligible wealth coefficient. This is consistent with Latané's result, according to Meltzer, except the elasticity of -1.78 is much higher, "as a consequence of the measurement procedure."

SOME OTHER RESULTS

Lawrence Klein, in presenting some empirical results concerning the inverse of velocity $(1/V)$,[12] introduced such variables as the yield on long-term bonds (r) and the change in prices for the previous period $(p - p_{-1})$, where p was the implicit deflator for Gross National Product. Klein's analysis of quarterly data for the United States (1948–59) yielded, as a part of a larger model, this equation:

---

[12] See Klein, "Stocks and Flows in the Theory of Interest," in *The Theory of Interest Rates*, F. H. Hahn and F. P. R. Brechling, eds., (London: Macmillan and Co., Ltd., 1965), p. 150.

$$1/V = 0.815 - 0.074r - 1.38(p - p_{-1}).$$

The coefficients and their signs suggest that velocity and the rate of interest varied directly in the post-World War II years.

The Latané (or Latané-Tobin) Explanation for the Velocity–Interest Rate Association

In attempting to explain the results reflecting a covariation in velocity and the rate of interest Latané comments in his 1960 article, as follows:

> For many purposes bonds are excellent substitutes for money. This easy interchangeability is recognized in much *corporate financial reporting* where cash and governments are lumped together as liquid assets. . . . Money is held largely to facilitate transactions. Its yield is imputed from the convenience and utility of holding cash balances. The yield from bonds, after administrative costs, is balanced at the margin with the imputed yield from money. *When interest rates are high, wealth-holders economize on their cash balances thus leading* to increases in the turnover of money [italics added].[13]

The analysis is straightforward: high interest rates encourage

---

[13] Latané, "Income Velocity and Interest Rates," *op. cit.*, p. 446.

For a similar and, as matters turn out, an incorrect view of what causes a rise in the turnover of the balances held by manufacturing corporations in particular as interest rates rise over the expansion phase of a cycle or secularly as over the post-World War II years in the United States, see George Garvy, "Money, Liquid Assets, Velocity and Monetary Policy," *Banca Nazonale del Lavoro Quarterly Review*, December 1964, pp. 323–338. The latter article is also reprinted in Richard A. Ward, ed., *Monetary Theory and Policy* (Scranton, Pennsylvania: International Textbook Company, 1966), pp. 217–229.

The Garvy explanation of the post-World War II rise in the turnover of the cash balances held by manufacturing corporations is also similar to an explanation by Ritter. See Lawrence S. Ritter, "The Structure of Financial Markets, Income Velocity, and the Effectiveness of Monetary Policy," *Schweizerische Zeitschrift für Volkswirtschaft und Statistik*, September 1962, pp. 276–289. For a contrary view, see William J. Frazer, Jr., "Monetary Analysis and the Postwar Rise in the Velocity of Money in the United States," *Schweizerische Zeitschrift für Volkswirtschaft und Statistik*, December 1963, pp. 584–596.

economy in the use of cash via a switching from cash to bonds, and the result is a rise in velocity.

To bolster the above view, Latané notes that "most deposits are held by large depositors who can adjust their balances readily." He continues with a notion about compensating balances whereby banks are said to get paid for their services to the large depositors "indirectly by the yield they can obtain from the depositors." The idea is that higher interest rates permit smaller compensating balances at the bank and this leads to a fall in required cash balances.[14]

In emphasizing the economies effected in the use of cash as rates rise, Latané then cites the analysis by James Tobin[15] in which the transactions demand for money varies inversely with the excess of the rate of interest over the cost of switching into and out of interest-bearing assets, other things being equal. The reason for the variation in demand, according to Tobin, concerns both the gain resulting from the transfer of cash to interest-bearing assets as interest rates rise and overcome the cost of switching into and out of interest-bearing assets and economies in the cost of switching. Assuming optimizing behavior for the economic units in question, Tobin summarizes the incentive for the more economical use of balances:

> When the yield disadvantage of cash is slight, the costs of fre-

---

[14] Such a notion, whereby large firms carry a smaller amount of bank loans and deposits in relation to their size and that this contributes to a higher turnover of balances, is not uncommon, but the bases for such a notion still may vary. See, e.g., William J. Frazer, Jr., "Firms' Demands for Money: The Evidence from the Cross-Section Data," *Staff Economic Studies*, No. 25 (Washington, D. C.: Board of Governors of the Federal Reserve System, 1967).

[15] See Tobin, "Interest Elasticity of Transactions Demand for Cash," *Review of Economics and Statistics*, August 1956, pp. 241–247.

Work by Baumol (William J. Baumol, "The Transactions Demand for Cash: An Inventory Theoretic Approach," *Quarterly Journal of Economics*, November 1952) is often associated with the Tobin article cited above. (See, for example, Allan H. Meltzer, "The Demand for Money: A Cross-Section Study of Business Firms," *Quarterly Journal of Economics*, August 1963, pp. 415–418.) The present references are confined to Tobin's article, however, since Latané cites Tobin.

quent transactions will deter the holding of other assets, and average cash holdings will be large. However, when the yield disadvantage of cash is great, it is worth while to incur large transactions costs and keep average cash holdings low. *Thus, it seems plausible that the share of cash in transactions balances will be related inversely to interest rates on other assets* [italics added].[16]

Now, there may be some doubt about whether empirically testable hypotheses should be attributed at all to the Tobin analysis in question. Nevertheless, a testable notion has been attributed to him by Latané and other authors.[17] It is simply this: *A rise in the rate of interest reduces cash balances relative to income and increases liquid security holdings relative to income and, conversely, a decline in the rate of interest increases cash balances relative to income and decreases liquid security holdings relative to income.* According to the Latané (or Latané-Tobin) explanation, velocity and the rate of interest vary directly over time; the ratio of cash to government securities varies inversely with the rate of interest over time; and the ratio of government securities to bank loans varies directly with the rate of interest over time where, according to some analyses, government-security holdings in relation to income (or assets) are a source of liquidity similar to a reduction in bank loans relative to income (or assets).

THE LATANÉ-CHRIST RESULTS AND MONETARY POLICY

Carl Christ in drawing upon his results and in implying a direct causal relationship between the changes in velocity and the rate of interest, in effect relates the sort of explanation outlined above to changes in monetary policy (defined as changes in the rate of interest). He notes that an increase in the rate of interest would lead to a decline in the demand for currency and demand deposits and that, with no change in the money stock, the rise in

---

16 Tobin, *op. cit.*, p. 242. Most of Tobin's paper on transactions demand is taken up with a proof of the possibility cited.

17 See Edward L. Whalen, "The Demand for Money: A Cross-Section Study of Business—Further Comment," *Quarterly Journal of Economics*, February 1965, p. 160; Meltzer, "A Cross-Section Study of Business Firms," *op. cit.*, p. 409.

the rate of interest would be associated with a rise in GNP. Continuing, he says, "This suggests that changes in the velocity of money in response to interest-rate fluctuations may be substantial enough to be of concern to the monetary authorities in their attempts to stabilize the economy."[18] Apparently this suggests that if the monetary officials could in some way raise the rate of interest independently of changes in income and the money stock, then the rise in the rate would lead to an increase in income. The flaw in this sort of analysis, and the subsequent Latané (or Latané-Tobin) explanation for the velocity–interest rate association, as revealed in subsequent sections, is that some causal factor may give rise to changes in both velocity and the rate of interest. Such an alternative explanation is suggested below in an outline of the Friedman-Schwartz review of the postwar rise in velocity and in the later section on the velocity–interest rate association and manufacturing firms.

FRIEDMAN AND SCHWARTZ ON THE LATANÉ RESULTS AND EXPLANATION

Friedman and Schwartz, along with the other authors cited, attribute an explanation to Latané. According to Friedman and Schwartz, Latané "has argued that the whole of the movement of velocity . . . can be accounted for by changes in interest rates [random perturbations aside], higher interest rates leading to economy in the use of money and so to higher velocities, and conversely."[19] On the other hand, they recognize no "necessary" or "irreconcilable" contradiction between his (M/Y)-r association and their views since, among other things, they define money to include the sum of currency plus adjusted demand deposits plus time deposits, and this may have some differential effect.[20] As revealed by some of Meltzer's results utilizing alternative defi-

---

[18] See Christ, *op. cit.*, pp. 203–204.

[19] Friedman and Schwartz, "Money and Business Cycles," *op. cit.*, p. 44. See, also, Friedman and Schwartz, *A Monetary History of the United States, 1867–1960, op. cit.*, p. 652.

[20] Friedman and Schwartz, "Money and Business Cycles," *op. cit.*, p. 44; and Friedman and Schwartz, *A Monetary History of the United States, 1867–1960, op. cit.*, p. 655.

nitions for money (i.e., using M_1, the usual measure, and M_2 for the Friedman-Schwartz measure), for instance,

$$\frac{\partial \ln M_1}{\partial \ln r} = -0.781 \qquad \frac{\partial \ln M_1}{\partial \ln W} = 1.01$$

for one multiple regression equation and, for another,

$$\frac{\partial \ln (M_2/p)}{\partial \ln r} = -0.50 \qquad \frac{\partial \ln (M_2/p)}{\partial \ln (W/P)} = 1.32$$

where, in addition to symbols defined earlier,

W is nonhuman wealth, and

P is the price level for assets obtained by computing the implicit price deflator from nominal and real wealth estimates by Raymond Goldsmith.[21]

Here, wealth becomes of greater importance and the interest rate less important in their respective associations with the demand for money under the broader definition. This is probably not surprising, since some of the switching from money balances (M_1) associated with a rise in interest rates has been said to involve a transfer to time deposits. Friedman and Schwartz recognize such a prospect.

Viewing the interest rate as a possible explanation of the postwar rise in velocity, Friedman and Schwartz note that it explains too much. "If interest rates account for the later postwar rise in the velocity of money, presumably they had a similar effect in the early postwar period." During the war velocity had declined; after 1946 it began its postwar rise (Sec. 2.1), but bond yields did not begin any appreciable rise until after 1950.[22] The explanation offered for the rise in velocity in the early postwar years, then, is as follows:[23]

---

[21] Meltzer, "The Evidence from the Time Series," *op. cit.*, p. 225.

[22] The postwar years 1946-50 comprised a period of pegged interest rates, as did the war years. See William J. Frazer, Jr. and William P. Yohe, *Introduction to the Analytics and Institutions of Money and Banking* (Princeton, N.J.: D. Van Nostrand Company, Inc., 1966), Sec. 24.3.

[23] Friedman and Schwartz, *A Monetary History of the United States, 1867–1960, op. cit.*, p. 643.

The unavailability of consumer durable goods during the later war years induced individuals to accumulate liquid assets instead. With respect to these goods, effective prices were certain to fall after the war, since their current prices were essentially infinite. There was, therefore, an incentive to accumulate money and other liquid assets to be used later to purchase goods not currently available. The expectation of a postwar-general price decline and the fear of a severe postwar depression worked in the same direction. The high wartime mobility of people and the frequent difficulty of acquiring goods when and as desired made high money balances more desirable than they would be in ordinary times for current purposes and not only as a store of value intended for future purchases. And presumably other factors were at work as well. Given that wartime phenomenon, an immediate postwar reaction involving the working down of excess balances of liquid assets in general and of money in particular was only to be expected.

Continuing, Friedman and Schwartz say that the postwar "movements in income and interest rates alone cannot explain the postwar rise in velocity." For the period before 1929, Friedman and Schwartz have sought the explanation of a secular decline in velocity in terms of a wealth hypothesis (Sec. 3.5), but they look for other explanations in the postwar years. They note that wealth and income were rising at a time when their wealth effect should have contributed to a further decline, and they note, too, that the postwar rise was more rapid than the interest rate could have produced.[24] They also consider, among other possibilities, the possible effect of the expected rate of change in prices (note 5, Sec. 2.1)—which, like the interest rate, could account for only a minor part of the postwar rise in velocity—and they suggest, furthermore, that the interest rate might simply have reflected any expected change in prices.

Finally, Friedman and Schwartz conclude, with full recognition of the inadequacy of the conclusion, as follows:

> Changing expectations about economic stability seem . . . a more plausible explanation of postwar movements in the velocity of money than any other factors. . . .[25]

---

[24] *Ibid.*, p. 655.
[25] *Ibid.*, p. 675.

They point out:

> The major virtue of cash as an asset is its versatility. It involves a minimum of commitment and provides a maximum of flexibility to meet emergencies and to take advantage of opportunities. The more uncertain the future, the greater the value of such flexibility and hence the greater the demand is likely to be. In a qualitative sense, an explanation of the movement of the velocity of money in these terms is consistent with both the 1929 to 1942 and 1942 to 1960 movements in velocity.[26]

5.2 THE VELOCITY–INTEREST RATE ASSOCIATION AND MANUFACTURING FIRMS

One may speculate about the group (or groups) of firms in the economy to which the Latané (or Latané-Tobin) explanation should be applied. Nevertheless, statements by Latané, Meltzer, and others, such as H. F. Lydall (Sec. 3.5), suggest that a likely group would be manufacturing firms, and, furthermore, data for such firms have been analyzed as a means of testing the Latané (or Latané-Tobin) explanation for the velocity–interest rate association against an alternative explanation. The alternative explanation in question is, in fact, the explanation presented earlier (Sec. 4.2) as an alternative to the conventional liquidity-preference explanation. This section, then, presents a review of some statistical results from the analysis of data for manufacturing firms, and a brief summary of an alternative explanation for a velocity–interest rate association as revealed by an analysis of data. The implications of the results and the explanation are given for the possible effect of changes in the rate of interest, possibly by the monetary officials.

SOME STATISTICAL RESULTS

In dealing with velocity for manufacturing firms, sales are used as a substitute measure for income. Otherwise, the analyses involve the yield on high-grade corporate bonds, as in the original Latané analyses, and data for cash, government securities, and bank loans, as they would appear on balance sheets for manufacturing

---

[26] *Ibid.*, p. 673.

firms. The substitution of sales for income is supported, in part, by the correlation between sales and GNP. Regressing time-series data for sales at an annual rate (seasonally adjusted) on GNP at an annual rate (seasonally adjusted) for the years 1952–64, following a logarithmic transformation of the data, yields a regression coefficient of 0.96 and a coefficient of determination of 0.73.

Other relevant results for the analysis of quarterly data (seasonally adjusted, 1952–64) and concerning the Latané (or Latané-Tobin) explanation and the rate of interest, as an independent variable, are as follows:

Dependent Variable	Regression Coefficient	Coefficient of Determination
Ratio of sales to cash	1.0	0.85
Ratio of governments to bank loans	−1.12	0.49
Ratio of cash to governments	0.04	0.01

The balance-sheet data are for firms with assets over 10 million dollars, as reported by the Federal Trade Commission and the Securities and Exchange Commission.

The above results show a very strong velocity–interest rate association, a coefficient for the ratio of cash to government securities with the opposite sign from that implied by the Latané (or Latané-Tobin) explanation, and the coefficient for the ratio of cash to governments is almost zero and of the opposite sign from that implied by the Latané (or Latané-Tobin) explanation. The Latané (or Latané-Tobin) explanation is unsupported by the statistical results, but the above results are consistent with an alternative explanation.

An Alternative Explanation

The alternative explanation recognizes two broad classes of assets, and the role of government securities relative to other assets as a source of liquidity similar to a reduction in bank loans relative to other assets. The two broad classes of assets are those with a fixed claim against future income, such as money balances and bonds, and those with a residual claim against future income, such as plant, equipment, and inventories. In response to increases in sales (or asset size, since the two are highly correlated[27]), all the classes of assets increase, but the classes in relation to sales (or total assets) vary in response to changes in the rates of return from additions to the various classes of assets, after allowance for risk, liquidity, and other elements comprising the various returns, as set forth in various sources.[28] The flows, or additions to the various classes of assets, as well as bank loans, are constant at stable equilibrium at a moment in time but most frequently the flows vary in response to changes in the rates of return on additions to the various classes of assets and in response to changes in the rate of interest. In this context, the rate of return is the rate for relating a prospective flow of returns from some additional assets to the given supply price or cost of the additional assets, and the rate of interest is the given rate determining the value of the additional assets in relation to the prospective returns. These are the usual supply-price (= constant), present-value concepts associated with investment demand.[29] Changes in the latter rate of interest are indicated by changes in the rate of interest used in the regression results reported above. Changes in the rate of interest may reflect changes in the rate of return, since changes in

---

[27] For example, a regression of sales on asset size shows a regression coefficient of 1.02 and coefficient of determination of 0.96 when the data used are those reported by the 500 largest industrial corporations in 1962. Also, using time-series data of the type analyzed in generating the results in this section, sales and total assets (seasonally adjusted) have a regression coefficient of 1.06 and a coefficient of determination of 0.97, and using the same data after a logarithmic transformation the regression of sales on total assets results in a regression coefficient of 0.82 and a coefficient of determination of 0.96.

[28] See, e.g., William J. Frazer, Jr., and William P. Yohe, *op. cit.*, Secs. 4.1, 5.4, and 17.4.

[29] Recall (from introductory monetary economics, as in Frazer and Yohe, *op. cit.*, Secs. 4.1, 5.4, and 17.4.) that

$$CV = \frac{R_1}{(1+i)^1} + \frac{R_2}{(1+i)^2} + \ldots + \frac{R_n}{(1+i)^n}, \quad i = \text{const.}$$

$$C = \frac{R_1}{(1+r)^1} + \frac{R_2}{(1+r)^2} + \ldots + \frac{R_n}{(1+r)^n}, \quad C = \text{const.}$$

where CV is the present value; C is supply price (or cost); $R_1, R_2, \ldots, R_n$ is the various flows for expenditures in response to imbalances at some previous equilibrium between the rate of return and the rate of interest give rise to changes in the rate of interest.

The prospective flows of returns relating the rate of interest to the value of additional assets as well as relating the rate of return to the supply price (or cost) of additional assets are subject to the influence of a variety of factors. A prospective rise in prices, for instance, increases the returns from assets with a residual claim against future income, and, given the rate of interest and prevailing supply prices, the increase in prospective returns implies an increase in the rate of return relative to the rate of interest or an increase in the value of the residual-claim assets relative to their supply price, given the rate of interest and the supply price. The prospective rise in prices has the reverse effect on the prospective flow of returns from assets with a fixed claim against future income.

The prospective rise in prices, in the context of the above analysis, would contribute to a rise in the velocity of money and a decline in noncash liquid asset holdings and their substitutes in relation to income (or asset size). It is, no doubt, the factor introduced in the Klein equation:

$$1/V = 0.815 - 0.074r - 1.38(p - p_1).$$

It is also the factor others have introduced, on other occasions, in the form of the rate of change in the price level, but in addition to prospective price changes a whole host of factors may impinge on the prospective returns to introduce imbalances at some previous equilibrium in the relationships between the rates of return and the rate of return relative to the rate of interest. In the case of the post-World War II years, Friedman and Schwartz mention greater certainty about the future. Other additional factors include economies of automation, changes in the tax credit

---

the prospective flow of returns; i is the rate of interest; and r is the rate of return.

Proceeding from equilibrium $(i = r)$ in response to a change in $R_1, R_2, \ldots, R_n$ and with i constant and C constant, either

                    $r > i$, and the flows of expenditures expand

or $i > r$, and the flows contract.

for additional capital expenditures, accelerated depreciation, labor costs, and so on.[30]

The above results from analyses of quarterly data for manufacturing corporations would tend to support the present explanation. The various tendencies—that for cash and governments to decline relative to sales (income or assets) as interest rates rise, and that for the ratio of government securities to bank loans to decline as interest rates rise—are consistent with the present explanation of the velocity–interest rate association. The above statistical results warrant the following conclusions: (1) Changes in the rate of interest do not contribute primarily to changes in velocity via their influence on a form of switching between cash and liquid non-cash assets such as government securities. (2) Changes in yields on capital goods contribute to changes in both velocity and the rate of interest.

THE EFFECTS OF CHANGES IN THE RATE OF INTEREST

As for the effects of changes in the rate of interest, possibly by the monetary officials, the present explanation suggests that the changes may have an effect on expenditures for assets with a residual claim against future income and, therefore, on the velocity of money. The present explanation and the results, on the other hand, suggest that the changes in yields (as rates) on capital goods contribute primarily to both changes in the rate of interest, possibly by the monetary officials, and the velocity of money.

5.3 VELOCITY, THE AVAILABILITY
DOCTRINE, AND SOME EMPIRICAL FINDINGS

The association between velocity and the rate of interest is revealed in a variety of forms: the association between the inverse of velocity and the rate of interest; the association between inverse velocity and the inverse rate of interest; and the direct association between velocity and the rate of interest. The association presently considered is simply the association between the velocity of money balances and the rate of interest. Professor Rousseas is

---

[30] See Frazer and Yohe, *op. cit.*, Secs. 5.4 and 17.3.

one of the writers to deal with the association in this form. He touches upon several issues surrounding it.[31] For one, he introduces the availability doctrine and a notion of the effectiveness of credit tightness as the doctrine relates to the association. This we review along with empirical results and views relating to the question of the velocity–interest rate association.

In this section, a short-term interest rate—such as that on Treasury bills—should be thought of as an indicator of credit ease or tightness.[32] Also, a policy is a goal at the operating level, and the monetary officials confront a number of them.[33] In the present context, however, "monetary policy" concerns credit ease or tightness.

THE V-CURVE

Professor Rousseas deals with a velocity–bill rate (V-i) association in terms of empirically illustrated figures[34] and an association in the form of a so-called V-curve. In this context, velocity (V) and the bill rate (i) vary coincidentally; as the rate rises, a velocity ceiling is approached (i.e., V-curve becomes asymptotic in a vertical direction), and the ceiling is subject to possible shifts—all as sketched in Figure 5–2. Rousseas, like Latané in his earlier paper (Sec. 5.1), does not want to introduce a causal arrow (i.e., $\Delta i \to \Delta V$). Instead he uses short-term interest rates as indicators of the state of credit availability, and he speculates "that much of the idle cash balances activated during boom periods are not in direct response to interest rate changes."[35] [*Note:* Since the measure on the horizontal axis is the inverse of

---

[31] Stephen W. Rousseas, "Velocity Changes and the Effectiveness of Monetary Policy, 1951–57," *Review of Economics and Statistics,* February 1960, pp. 27–36; Peter L. Bernstein, "The Response of Income Velocity to Interest Rate Changes: A Comment," *Review of Economics and Statistics,* November 1960, pp. 453–455; and Stephen W. Rousseas, "Rejoinder," *Review of Economics and Statistics,* November 1960, pp. 455–457.

[32] See Frazer and Yohe, *op. cit.,* Sec. 24.2.

[33] *Ibid,* Sec. 24.1.

[34] There are three such curves involving postwar data, two by Rousseas and one by his discussant. See Rousseas, "Velocity Changes," *op. cit.,* p. 31, and p. 33; and Bernstein, "The Response of Income Velocity," *op. cit.,* p. 454.

[35] Rousseas, "Rejoinder," *op. cit.,* p. 456.

the ratio of the money stock to income (M/Y), the V-curve slopes in the opposite direction from the line in Figure 5–1.]

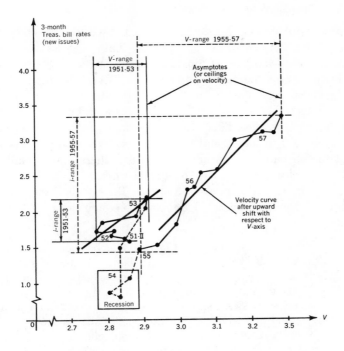

Figure 5–2. The Velocity–Interest Rate Association and the Velocity–Ceiling.

A CEILING ON VELOCITY

The view of a ceiling on velocity is implicit in the availability doctrine. The doctrine was an attempt to explain the effectiveness of monetary policy under early postwar conditions.[36] Major components of the doctrine, as summarized by Rousseas, are

(i) the shift in emphasis from the rate of interest to the availability of credit, i.e., from the demand to the supply side of the

---

[36] See Frazer and Yohe, *op. cit.*, Sec. 25.3.

money market, (ii) the increased sensitivity of the financial community to the pressures of the central bank, and (iii) the willful creation and manipulation of uncertainty in the money market by the monetary authorities.[37]

A major emphasis in the doctrine was upon the restrictive effect of small rises in the rate of interest. This was to operate via credit lenders—holders of government securities—who were allegedly reluctant to realize capital losses from the disposition of their government securities when interest rates were up and bond prices down (the "pinning-in" effect).[38] Under tight credit conditions, banks were less likely to engage in switching from government securities to loans, and thus balances were simply less likely to get in the hands of spenders. In effect, there was a ceiling on velocity, resulting from a rise in interest rates.

Another monetary analyst—Lawrence Ritter—discusses the ceiling and the effectiveness of monetary policy in the 1950's as follows:

> . . . when interest rates are low and idle balances large, a small rise in rates is likely to result in a large transfer of funds from hoards to active circulation, increasing velocity substantially. In this phase there is considerable truth in the "offset" viewpoint. But as interest rates continue to rise, due to continued monetary restraint and persistent demand for funds, idle balances are likely to approach minimum levels. Correspondingly, velocity is likely to encounter an upper limit, a rough and perhaps flexible ceiling, but a ceiling nevertheless. As it becomes increasingly difficult to obtain the release of additional funds from the now depleted idle balances, velocity will be subject to new constraints, economic activity will become increasingly sensitive to monetary policy and further expansion of GNP will be inhibited.[39]

Rousseas in effect centers arguments about a ceiling and the effectiveness of a rise in interest rates. He discusses the prospect

---

[37] Rousseas, "Velocity Changes," *op. cit.*, p. 34.

[38] On the effectiveness of the "pinning-in" effect see J. Aschheim, "Restrictive Open-Market Operations *Versus* Reserve-Requirement Increases: A Reformulation," *Economic Journal*, June 1963, pp. 262–265.

[39] Lawrence S. Ritter, "Income Velocity and Anti-Inflationary Monetary Policy," *American Economic Review*, March 1959, p. 128.

of a given velocity ceiling (the "asymptote") being compatible with various institutional arrangements. However, he maintains that the evolution of credit-market institutions—such as the evolution of nonbank financial intermediaries and others resulting from the innovativeness of the credit-granting institutions—will cause the ceiling to gradually move to the right.[40] He says, in effect, "Our problem still remains . . . the obsolescence of monetary controls in terms of constant institutional change," even if the gradually-moving, vertical asymptote exists.[41]

Latané, Meltzer, and Friedman have all commented on the ceiling for income velocity. Latané says, with reference to the upper part of Figure 5–1, that the data do not support Ritter's concept of a flexible ceiling over velocity. Continuing, he says, "within the range of experience (i.e., *V* as high as 4.26 and long-term interest rates as high as 5.17 as compared with *V* of 3.43 and *r* of 4.47 per cent in the second quarter of 1959), the interest elasticity of proportionate cash balances seems to be the same whether velocity is high or not."[42] Meltzer offered further confirmation of the absence of a ceiling; according to him, there is little support for Ritter's notion of a velocity ceiling for interest rates that have ranged from 2.35 to 5.31 per cent. The existence of a ceiling should, he said, be revealed by a comparison of the measured values for 1/*V* and the values predicted by one of his regression equations for 1/*V*. He found an excess of measured over predicted values when interest rates were above 5 per cent, but, according to him the excess of measures were not substantial enough to support the notion of a ceiling in the United States.[43] Reviewing the possible contributions of various developments in the 1950's to greater and greater confidence in the future, Friedman and Schwartz[44] simply suggest the prospect of an end to the postwar

---

[40] Rousseas, "Velocity Changes," *op. cit.*, pp. 32–33.

[41] Rousseas carries his discussion further. He maintains that credit policy conducted with general credit controls is ineffective; he recommends selective credit controls to counter velocity leakage. See Rousseas, "Velocity Changes," *op. cit.*, p. 35.

[42] Latané, "Income Velocity and Interest Rates," *op. cit.*, p. 449.

[43] See Meltzer, "The Evidence from the Time Series," *op. cit.*, p. 241.

[44] See *A Monetary History of the United States, 1867–1960, op. cit.*, pp. 674–675.

rise in velocity and a re-emergence of the long-term downward trend, in accordance with the wealth hypothesis, and their view of money as a luxury good.

Apparently, empirical evidence does not support the concept of a ceiling on velocity.

5.4   SELDEN, FRIEDMAN, AND MELTZER: VELOCITY, INTEREST RATES, AND OTHER MATTERS

A function due to Friedman, concerning a collection of essays by former students, and implying an 'association between velocity and various interest rates, was introduced in an earlier section (Sec. 2.1). In one of the essays, Richard Selden reported results from the regression of velocity on the cost of holding money (r_m), the cost of money substitutes (r_{ms}), and real income per capita (y/N), while Friedman's original money-demand function was simply a part of a broader discussion about the quantity-theory approach. Later, in the case of subsequent work, Selden made further comments about his earlier regression results, and Friedman dealt further with the demand for money and the velocity–interest rate association, as well as with such variables as population and "permanent" income. Meltzer, in turn, has dealt extensively with the Friedman analysis and results. In this section, then, we review some of Selden's results from regression analyses, and aspects of the Friedman and Meltzer works bearing on the velocity–interest rate question and related matters.

SELDEN ON INTEREST RATES AND VELOCITY

A representative regression equation from Selden's analyses of data covering the years 1919 to 1951 is as follows.[45]

$$V_y = 0.800 + 0.0831\, r_m + 0.0002\, \frac{y}{N} - 0.1445\, r_{ms}$$

where the variables are the same as defined above. In the context of the equation, the results indicate that the cost of money

---

[45] See Richard T. Selden, "Monetary Velocity in the United States," *Studies in the Quantity Theory of Money*, Milton Friedman, (ed.) (Chicago, Illinois: University of Chicago Press, 1956), p. 217.

substitutes is an important factor in the regression. Given the definition for r_{ms}—bond yields minus yields on 4–6 month commercial paper—and the usual facts about the behavior of yields on long- and short-term instruments over the cycle,[46] furthermore, a negative and small coefficient might be expected for two reasons: (1) the two yields in the definition should be expected to move in the same direction with velocity over the cycle, but (2) the yield on the short-term paper should be expected to fluctuate in a wider range. Thus r_{ms} is expected to be negative in the expansion phase and positive in the contraction phase.

Selden has some reservations about his regression results, but they do not particularly bear on the present questions. Selden, for example, refers to the "pitfalls of attaching significance to correlation analysis of time series,"[47] but the results are still useful in that they reflect the behavior of the time series. Also, in a later work—while referring to velocity in relation to such measurable variables as interest rates, yields on money substitutes, and real income per capita—Selden says that his earlier "regression equations have performed poorly for later years."[48] He appears to emphasize the inapplicability of the luxury-goods hypothesis (Sec. 3.5). The postwar rise in velocity, he says "is all the more puzzling because the major factor thought to be responsible for the earlier downward trend—advancing per capita real income [i.e., y/N]—has continued to operate since the end of the war."

FRIEDMAN ON INTEREST RATES AND VELOCITY

In 1959 Friedman presented a secular analysis of the demand for money. His data covered the period 1870–1954, and, among other things, he reported on cyclical changes in interest rates and velocity, as follows:

The yield on corporate bonds is correlated with the real stock of

---

[46] For review of the cyclical behavior of velocity and yields on short and long-term debt instruments, see Milton Friedman, "The Demand for Money: Some Theoretical and Empirical Results," *Journal of Political Economy*, August 1959, pp. 344–347. See also Frazer and Yohe, *op. cit.*, Chapter 4 and Sec. 5.4.

[47] Selden, "Monetary Velocity in the United States," *op. cit.*, p. 215.

[48] Selden, "The Postwar Rise in the Velocity of Money," *op. cit.*, p. 44.

money and velocity in the expected direction; a rise in bond yields tends to reduce the real stock of money demanded for a given real income—that is, to raise velocity—and conversely.

However, Friedman also concludes from his secular analysis involving "permanent" income that bond yields "play nothing like so important and regularly consistent a role in accounting for changes in velocity as does real income."[49] On this latter point there are empirical differences between the Friedman results and later results by Meltzer.

MELTZER ON FRIEDMAN'S DEMAND RELATION

To deal with the empirical differences between the Friedman demand relation, as outlined in his 1959 article, and the later Meltzer demand relation, Meltzer compares results from three equations:

(1) $$\ln \frac{M_2}{Np} = \alpha + \beta \ln r + \gamma \ln \frac{W}{NP}$$

(2) $$\ln \frac{M_2}{NP_p} = a + b \ln \frac{y_p}{N}$$

(3) $$\ln \frac{M_2}{p} = A + B \ln r + C \ln \frac{W}{P}$$

where M_2 is money balances plus time deposits, N is population, M_2/Np is real per capita money balances, M_2/NP_p is real per capita permanent money balances, M_2/p is real aggregate money balances, y_p/N is real per capita permanent income, W/NP is real per capita wealth, W/P is real aggregate wealth, y_p $(= rW)$ is permanent income (Sec. 2.2), r is the rate of interest, p and P are both averages of prices (only for deflating different stocks, such as the money stock and the stock of wealth), and α, β, γ, a, b, A, B, and C are parameters to be estimated. The annual data analyzed by Meltzer, as a means of estimating the latter parameters, were supplied by Anna J. Schwartz.[50] They were those used by Friedman and Schwartz in their monetary history.[51] With respect to the data

[49] Friedman, "The Demand for Money," *op. cit.*, p. 345.
[50] Meltzer, "The Evidence from the Time Series," *op. cit.*, note 32, p. 235.
[51] See Friedman and Schwartz, *A Monetary History of the United States 1867–1960, op. cit.*

in question, the variables ln M_2/Np, ln M_2/NP_p, and ln M_2/p, are regressed on other variables in Eqs. (1), (2), and (3), but the results also reveal information about the velocity of money, since a negative coefficient for the interest rate suggests that a rise in the rate reduces the stock of money demanded for a given income— that is, a rise in velocity—and so on. The major empirical results from the analyses of the annual data, using Eqs. (1), (2), and (3), respectively, are summarized in Table 5–1.

Table 5—1. Coefficients of Regression (β, γ, b, B and C) and Determination (R^2) for Equations (1), (2), and (3)

	Equation (1)			Equation (2)		Equation (3)		
	β	γ	R^2	b	R^2	B	C	R^2
1900–58	−0.52	1.62	0.97	1.59	0.95	−0.50	1.32	0.99
1900–29	−0.32	1.75	0.94	1.37	0.96	−0.42	1.41	0.98
1930–58	−0.71	1.24	0.94	1.39	0.88	−0.72	1.12	0.96
1950–58	−0.03	−2.78	0.44	−0.51	0.88	−0.65	0.54	0.75

Source: Adapted from Meltzer's Table 3 (See Allan H. Meltzer, "The Demand for Money: The Evidence from Time Series," *Journal of Political Economy*, June 1963, p. 236.)

Now, the stock of money being used in the present analyses is the Friedman M_2 stock, and, as noted earlier (Sec. 5.1), its use reveals a stronger wealth effect than the use of the stock M_1. Nevertheless, Meltzer's results from the analyses of Friedman-Schwartz data reveal some interesting facts, as Meltzer would point out: the parameter estimates for Eq. (3) for different time periods are more stable proportions of their 1900–58 values and at least always carry the same sign; the inclusion of the variable N in Eq. (1) raises the values for γ over those for C in Eq. (3) and contributes to a change in the sign for γ in the period 1950–58; and the coefficients of determination for equation (3) are usually larger than those in equation (2) involving permanent income, the striking exception being the period 1950–58 "when permanent per capita money balances are *negatively* related to permanent per capita income.[52]

---

[52] Meltzer, "The Evidence from the Time Series," *op. cit.*, pp. 235–236.

As Meltzer concludes, "Interest rates do enter significantly into the demand function for money." He also notes that the differences between his results and Friedman's "stem from the measurement procedures." They are dealt with later (Secs. 6.1, and 6A.1).

The present Meltzer results reveal that the interest rate is a significant determinant in the demand function for money. The results, in combination with the earlier results attributed to Meltzer (Sec. 5.1), moreover, indicate that the rate of interest is a more significant variable than real wealth when the M_1 stock of money is used rather than the M_2 stock. The Meltzer analyses of time series, however, do *not* say anything about whether the changes in the rate of interest *cause* changes in velocity. They simply confirm the presence of generally expected variations in velocity, interest rates, and income.

Finally, there are several side issues. For one, the analytical results concerning the population variable N lead Meltzer to reject a Friedman assumption that the demand function for money is homogeneous of degree one with respect to population. For another, we may note that the negative or low positive values during the period 1950–58 for γ ($= -2.78$) in Eq. (1), b ($= -0.51$) in Eq. (2), C ($= 0.54$) in Eq. (3) reflect the failure of the wealth hypothesis to predict even the direction of the postwar trend for velocity. In the confrontation with these facts, Friedman and Schwartz fall back on the precautionary motive and greater certainty about the future as an explanation of the postwar rise in velocity. They note, too, that this is reflected in the rate of interest.

5.5   SUMMARY

The velocity–interest rate association appears and reappears in the results from regressing inverse velocity on the inverse rate of interest; in the results from regressing the log of inverse velocity on the log of the rate of interest; in the results from regressing the ratio of corporate sales to corporate cash on the long-term rate of interest, after a logarithmic transformation of the data; in Professor Rousseas' V-curve and in some multiple regression results, including those for the stock of money. The Christ-Latané results from regressing inverse velocity on the inverse rate of interest reveal that velocity and the rate of interest move in the same direction, and that 76 per cent of the variation in velocity is explained by changes in the rate of interest. Christ says the relationship is stable, and cites a remarkable occurrence in the brief history of econometric equations—namely, when new points were added to his results from earlier analysis, the new points were closer to the regression line than the points of the original sample period. Latané, in his later results, finds that about 88 per cent of the variation in the log of inverse velocity is explained by changes in the long-term rate of interest. His results support the prospect of percentage changes in velocity being associated with equal percentage changes in the rate on long-term, high-grade corporate bonds; and, dealing only with the nonfinancial business sector, we find from a review of analyses of quarterly data that sales and GNP are highly correlated, and that percentage changes in velocity (defined as the ratio of sales to cash) are associated with equal percentage changes in the rate of interest. Meltzer says the results from regressing velocity (or its inverse) on the rate of interest are not as significant for the early decades of this century as for the later decades, but, his results from regressing the ratio of the money stock to "permanent" income on the rate of interest and nonhuman wealth are consistent with Latané's.

Multiple regression results due to Lawrence Klein and Richard Selden, as well as some results due to Friedman and Friedman and Schwartz, also are consistent with the existence and recurrence of a strong velocity–interest rate association. Selden has regressed the velocity of money on variants of rates of interest, and the results support the velocity–interest rate association, but he expresses reservations due to "pitfalls of attaching significance to correlation analysis of time series," and the failure of the wealth hypothesis to predict the post-World War II rise in the velocity of money. Friedman finds that the yield on corporate bonds is correlated with the real stock of money and velocity in the expected direction, but he does not attribute as important a role to the rate of interest as he does to real income in the determination of the demand for money. Working with Friedman's demand relationship, however, Meltzer finds that Friedman's special results "stem from the measurement procedures." He finds, in particular, that broadening the money stock to include time deposits weakens the velocity–interest rate association, and that population is a poor predictor of the demand for money. Christ, too, has mentioned the tendency for the rate of interest to explain less of the variation in inverse velocity when including time deposits as a part of the money stock in the velocity ratio. This tendency is attributed to the possibility of some switching between money balances and time deposits in response to changes in the rate of interest.

The velocity–interest rate association may be cited as simply a covariation in the respective variables, independent of any causal relationship between the variables. Latané did this in his earlier work. On some other occasions, however, explanations that imply causal relationships are given for the velocity–interest rate association. Usually, these explanations have some relevance to questions concerning the effect of changes in the rate of interest (possibly by the monetary officials) on velocity. In presenting an explanation for the velocity–interest rate association in his later work, Latané drew on an analysis by Tobin. This Latané (or Latané-Tobin) explanation mainly concerns economies effected in the transactions demand for money in response to an increase in the rate of interest, and it suggests that nonfinancial corporations are a likely group to which the explanation applies. A higher rate of interest provides inducement for switching some portion of cash into bonds, and, conversely, a lower rate of interest weakens the inducement. The explanation predicts then a change in cash in relation to income and, therefore, changes in velocity—all in response to changes in the rate of interest. It would also predict changes in the ratio of cash to bonds in response to changes in the rate of interest, and, given the prospect of some portion of government-securities holdings being substituted for a decline in bank loans, the ratio of government-securities holdings by business firms to bank loans would appear to be positively related to the rate of interest.

The Latané (or Latané-Tobin) explanation is inconsistent, however, with the results from the analysis of quarterly data for nonfinancial business firms, even though the explanation would seem to be especially applicable to such firms. Analysis of time-series data for manufacturing firms shows no significant relationship between the ratio of cash to governments and the rate of interest, and the ratio of government securities to bank loans varies inversely with the rate of interest over time.

A notion concerning the effect of changes in the rate of interest (caused possibly by the monetary officials) on the velocity of money is expressed by Christ. He notes that an increase in the rate of interest would lead to a decline in the demand for money and that, with no change in the money stock, the rise in the rate would be associated with a rise in GNP. This, he says, may concern "the monetary authorities in their attempt to stabilize the economy."

The notion of a ceiling on the velocity of money also concerns changes in the rate of interest (possibly by the monetary officials) and the effectiveness of monetary policy. Increases in the rate of interest are supposed to activate idle balances; but at some rate idle balances become depleted and velocity reaches a ceiling. In the context of this explanation of a rise in velocity and a ceiling, some maintain that institutional evolution will cause the ceiling to gradually move. Such notions arose in connection with the availability of credit doctrine, whereby increases in the rate of interest were supposed to meet a ceiling on velocity and, via a "pinning-in" effect on credit-granting institutions, constrain further increases in expenditures and reduce the availability of credit. Apparently, empirical evidence does not support the theory of a ceiling on velocity, in part, because the evidence does not support the notion that a rise in interest rates causes an activation of idle balances, and, in part, because the interest elasticity of proportionate cash balances seems to be sufficiently unchanged by changes in the rate of interest.

Friedman and Schwartz appear to suggest the prospect of a ceiling in their anticipation of an end to the postwar rise in the velocity of money. Their explanation for the ceiling follows from their wealth hypothesis whereby the long-term trend is downward for percentage changes in the demand for money in response to percentage changes in income (or wealth). Indeed, in explaining the postwar rise in the velocity of money, Friedman and Schwartz cite factors other than income (wealth) or even the rate of interest. They cite greater certainty about the future.

The Friedman-Schwartz explanation of the post-World War II

rise in velocity is inconsistent with the Latané (or Latané-Tobin) explanation of movements in velocity. The Latané argument that higher interest rates lead to economy in the use of money and to higher velocities explains too much, they say. The emphasis by Friedman and Schwartz on certainty about the future as a determinant of velocity is consistent with other observations and explanations. It is consistent with Rousseas' statement that much of the idle balances activated during boom periods are not in direct response to interest rate changes, and with an alternative to the Latané (or Latané-Tobin) explanation for the velocity–interest rate association, as it concerns nonfinancial business firms.

As an alternative to the Latané (or Latané-Tobin) explanation for the velocity–interest rate association, a form of switching between assets with a fixed claim against future income and assets with a residual claim is combined with the narrower notion of switching between cash and bonds in relation to changes in interest rates. In the alternative explanation, changes in velocity result primarily from changes in the rate of return on additions to inventories, plant and equipment, in response to a possible variety of factors (tax credits, price-level changes, and so on) and in relation to the rate of return on additions to other assets or the rate of interest. In effect, as the rate of return on additional capital goods rises, income and total assets increase, and cash and government-securities holdings by manufacturing firms increase, too, but not in proportion to the rise in income. In such an expansion, then, the velocity of money rises (or cash as a proportion of income declines). This explanation is consistent with results from regressing the ratio of cash to governments on the rate of interest, with other analyses of data for manufacturing firms, and with the negative coefficient for price-level changes in a multiple regression result due to Lawrence Klein.

In the latter explanation, changes in the rate of interest, possibly by the monetary officials, have some effect on expenditures. The explanation and the statistical results, however, suggest that the changes in yields (as rates) on capital goods contribute primarily to both changes in the rate of interest and the velocity of money, at least insofar as the corporate manufacturing sector is concerned.

Chapter 6

STABLE DEMAND RELATIONS, STATISTICAL RESULTS, AND ELEMENTS OF THEORY

The concept of wealth as the capitalized value of prospective income—as introduced earlier (Sec. 3.5), and as presently reviewed (Sec. 6.1)—anticipates a review of a Friedman demand relation and problems in regression analyses of time series for wealth, income, and the rate of interest. Following analysis due to Meltzer, the Friedman demand relation is reviewed (Sec. 6.2) as being, among other things, conceptually similar to Meltzer's demand relations. This is then followed by a review of Meltzer's demand relations and his widely discussed evidence from time series (Sec. 6.3) and reviews of Laidler on the empirical definition of money (Sec. 6.4) and Chow on the long- and short-run demand (Sec. 6.5).

Results due to both Friedman and Meltzer, as well as the others, involve statistical problems in the analysis of time series; each emphasizes the analysis of time series, and each emphasizes the analysis of time series over long periods. As these matters may loosely suggest, the over-all results in question bear more directly on broad issues rather than on questions of the implementation and effectiveness of monetary policy in the short run. The broad issues involve the "luxury" goods hypothesis of the demand for money, the effects of specifying a stock of money to include time deposits, the homogeneity of the demand relation, and questions about whether specific sets of variables adequately specify a "stable" demand function. With reference to the demand function, the term *stable* has come to mean either (1) that regression coefficients involving demand relationships are constant from period to period, or (2) that parameter estimates for different periods

139

appear to be drawn from the same population. Some also wish to imply that enough variables are included in the demand function to account for most of the variation in demand. The search for a stable demand function has been motivated in part, by the desire to advance economics as an empirical science, and possibly, in part, by the desire to find satisfactory rules as guides in the formation of monetary policy.

The most explicit statement of a stable demand function by Friedman involves the real stock of money per capita and real permanent income per capita. Via his wealth hypothesis, the former variable increases more than in proportion to the latter, but the hypothesis apparently fails to predict the post-World War II rise in velocity, and Friedman later (along with Anna Jacobson Schwartz) introduces greater certainty about the future to deal with the post-World War II rise in velocity. Meltzer notes several reasons for the failure of Friedman's demand equation to predict relationships in the post-World War II years—the most important factors being the use of the definition of money to include time deposits in the regression analyses, and the inadequacy of the population variable as a predictor. In his alternative analysis, Meltzer emphasizes the regression of the money stock on wealth (or income) and the rate of interest, and the results reflect good fits to the logarithmically transformed data. The various results, including elasticity coefficients, tend to support the predictions as to direction and magnitude that would follow from the broad underlying foundations of monetary economics (Sec. 3.3), but they are also no more than consistent with a possibility mentioned earlier (Sec. 5.2)—namely, that changes in the ratio of income to cash and the rate of interest both reflect some changes in the rate of return on real capital as affected by a variety of factors.

Laidler and Chow, too, deal with empirical demand functions[1] concerning, respectively, the question of the most appropriate empirical definition of money as judged primarily by regression results

---

[1] David Laidler, "Some Evidence on the Demand for Money," *Journal of Political Economy*, February 1966, pp. 55–68; and Gregory C. Chow, "On the Long-Run and Short-Run Demand for Money," *Journal of Political Economy*, April 1966, pp. 111–127.

involving alternative statistical definitions of the money stock, and demand functions of the type initially dealt with by Friedman and Meltzer. Chow, in particular, draws "attention to the possibility of treating the demand for money as a special case of the demand for durable goods," and he has introduced a mechanism for dealing with a distinction between a long-run or equilibrium demand and a short-run demand. The particular treatment of the demand for money as a durable good, however, is primarily motivated by Chow's work on statistical demand functions for automobiles. Chow notes with respect to his evidence on the long-run demand for money, that "the results . . . are in agreement with the findings of previous authors that much of the variation in the demand for money can be explained by the interest rate and an income variable, be it permanent income, wealth, or current income." His results on the short-run demand indicate a less pronounced role for the permanent-income variable.

A net result of analyses reviewed in this chapter on the positive side is simply support for the broad underlying foundations of monetary economics. The variables "explaining" the demand for money remain to be adequately specified. Apparently, the search for a demand equation involving these variables and stable coefficients must proceed. In the appendix to this chapter, therefore, we continue to deal with the following: criticisms of aspects of Friedman's approach; a possible explanation for the "denigration of the influence of interest rate movements," and his evaluation of other possible determinants of the demand for money, including, among others, the rate of change in prices as a measure for changes in the rate of return on real capital. The discussion in the appendix takes the form, in particular, of a review of Meltzer's attempt to state explicitly the monetary theory implicit in Friedman and Schwartz's *A Monetary History* and in related works.

6.1 WEALTH, THE CAPITALIZED VALUE OF INCOME

Among the fundamental notions that appear and reappear in considerations of a demand function for money is that of wealth as the discounted value of a prospective stream of income. A review of this notion, in fact, may lead to a review of Friedman's definition of "permanent" income, the effects on the demand for money that get submerged in the definition, interrelationships between stock and flow variables for wealth and income particularly, and the prospect for serial correlation and multicollinearity in multivariate analyses concerning the demand for money and time-series data.

WEALTH, INCOME, AND PERMANENT INCOME

Wealth (W) may be defined as the discounted value of the prospective stream of income (Y). This may be denoted as a perpetuity—namely, $W = Y/r$—where current income or GNP is the prospective stream to be discounted by a current rate of interest (r). Friedman has used this definition in several contexts (Sec. 3.5), and he has also defined expected (permanent) income as rW. However, in time-series investigations, as indicated by the earlier definition of permanent income (Sec. 2.2), and as noted by several writers, a theory of expectations is added. Mincer notes, for example, that this theory "leads to a definition of permanent income as a weighted average of current and past incomes."[2] Meltzer, too, notes that the permanent yield (Y_p) on wealth is measured by "an exponentially weighted average of past incomes,"[3] but, at times, he simply takes the definition of permanent income as the "income flow resulting from a stock of wealth." Mincer, facing a problem of statistical measurement, takes "expected or normal income as the income a family receives per unit of time during which its labor input is 'normal.' " This translates into income at the average level of employment. The use of some average of income, in combination with the definition of the velocity of money as the ratio of income to the stock of money, should suggest that a lot of the change in velocity is washed out by the use of the substitute measure. Further, the earlier velocity–interest rate association (Sec. 5.1), in combination with the use of the substitute measure for income, should suggest the prospect of a much weaker association

---

2 See Jacob Mincer, "Employment and Consumption," *Review of Economics and Statistics,* February 1960, note 4, p. 21.

3 Allan H. Meltzer, "The Demand for Money: The Evidence from the Time Series," *Journal of Political Economy,* June 1963, note 31, pp. 234–235.

between the interest rate, velocity and/or the demand for money in analyses employing the "permanent" income measure.

Finally, viewing 1963 as a representative year, we may note that roughly about 60 per cent of GNP could be represented as due to human capital (as indicated by compensation of employees as a percentage of GNP). This is of no particular consequence, but over-all it indicates that human capital is a larger proportion of total capital than nonhuman capital. This fact should provide some perspective on analyses involving the income-wealth framework (i.e., $Y = rW$) and utilizing estimates for nonhuman capital.

Wealth (a Stock) and Income (a Flow)

As noted earlier (Sec. 3.5), wealth is a stock variable; income is a flow variable; and the increments in wealth, apart from adjustments in value (i.e., $r = $ constant), are due to the flow of the unconsumed or capital enriching portion of income. Thus, with $r = $ constant, we expect wealth to vary directly with income unless the capital enriching portion of income is so unusually small as to fail to provide for the depreciation of the physical capital, and, even with income and the rate of interest tending to vary positively over reference cycles, we expect wealth to vary directly, remain unchanged, or decline, depending on whether $\frac{\Delta Y}{Y} \Big/ \frac{\Delta r}{r} \gtreqless 1$. Further, in the very long run, as when the scale of operation may be doubled (Sec. 3.5), we expect roughly equal proportional changes in income and wealth with the rate of interest remaining unchanged.

All of this suggests several points of possible importance. For one, the fact that marginal changes in the relative large wealth variable result from the relatively small flow variable for income suggests that percentage changes in income will be more volatile when interest rates change only modestly.[4] For another, the scale changes—interest rates constant—suggest that percentage changes in wealth and income respectively are the same. For still another, our reasoning suggests that wealth and income are likely to be highly correlated in contrast to the rate of interest and income (or

---

[4] Compare Lydall on Hansen, Sec. 3.5 of this text.

wealth) in the long run. And, finally, given the cyclical behavior of velocity (Y/M) and interest rates (Sec. 5.1 and 5.2) and the analytical result whereby these possibly respond to the same change in the setting (Sec. 5.2), we expect some serial correlation between interest rates, the demand for money, income, and wealth.

These latter prospects are borne out by results from analyses of data. Courchene and Shapiro recognize problems of serial correlation in Meltzer's analyses of time series,[5] and Meltzer concedes the presence of serial correlation and multicollinearity (Secs. 2A.4, 2A.5) in his extensive analyses of time series.[6] Even in his initial paper on the evidence from time series, Meltzer recognized the difficulty in the interpretation of the evidence "owing to substantial multicollinearity due to the high correlation between real income and real wealth."[7] All of this gains part of its present import simply by serving as a means of emphasizing the need for caution and proper allowances in evaluating the evidence from time series about the determinants of the demand for money. The possible serial correlation between income and the rate of interest and the prospect that changes in velocity and interest rates both reflect some changes in the setting suggest, in particular, that the interest rate may not "explain" changes in the demand for money, even though its presence in multiple regression analyses tends to account for some additional portion of the variation in the demand for money.

6.2   A FRIEDMAN DEMAND RELATION AND MELTZER ANALYSES

The Friedman demand relation is originally formulated for a simple regression analysis. Even so, Meltzer views it as being conceptually similar to his own demand relations, as involving more than one independent variable, and as involving a concealing meas-

---

[5] T. J. Courchene and H. T. Shapiro, "The Demand for Money: A Note from the Time Series," *Journal of Political Economy*, October 1964, pp. 489–500.

[6] See Allan H. Meltzer, "A Little More Evidence from the Time Series," *Journal of Political Economy*, October 1964, pp. 505–507.

[7] See Meltzer, "The Evidence from the Time Series," *op. cit.*, p. 233.

urement procedure. He gives the Friedman relation an alternative formulation and presents some results from multiple regression analyses. In either the simple or multiple regression form, however, the relation fails to anticipate even the direction of postwar movements in the velocity of money. This section is a review of these matters—the Friedman relation, the concealing measurement procedure, the alternative formulation of the relation, and statistical results.

THE DEMAND RELATION

Friedman's demand function is concerned with the relationship between secular changes in the real stock of money per capita (M/NP) and real permanent income per capita (Y_p/NP_p). He approximates this functional relationship by the equation

$$\frac{M}{NP_p} = \gamma \left(\frac{Y_p}{NP_p} \right)^\delta$$

Taking the logarithm of both sides,

$$\ln \left(\frac{M}{NP_p} \right) = \delta \ln \left[\gamma \frac{Y_p}{(NP_p)} \right]$$

and differentiating with respect to the logarithm of the bracketed term, the elasticity of the demand for money becomes δ.[8] Friedman also notes (1) that average values over complete reference cycles were used as the elementary observations in a simple regression analysis; (2) that the observations concerned twenty cycles "measured from trough to trough and covering the period from 1870 to 1954"; (3) that money was defined to include time deposits (denoted presently as M_2 stock); and (4) that the measures for income and prices involved Simon Kuznets' estimates.

The results from Friedman's analysis of data were a correlation coefficient of 0.99 and a computed elasticity of 1.8 (i.e., $\delta = 1.8$). He notes that they support the "luxury" goods hypothesis (Sec. 3.5), if the results are interpreted as "reflecting movements along a stable demand relation." However, Friedman says that "the

---

[8] See Milton Friedman, "The Demand for Money: Some Theoretical and Empirical Results," *Journal of Political Economy*, August 1959, p. 336.

high correlation does not justify much confidence" in the validity
of the demand estimate, "because of the strong trend element in
the two series." Nevertheless, Friedman views the "luxury" goods
hypothesis as a principal explanation of a secular decline in the
velocity of money, and, later, analyzing the rise in velocity after
1951, brings into question the stability of his demand relation.
"Why," he says along with Anna Jacobson Schwartz, "should
velocity instead have continued to rise?"[9] They appear to invoke
a variant of the precautionary motive (Sec. 3.4)—or greater certainty about the future—as the explanation. "Changing expectations about economic stability," they conclude, "seems . . . a more
plausible explanation of postwar movements in the velocity of
money. . . ."[10] His equation, as an alleged definition of a stable
demand relationship, failed to predict the rise in velocity after
1951.

MELTZER ON THE FRIEDMAN DEMAND RELATION

Meltzer views Friedman's demand relation as conceptually similar to his own. He proceeds to give the Friedman relation an
alternative formulation and to conduct tests to determine the
relevance of his own and Friedman's demand relation.

Following Friedman, he lets $Y = rW$ or $W = Y/r$, and proceeds
with the equation

(1) $$M = g(r)W$$

The latter equation defines the demand for money as some variable proportion $g(r)$ of wealth, where the proportion is some function of the rate of interest. Substituting Y/r for W in the latter
equation, $M = g(r) Y/r$, and substituting permanent income Y_p
for income Y, we get

$$M = \frac{g(r) Y_p}{r}$$

---

[9] Milton Friedman and Anna Jacobson Schwartz, *A Monetary History of
the United States, 1867–1960,* (Princeton, New Jersey: Princeton University
Press, for the National Bureau of Economic Research, 1963), p. 644.

[10] *Ibid.,* p. 675. Friedman uses the term "precautionary motive" in his
1959 article. See "The Demand for Money," *op. cit.,* p. 349.

Now, if $g(r)/r$ is approximately constant, this equation becomes

(2) $$M = kY_p$$

[Note that $g(r)/r$ could reflect some portion of the association between inverse velocity and the rate of interest as in an earlier section (Sec. 5.1).]

To proceed in comparing Friedman's relation with his own, Meltzer divides Eqs. (1) and (2) by population N and prices p (or permanent prices P_p), introduces a few constants, and takes logarithms to get

(1) $$\ln \frac{M_2}{Np} = \alpha + \beta \ln r + \gamma \ln \frac{W}{NP}$$

(2) $$\ln \frac{M_2}{NP_p} = a + b \ln \frac{W}{NP}$$

where P is a special deflator for nonhuman wealth. [Note that the factor $g(r)/r$ gets submerged in constants in Eq. (2) and appears as a term in Eq. (1).]

As it turns out, the results of regressions involving these two equations were reviewed earlier (Sec. 5.4, Table 5-1). From the review, we recall several things. For one, the analytical results concerning the population variable N lead Meltzer to reject the implicit Friedman assumption of a homogeneous demand function of degree one with respect to population. For another, we note that the negative or low positive values during the period 1950–58 for γ ($= -2.78$) in Eq. (1), b ($= -0.51$) in Eq. (2), and C ($= 0.54$) in Eq. (3) reflect the failure of the wealth hypothesis to predict the direction of the postwar trend in velocity. For still another, the role of the interest rate appears significant in the earlier Eq. (3), but, according to Meltzer, "Friedman's conclusion that interest rates play a small role in the demand function for money seems to stem from the measurement procedure he employs."[11]

Dealing with relations involving questions similar to those just dealt with, Chow provides, among others, the following regression equation:

---

[11] Meltzer, "The Evidence from the Time Series," *op. cit.*, p. 235.

$$\ln M = -1.072 + 0.2022 \ln N + 0.1595 \ln P$$
$$\quad\quad\quad (0.2555) \quad\quad\quad (0.2453)$$
$$+ 0.9332 \ln Y_p - 0.7673 \ln r \quad\quad R^2 = 0.9966$$
$$(0.1657) \quad\quad\quad (0.0592)$$

where he analyzes "annual data from 1897 to 1958 (excluding the war years 1917–19 and 1941–45)," and where M is "currency and demand deposits adjusted in the middle of the year," N is "total population (including armed forces overseas from 1930 on) residing in the United States, in the middle of the year," P is a consumer price index, 100 per cent for 1954, Y_p is "Friedman's aggregate real permanent income, multiplied by the above price index P," and r is the "yield on twenty-year corporate bonds."[12] Citing the results concerning this latter equation, Chow notes that neither the regression coefficient for $\ln N$ or $\ln P$ is statistically significant, and he views the coefficient of $\ln Y_p$ as confirmation of a unit income elasticity hypothesis. The lack of significance of the regression coefficient for $\ln N$ would support Meltzer in his rejection of a homogeneous demand function of degree one in population. The regression coefficient for $\ln r$, further, would appear to be

---

[12] See Chow, *op. cit.*, pp. 118–119. Chow's sources of data are set forth in his Appendix A (Chow, *op. cit.*, p. 128). The money supply series for the years 1897–1957 is from U.S. Bureau of the Census, *Historical Statistics of The United States: Colonial Times to 1957* (Washington, D.C.: U.S. Bureau of the Census, 1960), p. 646, Series 267. For the period since 1958 the money supply is from the Federal Reserve Bulletin. Total population series for the years 1897–1929 and 1930–57 is from the Bureau of the Census, *op. cit.*, p. 7, Series 2, and Series 1. The latter series for the years beginning in 1958 is from *Statistical Abstract of the United States* (Washington, D.C., 1960). The price index of consumers expenditures, 1954=100, is that used by Friedman and Meiselman (see Milton Friedman and David Meiselman, "The Relative Stability of Monetary Velocity and the Investment Multiplier in the United States, 1897–1958," *Stabilization Policies: Commission on Money and Credit* [Englewood Cliffs, New Jersey: Prentice-Hall, Inc., 1964], Table B-1, col. 6). The permanent implicit price index of net national product, 1929=100, was supplied by Milton Friedman and Anna J. Schwartz. The series for the yield on twenty-year corporate bonds, 1897–1899 is that reported by the Bureau of the Census, *op. cit.*, p. 656, Series 332. The latter is multiplied by 0.85 for linkage for the years 1900–56 with the Census Series 346 (Census, *op. cit.*, p. 657) and for the years 1957–58 with the series in *Statistical Abstract, op. cit.*, p. 466.

consistent with Meltzer's conclusion (Sec. 5.4) that "interest rates do enter significantly into the demand function for money."

6.3 MELTZER'S DEMAND RELATIONS AND EVIDENCE FROM TIME SERIES

Meltzer's equations and his reporting of evidence from time series have primarily been concerned with the long-run characteristics of the demand function for money,[13] and with broad theoretical issues. His conclusions concern, in particular, the homogeneity of the demand for money with respect to prices and assets, the stock of money providing the most stable alternative demand relation, the specification of the independent variables yielding the most stable demand function, and the matter of determining the relative stability of alternative demand functions as a means of settling upon an appropriate specification of the money stock.

The Meltzer Equations

The basic Meltzer equation defining the demand for money is

$$(1) \qquad M = ar^b W_n^c$$

or alternatively, taking the logarithm from both sides,[14]

$$(1') \qquad \ln M = a + b \ln r + c \ln W_n,$$

where, apart from the constants a, b, and c and the variables M and r as defined above, W_n is nonhuman wealth.

Further, Meltzer reviews the ratio of human income to its capitalized value as a constant (i.e., $d = $ constant) and combines the yield on financial assets and physical assets (i.e., r^* and ρ) in a single variable r. Also, he views Eq. $1'$ as a "truncated" form of a more complete equation,[15]

---

[13] See Meltzer, "The Evidence from the Time Series," *op. cit.*, p. 223; and Meltzer, "A Little More Evidence from the Time Series." *op. cit.*, p. 505.

[14] As a strictly formal matter the equation should be written $\ln M = \ln a + b \ln r + c \ln W_n$, but since the term $\ln a$ is constant, it is sometimes simply denoted a.

[15] See Meltzer, "A Little More Evidence from the Time Series," *op. cit.*, pp. 504–505; and Meltzer, "The Evidence from the Time Series," *op. cit.*, p. 223.

$$\ln \frac{M}{P} = a + b \ln r + c \ln \frac{Y}{Y_p} + d \ln \frac{W_n}{P} + e \ln \frac{P}{p}$$

where, in addition to the terms defined earlier, P is the deflator of nonhuman wealth, and p is the income deflator. Equations (1) and (1') follow from the more complete equation and some of Meltzer's assumptions—namely, P/p, an index of interest rates can be combined with r, and Y/Y_p, the index of transitory income (or the ratio of Net National Product to Friedman's permanent income) can be approximated by a term equal to unity (with logarithm $= 0$).

In his analyses of data, Meltzer uses the following: alternative money stock variables (M_1, M_2) as mentioned earlier (Secs. 2.2, 5.1, and 5.4); Durand's basic yield on twenty-year corporate bonds for the interest rate variable r; and several alternative measures of nonhuman wealth, usually involving measures by R. W. Goldsmith.[16]

THE HOMOGENEOUS DEMAND FUNCTION

Results from analyses of data concerning the theoretical notion whereby the demand for money is homogeneous of degree one in prices and financial assets (Sec. 3.2) are reviewed below. The analyses in question utilize the M_1 money stock, the rate of interest (r), and the "consolidated net nonhuman wealth of the public."

Meltzer's initial regression estimates for the period 1900–58 are

(2) $\ln M_1 = -1.65 - 0.781 \ln W_n + 1.01 \ln W_n,$ $R^2 = 0.994$

Partial correlations: $- 0.88$ $+ 0.99$

(3) $\ln \dfrac{M_1}{P} = -1.48 - 0.949 \ln r + 1.11 \ln \dfrac{W_n}{p},$ $R^2 = 0.992$

Partial correlations: $- 0.93$ $+ 0.98$

Here we observe from Eq. (2) that the wealth elasticity of the

---

[16] See Meltzer, "The Evidence from the Time Series," *op. cit.*, p. 224, notes 19 and 20, p. 228 and note 23.

demand for money is very close to one.[17] Also, from Eq. (3), where the money balances and income are deflated, we observe only a modest change in the wealth elasticity.[18] These statistical results appear reasonably consistent with the notion of a homogeneous demand function of degree one in prices and assets: "a doubling of prices and the value of financial assets doubles the demand for nominal balances but leaves the demand for real balances unaffected."[19]

THE M_1 STOCK VERSUS THE M_2 STOCK

Continuing with the interest rate and wealth variables of Eq. (3), and adding time deposits to get the M_2 stock of money,

$$(3^*) \qquad \ln \frac{M_2}{p} = -1.98 - 0.50 \ln r + 1.32 \ln \frac{W_n}{P}, \qquad R^2 = 0.994$$

Partial correlations: −0.82   +0.99

---

[17] As a check on Meltzer's calculations involving Eq. (2), Chow presents the following regression (see Chow, *op. cit.*, p. 119):

$$\ln M = -2.186 - 0.7059 \ln r + 1.038 \ln W_n, \qquad R^2 = .9946$$
$$ (0.0562) \quad\;\; (0.012)$$

where, in addition to the Chow variables defined earlier (Sec. 6.2), W_n is total nonhuman wealth. As Chow notes (Chow, *op. cit.*, p. 120), the same variables are used as in Meltzer's Eq. (2), "except that his [Meltzer's] wealth variable is at the *end* of each year and that his observations are from 1900 to 1958, including war years." Continuing, Chow concludes, "Meltzer's coefficients of the corresponding equation are . . . not too far from ours." Chow's nonhuman wealth variable is the "mean of two nearest beginning-of-year figures." His wealth series comes from several sources, including two due to Goldsmith (see Chow, *op. cit.*, Appendix A, pp. 128–129).

[18] An index of interest rates, P/p, has been combined with r for the regression estimates in Eq. (3). Meltzer says "this results in a somewhat higher estimate for the coefficient of $\ln r$ in (3) than in (2)." See Meltzer, "The Evidence from the Time Series," *op. cit.*, p. 225.

[19] Meltzer, "The Evidence from the Time Series," *op. cit.*, p. 227. Meltzer also refers to such results elsewhere in discussing the Friedman-Schwartz monetary history. (See Allan H. Meltzer, "Monetary Theory and Monetary History," *Schweizerische Zeitschrift für Volkswirtschaft und Statistik*, December 1965, pp. 409–411).

Note, by comparing the interest rate and wealth coefficient of this equation with those in Eqs. (2) and (3), that "the interest rate and wealth elasticities differ substantially depending on the definition of money balances used."[20] When time deposits are added to the stock of money, in other words, the regression results show a drop in the size of the interest rate coefficient and an increase in the wealth coefficient.

From the above and similar types of evidence, Meltzer draws several conclusions. For one, the wealth elasticity increases when the definition of money is broadened to include time deposits. Thus, he says, Friedman's conclusion that money is a "luxury" good (Secs. 2.2 and 3.5) "relates to the particular definition of money that Friedman uses."[21] For another, the negative interest rate parameter is smaller under the broader definition of money. This suggests that some of the association between interest rates and the demand for money is submerged in the possible switching between time and demand deposits as interest rates change.[22]

The conclusions are also supported by additional analyses of similar time series for the periods 1900–58, 1900–49 and 1900–29. These are due to Courchene and Shapiro (Sec. 2A.4).[23]

---

[20] Meltzer, "The Evidence from the Time Series," *op. cit.*, p. 235.

[21] Meltzer, "The Evidence from the Time Series," *op. cit.*, p. 238. Chow also supports Meltzer's conclusion. He presents the following regression equation:

$$\ln M = -0.7471 + 0.06806 \ln N + 1.037 \ln Y_p - 0.7427 \ln r, \qquad R^2 = .9966$$
$$ (0.14948) \quad\ \ (0.040) \qquad (0.0452)$$

where the variables are those defined earlier (Sec. 6.2). Chow says (Chow, *op. cit.*, p. 119), "Meltzer has advocated the unit income elasticity hypothesis, explaining that the higher elasticity found by Friedman is due to the broader definition of money used."

[22] This prospect of switching between time and demand deposits in response to interest rate changes has been noted earlier (Sec. 5.1). In neither case, however, should the prospect necessarily be inconsistent with the findings for the business sector (Sec. 5.2) of an absence of switching between cash balances and government securities in response to interest rate changes. The difference in the findings may be due to sector differences comprising the aggregates for the economy as a whole, and/or they may be due to the nature of the difference between time deposits and marketable government securities as debt instruments. Time deposits, exclusive of negotiable time certificates of deposit, are essentially different from marketable government bonds—they do not decline in value (or market value) as the bonds do in response to a rise upward as market yields rise.

[23] See "A Note from the Time Series," *op. cit.*, p. 499 and Meltzer's

THE STABILITY OF ALTERNATIVE DEMAND RELATIONS

Meltzer further concludes that the demand function for the stock of money balances M_1 is at least as stable as the demand functions involving broader definitions of the stock of money. He says that "the evidence does not suggest any compelling reason for broadening the definition of money,"[24] and he presents evidence to support the conclusion. Courchene and Shapiro, however, say that "regression estimates display no stability at all" when they estimate functions for shorter periods (10–15 years).[25]

Some of the Courchene-Shapiro results for longer periods are as follows:[26]

$$\ln \frac{M_1}{P} = a + b \ln r + c \ln \frac{W_n}{P}$$

Period	b-Value	c-Value	R^2	Correlation coefficient for independent variables
1900–58	−1.001	1.150	0.98	−0.46
1900–29	−0.317	0.876	0.90	0.82
1920–58	−1.001	1.161	0.97	−0.60
1930–58	−1.214	1.260	0.96	−0.23

$$\ln \frac{M_2}{P} = a + b \ln r + c \ln \frac{W_n}{P}$$

Period	b-Value	c-Value	R^2	Correlation coefficient for independent variables
1900–58	−0.579	1.329	0.98	−0.46
1900–29	−0.454	1.420	0.98	0.82
1920–58	−0.696	1.106	0.97	−0.60
1930–58	−0.794	1.147	0.96	−0.23

comments on their results in "A Little More Evidence from the Time Series," *op. cit.*, pp. 504–508. See also, Meltzer's Table 2, "A Little More Evidence from the Time Series," *op. cit.*, p. 507.

24 Meltzer, "The Evidence from the Time Series," *op. cit.*, p. 227.

25 See Courchene and Shapiro, "A Note from the Time Series," *op. cit.*, note 11.

26 *Ibid.*, Table 1.

A comparison of the coefficients for the period 1900–29 with the 1920–58 and 1930–58 periods shows some instability. Even so, Meltzer's earlier point that the wealth elasticity increases and the negative interest elasticity declines when M_2 rather than M_1 balances are regressed on the variables gains additional support by the Courchene-Shapiro results.

ESTIMATES USING INCOME

In arguing for the stability of his demand function vis-à-vis other alternatives, Meltzer presents results concerning $M_1 = f(r, Y)$ as do Courchene and Shapiro. These may be contrasted with the immediately preceding Courchene-Shapiro results from the regressions of $\ln M_1$ on $\ln r$ and $\ln (W_n/P)$, and with some of their additional results.

The Meltzer results in question are as follows:

	$\ln \dfrac{M_1}{P} = a + b \ln r + c \ln \dfrac{Y}{P}$		
Period	b-Value	c-Value	R^2
1900–58	−0.79	1.05	0.86
1900–29	−0.05	0.07	0.86
1930–58	−0.69	0.94	0.52

The Courchene-Shapiro results are these:

	$\ln \dfrac{M_1}{P} = a + b \ln r + c \ln \dfrac{Y}{P}$			
Period	b-Value	c-Value	R^2	Correlation coefficient for independent variables
1900–58	−0.674	0.971	0.98	−0.51
1900–29	−0.233	0.739	0.90	0.80
1920–58	−0.664	0.934	0.97	−0.73
1930–58	−0.544	0.940	0.96	−0.55

[*Note:* Meltzer used Net National Product $(=Y)$ and Courchene and Shapiro used Gross National Product $(=Y)$.]

A comparison of these results with the previous Courchene-Shapiro results from regressing $\ln M_1$ on $\ln r$ and $\ln (W_n/P)$ reveals about the same instability in the results. Meltzer, however, shows smaller coefficients of determination when income is used rather than nonhuman wealth. These contrasting results concern Meltzer's conclusion that "the demand function for money is more stable when the function is formulated in terms of a wealth constraint rather than an income constraint."[27] Courchene and Shapiro conclude, on the other hand, that neither "specification of the function yields estimates of the relevant coefficients which are surprisingly 'stable' for different time periods. . . ." They say, "The wealth constraint *might* appear to provide a slightly better alternative but the choice is not clear cut."[28]

Meltzer, in his reply to Courchene and Shapiro, presents some additional results. These are from analyses of data that exclude the wars 1942–51, and that involve his more complete version of the "truncated" equation (1). Meltzer then concludes that "the demand function for currency plus demand deposits, M_1, is at least as stable as the demand functions that use alternative definitions."[29]

SOME EVIDENCE FROM QUARTERLY DATA

Some evidence is available on money demand relations for the years 1947–58 that involves the Meltzer type of equations. This evidence concerns analyses of quarterly data and it especially involves serious statistical and practical problems. On the statistical side, there are the earlier problems of serial correlation and multicollinearity (Secs. 2A.4 and 2A.5), possibly compounded for the short period,[30] and on the applied side, the interest rates entering

---

27 Meltzer, "The Evidence from the Time Series," *op. cit.*, pp. 233–234.

28 Courchene and Shapiro, "A Note from the Time Series," *op. cit.*, p. 501. At this stage in the defense of their point that "the evidence from the time series is far less clear" than Meltzer suggests, the latter authors introduce the "Chow" test. In reply Meltzer notes, however, that "the Chow test is inapplicable where there is serial correlation of the residuals." See Meltzer, "A Little More Evidence from the Time Series," *op. cit.*, p. 506.

29 Meltzer, "A Little More Evidence from the Time Series," *op. cit.*, p. 508.

30 See Meltzer, "The Evidence from the Time Series," *op. cit.*, p. 222.

the analysis reflected developments during the "pegged rate" episode for about half of the years 1947–58. The article, by H. R. Heller,[31] reporting the evidence from the quarterly data, moreover, is somewhat frustrating. For example, his statement, "in the downswing, money balances decrease percentagewise," is inconsistent with the observations (Table 2.1) showing a rise in money balances for two of the three recessions during the period 1947–58.[32]

SOME MELTZER CONCLUSIONS IN PERSPECTIVE

Meltzer's time-series analyses are affected by the presence of serial correlation and multicollinearity. They deal more or less adequately, nevertheless, with some important matters. His results are consistent with the notion of a homogeneous demand function of degree one in prices and assets. They are also, along with those of Courchene and Shapiro and, later, Chow, consistent with the view that Friedman's "luxury" goods hypothesis is the result of his use of a money stock that includes time deposits. From the results presented thus far Meltzer further appears warranted in the view that demand relations involving the narrower M_1 stock of money are at least as stable as those involving broader measures of the stock of money. Laidler's results, as reported below (Sec. 6.4), moreover, provide further evidence on this point.

On the less positive side, questions remain concerning the specification of a stable demand function. The wealth in Meltzer's demand function is unlikely to deal much better with the postwar rise in the velocity of money than the wealth variable in Friedman's function (Sec. 6.2), and the coefficients for the rate of interest in the Meltzer regression results are unlikely to be any more satisfactory as an explanation of the demand for money than Latané's unitary elasticity measure for changes in the stock of

---

[31] "The Demand for Money: The Evidence from the Short-Run Data," *Quarterly Journal of Economics*, May 1965, pp. 291–303.

[32] With respect to the Heller results, Kaufman and Latta report as follows: "Attempts to replicate his [Heller's] results . . . resulted in the discovery of an error in the computation of the coefficients." See George G. Kaufman and Cynthia M. Latta, "The Demand for Money: Preliminary Evidence from Industrial Countries," *Journal of Financial and Quantitative Analysis*, September 1966, note 12.

balances as a proportion of income with respect to changes in the rate of interest. Also, as Courchene and Shapiro note, surprisingly good estimates of the demand for money are provided without using interest rates. They find that real income alone will account for 95 to 96 per cent of the variance in the real M_1 and M_2 money stocks, respectively, for the period 1900–58.[33] They get similar results for real nonhuman wealth alone.

6.4 LAIDLER ON THE EMPIRICAL DEFINITION OF MONEY

Laidler relies primarily on regression equations involving the alternative equation forms in dealing with the question of whether the money stock as usually defined or the money stock as defined to include time deposits provides the most adequate definition of money. He wishes to compare the regression results corresponding to the respective forms in arriving at the best statistical definition of money. The forms of the regressions are as follows:[34]

Nonhuman wealth hypothesis:

$$M_t - M_{t-1} = b_1 Y_{p,t-1/2} + b_2 Y_{T,t-1/2} + b_3(r_t - r_{t-1})$$

Permanent income hypothesis:

$$M_t - M_{t-1} = b_1(Y_{p,t} - Y_{p,t-1}) + b_2(r_t - r_{t-1})$$

Orthodox hypothesis:

$$M_t - M_{t-1} = b_1(Y_t - Y_{t-1}) + b_2(r_t - r_{t-1})$$

where $M_t - M_{t-1}$ is the first difference in the series for the money stock, Y_p is permanent income, Y_T is transitory income (i.e., measured income less permanent income), r is the rate of interest, t is time, and $t - 1$ and $t - \frac{1}{2}$ represent variables lagged by one and by one-half periods, respectively.[35] The half-period lag in the

---

[33] Courchene and Shapiro, "A Note from the Time Series," *op. cit.*, note 15.

[34] Laidler, *op. cit.*, p. 59.

[35] In continuous forms involving the stock variables rather than the flows (i.e., first differences in discrete series), Laidler denotes the functions involving the respective regression forms as follows:

flow variables Y_p and Y_T is simply to center the flows in the period in which they occur. The name for the first hypothesis is derived from the role of the flow variables as proxies for permanent and transitory components of nonhuman wealth. The name for the second comes from the role of permanent income. The name for the third comes from the inclusion of the first differences of variables implicit in liquidity-preference analysis (Sec. 3.3).

As the names of the preceding equations and hypotheses suggest, Laidler is interested in analyzing first differences. In the first equation, flow variables are included for permanent income and transitory income, but these are simply first differences when one is considering the stock quantities they imply. Laidler is in effect using permanent income and permanent transitory income as substitute variables for increments in nonhuman wealth. He notes that the use of first differences avoids some problems in the summing of these flow variables as a means of converting them to stock variables. "In particular," he says, "the permanent income series is a statistical artifact . . . a proxy for the 'true' variable." Further, "Any errors in this variable are also of necessity present in the transitory income data." Thus, he says, "To sum either would involve the cumulation of errors." This problem, among others, influences Laidler's choice of a regression equation without the use of logarithms. Also, as the names for the hypotheses imply,

$$M_d = F\left[\int_{-\infty}^{t}(1-k)\,Y_p,\quad \int_{-\infty}^{t}(Y_T-C_T),r\right]$$
$$M_d = g(Y_p,r)$$
$$M_d = G(Y,r)$$

where, in addition to the variables defined for the discrete equations, M_d is the stock of money demanded, k is constant consumption as a proportion of income, $1-k$ is proportion of permanent income going to saving, and C_T is transitory consumption.

In the first of these functions, the first integral represents nonhuman wealth as accumulated savings out of permanent income. It is in effect a summation of flows from an early time to the current time. The second integral is in effect a summation of the difference between transitory income and transitory consumption. Laidler recognizes the second of these functions as that employed by Friedman, only with an interest rate variable added. The third function simply suggests the liquidity-preference analysis (Sec. 3.3).

the rate of interest in Laidler's analyses takes a subordinate role. As he notes, "to include the rate of interest in a linear relationship suggests that its effect is merely additional to that of other variables, and that its importance as a determinant of the demand for money declines as the money stock increases." Continuing, he says, "the only defense of the procedure is that it has been used by others with reasonable success and that the role of the rate of interest is not the primary matter under investigation in the present tests."

In examining regression results concerning the preceding equation forms, Laidler concludes that the inclusion of time deposits in the definition of money improves the "explanatory" power of the various sets of independent variables in question. He is concerned as well with the stability of regression coefficients, particularly those involving the broader definition of money. He says, with reference to Meltzer's results (Sec. 6.3), "Past results have tended to show that the addition of time deposits made no significant contribution to the explanatory power of any hypotheses." Laidler's conclusion, then, is directly in contrast to Meltzer's. He says, however, "There is no statistical contradiction here, for earlier tests were performed on the levels of the data, and one might expect first differences to be a more sensitive tool in discovering such discrepancies."

By the regression criteria employed, the nonhuman wealth hypothesis performs best for time deposits alone. The permanent income and orthodox hypotheses do a bit better in other respects. Laidler then recognizes the ambiguous nature of time deposits. We quote him, as follows:

That they [time deposits] are a less liquid asset than currency and demand deposits is beyond question, and the outcome of the regressions for time deposits alone suggests that a different theory from that which explains the demand for money does better in explaining the demand for such assets [i.e., time deposits]. The only interpretation for this apparent contradiction of the other evidence is that time deposits fulfil more than one role.[36]

---

[36] Laidler, *op. cit.*, p. 66.

Continuing, Laidler recognizes an element of arbitrariness in the statistical definition of money. He would, however, choose the definition of money excluding time deposits because time deposits fulfill a role of assets other than money.

Regression results of the type Laidler presents as a result of the analysis of annual data[37] are shown in Tables 6–1, 6–2, and 6–3.[38] As the results in the tables reveal, "the non-human wealth hypothe-

---

[37] "The permanent income series used is Friedman's per capita expected real income, while measured income is represented by Kuznet's per capita net national product, variant III. This latter series was selected because it forms the basis of the permanent income estimates. Transitory income is merely the difference between these two series. The variables chosen to represent the rate of interest is the rate on 4–6 months commercial paper." (See Laidler, op. cit., p. 57) As Laidler also notes, the latter choice is perhaps a bit unusual. He says it "was prompted by the fact that a short rate seemed a more appropriate proxy for the opportunity cost of holding money than a long rate, and partly because the variable performed slightly better than the yield to maturity on 20-year bonds in a series of preliminary tests."

Laidler's regression for the respective hypotheses involved the same sources and methods of data handling. "The various income variables employed," he says, "all result from the manipulation of the same basic series." In this respect, he says, "One of the major problems associated with the comparative testing of economic theories is avoided. There is no question here of a theory winning a competition with rivals because there happens to be more accurate data available to measure the particular variables that it employs."

[38] Laidler's results involve some special methods. He describes these as follows:

The theories in question all imply that regressions should have zero intercepts, and all the functions reported here were constrained to this form. A further justification for this is that first-differenced data include a great deal of error. Since zero-intercept regessions coefficients are computed from the moments of the variables about zero, rather than about their means, the effect of error is diminished by using this procedure. Many tests were performed on all the theories using intercepts, and the result was usually a significantly positive intercept and implausibly low regression coefficients. Since most of the regression coefficients obtained with zero intercepts were a priori reasonable, and since there is little doubt that the data contain a great deal of error, it was concluded that the regressions reported here gave the more accurate reflection of the economic relationships involved.

(See Laidler, op. cit., note 10, p. 59.)

sis performs best for time deposits alone." In Table 6-1 the coefficients of determination are higher for the regressions involving time deposits alone. In the case of money excluding time deposits in that

Table 6-1. The Nonhuman Wealth Hypothesis[*]

Time Period	$b_1 Y_{pt-1/2}$	$b_2 Y_{Tt-1/2}$	$b_3(r_t-r_{t-1})$	R^2
	Money Defined to Include Time Deposits			
1920–60	0.010 (0.005)	0.348 (0.080)	−10.347 (3.694)	0.401
1920–40	0.021 (0.006)	0.287 (0.086)	− 6.765 (4.200)	0.388
1947–60	0.004 (0.008)	0.387 (0.178)	−10.014 (7.315)	0.336
	Money Defined to Exclude Time Deposits			
1920–60	0.002 (0.004)	0.198 (0.071)	− 6.892 (3.240)	0.255
1920–40	0.013 (0.005)	0.117 (0.075)	− 4.084 (3.658)	0.131
1947–60	−0.001 (0.006)	0.316 (0.129)	− 3.543 (5.328)	0.352
	Time Deposits			
1920–60	0.007 (0.002)	0.150 (0.033)	− 3.455 (1.521)	0.403
1920–40	0.007 (0.003)	0.170 (0.040)	− 2.681 (1.947)	0.506
1947–60	0.006 (0.003)	0.070 (0.067)	− 6.471 (2.739)	0.359

[*] R^2 here and in Tables 6-2 and 6-3 is defined as 1 minus the ratio of the summed squared residuals to the summed squared deviations of the dependent variable about its mean. Since the mean of the residuals of a zero-intercept regression is not equal to zero, this statistic may take negative values. Rather than the absolute explanatory power of the regression equation, it measures its explanatory power relative to that of the hypothesis that the dependent variable is equal to its own mean. The statistic is adequate for the purpose to which it is put here, of ordering the explanatory power of competing hypotheses.

Source: David Laidler, "Some Evidence on the Demand for Money," *Journal of Political Economy*, February 1966, p. 61.

table, a significant negative coefficient for permanent income even appears for the period 1947–60. In Tables 6–2 and 6–3, the permanent income and orthodox hypotheses are shown to yield regression coefficients with a consistency in the expected signs. The coefficients of determination, however, are a bit higher for the results concerning the permanent income hypothesis, except for the empirical definition of money excluding time deposits for the postwar, 1947–60 period. The regression coefficients for the first differences in the income variables in Table 6–2 and 6–3 are reasonably stable from period to period, although the coefficients of determination for the various regressions behave somewhat erratically, especially for the postwar, 1947–60 period. The re-

Table 6–2.   The Permanent Income Hypothesis

Time Period	$b_1(Y_{pt}-Y_{pt-1})$	$b_2(r_t-r_{t-1})$	R^2
	Money Defined to Include Time Deposits		
1892–1960	0.622	− 7.197	0.420
	(0.097)	(1.946)	
1892–1916	0.606	− 3.690	0.457
	(0.097)	(1.134)	
1920–60	0.657	−11.256	0.452
	(0.133)	(3.513)	
1920–40	0.660	− 9.220	0.454
	(0.134)	(3.671)	
1947–60	0.662	−16.842	0.116
	(0.352)	(8.210)	
	Money Defined to Exclude Time Deposits		
1920–60	0.394	− 7.573	0.283
	(0.120)	(3.161)	
1920–40	0.373	− 6.581	0.194
	(0.119)	(3.260)	
1947–60	0.482	−10.639	−0.402
	(0.327)	(7.625)	
	Time Deposits		
1920–60	0.263	− 3.683	0.333
	(0.061)	(1.599)	
1920–40	0.286	− 2.639	0.417
	(0.071)	(1.958)	
1947–60	0.180	− 6.203	0.261
	(0.122)	(2.861)	

Source: David Laidler, "Some Evidence on the Demand for Money," *Journal of Political Economy,* February 1966, p. 62.

Table 6–3. The Orthodox Hypothesis

Time Period	$b_1(Y_t - Y_{t-1})$	$b_2(r_t - r_{t-1})$	R^2
	Money Defined to Include Time Deposits		
1892–1960	0.212	− 5.648	0.255
	(0.048)	(2.165)	
1892–1916	0.187	− 2.672	0.223
	(0.041)	(1.329)	
1920–60	0.232	− 9.077	0.281
	(0.071)	(3.947)	
1920–40	0.260	− 6.837	0.220
	(0.078)	(4.293)	
1947–60	0.177	−14.641	−0.037
	(0.158)	(8.853)	
	Money Defined to Exclude Time Deposits		
1920–60	0.180	− 6.761	0.274
	(0.056)	(3.121)	
1920–40	0.194	− 5.654	0.258
	(0.055)	(3.059)	
1947–60	0.151	− 9.486	−0.512
	(0.140)	(7.884)	
	Time Deposits		
1920–60	0.052	− 2.316	0.024
	(0.034)	(1.899)	
1920–40	0.066	− 1.182	0.037
	(0.044)	(2.460)	
1947–60	0.027	− 5.156	0.144
	(0.055)	(3.064)	

Source: David Laidler, "Some Evidence on the Demand for Money," *Journal of Political Economy*, February 1966, p. 62.

gression coefficients for the first differences in the money stock, including time deposits, with respect to the first differences in permanent income are surprisingly stable for the periods shown in Table 6–2—that is, the partial regression coefficients 0.622, 0.606, 0.657, 0.660, and 0.662 are surprisingly stable. The standard error of the regression coefficient increases considerably, however, for the 1947–60 period and the permanent income hypothesis yields relatively more stable regression coefficients than the orthodox hypothesis.

6.5 CHOW ON THE LONG- AND SHORT-RUN DEMAND

Chow advances the notion that "one of the major weaknesses in the available theoretical formulations of demand functions for money seems to be the failure to distinguish between long-run equilibrium demand by introducing a mechanism for the adjustment of the actual stock of money to its equilibrium level." Thus Chow introduces a mechanism for making the distinction, but his mechanism depends on his assumption of the equilibrium demand function, namely[39]

(1) $$M_t^* = b_0 + b_1 A_t + b_2 r_t$$

where M^* is the estimated equilibrium money stock, A is the relevant income or wealth variable, r is the rate of interest, and the subscript t denotes the current time. Chow is particularly con-concerned with the Friedman and Meltzer functions as formulated above (Secs. 6.1, 6.2, and 6.3).[40]

Chow's mechanism for dealing with the adjustment process and his results are of interest. The regression results, however, may be viewed independently of the particular mechanism that leads him to formulate a so-called short-run demand function. Chow's adjustment mechanism depends on the assumption of a time lag in the adjustment of demand to "equilibrium" or an imbalance between the desired stock of money (M^*) and the actual stock held in the previous period (i.e., M_{t-1}), when the desired stock is the stock estimated by his equilibrium demand function set forth above. Indeed, his mechanism consisting of a "long-run" or so-called equilibrium component and a "short-run" component in the right-hand member is

(2) $$M_t - M_{t-1} = \underset{\substack{\text{long-run} \\ \text{component}}}{c(M_t^* - M_{t-1})} + \underset{\substack{\text{short-run} \\ \text{component}}}{d(A_t - A_{t-1})}$$

where $M_t - M_{t-1}$ is a change in the money stock, $c(M_t^* - M_{t-1})$

---

is a fraction of the difference between the so-called equilibrium stock and the stock of the previous period, and $d(A_t - A_{t-1})$ is a fraction of change in total assets $(A_t - A_{t-1} = \Delta$ total assets or savings). Upon substituting the right-hand member of Eq. (1) for M_t^* in Eq. (2), and upon rearranging terms, we get

(3)
$$M_t = cb_0 + cb_1 A_t + cb_2 n_t + (1 - c)M_{t-1} + d(A_t - A_{t-1})$$

Now, Eq. (3) becomes the equation for which regressions are run for studying the short-run demand, even though Chow proceeds to study short-run demand by dropping the terms $d(A_t - A_{t-1})$.

Using annual data and substituting different variables for A_t in Eq. (3), after dropping the term $d(A_t - A_{t-1})$, Chow reports such results as the following:

$$\ln M_t = 0.3180 + 0.4987 \ln Y_p - 0.4644 \ln r + 0.5056 \ln M_{t-1},$$
$$(0.0758) \qquad (0.0512) \qquad (0.0697)$$
$$R^2 = 0.9985$$

$$\ln M_t = 0.4893 + 0.4328 \ln W_n - 0.4111 \ln r + 0.5580 \ln M_{t-1},$$
$$(0.0771) \qquad (0.0508) \qquad (0.0723)$$
$$R^2 = 0.9983$$

where, in addition to the Chow variables defined earlier (Sec. 6.2), W_n is total nonhuman wealth in current dollars. Here in comparing the results for the two equations, Chow notes that permanent income turns out to yield a slightly higher regression coefficient than the nonhuman wealth measure. Also, this difference in the performance of the two variables is reflected in the following additional equation,

$$\ln M_t = 0.07363 + 0.1715 \ln W_n + 0.02281 \ln Y - 0.3704 \ln r$$
$$+ 0.5222 M_{t-1}, \qquad R^2 = 0.9989$$

where, as Chow notes, the current income variable yields a higher coefficient than the nonhuman wealth variable, and the value of the t-ratio (i.e. slope parameter/standard error of the regression coefficient) of 2.157 for the wealth variable is less than that of 4.140 for the current-income variable. Next,

$$\ln M_t = 0.3067 + 0.06158 \ln Y_p + 0.3274 \ln Y - 0.3325 \ln r$$
$$(0.14284) \qquad (0.0940) \qquad (0.0597)$$
$$+ 0.5878 \ln M_{t-1}, \qquad R^2 = 0.9988$$
$$(0.0669)$$

With respect to this equation, Chow notes that the coefficient of the permanent income variable is smaller than the standard error, while the coefficient for current income is positive and significant This result he cites as supporting the view that "permanent income explains the total stock of money better than current income when short-run adjustments are not allowed for." Chow concludes, "Permanent income is more important in equilibrium demand, and current income is more important in short-run *changes* in demand." Chow's special measurement procedure is involved, but his conclusion still supports the contention that Friedman's measurement procedure obscures some of the short-run changes in the demand for money.[41]

6.6   SUMMARY

In summary, the conclusions reached from the analytical and statistical results reviewed in this chapter are these:

(1) Population is a poor predictor of the demand for money.

---

[41] Commenting on one aspect of Chow's measurement procedure—that of introducing a lagged variable in an equation of the form of Eq. (3)—Hamburger makes the following point: namely, the introduction of the lagged variable accomplishes a purpose similar to that accomplished by the introduction of Friedman's measure of permanent income. Hamburger says that "Friedman's measurement of permanent income is generally introduced into a regression equation for the express purpose of allowing for a lag in the adjustment of the dependent variable to changes in income." (See Michael J. Hamburger, "The Demand for Money by Households, Money Substitutes and Monetary Policy," *Journal of Political Economy,* December 1966, note 6.) Thus, it would seem that Chow compounds the allowance for lagged adjustment in the amount of money demanded by introducing permanent income as a variable in an equation with a lagged variable. The introduction of the permanent income variable itself, however, should not alter the Chow conclusions that rely on a comparison of coefficients in the context of his particular analysis.

(2) The wealth hypothesis fails to predict the direction of the post-World War II trend in the velocity of money.

(3) Friedman's empirical support for the "luxury" goods hypothesis is a result of his use of a money stock that includes time deposits.

(4) The demand for money is homogeneous of degree one in prices and assets, as the broad underlying foundations of monetary analysis lead us to expect.

(5) Regression results due to Meltzer and to Courchene and Shapiro and involving the addition of time deposits to the stock of money reflect a decline in the size of the interest-rate coefficient and an increase in the wealth coefficient.

(6) The demand function for the stock of money balances narrowly defined is at least as stable as the demand function for the stock of balances broadly defined to include time deposits when variables for income and interest rates are used in regression analyses, following logarithmic transformations of the data.

(7) The inclusion of time deposits in the empirical definition of money yields stable coefficients for a number of periods for permanent income in linear regression analyses of first differences. The particular analyses in question, however, indicate the presence of a role for time deposits as a nonmonetary asset, and they indicate, as well, an element of arbitrariness in the statistical definition of money.

(8) Estimates of slope parameters concerning demand functions of the type dealt with by Friedman and Meltzer display greater instability over shorter periods.

(9) Formulating the demand function in terms of wealth rather than income increases the stability of the function somewhat, according to Meltzer. This is consistent with monetary analysis. However, Courchene and Shapiro do not find the choice clear-cut as a result of statistical results.

(10) The introduction of the Chow mechanism for distinguishing between the long- and short-run demand for money

indicates interesting results from analyses of annual data: namely, permanent income is more important than current income in the long-run framework, and current income is more important in the short-run framework.

(11) The rate of interest and real nonhuman wealth in one instance, and the rate of interest and real income, in another, are somewhat correlated over time.

(12) The latter results, other results, and analysis suggest that changes in the rate of interest do not "explain" changes in the velocity of money over time in the operational as distinct from the computational sense.

Again and again results from analyses concerning money-demand functions with interest rate and income variables indicate that much of the variation in the demand for money can be "explained," at least in the computational sense. Such results are consistent with the broad outlines of monetary analysis. It would appear from this conclusion and the others that the soundness of the broad analytical foundations of monetary economics is affirmed. In the context of that framework, changing the scale of operation calls for equal proportional changes in the stock of money, total assets (or wealth), and the flow of income. Such changes and the unit elasticities they imply are reflected in the various analyses of data over long periods of time. The rate of interest does not change in response to the scale changes, but, a change in the rate of return on additions to real capital in response to various factors will apparently give rise to changes in income and assets such that the velocity of money and interest rates increase when the stock of money increases less than in proportion to income. In the latter instance, percentage changes in velocity are apparently paralleled by equal percentage changes in the rate of interest. These changes, too, appear to be supported by a range of empirical results.

Appendix to Chapter 6

THE VELOCITY OF MONEY,
SOME MEASUREMENT PROCEDURES,
AND SELECTED ASPECTS OF
MONETARY THEORY

In the first section of this appendix (6A.1), we review Milton Friedman's measures for observed and computed velocity, a resulting residual element in the cyclical behavior of velocity, and a hypothesis attributed to Friedman by Ronald Teigen in an evaluation of the portion of Friedman's work in question. This review permits us to do several things: to introduce a portion of Friedman's work upon which Allan Meltzer draws in setting forth some monetary theory; to present some further conclusions concerning velocity; and to reintroduce a tentative conclusion concerning the rate of interest as a determinant of the demand for money.

In the second section of this appendix (6A.2), we review Allan Meltzer's statement of the implicit theory of price and income determination that emerges from the monumental monetary history by Milton Friedman and Anna Jacobson Schwartz, and from related papers.[1] As Meltzer notes, his interpretation of their work may not result in a completely correct statement of the authors'

---

[1] See, in particular, Milton Friedman and Anna Jacobson Schwartz, *A Monetary History of the United States, 1867–1960* (Princeton, New Jersey: Princeton University Press, 1963); Milton Friedman, "The Demand for Money: Some Theoretical and Empirical Results," *Journal of Political Economy*, August 1959, pp. 327–351; and Milton Friedman and Anna Jacobson Schwartz, "Money and Business Cycles," *Review of Economics and Statistics*, Supplement, February 1963. The article in which Meltzer's statement of the monetary theory implicit in the latter works appears is "Monetary Theory and Monetary History," *Schweizerische Zeitschrift für Volkswirtschaft und Statistik*, December 1965, pp. 404–422.

theory, but the authors do not present their theory, and their discussions suggest that they use one. Meltzer's statement of their theory does two things: suggests the source of some of the conclusions in the Friedman-Schwartz history—"particularly the denigration of the influence of interest-rate movements and the denial of an important role to interest rates in the demand function for money"; and "leads to an understanding of the central role that the stock of money plays in the author's analysis of income and employment. . . ."[2]

Like a number of economists, Meltzer is quite lavish in his praise of the Friedman-Schwartz history and the Friedman contributions to monetary economics. In most respects the insights and work of Friedman have been the basis or point of departure for major portions of work on the demand for money since Keynes, including especially the work on empirical demand functions for money. Our evaluations of work due to Friedman may not always reflect the importance of his role, however, perhaps in part because he excels in provoking controversy and in stimulating others to do further work on the various points of controversy.

The review of aspects of Friedman's work in the first section of this appendix and the related review of Meltzer's statement of the monetary theory implicit in the Friedman-Schwartz history and related papers should help in two respects: first, to set empirical results concerning the demand for money in better perspective; and, second, to isolate more explicitly the short-run or cyclical type of phenomena concealed in the emphasis on secular-demand relationships.

The major conclusions that Meltzer arrives at in attempting to present an explicit statement of the theory implicit in Friedman and Schwartz's discussions are:

(1) In using a broad definition of the money stock that includes time deposits, they conceal some of the effects of interest-rate changes on the supply of money and the velocity of money.

(2) Friedman and Schwartz fail to treat systematically factors invoked to explain some special historical episodes.

---

[2] Meltzer, *op. cit.*, pp. 404–405.

(3) In the light of their treatment of the demand for money as a function of real per capita income, and in view of the hypothesis whereby the demand for money increases at a faster rate than real per capita income, it is difficult to accept the Friedman-Schwartz emphasis on greater certainty about the future as an explanation of the post-World War II rise in velocity.

(4) The long-run theory attributed to Friedman and Schwartz is primarily a theory of the price level rather than a theory of fluctuation in output—i.e., the theory is basically classical.

(5) Some so-called "transitory" changes in income are excluded from analysis by the Friedman-Schwartz approach. These changes, Meltzer says, are another name for the business cycle. The explanation for cyclical changes is not carefully integrated with the long-run theory.

(6) The core of the Friedman-Schwartz explanation of depression or inflation is that "major changes in the growth rate of the money supply produce large short-run changes in the growth rate of real income or prices."

(7) In the Friedman-Schwartz explanations of deep depressions, interest rates acquire a prominent role, although they are excluded from the long-run theory. Large increases in the rates or the rate structure reduce the money supply through their influence on the desired reserve and currency ratios.

Among the relationships between selected topics in the respective sections of this appendix are:

(1) That between the possibility of obscuring cyclical changes in the velocity of money through Friedman's measurement procedures (Sec. 6A.1), and the Meltzer criticism of the concealment of cyclical changes in the Friedman-Schwartz treatment of "transitory" income (Sec. 6A.2).

(2) That between the failure of Friedman and Schwartz to deal with the rate of return on physical goods as a part of their long-run theory (Sec. 6A.2), and the practices of relating the rate of change in prices to the return on physical goods (Sec. 6A.1) and of dealing with the rate of change in

prices only in connection with inflationary episodes (Sec. 6A.2).

(3) That between Friedman's rejecting a Keynesian (interest-responsive) demand for money function, as described by Teigen (Sec. 6A.1), and the prospect that both interest-rate changes and velocity changes are responding to some other set of changes, such as the rate of return on real capital and the factors affecting that rate.

With respect to the first relationship between topics, it is apparent that some cyclical changes are obscured in both instances and that both concern velocity. With respect to the second, the rate of return on physical capital as a determinant of the demand for money apparently gets submerged in the role of the rate of change in prices as a determinant of the demand for money and the latter factor is invoked mainly to deal with inflationary episodes. Finally, with respect to the third relationship, Friedman is possibly correct in neglecting the rate of interest as an explanatory variable, in view of the prospect that both velocity and bond yields are responsive to changes in the rate of return on real capital (Sec. 5.2).

6A.1   FRIEDMAN'S OBSERVED AND MEASURED VELOCITY

In the text of the chapter (Sec. 6.2), we noted Friedman's equation for the real stock of money per capita, i.e.,

(1) $$\frac{M}{NP_p} = \gamma\left(\frac{Y_p}{NP_p}\right)^{\delta}$$

and his computed elasticity of the demand for money (i.e., $\delta = 1.8$). From this equation and the definition for velocity, Friedman is also able to write an equation for velocity, namely,[3]

(2) $$V = \frac{Y}{Y_p}\frac{1}{\gamma}\left(\frac{Y_p}{N}\right)^{1-\delta}$$

and insert numerical values for parameters such that

---

[3] See Friedman, "The Demand for Money," *op. cit.*, p. 337.

$$(3) \qquad V^* = \frac{1}{0.00323} \left(\frac{Y_p}{N}\right)^{-1.810} \frac{Y}{Y_p}$$

where V^* is measured velocity, and values for V^* computed from Eq. (3) are computed measured velocities. When values for computed measured velocity are plotted as a time series along with a time series for observed measured velocity, a result is Figure 6A–1.

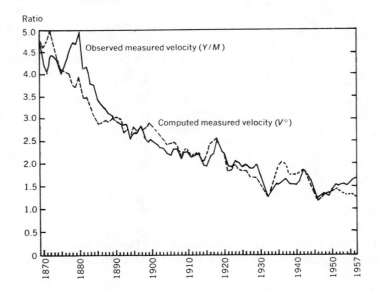

Figure 6A–1. Observed and Computed Measured Velocity, Annually, 1869–1957.

Friedman calls the differences between the two series, as reflected in the ratio of observed measured velocity to computed measured velocity "the residual element in the cyclical behavior of velocity that requires explanation."

Friedman says the isolation of the residual element is a major significance of the analysis in question. Apparently he says this because it enables us "to eliminate the largely spurious movements of velocity that have hitherto masked the economically significant movements."[4] We would likely view this residual element, however, as a part of cyclical changes in the velocity of money that have been obscured by Friedman's method of estimating the parameters in Eq. (3) from average values over whole reference cycles. Average values over cycles, of course, would be more stable than the values being averaged.

With respect to the discrepancies between the cyclical behavior of measured and permanent income, we quote Friedman as follows:

> For the cyclical analysis, permanent income need not itself be stable over a cycle. It may rise during expansions and fall during contractions. Presumably, however, it will rise less than measured income during expansions and fall less during contractions. Hence, if money holdings were adapted to permanent income, they might rise and fall more than in proportion to permanent income . . . yet less than in proportion to measured income. . . .[5]

This sort of analysis helps Friedman to deal with the discrepancy between his secular results (including the long-run tendency for the demand for money to increase more than in proportion to income in the pre-World War II years) and cyclical tendencies,[6] as revealed by earlier velocity studies, such as rises in income velocity during cyclical expansions as real income rises and declines in income velocity in cyclical contractions as real income falls.

In the further reporting of the results of his work, including portions with Anna Jacobson Schwartz, Friedman recognizes possible determinants of the demand for money other than those introduced in Eq. (1). He says, "One alternative to holding money is to hold securities; another, to hold physical goods." He relates the return on bonds to the first alternative and the rate of change in the average of prices to physical goods, but he de-emphasizes the role of the rate of interest and notes the limitation

---

[4] *Ibid.*, p. 343.
[5] *Ibid.*, pp. 333–334.
[6] *Ibid.*, p. 327.

of selected attempts to isolate the effect of the rate of change in prices. On interest rates, Friedman concludes as follows:

> In our secular analysis, we have found that the yield on corporate bonds is correlated with the real stock of money and velocity in the expected direction: a rise in bond yields tends to reduce the real stock of money demanded for a given real income—that is, to raise velocity—and conversely. Bond yields, however, play nothing like so important and regularly consistent a role in accounting for changes in velocity as does real income.[7]

In dealing with the Friedman analysis of the demand for money, Teigen evaluates a hypothesis and presents some results of his own on the relationship between observed velocity and computed velocity.[8] The hypothesis Teigen attributes to Friedman is this: "First a Keynesian (interest-responsive) demand for money function cannot explain what Friedman considers to be contradictory secular and cyclical behavior of income velocity, and secondly, that even a classical money demand function must be recast into his 'permanent income' approach before it can adequately account for this behavior." Continuing, Teigen says, Friedman attempts to support his hypothesis by demonstrating that computed velocity is a fair approximation to observed velocity. Teigen then demonstrates an alternative approach, "using an interest-responsive demand-for-money function . . . and the usual definition of the money stock." His result is a computed velocity that approximates observed velocity more closely than Friedman's computed velocity, and his data are for quarterly dates over the post-World War II years. Teigen concludes as follows:

> Friedman's hypothesis appears to be inferior in terms of empirical support. We believe we have demonstrated that an interest-responsive demand-for-money function, used within the context of a structural model of the monetary sector, is effective in explaining the movement of velocity through time, contrary to Friedman's assertion.

---

[7] *Ibid.*, p. 345. (See p. 332, also).

[8] See Ronald L. Teigen, "Demand and Supply Functions for Money in the United States: Some Structural Estimates," *Econometrica*, October 1964, pp. 495–498.

From the above review of portions of Friedman's and Teigen's respective works, and from earlier statistical results and analysis concerning the velocity–interest rate association (Secs. 4.2 and 5.2), we may conclude, briefly, as follows:

(1) Friedman's procedures isolate a residual amount of cyclical variation in velocity.

(2) Possibly, in part, because of these procedures Friedman attributes only a small role to the rate of interest as a determinant of the demand for money.

(3) The rate of interest possibly does not account for variations in velocity as Friedman suggests, nor does it "explain" changes in velocity as Teigen concludes, in view of the findings (Secs. 4.2 and 5.2) that the ratio of cash to bonds does not decline as interest rates rise, at least for the corporate manufacturing sector.

6A.2   MONETARY THEORY AND MONETARY HISTORY

Meltzer's review of the Friedman-Schwartz work(s) is in several parts—the money supply; velocity and the demand for money; the long-run relation of money to prices and income; and the analysis of economic instability. In review, Meltzer attempts to make explicit the theory implicit in the author's explanations of monetary phenomena as revealed by statistical data for the money stock, income velocity, and a host of other measures. He achieves, in fact, a systematic statement of the long-run relation of money and prices implicit in the Friedman-Schwartz work(s), but he is critical of some of the same procedures and the frequent need to introduce special factors of an exogenous or *ad hoc* character to explain cyclical developments and special historical episodes. Lurking in the background of many of the criticisms is a rather idealistic (or hopeful) view of the prospect of a systematic framework involving a consistent explanation of the demand for money and changes in velocity.

THE MONEY SUPPLY

The money-supply equation around which Friedman and Schwartz center their arithmetic accounting of the money supply and around which Meltzer centers his review of the Friedman-Schwartz analysis of money-supply changes is[9]

$$M = \frac{1 + k}{r + k} B$$

where

M is the money supply (currency plus demand deposits plus time deposits),

k is the ratio of currency held to other forms of money,

r is the weighted average reserve ratio, and

B is bank reserves and the monetary base.

In discussing this equation, Meltzer points out that it plays two quite different roles in the Friedman-Schwartz history. He notes that it leads to two concepts of the money supply: (1) an "expected" supply and (2) an actual supply. In the first instance, B, r and k are "proximate determinants" and Friedman and Schwartz are said to indicate the principal factors on which they are assumed to depend. This procedure, Meltzer says, "makes r and k desired ratios and converts the money-supply equation into a statement about the quantity of money that is expected to result from the behavior of banks, the public and the policymakers." In the second instance, the equation is used as an "arithmetical" relation, "a framework for dividing changes in the money supply into changes produced by variations in B, r and k." The "actual" and "expected" long-run money supply, of course, would become approximately equal, "if B, r, and k always adjusted rapidly to changes in the variables on which they depend."

Meltzer points out, however, that "many of the interesting episodes in U. S. monetary history are those in which the expected and actual money supply are not equal." There have, Meltzer

---

[9] The supply equation is derived from a system of four additional equations and presented in Appendix B of the Friedman-Schwartz history. (See Meltzer, *op. cit.*, 405–406.) For a similar and more complete supply equation and its derivation, see William J. Frazer, Jr., and William P. Yohe, *Introduction to the Analytics and Institutions of Money and Banking* (Princeton, New Jersey: D. Van Nostrand and Company, 1966), pp. 24–48.

notes, "been periods of bank 'runs' and bank failures as well as periods in which banks accumulated a relatively large volume of reserves." Meltzer then does several things: he notes that the introduction of r and k as desired ratios affects the propriety of regarding them as relatively exogenous variables; he notes that the expected money supply is dependent on interest rates and/or other variables, if the latter variables affect the desired reserve and currency ratios; and he then notes that real income and prices depend on interest rates, since they depend at least partially on the money supply. Thus, Meltzer concludes, "The procedure used by Friedman and Schwartz permits them to ignore the systematic effect of interest rates (and other variables) on the money supply and hence on the equilibrium levels of real income and prices."

Three examples of the Friedman-Schwartz treatment of interest rates on the supply side are cited by Meltzer. For one, the Friedman-Schwartz use of the definition of money to include time deposits at commercial banks obscures the possibility of switching between demand and time deposits in response to interest-rate changes. For another, the neglect of the distinction between borrowed and unborrowed reserves, which, according to Meltzer, avoids the influence of interest rates on borrowed reserves. For still another, the ratios r and k are made dependent on a number of other variables described as endogenous, but the influence of these is given no long-run or persistent role in monetary history.

The main criticisms of the Friedman-Schwartz treatment of the money supply that emerge from Meltzer's review are, in brief, their neglect of the possible effect of the interest rate on switching between demand and time deposits, and the absence of a systematic inclusion of the special factors that are invoked to deal with special episodes. The link between the money supply and the interest rate is velocity, and the Friedman-Schwartz treatment of the money supply is presumed to conceal some of the relationship between velocity and the rate of interest. This charge of a possible concealment of a particular influence of the rate of interest on velocity is in part supported by some of Meltzer's results presented in Chapter 6 (Sec. 6.2) and by some of the earlier results due to Christ (Sec. 5.1). The criticism that Friedman and Schwartz fail to introduce systematically some of the factors invoked on an *ad hoc* basis to explain some developments appears to follow from a rather idealistic (or hopeful) view of what may be accomplished by monetary economists in the way of an equation for a completely endogenously determined money supply.

VELOCITY AND THE DEMAND FOR MONEY

The principal sources for the Friedman-Schwartz analysis of velocity or the demand for money are the 1959 Friedman article cited earlier (Sec. 6A.1) and Chapter 12 of the Friedman-Schwartz history. The latter draws from and expands upon the 1959 article in which Friedman distinguished between measured and permanent velocity, and in which Friedman advanced "per capita permanent real income" as the principal determinant of permanent velocity. In the 1959 article, permanent velocity (V_p) is defined as the ratio of permanent income to the stock of money (Y_p/M), or as the ratio of permanent aggregate income in real terms to the permanent aggregate stock of money in real terms (y_p/m_p), where

$$\frac{y_p}{m_p} = \frac{1}{\gamma}\left(\frac{y_p}{N}\right)^{1-\delta}.$$

Also, by the definition of velocity

(4) $$V = \frac{Y}{M}$$

and

$$\frac{Y}{M} = \frac{Y}{Y_p}\frac{Y_p}{M} = \frac{Y}{Y_p}V_p$$

so that

(4.1) $$V = \frac{Y}{Y_p}\frac{1}{\gamma}\left(\frac{y_p}{N}\right)^{1-\delta}$$

as in Eq. (2).

Measured velocity is the product of the ratio of income to permanent income (Y/Y_p) and permanent velocity (V_p), and the differences in observed measured velocity and computed measured velocity, as in Eq. (4) and (4.1) and as in Figure 6A–1, concern the measurement procedure in Eq. (4.1). Over long periods, the two concepts of velocity are closely related, but they diverge in the short run and during the post-World War II period of rising velocity.

In the Friedman-Schwartz history a variable is added to permanent per capita real income to help explain the postwar rise in velocity, since rising per capita real income (or the wealth hypothesis) fails to predict it, as noted on other occasions (Sec. 6.3). The variable added is changing expectations or greater certainty about the future. The resulting velocity relationship provided by Meltzer is

$$V_p = a\left(\frac{y_p}{N}\right)^b S, \qquad 0 > b > -1$$

where

V_p is permanent velocity,

y_p is real permanent income,

S is a measure of expectations about economic stability, and

N is population.

Meltzer then notes that the emphasis on S is difficult to accept in the context of the Friedman-Schwartz theory. In Meltzer's analysis, Y and Y_p converge and the ratio Y/Y_p approaches unity, and the difference between V and V_p, as in Eq. (4), should have been smaller during the postwar period rather than larger, since the public expects and experiences smaller fluctuations in income.

THE LONG-RUN RELATION OF MONEY TO PRICES AND INCOME

According to Meltzer, "the money supply and demand equations above are a part of a macro-economic theory that underlies the authors' [Friedman and Schwartz] analysis of prices and income changes in the U.S." Restating the supply and demand equations and adding some additional equations, Meltzer's system of equations for the Friedman-Schwartz theory would appear as follows:

(5) $$M = \left(\frac{1 + k}{r + k}\right)B$$

(6) $$V_p = a\left(\frac{y_p}{N}\right)^b S, \qquad 0 > b > -1$$

(7) $$Y_p = MV_p$$

$$(8) \qquad y_p(T) = \beta \int_{-\infty}^{T} e^{\beta(t-T)} \, y_t \, dt$$

$$(9) \qquad P = \frac{Y_p}{y_p}$$

where, given the variables already defined in this section, only Eqs. (8) and (9) need further elaboration. Equation (8) says that an estimate of expected income at time T is given by a weighted average of past incomes, the weights declining exponentially and being equal to $e^{\beta(t-T)}$. There t is the time of the observation being weighted, e is the base of the natural system of logarithms (i.e., $e \approx 2.7$), and the numerical value of β was estimated to be 0.4 in Friedman's work on the consumption function.[10] In Eq. (9), the price level (P) is obtained from nominal permanent income (Y_p) in Eq. (7) and the real permanent income measure (y_p) in Eq. (6). The system of Eqs. (5) through (9) determines M, V_p, Y_p, y_p, and P to a first approximation, given B, r, k, N, and lagged real income (y).

Observing the Friedman-Schwartz long-run model as he has presented it, Meltzer notes the absence of "interest rates, the yield on real capital and similar variables representing the operation of relative prices on portfolio allocations. . . . If they were included," he continues, "some additional equations would have to be introduced, and Friedman and Schwartz would be forced to develop their analysis of the real sector of the economy and of the determinants of real income in greater detail." Thus, Meltzer concludes, "The long-run theory is primarily a theory of the price level and not a theory of the real sector."

Having set forth the long-run theory, Meltzer notes its relevance to short-run fluctuations in income and to the possible conduct of monetary policy. The application of the model to the short run is complicated, in part by the fact that Friedman and Schwartz do not deny the importance of changes in interest rates and relative

---

[10] See Milton Friedman, *A Theory of the Consumption Function* (Princeton, New Jersey: Princeton University Press, for the National Bureau of Economic Research, 1957), pp. 146–147. See also Meltzer, *op. cit.*, p. 415, and Friedman, "The Demand for Money," *op. cit.*, pp. 337–338.

prices in the short run. Thus, Meltzer says "If I judge correctly, the authors suggest that the long-run model is applicable to periods that are not subject to marked instability in the growth rate of the money supply." He lists the following arguments to support their position:[11]

(1) The empirical equations hold subject to error. The omitted variables will influence the size of the errors if the model is used in any particular year.

(2) Changes in expectations may modify the value of β to be used in the estimate of permanent income applicable to a particular year. Transitory and permanent income are approximations; the value of $\beta = 0.4$ is not presented as a constant imposed on the economic system. It is obtained by numerical methods and may change slightly from year to year if there are minor changes in expectations..

(3) The value of transitory income in the current year is not known a priori. This introduces an additional source of error into the level of prices, etc., estimated from the model.

"Moreover," Meltzer says, "the five equations go a long way." And, continuing, "besides, the consumption function provides much of the missing information for both short- and long-run analysis." With respect to the five equations, Meltzer says the following:[12]

Lagged real income gives the value of real permanent income, and the money equations determine the price level to a first approximation once permanent real income has been computed. To obtain more, a variety of interest rates, yields, prices, etc., are required. In the judgment of the authors [Friedman and Schwartz] two or three more equations for investment, consumption, and "the" interest rate will not do. They see the real sector as far too complicated to be approximated by such simple hypotheses. For them there is more than one kind of investment, more than one interest rate that has to be determined. Even if all of the relations could be formulated consistently, where would one get the data to estimate the parameters?

Referring to the consumption function (from *A Theory of the*

---

[11] Meltzer, *op. cit.*, p. 416.
[12] *Ibid.*

Consumption Function), Meltzer says that the reference is in effect parenthetical to the Friedman-Schwartz monetary history. He believes, nevertheless, that it is germane to the theory underlying the monetary history, and he may be quoted as follows:[13]

> From permanent income and the consumption function the amount of permanent income not consumed in the current year can be estimated; this is the (approximate) aggregate value of the addition to wealth, the amount saved by the community up to the transitory component. The equality of saving and investment implies that the amount saved is an estimate of the amount invested by business and households up to the transitory component in saving. Again, one equation does a large part of the work of many and, if my interpretation of the authors' position is correct, obviates (for them) the need for additional equations expressing the households' demand for each of a number of durable goods, business' demand for plant and equipment, etc. If we are willing to ignore "transitory" changes, there is little more that we need to know for the prediction of aggregate real income and the price level in most years.

In view of the role of "transitory" changes, however, Meltzer is unwilling to ignore them. He says several things about these changes: that they are another name for the business cycle; that a part of past "transitory" income is included in current permanent income; and that the difference between real and permanent income has at times been quite large. Errors in the money demand function, he continues, are quite large at times and estimates of these suggest we cannot neglect the transitory component of income in seeking to understand the cyclical behavior of income and prices.

Looking at the model consisting of Eqs. (5) through (9) as a guide to policy, Meltzer suggests, we need not look very far. We quote him as follows:[14]

> By operating on the monetary base, we can, given r and k, make the money supply what we want it to be. But despite the "arithmetical" method of determining the money supply by combining

---

13 *Ibid.*, pp. 416–417.
14 *Ibid.*, pp. 417–418.

r, k and B, it is quite clear from the authors' discussion that r and k have lives of their own. Hence neither the reader nor the authors can be certain that by controlling B they will in fact get the money supply in the short-run that will keep income rising and prices stable. Again, the problem is easily resolved. Just look at the money supply. Since lagged income is the principal determinant of permanent income, there is nothing else in equations (5)–(9) that is a better guide to price stability. In fact, there is nothing else for a policy-maker to change.

The policy question left open to us, Meltzer continues, "is whether we set the growth rate of the money stock once and for all time, control it on a daily basis, or choose some intermediate monetary policy." Meltzer further notes the following: that in the view of Friedman and Schwartz we have no better lever for stabilizing income than stabilizing the growth rate of the money stock; that Friedman would not be unhappy if the reader of A Monetary History finds rules superior to the judgment exercised by officials in dealing with crucial episodes in history; and that a central element of crucial importance in A Monetary History is the notion of steady monetary growth as a means of damping fluctuations in transitory income and reducing the need for better information about the real sector.

THE ANALYSIS OF ECONOMIC INSTABILITY

The most illuminating portions of the Friedman-Schwartz analysis of economic instability are those dealing with deep depressions, according to Meltzer's review. The theory in the previous section becomes applicable to inflationary episodes, if a modification is introduced in the form of expectations of price changes as indicated by the rate of change in prices. Even so, the core of the Friedman-Schwartz explanation of depression or inflation consists of "major changes in the growth rate of the money supply" that "produce large short-run changes in the growth rate of real income or prices," and for the most part, the analysis of instability is an analysis of major depressions. The characteristics of the latter analysis as outlined by Meltzer are these:

(1) "A detailed account of the reasons for the decline in the money supply."

(2) "The empirical generalization that large declines in the money supply or its growth rate induce large declines in real income and industrial production. Sudden increases in the rediscount rate in 1920 and in 1931 and the doubling of reserve requirements in 1936–1937 are," according to Meltzer, "examples of policy changes that cause larger contractions in the money supply than could be expected from the long-run relation of the money supply to the monetary base."

(3) In the explanation of deep depressions, variables excluded from the long-run model, such as interest rates, acquire a prominent position. Meltzer cites, as an example, large increases in the discount rates in 1920 and again in 1931 and the description of their effect on market interest rates and banks' desired reserve positions. In these instances, "the short-run response of the money supply to the monetary base is reduced or made negative by the influence on the desired reserve and currency ratios of interest rates, rediscount rates, currency drains, bank failures, etc."

Chapter 7

BUSINESS FIRMS' DEMANDS
FOR MONEY

In two earlier chapters some statistical results concerning business firms' demands for cash were introduced and, indeed, Selden's method for relating sector velocities to aggregate velocity was reviewed along with the possible importance and role of sectoral analyses (Sec. 2.2). We now turn to some analyses of firms' demands for cash and to results from analyses of cross-section and time-series data for the business sector. Two succeeding chapters, too, deal with sectors of the economy—the transactions demand for money balances by business firms and subsequently the consumer sector's demand.

A number of articles and other works have dealt with firms' demands for cash (or cash and liquid securities). A portion of them have been almost entirely empirical,[1] and others have dealt with various aspects of monetary theory—including those involving the motives for holding money balances, the simple quantity theory, and the effects of changes in the rate of interest. Apart from some papers previously introduced (Sec. 4.2) and the closely related papers dealing with the transactions demand for cash in the next

---

[1] See, e.g., Allan W. Heston, "An Empirical Study of Cash, Securities, and Other Current Accounts of Large Corporations," *Yale Economic Essays,* Spring 1962; and Ernest Bloch, "Short Cycles in Corporate Demand for Government Securities and Cash," *American Economic Review,* December 1963.

For another study dealing with the Bloch, Heston, and some related studies, see Michael E. Levy, *Cycles in Government Securities: II. Determinants of Changes in Ownership,* Studies in Business Economics Number Eighty-Eight (New York: National Industrial Conference Board, Inc., 1965), Chapter 4.

186

chapter, these articles and works involving various aspects of theory have been due primarily to Allan Meltzer[2] and the present author.[3] In this chapter, consequently, we first review portions of the works on business firms by the latter authors, and then review empirical results concerning testable hypotheses, notably:

(1) The asset size (or sales) elasticity of the demand for money is approximately unity to a first approximation.

(2) The asset size (or sales) elasticity of the demand for money is significantly less than unity to a first approximation.

(3) A rise in the market rate of interest is related to a rise in velocity and a form of switching from cash into marketable bonds such as government securities.

(4) A rise in the market rate of interest is related to a rise in velocity and a form of switching from both cash and govern-

---

[2] See Allan H. Meltzer, "The Demand for Money: A Cross-Section Study of Business Firms," *Quarterly Journal of Economics,* August 1963; and Allan H. Meltzer, "Reply," *Quarterly Journal of Economics,* February 1965. For an additional study and comment on Meltzer's study see, G. S. Maddala and Robert C. Vogel, " 'The Demand for Money: A Cross-Section Study of Business Firms': Comment," *Quarterly Journal of Economics,* February 1965; and Edward L. Whalen, "Further Comment," *Quarterly Journal of Economics,* February 1965.

[3] See, e.g., William J. Frazer, Jr., "Monetary Analysis and the Postwar Rise in the Velocity of Money in the United States, *Schweizerische Zeitschrift für Volkswirtschaft und Statistik,* December 1964; William J. Frazer, Jr., "The Financial Structure of Manufacturing Corporations and The Demand for Money: Some Empirical Findings," *Journal of Political Economy,* April 1964; William J. Frazer, Jr., "Some Comments on Professor Ritter's Interpretations of Keynes and Changes in Income Velocity, *Schweizerische Zeitschrift für Volkswirtschaft und Statistik,* March 1963; William J. Frazer, Jr., *The Liquidity Structure of Firms and Monetary Economics* (Gainesville, Florida: University of Florida Press, 1965); William J. Frazer, Jr., and William P. Yohe, *Introduction to the Analytics and Institutions of Money and Banking* (Princeton, New Jersey: D. Van Nostrand Company, Inc., 1966), Chapter 17; William J. Frazer, Jr., "Firms' Demands for Money: The Evidence from the Cross-Section Data," *Staff Economic Studies,* No. 25 (Washington, D.C.: Board of Governors of the Federal Reserve System, 1967).

ments into other classes of assets such as plant and equipment.

In effect, the first hypothesis may be tested against the second, since the two call for different asset size (or sales) elasticity measures as a first approximation, and the third hypothesis may be tested against the fourth, since the third calls for a negative relation between the ratio of cash to governments and the rate of interest, and the fourth calls for no such relation. Meltzer and some others analyzing data for firms by industry groups have presented results in support of the first hypothesis, and some results have been shown to support the second hypothesis, but clearly the results cannot support both hypotheses (1) and (2).

We will deal with the problem raised by the prospect of results supporting both hypotheses (1) and (2). With respect to hypotheses (3) and (4), we will review results concerning the variation in velocity and the rate of interest and the association between the rate of interest and the ratio of cash to governments and similar types of securities held by business firms.

7.1 MELTZER'S MODEL, MONETARY ANALYSIS, AND HYPOTHESES

Meltzer's work on business firms' demands for cash[4] centers about a single-equation model. In this section, we review the model. We also review the following: some analysis implied by incidental remarks relating to the model and the model itself; the hypotheses following from Meltzer's model and analysis; and the possible relationship between the motives (Sec. 3.4) for holding money and Meltzer's analysis.

THE SINGLE EQUATION MODEL

The model for the demand for balances by the ith firm in the jth industry is, in its most complete form,

(1)
$$M_{ij} = \frac{kr^\alpha}{(K_{ij}\rho_j)^\beta} S_{ij}^\beta$$

---

[4] See Meltzer, "A Cross-Section Study of Business Firms," *op. cit.*, and Meltzer, "Reply," *op. cit.*

or, taking the logarithm of both sides,

(2) $\ln M_{ij} = \ln k + \alpha \ln r - \beta \ln (K_{ij}\rho_j) + \beta \ln S_{ij}$

where

M_{ij} is the cash balances of a particular firm (i.e., the ith firm in the jth industry),

r is a "market rate of interest,"

S_{ij} is the "sales or gross income of the firm" [and also a substitute variable for nonhuman wealth (W_{ij}), where $S_{ij} = \rho_j W_{ij}$],

K_{ij} "varies over the cycle with changes in demand for the firm's product and changes in the capital-labor ratio,"[5]

ρ_j "is the internal rate of return on assets for an industry or class of firms."[6]

Equations (1) or (2), as Meltzer notes, allow for the possibility of "a decrease in velocity [i.e., the sales to cash ratio] for particular firms despite a rise in the external rate of interest or a slight increase in sales." However, he does not believe such "perverse" movements will dominate sector velocities, and he used the model to predict selected sets of changes in the demand for money by business firms, both at a given time and over time. The major relation that Meltzer deals with on a cross-section basis involves the money stock and sales. Treating all the other variables in Eq. (2) as constant, he writes $M_{ij} = \gamma_{ij} S_{ij}^{\beta}$, or $\ln M_{ij} = \ln \gamma_{ij} + \beta \ln S_{ij}$, and views the sales elasticity of the demand for money as approximately one (i.e., $\beta \approx 1.0$). This is consistent with a view that he defends at a later date,[7] namely, the sales elasticity of the demand

---

[5] Whalen says "K is a compensatory variable which accounts for the business cycle and changes in the capital/labor ratio." See Whalen, *op. cit.*, p. 161.

[6] Meltzer says his ρ "is similar to that used in discussion of the cost of capital by Franco Modigliani and Merton H. Miller." He cites their paper, "The Cost of Capital, Corporation Finance, and the Theory of Investment," *American Economic Review*, June 1958.

[7] See Karl Brunner and Allan H. Meltzer, "Economies of Scale in Cash Balances Reconsidered," *Quarterly Journal of Economics*, forthcoming.

for money by business firms is approximately one and, as evidenced by the results from the cross-section data, the simple quantity theory provides a good first approximation to the relationship between firms' money balances and their sales. In reporting his empirical results from analyses of cross-section data, and in dealing with some alternative hypotheses introduced in the next chapter (Sec. 8.3), Meltzer has in effect concluded as follows: economies (i.e., sales elasticities less than one) "are neither so pervasive nor so large as those we would expect from the Baumol and Tobin models, . . . and there is almost no evidence of diseconomies of scale [i.e., sales or wealth elasticities in excess of one] which approach in magnitude those which Friedman has suggested."[8]

The major relation that Meltzer deals with, in respect to time, involves firms' money stocks and a rise in the "market (or external)" rate of interest (r). Referring to his statistical model, Eq. (1), he notes the complexity of the relationship between business cash balances and sales over time—first, because K varies over the cycle, and second, because of the need to consider changes in ρ as well as in r. Even so, given the latter variables as constant, Eq. (1) can be written

$$(3) \qquad \ln M_{ij} = \ln (\text{const.}) + \alpha \ln r + \beta \ln S_{ij}, \qquad \alpha < 0$$

Hence the interest elasticity of the demand for money is α. According to Meltzer's time-series findings,[9] $\alpha \approx -0.9$, or the interest elasticity of the demand for money is approximately unity.

As Meltzer says, "α is negative." Continuing, he says, "A rise in market (or external) rates which accompanies an increase in sales will result in a less than proportional increase in cash balances." This, as well as Eq. (3), "suggests that velocity will increase in prosperity and fall in depression." According to Meltzer, "This result is similar to those obtained by Baumol, Tobin, and Friedman,"[10] and, according to the subsequent analyses due to Baumol

[8] Meltzer, "A Cross-Section Study of Business Firms," *op. cit.*, p. 420.

[9] See Allan H. Meltzer, "The Demand for Money: The Evidence from the Time Series," *Journal of Political Economy*, June 1963.

[10] Meltzer, "A Cross-Section Study of Business Firms," *op. cit.*, p. 408.

and Tobin (Secs. 8.1 and 8.2), a rise in the market rate of interest results in a form of switching from cash to securities such that the velocity of cash increases and the ratio of cash to governments decreases.

THE ANALYSIS (THEORY)

Meltzer is inclined to view questions concerning the economies of scale in the use of cash as primarily empirical in nature and, in any event, he does not elaborate upon the analysis underlying Eq. (1) and implicit in many of his remarks. However, a reconstruction of the analysis implicit in his equation and remarks would seem to run along the ensuing lines: Firms' managers are reasonably rational and prefer more assets to less; the choice of assets is subject to the constraint imposed by the total for their nonhuman capital or assets "in use"; and the capital may vary directly with sales, but at varying rates. The capital may vary directly with sales, but at varying rates, because $K_{ij}\rho_j$ varies with the phases of the cycle; because $S_{ij} = K_{ij}\rho_j W_{ij}$; and because the value of a firm is given by capitalizing the expected stream of returns by the appropriate rate (i.e., ρ)[11] and the factor K_{ij}. Also, from Eq. (1), the money balances vary inversely with the product $K_{ij}\rho_j$, and directly with sales. Thus, the rise in the velocity of money is complicated by the factor $K_{ij}\rho_j$, but the effect of this factor simply reinforces the effect of the external rate of interest on the velocity of money.

THE HYPOTHESES

However viewed, the theory implicit in Meltzer's study of business firms and his incidental remarks lead to two testable hypotheses in which we presently have an interest. These are hypotheses (1) and (3) as introduced at the outset of this chapter—namely, the sales elasticity of the demand for cash by business firms is unity as a first approximation; and a rise in the market rate of interest, via a form of switching between cash and marketable securities, contributes to a rise in the sales-to-cash ratio and a decline in the ratio of cash to marketable securities.

---

[11] See footnote 6.

THE MOTIVES

Meltzer cites Keynes's references in his Treatise[12] to the demand for money and speculative transactions in capital goods or commodities by business firms. After mentioning "the motives for which business firms hold money," Meltzer says Eq. (1) does not "depend on any assumption about reasons for holding money." Later Whalen questions Meltzer's avoidance of the role of motives affecting the demand for cash by firms,[13] and in reply Meltzer notes that "hypotheses based on 'motives analysis' are rejected in comparison with any number of alternative demand functions for money."[14] One may point out, nevertheless, that motives could be involved in Meltzer's analysis, even though he may consciously avoid references to them. For example, the relation between cash balances and sales (or Meltzer's sales elasticity of one) may imply changes in the need for balances to satisfy all of the motives and equal proportional changes in sales or asset size. Cyclical changes in Meltzer's factor $K_{ij}\rho_j$, furthermore, may parallel changes in the speculative demand for inventories, equipment, and so on, and a form of switching from assets with a fixed claim against future income such as cash and bonds; the internal rate of return (ρ_j) may vary with the market rate of interest and changes in K_{ij} in response to the impact of expected price-level changes on the stream of returns from additional capital goods.

In early 1966 the prospect of inflation was widely discussed in the press, bank newsletters, and so on,[15] possibly in response to the prospect of large government expenditures on both military

---

[12] See John Maynard Keynes, *A Treatise on Money*, Vol. I (London: Macmillan and Co., Limited, 1930), pp. 45–49.

[13] See Whalen, *op. cit.*, pp. 160–162.

[14] Meltzer, "Reply," *op. cit.*, p. 163. Meltzer cites K. Brunner and A. H. Meltzer, "Predicting Velocity: Implications for Theory and Policy," *Journal of Finance*, May 1963.

[15] In an April survey of university and business economists by the Chase Manhattan Bank, 86 per cent of the university economists and 94 per cent of the business economists expressed the view that inflation was under way in the United States. See The Chase Manhattan Bank's *Business in Brief*, No. 68, June 1966.

and domestic programs. At about the same time, in the annual surveys appearing in the spring of 1966, planned capital outlays by business firms were reported as being about 17 per cent above those for the previous year, and it was not uncommon for some of those involved in the purchase of real capital goods to cite the need to effect contracts for future purchases as a means of avoiding losses and realizing gains from inflationary effects on the value of real capital assets. The effects of expected price-level changes and other factors on the velocity of money, speculative shifts between classes of assets, and the growth of assets are a formal part of the subsequent analysis of business firms' demands for money.

7.2 ADDITIONAL ANALYSIS: A MODEL AND SOME ALTERNATIVE AND ADDITIONAL HYPOTHESES

This section contains an outline of some additional analysis pertaining to the behavior of nonfinancial business firms, especially firms with assets of sufficient size to make expert management and operations in marketable debt instruments worthwhile. In the context of the analysis, we introduce the prospect of a wealth or "luxury" goods effect on over-all liquidity, and deduce the first alternative hypothesis, hypothesis (2) as set forth in the introduction to the chapter. Hypothesis (4), also as set forth earlier, is then shown to follow from the analysis, given a form of switching between broad classes of assets. A single equation model implied by the analysis and hypotheses is presented.

THE ANALYSIS

The additional analysis involves, briefly, three sets of equilibrium conditions: the first concerns the choice of assets, subject to a constraint imposed by total assets; the second concerns the choice of some alternative means of obtaining funds, subject to constraint; and the third contains a Keynesian, investment-demand type of equilibrium, in combination with the first two sets of conditions. The analysis ultimately involves, then, an over-all set of equilibrium conditions pertaining to both rates of return on additional assets and external rates of interest as rates for relating the prospective flows of returns from additional assets to their

present value. The prospective returns are subject to the influence
of a variety of factors. Some specific factors are mentioned and
related to a form of switching between broad classes of assets—
assets with a contractual or fixed claim against future income,
such as cash and bonds, and assets with a residual claim against
future income, such as plant and equipment.

In the establishment of the first set of equilibrium conditions,
the following axioms and definitions are taken as given: (1)
axioms—rationality and the preference of managers to manage
more assets rather than less; (2) total assets as a constraint—
including such assets as cash (M), government securities and
similar marketable-type assets (G), inventories (I), and plant and
equipment (P); (3) flows of prospective returns $(R's)$ from additional assets, including absolute dollar amounts and psychological
returns associated in varying degrees with the convenience and
security (the inverse of risk) in holding certain assets; and (4)
the satisfaction or utility (U) to be maximized from holding assets
as some increasing function of the classes of assets, e.g.,
$U = f(M,G,I,P)$. The constraint within which the choice must be
made may be considered as the sum of the assets in question, and
the constrained function becomes

$$g(M,G,I,P) = P_M M + P_G G + P_I I + P_P P$$

or in implicit form

$$g(M,G,I,P) - P_M M - P_G G - P_I I - P_P P = 0$$

where

P_M is 1 (or the price per dollar),

P_G is the price per bond,

P_I is the price per unit of inventories, and

P_P is the price per unit of plant and equipment.

Continuing, the Lagrangian function to be maximized becomes

$$L(M,G,I,P,r) = f(M,G,I,P) + r[g(M,G,I,P) - P_M M - P_G G \\ - P_I I - P_P P],$$

where r is the Lagrangian factor of proportionality.

Now, the first-order conditions for the constrained maximum are:[16]

$$\frac{\partial L}{\partial M} = \frac{\partial U}{\partial M} - rP_M = 0$$

$$\frac{\partial L}{\partial G} = \frac{\partial U}{\partial G} - rP_G = 0$$

$$\frac{\partial L}{\partial I} = \frac{\partial U}{\partial I} - rP_I = 0$$

$$\frac{\partial L}{\partial P} = \frac{\partial U}{\partial P} - rP_P = 0$$

$$\frac{\partial L}{\partial r} = g(M,G,I,P) - P_M M - P_G G - P_I I - P_P P$$

Hence, upon dividing the first four of these equations by their respective prices, and rearranging terms,

$$\frac{\partial U/\partial M}{P_M} = \frac{\partial U/\partial G}{P_G} = \frac{\partial U/\partial I}{P_I} = \frac{\partial U/\partial P}{P_P} = r$$

As it turns out, the numerators of these ratios are nothing more than the streams of returns (i.e., the R's) from acquiring additional assets in the respective classes and the r's corresponding to each of the ratios are nothing more than the rates of return for relating the various flows of returns to their present value. For the entire asset structure, then, equilibrium exists when the rates of return from acquiring additional assets in the various classes are equal,[17] and the percentages of assets in the various asset accounts may vary in response to discrepancies in the rates of return as a means of bringing about a new equilibrium structure.

The second set of equilibrium conditions involves the following: the dual to optimizing behavior, namely, minimizing or economizing in the case of costs; an outflow of funds to be minimized as

---

[16] Second-order conditions are assumed to be satisfied.

[17] For a slightly more detailed account of an equilibrium asset structure and the various elements entering into the returns and rates, see Frazer and Yohe, *op. cit.*, pp. 51–56 and pp. 368–370.

some function, for example, of bank loans (T), bonds (B), and stocks (S); a constraint function; and so on. The constraint function is, in the present instance,

$$g(T,B,S) = P_T T + P_B B + P_S S$$

where P_T is the price per unit of bank loans, P_B is the price per unit of bonds, and P_S is the price per unit of stocks. The Lagrangian function then becomes

$$L(T,B,S,i) = f(T,B,S) + i[g(T,B,S) - P_T T - P_B B - P_S S]$$

where i denotes the Lagrangian multiplier. Taking the first partial derivatives of the latter function and setting them equal to zero, the necessary conditions for a constrained minimum follow:

$$\frac{\partial L}{\partial T} = \frac{\partial U}{\partial T} - i P_T = 0$$

$$\frac{\partial L}{\partial B} = \frac{\partial U}{\partial B} - i P_B = 0$$

$$\frac{\partial L}{\partial S} = \frac{\partial U}{\partial S} - i P_S = 0$$

$$\frac{\partial L}{\partial i} = g(T,B,S) - P_T T - P_B B - P_S S = 0$$

Upon dividing the first four equations of the latter system by the respective prices,

$$\frac{\partial U/\partial T}{P_T} = \frac{\partial U/\partial B}{P_B} = \frac{\partial U/\partial S}{P_S} = i$$

and i is the rate of interest or the fundamental cost of obtaining funds from the financial markets. These equilibrium conditions say, in words, that the outflows of returns to the various sources of funds in question are a minimum when the rates from the respective sources are equal. The rates, of course, include risk premiums and elements for the drain or loss of liquidity imposed by the resort to the various sources of funds.

In the third stage of this analysis, profits are a maximum under reasonably competitive conditions,[18] when the rates of return from additional instrumental capital are just equal to the rate of interest for relating the flows of returns on additional capital to their present value. Here we have arrived at an equilibrium structure of rates:

$$r = i;$$
$$q_M - c_M + l_M =$$
$$q_G - c_G + l_G =$$
$$q_I - c_I + l_I =$$
$$q_P - c_P + l_P = q_T - c_T + l_T$$
$$= q_B - c_B + l_B$$
$$= q_S - c_S + l_S$$

where the q's are yields, the c's are carrying costs, the l's are liquidity elements, and the subscripts refer to the various classes of additional assets and the various sources of funds. Moreover, both sets of rates reflect risk factors as a part of the yields and separate liquidity elements (or their implied inverse, risk).

Upon ranking assets, according to the decreasing order of their liquidity return, and claims against the firm, according to the decreasing order of their drain on liquidity:[19]

	Inflows		Outflows	
	$q - c$	l		l
	0	+		−
Cash (i.e., money balances)		↑	Bank loans	
Government securities, and			Bonds	
similar noncash liquid			and	
assets			mortgages	
Instrumental capital				
(inventories,				
plant and equipment)	↓		Capital stock ↓	
	+	0		0

There is, as Keynes said, nothing to show for these liquidity

---

[18] See, e.g., Frazer and Yohe, *op. cit.*, pp. 383–388.

[19] See Frazer, *The Liquidity Structure, op. cit.*, pp. 14–16, and Frazer and Yohe, *op. cit.*, pp. 354–356.

elements, but they represent security and convenience. Among the above accounts—accounts reflecting choices as distinct from the more mechanically determined trade and tax-liability accounts— the ones reflecting the highest liquidity elements are cash and governments, and the one reflecting the largest drain on liquidity is bank loans. Thus, as one measure of noncash liquidity (or near moneyness), we use the ratio of government securities (including other similar noncash liquid assets, such as negotiable certificates of deposit) to bank loans.

The three stages of this analysis, so far, suggest an elaborate version of a Keynesian investment-demand model. This is notably the model implying the situation in which the inducement for managers to vary the flow of expenditures depends upon either of two sets of imbalances: an imbalance in the capital value (CV) and the contractual supply price or cost (C) of a given amount of instrumental capital, or an imbalance in the rate of interest for discounting the prospective returns from a given amount of instrumental capital and the rate of return for relating the prospective returns to the supply price of the capital. Where the streams of returns take a finite form[20]

$$CV = \frac{R_1}{(1+i)^1} + \frac{R_2}{(1+i)^2} + \cdots + \frac{R_n}{(1+i)^n}$$

$i =$ constant, since it is exogenously determined (i.e., determined by the credit conditions the monetary authorities effect in the financial markets)

$$C = \frac{R_1}{(1+r)^1} + \frac{R_2}{(1+r)^2} + \cdots + \frac{\dot{R}_n}{(1+r)^n}$$

$C =$ constant, since it is a cost at which a contract may be entered into with a builder or supplier of instrumental capital at a given time.

---

[20] In the case of these finite streams of returns, it may be shown that as $n \to \infty$, $CV = R/i$ and $C = R/r$, or $i = R/CV$ and $r = R/C$. Also, $r = \dfrac{\partial U/\partial P}{P_P}$, as in the case of the analysis involving Lagrangian functions above. See Frazer and Yohe, *op. cit.*, pp. 51–56.

Now these prospective returns, as just denoted, are subject to the effect of a variety of factors. Common among these is the prospect of inflation or deflation, usually included in models as a change in prices during the previous period or as a rate of change in prices. But other factors may be listed—e.g., changes in the tax credit for additional capital expenditures, changes in the time permitted for the write-off of new capital, labor costs, varying degrees of uncertainty about the future, news concerning tax and military developments, exhortation on the part of the President of the United States, and so on.

To illustrate the role of the outside factors, a news item suggesting inflationary prospects could be introduced. Proceeding from equilibrium (i.e., $CV = C, r = i$), a not unlikely effect of the inflationary prospects would be an increase in the prospective returns from assets with a residual claim against future income, such as plant and equipment, as mentioned earlier. Therefore, with C = constant and i = constant, at the present, $CV > C$ and $r > i$. This is the inducement for an expanded flow of expenditures on instrumental capital, a build-up in the backlog of planned capital outlays, and the accumulation of some liquid funds for asset expansion. The expanded flow of expenditures, of course, contributes to the return to equilibrium, along with any increase in the cost of funds for asset expansion. The prospect of deflation would have the reverse set of effects, and besides there are other factors too.

THE HYPOTHESES

Hypothesis (2), as set forth in the introduction to the present chapter, follows from the above analysis upon the introduction of one of the previously defined motives for holding money (Sec. 3.4) and a Friedman-type wealth effect on over-all liquidity. Hypothesis (2) particularly involves the preceding notion of a liquidity structure in which cash and governments possess large liquidity elements and in which bank loans reflect a drain on liquidity. The motive, in the present instance, is the precautionary motive according to which cash is needed to meet a subsequent liability such as a bank loan. As the wealth effect operates to increase liquidity, it results in a reduction in bank loans relative to asset size and a reduction in the need for cash to meet the reduced liability. The cash is, in effect, released for the purchase of government securities (including, as an accounting category, other similar types of liquid assets). A net result is hypothesis (2). Cash decreases in relation to asset size (and presumably sales), and the ratio of government securities to bank loans increases.[21]

Hypothesis (4), as set forth in the introduction to the present chapter, follows from the analysis in the preceding subsection upon the recognition of the prospect of switching between broad classes of assets in response to factors operating upon the inducement for managers to vary the flow of expenditures. In the case of the prospect of inflation, the switching of funds from cash- and bond-type assets into residual-claim-type assets may proceed, and, in addition, funds will likely be sought and obtained from other sources for asset expansion as well. At least, the analysis suggests these changes, and increases in total assets as well, in response to prospective price changes and an imbalance between the value of instrumental capital and its supply price. Purchasers, one might say, are committing their respective firms to more contracts, and capital budgets are increasing, at the same time as sales and total assets. A net effect of the switching and the changes, then, is a decline in cash and governments (or similar type assets) as a percentage of total assets (or sales), and a rise in the sales-to-cash ratio. The reverse set of changes too may hold in response to different outside developments, but we have explained a rise in velocity without resorting to the prediction of a decline in the ratio of cash to governments.

The switching phenomenon, as outlined, is a bit oversimplified. One complicating factor is the planning of the financing of the capital expenditures. As capital budgets begin to expand at an increasing rate, there is the prospect of a build-up in liquidity, possibly serving to offset temporarily the effect of the forces giving rise to the reductions in liquidity and the switching-out of assets of the fixed-claim type. As the financing of the asset

---

[21] For an early statement of the hypothesis, see Frazer, "The Financial Structure of Manufacturing Corporations," *op. cit.*, pp. 176–183. For a later statement, see Frazer, "Firms' Demands for Money," *op. cit.*

expansion takes place, external funds are likely to be sought by the respective firms, as previously noted. Internal funds are initially one source, but funds may be raised in the capital markets and returned to the money and credit markets, too, as firms build up liquidity. Later this liquidity serves as a source of funds, but all phases of the above activity place pressure on the suppliers of funds and on the banking system to supply the suppliers and business firms directly, in some instances. As a rule, the expansion of credit and money is not forthcoming in the amounts necessary to maintain constant market rates of interest, or a constant velocity of cash, for that matter. Indeed, the fact that sales during these periods of accelerated asset expansion usually are rising at a faster rate than the money stock is, in itself, possibly indicative of a degree of credit restriction.

The investors in the securities markets and the suppliers of funds also may respond to the same sort of factors as business managers, and the converse set of circumstances, too, may hold. Nevertheless, a conclusion ensues—changes in the velocity of corporate cash and interest rates are both responding to the same sets of changes in the setting. The explanation, in sum, involves switching among broad classes of assets, in response mainly to outside factors rather than a switching between cash and governments as interest rates rise. In accordance with hypothesis (4) as set forth at the outset there is a rise in velocity and interest rates, but there is no negative association between the rate of interest and the ratio of cash to governments.

THE SINGLE EQUATION MODEL

The single equation model for firms' demands for money implied by the above analysis and hypotheses would simply be

$$M_{ij} = \gamma r^\alpha A_{ij}^\beta, \quad \beta < 1, \alpha < 0$$

or in logarithmic form

$$\ln M_{ij} = \ln \gamma + \alpha \ln r + \beta \ln A_{ij}, \quad \beta < 1, \alpha < 0$$

where

M_{ij} is the cash balances of the ith firm and the jth industry,

r is a market rate of interest,

A_{ij} is the asset size of the ith firm in the jth industry,

α is simply the ratio of the percentage change in a single firm's cash holdings to the percentage change in the market rate of interest, and

β is the asset size elasticity of the demand for cash.

The single equation model is interpreted as applying to the ith firm in the jth industry, but this poses no special difficulty. We expect most firms to respond to the same changes in the setting and to the same factors during cyclical and secular phases of the post-World War II variety. The model, then, is viewed as being applicable to the sector comprising nonfinancial business firms, especially those in excess of some minimum size that begins to make expert cash management and operations in government securities worthwhile.

7.3   EVIDENCE FROM CROSS-SECTION AND TIME-SERIES DATA

In this section we review evidence from empirical data dealing with the four hypotheses listed in the introduction to the chapter. Two of these—hypotheses (1) and (3)—concern results due to Meltzer and Maddala and Vogel, and the other two—hypotheses (2) and (4)—have been shown to follow from the analysis of the preceding section. In reviewing evidence dealing with these hypotheses, it is also important to review support for some special propositions, in part with the view to explaining what would otherwise appear as a possible inconsistency in results from data for firms by industry groups and for firms by asset size. The propositions are as follows:[22]

(1)   The relation between changes in cash balances and changes in sales is such that cash balances at first increase in greater proportion than sales or assets and after a point in lower proportion (i.e., the velocity of cash at first declines and then rises).

---

[22] Frazer, "Firms' Demands for Money," *op. cit.*

(2) Meltzer and Maddala and Vogel were led astray by analyzing data for some industry groups in which cash varied significantly more than in proportion to sales and for some in which cash varied significantly less than in proportion to sales.

(3) Differences in manufacturing industries' demands for cash can be explained by differences in firm sizes.

SALES AND ASSET-SIZE ELASTICITIES

Meltzer's evidence from the cross-section data led him to conclude as follows: "The results suggest strongly that the cross-section demand for money by firms is a function of sales, to a first approximation linear in the logarithms and unit elastic."[23] Maddala and Vogel also engaged in a similar study and concluded, among other things, that "Meltzer's model is true to a first approximation," and "that it is possible to draw stronger conclusions than he [Meltzer] about the behavior of cash holdings of business firms."[24] Both Meltzer, and Maddala and Vogel, however, relied heavily on results from the analysis of data for industry groups, and they emphasized the results from regressing cash on sales after a logarithmic transformation of the data, although Maddala and Vogel mention "the inappropriateness of using sales as a surrogate for wealth" and analyze some data for log cash and log asset size. Further, in reporting their results these analysts hint at the prospect that some industries with small-firm populations have elasticities greater than unity for cash with respect to sales, and that some industries with predominantly large firms have elasticities less than unity.[25]

The above analysts analyzed a large amount of data. Some of the representative results are shown in Table 7–1, for an equation of the form $\ln M_{ij} = \ln \gamma_{ij} + \beta \ln S_{ij}$, where sales elasticity $= (\partial \ln M_{ij}/\partial \ln S_{ij}) = \beta$. In reviewing such results in a November 1966 article, Brunner and Meltzer may be quoted as follows:

---

[23] Meltzer, "A Cross-Section Study of Business Firms," *op. cit.*, p. 420.
[24] Maddala and Vogel, *op. cit.*, p. 153.
[25] See Meltzer, "A Cross-Section Study of Business Firms," *op. cit.*, p. 416; and Maddala and Vogel, *op. cit.*, pp. 156–157.

Table 7–1. Distribution of Sales Elasticity Coefficients from 126 Log Regressions* for Industry Groups

Range	1938	1944	1946	1951	1953	1954	1955	1956	1957	Total
1.241–1.270	2									2
1.211–1.240	1									1
1.181–1.210										0
1.151–1.180	5		1							6
1.121–1.150	4	1		1						6
1.091–1.120	1		2					1		4
1.061–1.090		2	4	1	1	3	1		1	13
1.031–1.060		5		8	5	7	5	4	3	37
1.001–1.030		4	3	1	4	2	6	6	5	31
0.971–1.000	1		2	2	3	1	2	2	3	16
0.941–0.970			1	1	1				1	4
0.911–0.940		1	1					1	1	4
0.881–0.910		1				1				2
Mean	1.157	1.040	1.042	1.035	1.020	1.033	1.026	1.020	1.010	1.042

* All coefficients (β) significantly different from zero.
Source: Allan H. Meltzer, "The Demand for Money: A Cross-Section Study of Business Firms," *Quarterly Journal of Economics*, August 1963, p. 411.

The elasticities of cash with respect to sales were computed for 14 industry groups in each of nine years. The cross sections are based principally on data from *Statistics of Income*. The mean value of the elasticity for each year ranges from 1.01 to 1.16. The mean of the 126 regressions is 1.04. Eighty per cent of the computed elasticities are above unity.[26]

However, it may be demonstrated in several steps that industry group data of the type Meltzer and Maddala and Vogel analyzed deal predominantly with industry groups populated by relatively small firms.[27] As a first step in such a demonstration, twenty-two industry groups of manufacturing firms were ranked according to the average-size firm in each group, and industry data were also shown for the ratio of cash to total assets and the ratio of business receipts to cash. The results included a ranking of firms, as in Table 7–2, and other results as revealed by the ranking of industry groups—namely, a declining ratio of cash to total assets, and a more erratic though nevertheless declining and subsequently rising ratio for business receipts to cash.

As a second step, cash was regressed on total assets and then business receipts, after a logarithmic transformation of the data, and these results were summarized, as in Table 7–2. The results there show: the regression (elasticity) coefficients for cash on asset size are predominantly and significantly less than one; the coefficients of determination are high in the latter instances; the coefficients for cash in relation to business receipts are somewhat less revealing than those for asset size, but six of the eight regression coefficients in excess of one appear in the first thirteen industry groups; and "up to the 13th industry group and an average-size firm of about 1.6 million, . . . half of the regression coefficients reflect elasticities greater than one (i.e., b's > 1), and only two of the nine beyond group 13 reflect such elasticities."

As a third step in demonstrating that Meltzer's results, as well as those due to Maddala and Vogel, were substantially affected by

---

[26] See Brunner and Meltzer, "Economies of Scale in Cash Balances Reconsidered," *op. cit.*

[27] See Frazer, "Firms' Demands for Money," *op. cit.*

Table 7–2. Cash with Respect to Total Assets and Business Receipts, Respectively, July 1961–June 1962: Results from Cross-Section Data for Industry Groups by Asset Size, after a ln Transformation of the Data

Industry groups ranked according to average-size firm in the group	Average-size firm (thousands of dollars)	Cash with respect to total assets Coefficients of		Cash with respect to business receipts Coefficients of	
		Regression (b)	Determination (r²)	Regression (b)	Determination (r²)
1. Apparel and other finished products made from fabrics and similar materials	298	0.77*	0.94	1.04	0.98
2. Furniture and fixtures	438	1.02	0.97	1.00	0.79
3. Printing, publishing, etc.	445	0.62	0.46	1.02	0.94
4. Other mfg. industries	464	0.79*	0.90	0.94	0.81
5. Leather and leather products	641	0.85*	0.95	0.94	0.91
6. Lumber and wood products	653	0.81*	0.87	0.88	0.73
7. Fabricated metal products (except machinery and transportation equip.)	739	0.85*	0.97	1.17	0.98
8. Machinery, except electrical and transportation equip.	1,119	0.69*	0.93	0.92	0.97
9. Stone, clay, and glass products	1,190	0.79*	0.95	1.00	0.94
10. Rubber and miscellaneous glass products	1,254	0.77*	0.98	0.91	0.98
11. Food and kindred products	1,280	0.85*	0.97	0.97	0.96

Industry					
12. Textile mill products	1,416	0.73*	0.96	1.04	0.90
13. Professional, scientific and controlling instruments; photographic and optical goods; watches and clocks	1,522†	0.69*	0.94	0.86*	0.96
14. Beverage industries	1,660	0.82	0.82	0.99	0.95
15. Electrical machinery, equip., and supplies	2,551	0.81*	0.96	0.88*	0.97
16. Chemical and allied products	2,584	1.02	0.97	0.93	0.98
17. Paper and allied products	3,187	0.71*	0.96	0.94	0.96
18. Transportation equip., except motor vehicles	4,009	0.80*	0.97	0.86*	0.97
19. Primary metal industries	6,294	0.78*	0.96	1.11	0.97
20. Motor vehicles and motor vehicle equipment	8,927	0.91	0.94	1.01	0.94
21. Petroleum refining and related industries	34,839	0.88	0.82	0.90	0.96
22. Tobacco manufacturing	39,558	0.73*	0.93	0.78*	0.97
23. All manufacturing firms	—	0.85*	0.86	0.97	0.87

* Significantly less than one at the 5 per cent level of significance.
† The average-size firm for all manufacturing groups is $1,590 thousand.

Note: There are twelve asset-size classes for firms in the U. S. Treasury's *Statistics of Income*. These in dollar amounts include the following: 1 to 50,000; 50 to 100,000; 100,000 to 500,000; 500,000 to 1,000,000; 1,-000,000 to 2,500,000; 2,500,000 to 5,000,000; 5 to 10 million; 10 to 25 million; 25 to 50 million; 50 to 100 million; 100 to 250 million, and 250 million and over. Some asset-size classes for several industry groups, however, have no firms in them because they are populated by either predominantly small or predominantly large firms.

Source of data: U. S. Treasury's *Statistics of Income, 1961–62* (Washington, D.C.: U. S. Government Printing Office, 1964).

their use of industry-group data, a frequency distribution was presented, as in Table 7–3. There a tally appears opposite the

Table 7–3. Frequency Distribution of Minimum Velocity for Twenty-Two Industry Groups

Moving average* of asset-size classes	Frequency of minimum value for the ratio of business receipts to cash
1 to 3	/
2 to 4	/
3 to 5	///
4 to 6	///
5 to 7	/////
6 to 8	///
7 to 9	////
8 to 10	/
9 to 11	/
10 to 12	

* There were three steps in the computation of the moving averages of the ratios for the size classes for each industry group: the first included finding the average-size firm and the business receipts per firm for the twelve asset-size classes; the second included taking a three-class moving average of each of the two sets of data obtained in the first step; and the third included finding the ratios for business receipts to asset size from the averages obtained in step two. The purpose of the moving average was to assure the occurrence of only one minimum ratio for each industry group.

Source of data: U. S. Treasury's *Statistics of Income, 1961–62* (Washington, D.C.: United States Government Printing Office, 1964).

size group for which a minimum velocity occurs in each of twenty-two industry groups. The minimum velocities are shown to occur with the maximum frequency for the size classes 5 to 7 (or between 1 million and 10 million dollars). Such occurrences are consistent with the prospect of a "tendency for velocity (business receipts to cash) to decline as firms increase in asset size and then to rise beyond some point as firms continue to increase in size." In fact, the regression coefficients for cash with respect to sales (after a logarithmic transformation of the data) are significantly less than unity for firms with assets over 10 million dollars, as shown in Table 7–4. Apparently, Meltzer and Maddala and Vogel found sales elasticity coefficients in excess of unity as a result of analyzing data for industries populated by relatively small firms. In addition to the coefficients for cash with respect to sales in Table 7–4, the table includes regression (elasticity) and determination coefficients for cash with respect to asset size, and regression and determination coefficients for the ratio of governments to bank loans with respect to asset size. These results support hypothesis (2), as set forth at the beginning of the chapter. As is apparent from the results in the table, the ratio of government securities to bank loans increases as firms increase in asset size beyond some minimum (namely, 10 million dollars), and cash increases less than in proportion to asset size (or sales).

The over-all results shown in the various tables support the special propositions outlined earlier: velocity (i.e., the sales-to-cash ratio) declines and then rises; Meltzer, as well as Maddala and Vogel, analyzed industry-group data for industry groups predominantly populated by small firms, as indicated by their results and the tendency for sales elasticity coefficients for the demand for money to exceed unity for industries populated by relatively small firms; and differences in manufacturing industries' demands for cash can be explained by differences in asset size. It is important to realize, with respect to these propositions and the related results, that an increasing number of sales elasticity coefficients in excess of unity for many industry groups is not necessarily increasing evidence in support of elasticity coefficients in excess of unity. The elasticity coefficients—as suggested by the use of the regression technique and the equation form $\ln M_{ij} = \ln \gamma_{ij} + \beta \ln S_{ij}$—concern any values the variable S_{ij} (or the substitute, asset-size variable A_{ij}) may take on, unless otherwise specified. In the case of the values the sales or asset-size variables are likely to take on, as indicated by the size of the existing firms, the asset-size values under 10 million, for which $\beta > 1$, include fewer than 1 per cent of the values the variable may likely take on. Meltzer's and Maddala and Vogel's results are affected by their study of industry groups with average-size firms of considerably less than 10 million dollars and, indeed, even less than the average of 1.5 million for the firms in industry group 13, in Table 7–2. In the test against alternatives—hypothesis (1) against (2)—hypothesis (2) is applicable for most of the values the size (or

Table 7–4. Cash with Respect to Sales, Cash with Respect to Asset Size, and the Ratio of Government Securities to Bank Loans with Respect to Asset Size: Results from Cross-Section Data for Firms by Asset Size

Year	Quarter	Cash with respect to sales for firms with assets of over 10 million dollars, after a ln transformation of the data — Coefficients of		Cash (per firm) with respect to asset-size of firms with assets of over 5 million dollars, after a ln transformation of the data — Coefficients of		Ratio (as a percentage) of government securities to bank loans with respect to asset-size for firms with assets of over 10 million dollars — Coefficients of	
		Regression (b)	Determination (r²)	Regression (b)	Determination (r²)	Regression (b)	Determination (r²)
1959	1	0.79*	1.00	0.87*	1.00	0.33†	0.97
	2	0.82*	0.99	0.87*	1.00	0.34†	0.97
	3	0.85*	0.99	0.86*	1.00	0.31†	0.98
	4	0.83*	0.99	0.86*	1.00	0.31†	0.97
1960	1	0.85*	0.99	0.89*	1.00	0.27†	0.97
	2	0.89*	0.99	0.89*	1.00	0.22†	0.97
	3	0.85*	0.99	0.87*	1.00	0.18†	0.97
	4	0.83*	0.99	0.87*	1.00	0.19†	0.97
1961	1	0.84*	0.99	0.88*	1.00	0.17†	0.97
	2	0.83*	1.00	0.87*	1.00	0.15†	0.98
	3	0.83*	0.99	0.86*	1.00	0.15†	0.98
	4	0.81*	0.99	0.86*	1.00	0.14†	0.98

Year	Quarter						
1962	1	0.79*	0.99	0.86*	1.00	0.17†	0.96
	2	0.79*	0.99	0.85*	1.00	0.18†	0.96
	3	0.81*	0.99	0.86*	1.00	0.16†	0.96
	4	0.84*	0.99	0.87*	1.00	0.17†	0.96
1963	1	0.78*	0.99	0.85*	1.00	0.17†	0.97
	2	0.80*	0.99	0.86*	1.00	0.17†	0.97
	3	0.82*	0.99	0.85*	1.00	0.15†	0.98
	4	0.84*		0.87*	1.00	0.17†	0.98

1964‡

* Significantly less than one at the 5 per cent level of significance.
† Significantly greater than zero at the 5 per cent level of significance.
‡ Changes in accounting classification of time certificates of deposit resulted in a change in the method of reporting cash and government securities (and similar liquid assets) in 1964.
Notes: The size classes in the FTC-SEC's *Quarterly Financial Report* include, in millions of dollars, under 1, 1 to 5, 5 to 10, 10 to 25, 25 to 50, 50 to 100, 100 to 250, 250 to 1,000, 1,000 and over.
Coefficients of determination of 1.00 are the results of rounding coefficients such as 0.99906565 for the fourth quarter 1963.
Data are from U. S. Federal Trade Commission and the Securities and Exchange Commission.

sales) variable may take on, though hypothesis (1) may apply in the special case of very small firms, relatively speaking.

VELOCITY, THE RATIO OF CASH TO GOVERNMENTS, AND THE RATE OF INTEREST

According to the more standard explanations of an increase in velocity (Secs. 4.1, 5.1), a rise in the rate of interest calls forth a form of switching from cash to governments (or similar types of liquid assets, such as negotiable certificates of deposit). As the above review (Sec. 7.1) of Meltzer's analysis reveals, Meltzer has supported that explanation. It may be identified with hypothesis (3), as set forth initially in the introduction to this chapter. An alternative explanation, on the other hand, attributes a rise in velocity and interest rates to a form of switching from both cash and governments to assets with a residual claim against income, possibly in response to the effect of outside factors on the prospective returns from a given flow of capital expenditures. It does not require a decline in the ratio of cash to governments, as in the more standard explanation; it may be identified with hypothesis (4). To the extent, moreover, that a reduction in bank loans in relation to assets is a form of liquidity, the shift out of liquidity as interest rates rise may also be reflected in a decline in the ratio of government securities to bank loans.

The empirical evidence concerning the latter hypotheses is shown in Table 7–5. It indicates a positive association between velocity and the rate of interest, as called for by both hypotheses (3) and (4). The results do not, however, reveal a negative association between the rate of interest and the ratio of cash to governments, as called for by hypothesis (3). The results, then, support hypothesis (4) over (3) and suggest a form of switching between broad classes of assets, including those with a residual claim against future income.

A complicating relation said to possibly affect the switching out of liquid assets as the backlog of planned outlays expands, or expands at an increasing rate, is that between liquidity and planned capital outlays (Sec. 7.2). In recognition of the possible

Table 7—5. Selected Ratios with Respect to the Rate of Interest, 1952–64: Quarterly Data (seasonally adjusted in ln Form

Ratios	Coefficients	
	Regression (b)	Determination (r^2)
Sales to cash	1.0*	0.85
Government securities to bank loans	–1.12*	0.49
Cash to government securities†	0.04	0.01

*Significantly different from zero at the 5 percent level of significance.
† The cash and government securities items are adjusted for the year 1964 (see note 1, *Quarterly Financial Report,* Fourth Quarter 1964, p. 50).
  Sources of data: Data for sales, cash, government securities, and bank loans are from the FTC–SEC's *Quarterly Financial Report,* and the data for the rate of interest are averages of daily figures for Aaa bond yields. The FTC–SEC data are for firms with 10 million dollars and over in assets.

presence of this relation, some results from a simple linear regression may be shown.[28] For example, regressing the ratio of government securities to bank loans on the ratio of planned capital outlays to total assets—after a logarithmic transformation of data exclusive of recession quarters plus two quarters forward from the trough and one quarter back from the peak—results in

> regression coefficient: 0.47
> coefficient of correlation: 0.46:[29]

Apparently there is some relation.

---

[28] For early results of this type from cross-section data, see Frazer, "The Financial Structure of Manufacturing Corporations," *op. cit.* pp. 180–182.

[29] The data are for the period 1952–64. Those for planned capital outlays are from the National Industrial Conference Board's series. for large firms (see *Quarterly Survey of Capital Appropriations: Historical Statistics,* National Industrial Conference Board). The data for total assets and the ratio of government securities to bank loans are for a similar group of firms—namely, the firms with assets over 10 million in the FTC-SEC's *Quarterly Financial Report.*

7.4   SUMMARY

Two sets of hypotheses have been introduced concerning firms' demands for money. The first set deals with the asset size (or sales) elasticity of the demand for money. One hypothesis in this set calls for a coefficient of unity, as a first approximation, and another calls for an elasticity coefficient of less than unity. The second set of hypotheses calls for an association between velocity and the rate of interest. One hypothesis in this set, however, leads to the prospect of a negative association between the ratio of cash to governments (or similar type liquid assets) and the rate of interest.

To deal empirically with these sets of hypotheses, evidence from both cross-section and time-series data are reviewed. The evidence, in the case of the cross-section data, supports the less than unitary asset size (or sales) elasticity hypothesis for the demand for money. The evidence from the time-series data for the period 1952–64 further supports the reoccurring association between velocity and the rate of interest, but there is no negative association between the ratio of cash to governments and the rate of interest. In fact, the standard hypothesis calling for switching between cash and governments is unsupported by the data. It fails the test against the alternative too, insofar as manufacturing corporations are concerned. Apparently, the form of switching paralleling changes in the rate of interest is between broader classes of assets—cash and liquid securities, on the one hand, and instrumental capital, on the other.

Evidence presented in papers by Meltzer and by Maddala and Vogel, resulting from the analysis of cross-section data for industry groups, has been shown to support a unitary sales elasticity coefficient of the demand for money. Further investigation, however, reveals the following: differences in manufacturing industries' demands for cash can be explained by differences in firm sizes; and industry groups populated by relatively small firms have greater than unitary sales elasticity coefficients, and other groups have other elasticities. What happens is that the velocity of cash at first declines and then rises, as firms increase in asset size. But the decline in velocity occurs only over a small fraction of the lower portion of the values the asset-size variable may take on. As firms increase in asset size beyond 10 million dollars, cash increases in lower proportion than sales, and cash continues to increase in lower proportion than asset size. As size increases this asset size of 10 million dollars occurs before the asset-size variable takes on one percent of its values.

Several bits of monetary analysis are reviewed in relation to the phenomena just outlined. Analysis due to Meltzer centers about a single equation model. For him the question of the sales elasticity of the demand for money is largely an empirical question. In the case of the velocity–interest rate association, he relies in part upon a rather common notion—the presence of a reward for holding balances in the form of securities rather than cash as the interest rate rises. In part, he notes the complexity of the relationship between cash balances and sales—first, because the ratio of capital to labor varies over the cycle, and second, because of the need to consider the "internal" rate of interest as well as the "market (or external)" rate. This sort of analysis, however, does not alter the testable notion Meltzer supports with respect to switching phenomena and the rate of interest.

Meltzer ignores the role of the motives for holding money, but this does not minimize the prospect of his analysis and results being consistent with some analysis involving motives. Indeed, the relation between changes in cash and changes in sales may imply equal proportional changes in various needs for balances to satisfy all the motives. And cyclical variations in cash in relation to assets in general may reflect a form of speculation—switching to avoid a "possible" loss or to realize a "possible" gain, such as may result from "prospective" price-level changes.

Additional analysis proceeds in three steps, and results in a somewhat complicated version of a Keynesian investment-demand model. As a first step, a constrained optimal, flow-of-returns equilibrium is shown to exist among assets when the rates of return from the various assets are equal. As a second step, the interest cost of obtaining funds is shown to be minimized when the rates of interest from the various sources are equal. As a third step, the preceding two sets of equilibrium conditions are related.

Equilibrium then revolves about the relationship between the value of additional assets and the cost or supply price of the assets or, alternatively, it revolves about the relationship between the rate of interest for discounting prospective returns from the flow of capital expenditures and the rate of return for relating the prospective returns to the cost of the given flow of capital expenditures. All of these rates are complicated by the presence of risk factors and liquidity elements. In fact, selected asset and liability accounts are ranked according to the magnitude of liquidity elements. The ratio of government securities to bank loans is cited as a good measure of noncash liquidity.

To deal with a less than unitary asset-size elasticity coefficient of the demand for money, a "wealth" effect and a variant of the precautionary demand for money are introduced. In the analytical framework the wealth effect on over-all liquidity proceeds to reduce bank loans relative to total assets, the decline in bank loans reduces the need for cash, and cash balances are released to government securities.

The prospective returns in the above analysis, further, are subject to the effect of a variety of factors—the tax credit, prospective price-level changes, and exhortation by the President of the United States, to list a few. These factors may affect the rate of return on additional capital and ultimately the rate of interest. In any event, imbalances between the latter rates provide the immediate inducement for altering the flow of expenditures, and they accompany a form of switching between two broad classes of assets—those with fixed claims against future income and those with residual claims. In the case of a prospective increase in the price-level, for example, the prospective returns from real capital tend to increase, and the value of the returns from fixed-claim assets—cash and so on—decreases. A net effect of these latter changes is a form of switching: both cash and governments decrease as a proportion of total assets. The expanded flow of expenditures, however, parallels increases in assets and sales, and cash and holdings of governments increase as a function of asset size. The need for funds for asset expansion results initially in some accumulation of liquidity and rather continuously in pressure on interest rates, given the tendency for credit conditions to tighten somewhat. This sort of analysis leads to the prospect of an association between velocity and interest rates, and a single equation model with elasticity coefficients for the rate of interest and asset size. It does not, however, call for a negative. relation between the ratio of cash to governments and the rate of interest. The switching phenomenon in question also involves the role of liquidity in relation to planned capital outlays. Evidence reveals its presence.

The two single equation models dealt with in the chapter differ mainly in two respects: first, with respect to the magnitude of the asset size (or sales) elasticity coefficients and, second, with respect to the explanation given for the negative interest elasticity coefficient. The models are interpreted as applying to the *i*th firm in the *j*th industry, but this poses no special difficulty in applying them to sectors. "Perverse" behavior by particular firms is not expected to dominate the sector aggregates; most firms are expected to respond to the same changes in the setting, the same factors during cyclical and secular phases of the post-World War II variety.

Chapter 8

THE TRANSACTIONS DEMAND FOR CASH: INTEREST ELASTICITY AND OTHER HYPOTHESES

The two most commonly cited papers on the transactions demand for cash are by William J. Baumol and James Tobin.[1] Because most writers cite the two papers as if they both dealt with an identical subject, they are related to each other in the present chapter. And indeed, Tobin said, in his 1956 paper, in making a late reference to the Baumol paper, that it was "a paper I should have read before writing this one but did not." In any event, a number of

---

[1] William J. Baumol, "The Transactions Demand for Cash: An Inventory Theoretic Approach," *Quarterly Journal of Economics*, November 1952; and James Tobin, "The Interest-Elasticity of Transactions Demand for Cash," *Review of Economics and Statistics*, August 1956.

For discussions of these works and analyses of data concerning notions contained in them, see, e.g., the following: Allan H. Meltzer, "The Demand for Money: A Cross-Section Study of Business Firms," *Quarterly Journal of Economics*, August 1963, pp. 409–418; Karl Brunner and Allan H. Meltzer, "Economies of Scale in Cash Balances Reconsidered," *Quarterly Journal of Economics*, August 1967; Karl Brunner and Allan H. Meltzer, "Predicting Velocity: Implications for Theory and Policy," *Journal of Finance*, May 1963, pp. 319–354; Edward L. Whalen, "A Cross-Section Study of Business Demand for Cash," *Journal of Finance*, September 1965, pp. 423–443; G. S. Maddala and Robert C. Vogel, " 'The Demand for Money: A Cross-Section Study of Business Firms': Comment," *Quarterly Journal of Economics*, February 1965, pp. 153–159; Edward L. Whalen, "Further Comment," *Quarterly Journal of Economics*, February 1965, pp. 160–162; Allan H. Meltzer, "Reply," *Quarterly Journal of Economics*, February 1965, pp. 162–165; William J. Frazer, Jr., "The Financial Structure of Manufacturing Corporations and the Demand for Money," *Journal of Political Economy*, April 1964, note 10, p. 178; Allan W. Heston, "An Empirical Study of Cash, Securities, and Other Current Accounts of Large Corporations," *Yale Economic Essays*, Spring 1962.

writers credit both Baumol and Tobin with common hypotheses, notably: (1) some form of an economies-of-size hypothesis, such that the transactions demand for cash increases less than in proportion to the volume of transactions, and (2) some form of interest-elasticity hypothesis, such that a rise in the rate of interest calls forth switching between cash and bonds. Tobin, however, said in his 1956 paper that "Baumol is mainly interested in the implications of his analysis for the theory of the transactions velocity of money at a given rate of interest, while the focus of this paper is on the interest-elasticity of the demand for cash at a given volume of transactions." Karl Brunner and Allan Meltzer also have re-emphasized this difference in reconsidering economies of size in cash balances.[2]

Although Baumol repeatedly mentions the "rational individual" and the "individual (or firm)," most writers dealing empirically with the various notions attributed to Baumol and Tobin view the notions as being primarily related to business firms. For this reason, and in view of the more likely potential applicability of the ideas to business firms, we tend to deal empirically with the notions in relation to business firms. In the first two sections of the present chapter, however, the main aspects of the analyses due to Baumol and Tobin are restated in detail, along with the rigorous critical evaluation of the respective analyses by Brunner and Meltzer.[3] The review of statistical results and the empirical evaluation of the analyses in question come in a third section. In that section,

---

[2] See Brunner and Meltzer, "Economies of Scale in Cash Balances Reconsidered," *op. cit.*

Note, the term "scale" as it applies to analysis and measurement has two common uses: (1) It applies to a series of marks at regular or graduated distances along a line that is used for measuring and computing; and (2) it refers to the proportion a model or drawing may have with respect to the thing it represents (Sec. 3.5). In the latter instance, for example, one may vary some or all the stock and flow variables in an economic model according to scale or in equal proportion. We are inclined in this work, therefore, to favor the use of the term in the latter instance, and to use the term "size" rather than "scale" when the only meaning intended is asset size, as in the case of the size of a firm, business unit, and so on.

[3] See Brunner and Meltzer, "Economies of Scale in Cash Balances Reconsidered," *op. cit.*

hypotheses due or attributed to Baumol and Tobin are tested against other hypotheses dealing with the particular phenomenon under consideration. These various additional, competing, or reinforcing hypotheses are due to Allan Meltzer, James Duesenberry, Milton Friedman, Irving Fisher, and others. For the most part, the Baumol and Tobin hypotheses, as well as most of the others, do not fare well in the review of statistical results and the test against alternatives. The important position attained by the Baumol and Tobin analyses, nevertheless, would appear to warrant the detailed consideration given to them.

A possible and subsequently unstated criticism of the combined Baumol and Tobin analyses is a common one made of analyses relying upon an arbitrary and rigid compartmentalization of the stock of money balances into separate transactions, precautionary, and speculative stocks of balances. This emphasis, of course, would be distinct from that upon the several motives and possible interrelationships between them. Earlier in the review of attempts to isolate specific stocks of "idle" and "active" balances, the criticism was of the arbitrary nature of such rigid compartmentalization (Secs. 4.1 and 4.2); but there is also the further prospect that the compartmentalization may conceal "interrelationships between the various motives for holding cash."[4] There is the prospect in particular of the motives being interrelated such that, for example, an increase in income exercises a luxury-goods or "wealth" effect on over-all liquidity, the latter in turn causing a reduction in the need for precautionary cash balances per se, and the latter in its turn altering the demand for transactions balances (or at least the functional relationship between cash balances and income), as outlined in a subsequent statement of an alternative hypothesis. Keynes said, "Money held for each of the three purposes forms . . . a single pool." Continuing, he said, "The holder is under no necessity to segregate [his stock of money] into three watertight compartments; for they need not be sharply divided even

---

[4] See, e.g., Whalen, "A Cross-Section Study of Business Demand for Cash," *op. cit.*, p. 433.

in his own mind, and the same sum can be held primarily for one purpose and secondarily for another."[5]

8.1 BAUMOL'S INVENTORY THEORETIC APPROACH

In dealing with the transactions demand for cash in his November 1952 article, Baumol drew upon analysis from the literature on inventory control. "A stock of cash is its holder's inventory of the medium of exchange, and like an inventory of a commodity," he said, "cash is held because it can be given up at the appropriate moment, serving then as its possessor's part of the bargain in an exchange." The simple model resulting from Baumol's application of inventory-control analysis involves the transactions demand for cash as dictated by rational behavior and as defined by a square-root equation, but the equation, as derived below, suggests various relationships between cash balances and other variables, both over time and on a cross-section basis. The suggested relationships and the assumptions of the model provide the basis for the major criticisms and evaluations of the model. These, as outlined subsequent to a review of the model, are by Karl Brunner and Allan Meltzer.

THE BAUMOL MODEL

The principal equation in Baumol's model is

$$(1) \qquad\qquad C = \sqrt{\frac{2bT}{i}}$$

where

C is cash obtained from the sale of security holdings (or from borrowing) at the beginning of a period and used evenly in effecting transactions over the period,

b is the noninterest costs of borrowing or making a cash withdrawal (i.e., b is Baumol's "broker's fee"),

T is the dollar amount paid out in a steady stream over a period, and

---

[5] John Maynard Keynes, *The General Theory of Employment, Interest, and Money* (New York: Harcourt, Brace and World, 1936), p. 195.

i is the interest rate on a loan or the opportunity cost of holding money rather than financial assets.

From the latter variables and definitions others follow and yield an equation which, when differentiated, yields Eq. (1). The other variables are

T/C: withdrawals over the course of one year (e.g., if $T = \$100$, then payments can be made by withdrawing \$50 every six months or \$25 every quarter),

$C/2$: the average cash holdings per period, since more than one-half are held in the first part of the period and less than one-half in the second,

$b(T/C)$: total cost in brokers' fees per annum, and

$i(C/2)$: annual interest cost of holding cash.

Summing the last two terms,

(2)

$$b\,\frac{T}{C} + i\,\frac{C}{2} = \begin{array}{l}\text{[Total cost per annum to individual (or firm)}\\ \text{in question for effecting transactions]}\end{array}$$

Upon differentiating Eq. (2) with respect to C, and setting the result equal to zero preparatory to finding the equation for the optimal (or minimum cost) stock of balances,

$$-b\,\frac{T}{C^2} + i\,\frac{1}{2} = 0$$

Then, solving the latter equation for C, we get Eq. (1). [*Note:* the broker's fee is constant in Eq. (2); it does not vary with the volume of transactions. Later it is shown to vary linearly with the quantity of cash handled and not to affect the results from differentiating Eq. (2).]

The simple analysis as it stands refers to two sorts of cases. According to Baumol these are "that of the individual (or firm) obtaining cash from his invested capital and that of the individual (or firm) spending out of borrowing in anticipation of future receipts."[6] In these cases, firms are restricted from receiving cash from the sale of their output, apparently because the Baumol problem depends on the noncoincidence of cash receipts and disbursements. In a third case, however, the individual (or firm) "has the option of withholding some of his receipts from investment and simply keeping the cash until it is needed." According to Baumol, "once this withheld cash is used up the third case merges into the first: the individual must obtain cash from his invested capital until his next cash receipt occurs." Here, the cash receipt is a periodic sort of thing that does not occur over the time period. It is, indeed, a potential source of difficulty because the receipt of funds from sales or receivables is likely to occur rather frequently or with some continuity or pattern over monthly or quarterly periods.

In the third case, Baumol does the following:

1. Lets I dollars be invested from the receipts and the remaining R dollars be withheld, either of which may be zero;

2. Lets the simple linear expression $b_w + k_w C$ be the broker's fee for withdrawing cash, where dollar amounts are withdrawn (note subscript w) and spaced evenly throughout the period, and where b and k are constants;

3. Lets $b_d + k_d I$ be the broker's fee for investing (or depositing) cash.

In this case, since the disbursements are continuous, the following occur: the R dollars withheld serve to make payments for that part of the period given by the fraction R/T; the average cash holding for that fraction of the period becomes $(1/2)R$; the interest cost from withholding the money becomes the product $i(R/T)(1/2)R$; and the total cost of withholding R dollars and investing I dollars becomes the sum of the interest cost from withholding money and the broker's fee for investing or depositing cash, namely,

$$i \frac{R}{T} \frac{1}{2} R + b_d + k_d I$$

[6] Baumol, *op. cit.*, p. 547.

or where $R = T - I$,

$$\left(\begin{array}{l}\text{Total cost of}\\ \text{withholding}\\ \text{money}\end{array}\right) \qquad \underbrace{\left(\frac{T - I}{2}\right)i\left(\frac{T - I}{T}\right)}_{\substack{\text{interest cost from}\\ \text{withholding money}}} + \underbrace{b_d + k_d I}_{\substack{\text{broker's fee}\\ \text{for investing}\\ \text{deposits}}}$$

Analogously, from the point of view of the withdrawal of cash from some source, such as an investment in securities, the following occur: the fraction of the period becomes (I/T); the average cash holding becomes $(1/2)C$; the interest cost from obtaining the cash becomes the product $i(I/T)$ $(1/2)C$; and the total cost of obtaining I dollars and paying the broker's fee on the fraction of cash withdrawn (i.e., I/C) becomes

$$\left(\begin{array}{l}\text{Total cost}\\ \text{of obtain-}\\ \text{ing money}\end{array}\right) \qquad \underbrace{\left(\frac{C}{2}\right)i\left(\frac{I}{T}\right)}_{\substack{\text{interest cost}\\ \text{from obtain-}\\ \text{ing money}}} + \underbrace{(b_w + k_w C)\frac{I}{C}}_{\substack{\text{broker's fee for}\\ \text{obtaining money}}}$$

The total cost of cash operations in this third case becomes the sum of the two expressions—the one for the total cost of money from receipts and the one for the total cost of obtaining money. Upon differentiating the sum of the two expressions with respect to C, setting the result equal to zero to find the extreme value, and solving the latter,

$$C = \sqrt{\frac{2b_w T}{i}}$$

where $b_w = b$ in Eq. (1), and where b_w is the fixed cost of withdrawing cash. Thus, as Baumol notes in this case, "the optimum cash balances after the initial cash holding is used up will again vary with the square root of the volume of transactions, as is to be expected by analogy with the 'living off one's capital' case."

Continuing with the task of investigating the optimum average cash balance before drawing on invested receipts, Baumol differentiates the total cost of cash operations with respect to I. Setting the result equal to zero,

$$-\left(\frac{T-I}{T}\right)i + k_d + \frac{Ci}{2T} + \frac{b_w}{C} + k_w = 0$$

or solving for $T - I$ (or R),

$$R = T - I = \underbrace{\frac{C}{2} + \frac{b_wT}{Ci}} + T\left(\frac{k_d + k_w}{i}\right)$$

$$C^2 = \frac{2b_wT}{i}$$

or dividing the latter expression by $2C$,

$$\frac{C}{2} = \frac{b_wT}{Ci}$$

Thus, substituting $C/2$ for b_wT/Ci in the expression for R,

$$R = \frac{C}{2} + \frac{C}{2} + T\left(\frac{k_d + k_w}{i}\right)$$

(3)
$$= C + T\left(\frac{k_d + k_w}{i}\right)$$

and we have the equation for the optimal average cash balances before drawing on invested receipts. According to Baumol, the first term in Eq. (3) is to be expected, "since if everything were deposited at once, C dollars would have to be withdrawn at the same moment to meet current expenses." On the one hand he says, "On this amount two sets of 'broker's fees' would have to be paid and no interest would be earned—a most unprofitable operation." On the other hand, no "brokerage fees" at all are paid on the C dollars, and the assumption of constant fees with $k_d = k_w = 0$ gets us into trouble. The assumption is a source of difficulty for Baumol's approach: Eq. (3) becomes $R = C$; the amount withheld from investment is never greater than C dollars because his strictly constant "broker's fee" implies the payment of the fee despite the absence of withdrawals or deposits; and, in the latter instance, "it pays to invest for any interest earning greater than zero."

The approach, we see, contains inconsistencies and highly restrictive assumptions. The writers mentioned below tend to emphasize these or modify them, in their evaluations of Baumol's approach. Baumol himself was somewhat modest about his square-root equation and its potential applicability to the real world. In fact, he minimized its relevance to a much greater extent than the wide range of references to the article in the economics literature would suggest. Baumol said the square-root equation was a "suggestive oversimplification" and noted the following with respect to the model (i.e., the equation and its accoutrements):

> It takes the distribution of the firm's disbursements over time to be fixed. . . . It assumes that there is one constant relevant rate of interest and that the "broker's fee" is constant or varies linearly with the magnitude of the sum involved. It posits a steady stream of payments and the absence of a steady stream of cash receipts during the relevant period. It deals only with the cash demand of a single economic unit and neglects interactions of the various demands for cash in the economy. It neglects the precautionary and speculative demands for cash.[7]

Despite his reservations, Baumol was inclined to draw conclusions from his equation (1) and related analysis, and other analysts have drawn some conclusions.[8] For one, Baumol in effect concluded that, given the price level, "the demand for cash rises less than in proportion to the volume of transactions." There are, he says, economies in the use of cash as firms increase in size.

In his reference to "the price level" he suggests a homogeneity of degree one for the demand for money with respect to the price level (Sec. 3.3). He says, "A doubling of all prices (including the 'broker's fee') . . . may be expected to double the demand for cash balances." Also, as the latter reference to the broker's fee suggests, Baumol was inclined to conclude that an increase in the broker's fee increases the demand for cash. And, finally, the ratio of transactions to cash or the velocity of money increases in response to increases in the rate of interest. This follows from

---

[7] *Ibid.*, p. 553.

[8] For a complete accounting of the conclusions drawn by Baumol himself, see Baumol, *op. cit.*

Eq. (1) and the possibility of interest earnings on securities exceeding the brokerage cost of transactions involving securities. The latter notion was not emphasized by Baumol, but it has been emphasized by others, especially those dealing with Baumol's analysis of the transactions demand for money and its similarity to the Tobin analysis introduced earlier (Sec. 5.1).[9]

CRITICISMS AND ANALYSIS DUE TO BRUNNER AND MELTZER

Brunner and Meltzer offer some criticisms concerning the logic and the role of the time period in Baumol's model of the transactions demand for money.[10] The main criticism concerns the model as an incomplete statement of individual firm behavior, its unsuitability for aggregation, and the portion of the domain for the asset-size (or volume of transactions) variable over which cash balances increase less than in proportion to increases in the asset-size (or volume of transactions) variable. The other Brunner-Meltzer criticisms include the following: the difficulty of reconciling Baumol's statements about the use of some cash receipts in the purchase of marketable securities as interest earnings exceed brokerage costs and statements about the existence of speculative balances; probabilistic statements by Baumol about "expected disbursements" that seem to imply the precautionary motive as well as the transactions motive; an analysis that "appears to merge a firm's 'transactions balances' with total money balances"; and the particular Baumol emphasis on balances distinguished according to the motives for holding them, when the evidence suggests the prospect of better statistical results from not attempting to distinguish balances according to motives.[11]

In their more devastating criticism of the Baumol model, Brunner and Meltzer introduce the problem resulting from the need to reconcile the time period with firms not being permitted to receive cash from sales (or payments from accounts receivable) during the

---

9 Tobin, *op. cit.*, p. 242.

10 See Brunner and Meltzer, "Economies of Scale in Cash Balances Reconsidered," *op. cit.*

11 Brunner and Meltzer cite an earlier paper in which they present a wide variety of results. For the earlier paper, see Brunner and Meltzer, "Predicting Velocity: Implications for Theory and Policy," *op. cit.*, pp. 319–354.

period. They view the time period as being very short or the prospect of receiving cash from sales during the period as very likely. In dealing with the difficulties imposed by this problem and the way Baumol attempts to handle it, Brunner and Meltzer obtain some interesting analytical results: a demand for money equation for which the square-root Eq. (1) appears as a special case; and an equation for the elasticity of the demand for money with respect to the volume of transactions that denies the prospect of economies of size in the management of cash balances by relatively large firms.

Brunner and Meltzer note that, to deal with the problem mentioned by them, Baumol presents the case resulting in Eq. (3) above. They note, too, the presence of two separate components of the average cash balances in this case—the amount $R/2$ that optimizing firms will withhold from investment during the transaction period with length R/T or $(T - I)/T$, and the amount $C/2$ held during the period of no receipts from sales (i.e., the period I/T). The separate components, then, suggest that the average money balances for a firm should be the weighted average of $R/2$ and $C/2$ and that the weights should be given by the proportions of the over-all period corresponding to the respective sets of balances. These weighted average balances (M) are denoted

$$M = \frac{R}{2}\left(\frac{T - I}{T}\right) + \frac{C}{2}\frac{I}{T}$$

and, substituting R from Eq. (3) in the latter expression,

$$M = \frac{C}{2} + \frac{R}{2i}(k_w + k_d)$$

Again substituting R from Eq. (3), Brunner and Meltzer get

$$(4) \qquad M = \sqrt{\frac{b_w T}{2i}\left(1 + \frac{k_w + k_d}{i}\right) + \frac{T}{2}\left(\frac{k_w + k_d}{i}\right)^2}$$

For Brunner and Meltzer the often-used, square-root Eq. (1) becomes a special case of Eq. (4)—namely, the case $k_w = k_d = 0$, where

k_w is the marginal cost of withdrawing cash [i.e.,
$d(b_w + k_wC)/dC$]

and

k_d is the marginal cost of depositing cash [i.e.,
$d(b_d + k_dI)/dI$].

Brunner and Meltzer point out, as we emphasized earlier, that the assumption $k_w = k_d = 0$ becomes troublesome once firms are permitted to receive cash from sales (or the repayment of accounts receivable). In part, the assumption becomes troublesome because there is an inducement to purchase securities at any interest earnings greater than zero.

Equation (4), furthermore, according to Brunner and Meltzer, either suggests a quantity-theory-of-money explanation of a firm's demand for money or it suggests an elasticity of one for money (M) with respect to the volume of transactions (T) for a large dollar amount of transactions. In the first instance, the term containing the square-root expression in Eq. (4) becomes zero, and $M = (\text{const.})\ T$, const. $= (1/2)\ [(k_w + k_d)/i]^2$, if the fixed cost of withdrawing cash is zero (i.e., $b_w = 0$). In the second instance, for given non-zero values of b_w, the elasticity of the money balances with respect to the volume of transactions [i.e., $\epsilon(M, T)$] is, as denoted by Brunner and Meltzer,

$$(5) \qquad \epsilon(M, T) = \frac{\left(1 + \dfrac{k_w + k_d}{i}\right)\sqrt{\dfrac{b_wT}{2i}} + \left(\dfrac{k_w + k_d}{i}\right)^2 T}{2\left(1 + \dfrac{k_w + k_d}{i}\right)\sqrt{\dfrac{b_wT}{2i}} + \left(\dfrac{k_w + k_d}{i}\right)^2 T}$$

Here, in Eq. (5), as the dollar volume of transactions approaches zero (i.e., $T \to 0$), the elasticity approaches one-half [i.e., $\epsilon(M, T) \to 1/2$]. Also, for large values of T, the elasticity approaches one as in the quantity theory of money (Sec. 4.1), and the economies move in the opposite direction from those posited by Baumol as firms increase in size (and dollar volume of transactions).

These are interesting results for they point to logical fallacies in the Baumol model. Brunner and Meltzer are inclined to view the results they deduce as being consistent with some of Meltzer's earlier findings of an absence of economies of size (i.e., a constant or decreasing velocity or sales-to-cash ratio) as firms increase in asset size.[12] The difficulty here, however, is that Meltzer obtained his results by fitting regression lines to logarithmically transformed data that emphasized firm sizes over the lower portion of the domain for the asset-size variable, as noted later. Other findings show that cash balances at first increase in greater proportion than sales or assets (i.e., velocity falls) and after a point in lower proportion,[13] as mentioned earlier (Sec. 7.3). Further, the analysis in the first instance in the preceding paragraph suggests that the velocity of money will rise in response to an increase in the rate of interest on securities as a result of a form of switching from cash balances to securities, and this result is not borne out by results from analyses of data reported in an earlier section (Sec. 5.2) dealing with the Latané-Tobin explanation for velocity changes.

8.2 TOBIN ON THE INTEREST ELASTICITY OF TRANSACTIONS DEMAND

Tobin's principal concern in the article usually linked with Baumol's on transactions demand is with the interest elasticity of the transactions demand for money. This concern was, indeed, implied earlier in the references to the Latané-Tobin explanation for the velocity–interest rate association (Secs. 5.1 and 5.2). Tobin's analysis, nevertheless, has also been used by analysts such as Meltzer as a basis for an economies-of-size hypothesis similar (or identical) to the Baumol hypothesis of the previous section,[14] and, more recently, Brunner and Meltzer have emphasized the primacy of the interest-elasticity hypothesis in the Tobin analysis and the prospect of neither economies nor diseconomies of size. In this

---

[12] See Meltzer, "A Cross-Section Study of Business Firms," *op. cit.*

[13] See William J. Frazer, Jr., "Firms' Demands for Money: The Evidence from the Cross-Section Data," *Staff Economic Studies,* No. 25 (Washington, D.C.: Board of Governors of the Federal Reserve System, 1967).

[14] See, e.g., Meltzer, "A Cross-Section Study of Business Firms," *op. cit.,* pp. 409–415; and Whalen "Further Comment," *op. cit.*

section, therefore, we will introduce briefly the Tobin analysis, review it in some detail, and review the Brunner-Meltzer "reconsideration" of the Tobin analysis. A review of results from statistical analyses concerning the hypotheses and other alternatives will appear subsequently (Sec. 8.3).

THE TOBIN ANALYSIS (AN OVER-ALL VIEW)

Tobin's interest-rate, transactions-demand notion, as set forth in his 1956 article, is essentially this: The transactions demand for money varies inversely with the excess of the rate of interest over the cost of switching into and out of interest-bearing assets, other things begin equal. By "transactions balances," Tobin means balances to satisfy the transactions motive as set forth earlier (Sec. 3.4)—namely, balances to "bridge the gaps in time between the receipts and the expenditures of economic units." Only in the present instance, this motive can be satisfied by holding bonds as well as money. As in the earlier outline of motives, "the amount of cash holdings needed for a given volume of transactions is taken as determined by the institutions and conventions governing the degree of synchronization of receipts and expenditures." Also, by "the rate of interest" Tobin means "the difference between the yield on bonds and the yield on cash," where the yield on cash is zero. This zero yield on cash distinguishes the yield on cash from that involving a liquidity element as in an earlier analysis (Sec. 7.2).

The reason for the variation in the demand for cash concerns mainly the gain resulting from the transfer of cash to interest-bearing assets as interest rates rise and overcome the cost of switching into and out of the interest bearing assets and leads to a hypothesis about the interest elasticity of the transactions demand for cash. Assuming optimizing behavior for the economic units in question, Tobin summarizes the incentive for the more economical use of balances:

> When the yield disadvantage of cash is slight, the costs of frequent transactions will deter the holding of other assets, and average cash holdings will be large. However, when the yield disadvantage of cash is great, it is worthwhile to incur large

transactions costs and keep average cash holdings low. Thus, it seems plausible that the share of cash in transactions balances will be related inversely to the interest rate on other assets.[15]

The other hypothesis sometimes associated with Tobin's analysis of the demand for money involves the prospect of economies of scale in the use of balances. According to this hypothesis there are economies in the use of cash relative to income and via a switching into bonds that result from an increase in income (or asset size). As we note later, this appears to follow from Tobin's notion that the number of switching transactions called for to maximize the revenue from bonds increases as income increases and contributes to a rise in the average transactions balances held in the form of bonds.

THE ANALYSIS IN DETAIL

The alternative assets include cash (C) and bonds (B). These are the same, except bonds are not a medium of payment, and bonds bear interest. There is, too, the highly restrictive assumption of an absence of risk from either a default on the bonds or a loss of value due to a rise in the rate of interest. For a switching transaction of x dollars, total cost of switching for a single transaction $= a + bx$, a and $b > 0$, where

a (a portion of the cost) is independent of the size of the financial transaction (i.e., a is the constant fixed cost component of transaction costs),

bx (the other part of the total cost) varies proportionally with the size of the financial transactions x, and

b is a fraction expressible as a rate per period such as one-fourth the rate of interest (r).

The total transactions balance $[T(t)]$ consisting of cash and/or bonds at a given time is equal to the product of the income Y received at the beginning $(t = 0)$ of the period and the expired fraction of the period $(1 - t)$, i.e.,

(1) $$T(t) = Y(1 - t), \qquad 0 \leqq t \leqq 1$$

---

[15] Tobin, *op. cit.*, p. 242.

Given the above, the individual's "average transactions balances" becomes

(2) $$T = \int_0^1 Y(1-t)\, dt = Y/2$$

Further $$Y = \int_0^1 Y(t)\, dt, \quad 0 \leqq t \leqq 1$$

where $Y(t)$ is viewed as the average of the flows of income (or expenditures) at the respective moments in the period, and where the flows accumulate to yield the income for the period. Income (Y) then is viewed as both income for the period and as the area under the line $T(t)$, as in Figure 8–1. Average transactions balances, moreover, are divided between cash and bonds, such that

(3) $$T(t) = B(t) + C(t), \quad B(t) \text{ and } C(t) \geqq 0$$

and

(4)
$$B = \int_0^1 B(t)\, dt, \quad C = \int_0^1 C(t)\, dt, \quad \text{and } B + C = T = 1/2Y$$

where B and C are, according to Tobin, "average bond holdings and cash holdings respectively."

The over-all problem set up by Tobin is "to find the relationship between B (and hence C) and the interest rate r," where

$B(t)$ and $C(t)$ are chosen by the individual so as to maximize interest earnings, net of transactions costs, and

r is the rate of interest per time period, no matter how short.

The relationship, according to Tobin, may be found by breaking down the over-all problem into three problems,[16] as outlined below, where

n is the number of transactions during a period,

R_n is the revenue from the optimal plan,

π_n is the net revenue (i.e., R_n − total cost of switching), and

n^* ("the optimal number of transactions") is the value of n for which R_n is a maximum.

---

[16] *Ibid.*

The Tobin Analysis (problem 1)

The first problem involves finding the times $(t_1, t_2, \ldots, t_n)$ and the optimal amounts of n switching transactions, such that the revenue from the bond purchases is maximized, given r and n. We proceed by considering the scheduling and sizes of two, three, and n switching transactions, for cases involving switching costs that are independent of asset size (i.e., $b = 0$). In these cases the costs are determined by the number of transactions, and, if there is one switching transaction from cash into bonds, then there must be at least one additional transaction from bonds back into cash.

The revenue optimizing schedule for two transactions (one into bonds and one out, $b = 0$) is shown in Figure 8–1. There half of the income Y received at the beginning of the period $(t = 0)$ is converted into bonds, and the bonds are held until further cash is needed at the middle $(t = 1/2)$ of the period. In the figure, the line $T(t) = Y(1 - t)$ represents the transactions demand for cash and bonds at any given t $(0 \leqq t \leqq 1)$; the area bounded by the respective axes and the line $T(t) = Y(1 - t)$ represents the sum of the average bond and cash holdings; and the area repre-

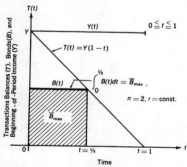

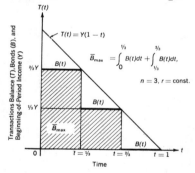

Figure 8–1. Scheduling of Switching Transactions to Maximize Revenue for a Cash-Bonds-Cash Round Trip Set of Transactions, $b = 0$.

Figure 8–2. Scheduling of Three Switching Transactions to Maximize Revenue: Into Bonds in One and Out in Two, $b = 0$.

senting the portion of balances held in bonds is a maximum for $B(t) = 1/2$, $t = 1/2$, since for any combination up to $t = 1/2$, the revenue increases in response to increases in the time the bonds may be held. Note, too, that for a given purchase of bonds [i.e., $B(t)$ = const.] it is always more profitable to purchase the bonds at the beginning of the period, since in no other way can the area $\bar{B}$ be a maximum and adequate cash be maintained for transactions.

If three switching transactions are permitted (i.e., $n = 3$), then the block of bonds initially purchased may be disposed of at two different times. In this case, as illustrated in Figure 8–2, the bonds held to maximize interest returns and to satisfy transactions needs for the second two-thirds of the period are represented by the area under the line $B(t)$, $0 \leqq t < 1/3$), and those held to maximize interest returns and satisfy transactions needs in the last one-third of the period are represented by the area under the line $B(t)$, $1/3 \leqq t < 2/3$. In general, for n transactions, the schedule for optimizing revenue involves the purchase of $[(n-1)/n]Y$ bonds at time zero, and their sale in equal installments of Y/n at times $1/n, 2/n, \ldots, (n-1)/n$. And, in general, the average bond holding ($\bar{B}_n$), revenue ($r\bar{B}_n$), and net revenue (i.e., $r\bar{B}_n - na$), respectively, are

$$(5) \qquad \bar{B}_n = \frac{n-1}{2n} Y, \qquad n \geqq 2$$

$$(6) \qquad R_n = \frac{n-1}{2n} Yr, \qquad n \geqq 2$$

$$(7) \qquad \pi_n = \frac{n-1}{2n} Yr - na, \qquad n \geqq 2$$

In taking account of the portion (i.e., bx) of the total switching transaction cost that varies with the size of the switching transaction x, some modifications of the above analysis are called for. To begin with, "every dollar of cash-bonds-cash round trip costs $2b$, no matter how quickly it is made," and this, along with other assumptions, means the following: (1) the interest earnings (i.e., rx) must exceed the variable portion of the round-trip switching cost (i.e., $2bx$) in order for the purchase of bonds to be worthwhile; and (2) the bonds must be held long enough for interest earnings to exceed the variable switching cost, and this requires a minimum time of $2b/r$ (e.g., minimum time = $1/2 = 2(.01)/.04$, where the rate of interest per the entire period is four per cent and the variable switching cost is one per cent). This case with variable

236   *The Demand for Money*

switching cost (i.e., $b > 0$) is the same as the previous cases without variable switching cost (i.e., $b = 0$), except for the following: the time at which revenue begins to exceed the variable switching cost is the minimum time t, $t = 2b/r$, rather than time zero; and the solution to the case proceeds as if total transactions balances were $Y - Y(2b/r)$ or $Y[1 - (2b/r)]$ rather than Y.

Figure 8–3. Scheduling of Three Switching Transactions to Maximize Net Revenue, $b = (1/4)r$.

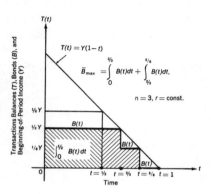

With the latter modifications, the case with $b > 0$ is the same as the earlier cases with $b = 0$. In other words, optimizing revenue involves putting $(n - 1)/n$ of the beginning balances into bonds, and selling these bonds in equal installments at $(n - 1)$ equally spaced dates. In a particular case, as in Figure 8–3, the effective beginning time is $t = 1/2$; the transactions balances to be distributed are in effect $(1/2)Y$; the initial purchase of bonds amounts to

$$\left(\frac{(n - 1)}{n}\right)\frac{1}{2}Y \quad \text{or} \quad \frac{2}{3} \cdot \frac{1}{2}Y = \frac{1}{3}Y$$

and half of the latter purchase is converted back into cash at two equally spaced dates, namely $t = 2/3$ and $t = 5/6$. In the figure, the balances in bonds serving to generate the earnings to meet the variable switching transactions cost correspond to the area under the line $B(t)$, $0 \leqq t < 1/2$, i.e.,

$$\int_0^{\frac{1}{2}} B(t)\ dt = \begin{array}{l} \text{(bond balances yielding interest to offset vari-} \\ \text{able switching transactions cost),} \end{array}$$

and

$$\bar{B}_{\max} - \int_0^{\frac{1}{2}} B(t)\, dt = \begin{array}{l}\text{(bond balances yielding revenue net of vari-}\\ \text{able switching transactions cost.)}\end{array}$$

For the general case corresponding to the special case with $b > 0$ Tobin proves the following:

(8) $\bar{B}_n = \dfrac{n-1}{2n} Y\left(1 - \dfrac{4b^2}{r^2}\right), \qquad n \geqq 2,\, r \geqq 2b$

(9) $R_n = \dfrac{n-1}{2n} Yr\left(1 - \dfrac{2b}{r}\right)^2, \qquad n \geqq 2,\, r \geqq 2b$

(10) $\pi_n = \dfrac{n-1}{2n} Yr\left(1 - \dfrac{2b}{r}\right)^2 - na, \qquad n \geqq 2,\, r \geqq 2b$

Note that for $b = 0$, Eqs. (8) to (10) became similar to Eqs. (5) to (7).

THE TOBIN ANALYSIS (PROBLEM 2)

The second problem involves finding the value of n for which π_n is a maximum, given r. As we know from basic economics and as Tobin indicates, this occurs at the value of n for which the difference between revenue R_n and cost na is a maximum, or at the value of n where marginal revenue (ΔR_n) is equal to marginal cost (i.e., the constant a in this case). Thus from Eq. (9),

$$\Delta R = \frac{1}{2n(n+1)} Yr\left(1 - \frac{2b}{r}\right)^2, \qquad n \geqq 2,\, r \geqq 2b,$$

where ΔR is marginal revenue, and the value of n at which $\Delta R = a$ is n^*, as illustrated in Figure 8–4. For $\Delta R = a$, we may also note

(12) $2n^*(n^* + 1) = \dfrac{1}{a} Yr\left(1 - \dfrac{2b}{r}\right)^2$

In addition, in the figure, we note values for revenue and marginal revenue at which $n = 2$, and we note the limits to revenue and marginal revenue as $n \to \infty$.

There are other possibilities than the solution for n^* in Figure 8–4. For example, net profit may be zero or negative, and the

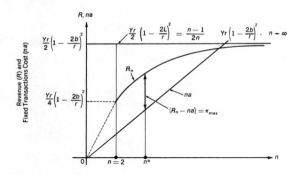

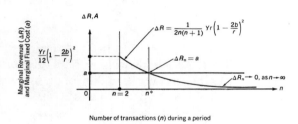

Number of transactions (*n*) during a period

Figure 8–4. The Determination of the Optimal
Number of Transactions.

optimal number of transactions is indeterminate for the values of n
between zero and 2.

THE TOBIN ANALYSIS (PROBLEM 3)

Problem 3 of the over-all problem set up by Tobin concerns
the effect of r on revenue, the dependence of n^* on r, the changes
in $\bar{B}$ and $\bar{C}$ as r changes, and the dependence of n^*, $\bar{B}$, and $\bar{C}$ on
income. To begin with, a number of relationships between the
various variables are apparent: revenue (R) varies directly with
the rate of interest (r) in Eqs. (9) and (11); the optimal num-

ber of switching transactions (n^*) varies directly with income (Y) and the rate of interest (r) in Eq. (12); and the average of transactions balances held in the form of bonds ($\bar{B}_n$) varies directly with the rate of interest (r) and the number of switching transactions (n) in Eq. (8). It is further apparent, from these relationships and from Eqs. (8) and (4), that "the optimal share of bonds in a transactions balance varies directly, and the share of cash inversely, with the rate of interest."

Thus, whether Tobin intended his theory to have empirical content or not, the notion of an interest elastic transactions demand for money, and one of the major hypotheses associated with the Tobin analysis should be clear—namely, a rise in the rate of interest induces switching between cash and bonds and gives rise to an increase in the ratio of income to cash. A second hypothesis associated with Tobin's analysis appears to follow from Eqs. (12) and (8)—namely, as income (or asset size) increases there will be economies effected in the use of cash via a switching into bonds. The economies in the use of cash in this case result from the effect of income on the optimal number of switching transactions and the effect of the number of switching transactions on the average of transactions balances held in the form of bonds.

BRUNNER AND MELTZER ON TOBIN'S ANALYSIS OF
ECONOMIES OF SIZE

The principal hypothesis in Tobin's analysis does not stand up well when tested against an alternative explanation, as earlier empirical results suggest (Sec. 5.2). Even so, the economies-of-size hypothesis would still appear to have some favorable prospects, at least when loosely interpreted and when dealing with results from the analysis of cross-section data. Brunner and Meltzer, however, consider rigorously Tobin's analysis and question its suitability for dealing even with cross-section changes, the rate of interest constant. They do this,[17] even though Meltzer has been one of the major analysts to deal empirically with economies of size of the Baumol-Tobin type.[18] Consequently, we review some aspects

---

[17] See Brunner and Meltzer, "Economies of Scale in Cash Balances Reconsidered," *op. cit.*

[18] See Meltzer, "A Cross-Section Study of Business Firms," *op. cit.*

of Brunner's and Meltzer's considerations of Tobin's analysis of economies of size. In particular Brunner and Meltzer compare the Tobin analysis to the quantity theory and find little conflict when both are applied to individual firms. They show "that to a first approximation each firm, operating according to the Tobin model, should regard its demand function for (transactions) money as unit elastic in the volume of transactions." They also deal with questions concerning "jump points" at which n^* changes or at which economies of size might exist in Tobin's analysis of the relationship between cash and income.

Brunner and Meltzer note that Tobin had previously defined $\bar{C}$ as in Eq. (4), so that $\bar{C} = (Y/2) - \bar{B}$, and so that upon substituting for $\bar{B}$ from Eq. (8),

$$(13) \qquad \bar{C} = \frac{Y}{2}\left[1 - \frac{n-1}{n}\left(1 - \frac{4b^2}{r^2}\right)\right], \qquad n \geqq 2, r \geqq 2b$$

Here, "as n becomes relatively large, cash balances will increase in direct proportion to the volume of transactions (or receipts) given b and r." Next, for $n < 2$ all balances are held in cash, i.e., $\bar{C} = (1/2)Y$, and cash balances still "increase in direct proportion to the volume of transactions" and for $n =$ constant in Eq. (13) the conclusion of direct proportional changes in cash and income still follows. Also, upon differentiating Eq. (13) with respect to Y and then dividing Eq. (13) by Y, Brunner and Meltzer show that

$$\frac{\partial C}{\partial Y} = \frac{1}{2}\left[1 - \frac{n-1}{n}\left(1 - \frac{4b^2}{r^2}\right)\right] \quad \text{and} \quad \frac{C}{Y} = \frac{\partial C}{\partial Y}$$

respectively, so that the percentage changes in income (i.e., $\partial Y/Y$) call forth equal percentage changes in cash (i.e., $\partial C/C$), as in the simple quantity theory. Thus, in reviewing the above instances where $\epsilon(C, Y) = 1$ for $n < 2$, n relatively large, and $n =$ constant, Brunner and Meltzer are led by the Tobin analysis "to expect neither economies nor diseconomies of scale in the holding of money balances."

However, Brunner and Meltzer continue to investigate changes in n, since they appear to be essential to the economies-of-size hypothesis in the Tobin analysis. They note several things: that Tobin restricts n^* as in Eq. (12) to integer values; that n^* will change only if income changes by a sufficient amount to raise it, r, b, and a

constant; that cash balances remain unit elastic with respect to income, between the points at which discrete changes in income take place; and that each time n^* increases by one, optimal cash balances shift down by a finite amount dependent on the constant terms. Such shifts in optimal cash balances and the line portraying equal proportional changes in cash in relation to income, as n^* changes by one unit, are illustrated in Figure 8–5,

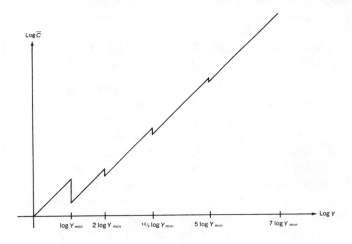

Source: Karl Brunner and Allan H. Meltzer, "Economies of Scale in Cash Balances Reconsidered," *Quarterly Journal of Economics,* August 1967.

Figure 8–5. The Relationship Between Percentage Changes in Cash and Income: "Jump Points" for Changes in the Optimal Number of Switching Transactions.

where Y_{min} is the minimum value of Y for successive values of n^*.

Brunner and Meltzer derive from Tobin's analysis equations for computing the amounts by which income must change in order to change the optimal number of switching transactions.[19] They then note these things: that unless sales double from one transactions

---

[19] See Brunner and Meltzer, "Economies of Scale in Cash Balances Reconsidered," *op. cit.*

period to the next, a firm just above the threshold level of sales at which n^* becomes 2 need not be concerned with the possibility that n^* may become 3; that the length of the transactions period is crucial; that a few transactions in a short period exhaust the possibilities of economies of size; and that as n^* increases, smaller downward shifts occur at each successive "jump point" in Figure 8–5. The authors conclude that the Tobin "analysis does not suggest the importance of economies of scale for individual firms with the perhaps minor exception of those that are close to a 'jump point.' "

8.3 STATISTICAL RESULTS AND THE BAUMOL, TOBIN, AND OTHER HYPOTHESES

The previous sections in this chapter have consisted largely of reviews and criticisms of analyses of the transactions demand for money by individuals and business firms. The analyses reviewed have been due mainly to Baumol and Tobin, and the evaluations of these analyses have come from a paper done jointly by Brunner and Meltzer. For the most part, the Brunner-Meltzer evaluation of the Baumol and Tobin analyses has been devastating as far as rigorous analysis and the derivations of the economies-of-size hypothesis are concerned. In the case of Baumol's analysis, Brunner and Meltzer have shown that the square-root formula is somewhat of a special case of a more general formula, and that the more general formula fails to reflect increasing economies in the use of cash balances as firms increase in sales (or size). In the case of the Tobin analysis, they show that a unit income elasticity of the demand for cash is most likely the case, especially as the number of switching transactions between cash and bonds increases. In the latter case, Brunner and Meltzer readily recognized the primacy of the interest-elasticity hypothesis over the income-elasticity hypothesis, but in neither instance did they question the analytical bases for the interest-elasticity hypothesis, except to question the applicability of the analysis to changes involving time.

The excessively restrictive assumptions of the Baumol and Tobin analyses and the analytical shortcomings in these, as emphasized by Brunner and Meltzer, doubtlessly have serious consequences for the analyses in question. In this section, however, we list the hypotheses associated with Baumol and Tobin as well as other alternative or possibly reinforcing hypotheses and survey the empirical evidence. The evidence consists entirely of that from the nonfinancial business sector of firms and in some instances simply the manufacturing sector. This is because of the availability of evidence and the tendency to associate the Baumol and Tobin analyses with business firms, especially those most likely to trade in government securities.

The hypotheses are presented in two lists—the first consisting of hypotheses involving the interest rate, and the second consisting of those involving receipts (income, sales, or asset size).

HYPOTHESES INVOLVING THE RATE OF INTEREST

Earlier (Sec. 3.3) we reviewed basic monetary analysis in which the elasticity of the demand for money with respect to the rate of interest was unity. The frequently cited association between the velocity of money and the rate of interest, moreover, supports this notion, and other results have reflected and reaffirmed this notion (Sec. 2.2). The explanations advanced for the elasticity measures, however, and the velocity–interest rate association have differed. Of the five explanations listed below, all lead to the prospect of some sort of direct relationship between the sales-to-cash ratio and the rate of interest. The first four depend on a significant decline in the ratio of cash to bonds as interest rates rise in the short or long run. Only the fifth is independent of the prospect of a significant decline in the ratio of cash to bonds as interest rates rise.

The hypotheses concerning the relationship between cash and the rate of interest include the following:

1. *Traditional liquidity preference analysis.* Traditional liquidity-preference analysis dealt with changes in the demand for money with respect to interest-rate changes in terms of a switching between cash and bonds (Secs. 3.3, 4.2), As interest rates rose there was greater inducement for switching out of cash and there was emphasis on the speculative demand for money. The higher rate meant a greater likelihood of a future rise in bond prices and the prospect of a capital gain.

2. *The Latané, Tobin, Baumol analyses.* The Latané, Tobin, and Baumol analyses all explain the interest elasticity of the demand for money in terms of switching between cash and bonds (Secs. 5.2, 8.1, and 8.2). In these explanations the emphasis is on the transactions demand and the reward in the form of higher rates from economizing on the use of cash. Instead of just suggesting a decline in cash in relation to income at higher rates, these explanations implied a decline in the ratio of cash to bonds, as did the liquidity-preference explanations.

3. *The Meltzer analysis.* In the Meltzer analysis involving an interest rate, treating changes in the capital-labor ratio as constant, $M = kr^{-\alpha}S^{\beta}$ or $\ln M = \ln k - \alpha \ln r + \beta \ln S$, where M and S are the stock of money and the flow of sales respectively for the ith firm in the jth industry, and r is the rate of interest. Here "a rise in market (or external) rates which accompanies an increase in sales will result in a less than proportionate increase in cash balances."[20] Apparently the effect of the rate of interest in this model is not too different from that in the liquidity and Latané, Tobin, and Baumol analyses, in that a rise in an external rate contributes to a rise in the sales-to-cash ratio.

4. *The Duesenberry analysis.* In another analysis due to James Duesenberry we are still led to expect switching between cash and bonds as the rate of interest increases, but in the Duesenberry analysis we expect shifts in the long run and "in response to changes in the average rate expected for a period of years—probably best measured by a fairly long moving average of past rates."[21] Duesenberry, moreover, also deals with the question of transactions costs, only somewhat differently from Baumol or Tobin. We may quote Duesenberry with respect to transactions costs and the hypothesis just cited as follows:

---

[20] See Meltzer, "A Cross-Section Study of Business Firms," *op. cit.*, p. 408.

[21] See James S. Duesenberry, "The Portfolio Approach to the Demand for Money and Other Assets," *Review of Economics and Statistics,* Supplement on the State of Monetary Economies, 1963, pp. 12–13.

The direct costs of transactions are only part of the cost of holding Treasury bills. If bills are held only for a few definite, large out-payments—e.g., tax payments—the only additional cost is a little thought on the part of the treasurer. But as soon as a firm embarks on a program of trying to earn interest by predicting cash inflows and outflows, and investing temporary excess funds, it has to bear some overhead costs to keep track of its cash position.

In entering on a program of investing short-term surpluses of funds and in deciding how far to carry it, a firm must balance the expected average return from its bill holdings (or an increment in them) against the overhead cost of controlling its cash position. The expected return will vary with the average rate of interest on bills expected over a period of years. The cost will vary with the tightness of the cash management.

. . . .

A rise in interest rates should push out both the extensive (size of firm) and intensive (closeness of cash management) margins and cause a shift from cash to bills. However, since the costs of cash management are mainly overhead costs, we do not expect much shifting between cash and bills in response to short-run fluctuations in the bill rate. Instead, we expect shifts in response to changes in the average rate expected for a period of years—probably best measured by a fairly long moving average of past rates. Moreover, some of the costs are costs of getting started and learning the tricks of cash management, so that a rise in bill rates may result in a shift from cash to bills. A later fall (even on a long-term basis) may not bring the cash-bill ratio back to its initial position.[22]

5. *An alternative analysis.* In an alternative analysis (Secs. 4.2, 5.2 and 7.2),[23] factors impinge on the prospective stream of returns from additional capital expenditures so as to contribute to an imbalance in the respective rates of return

[22] See Duesenberry, *op. cit.*, pp. 12–13.

[23] See, e.g., William J. Frazer, Jr., "Liquidity Preference, The Demand for Money, and Manufacturing Firms," *Quarterly Journal of Economics*, December 1966; and William J. Frazer, Jr. and William P. Yohe, *Introduction to the Analytics and Institutions of Money and Banking* (D. Van Nostrand Company, Inc., 1966), Chapters 4 and 17.

on various assets. These assets include those with a fixed claim against future income such as cash and bonds, and assets with a residual claim such as capital assets, and the yields (as rates) include allowances for risk, or liquidity, as well as carrying costs, so that at equilibrium the respective rates of return and the market rates of interest are equal. The factors impinging on prospective returns, then, contribute to imbalances in the respective rates of return on extra capital expenditures and liquid assets including bonds, such that the following occur in the case of a rise in the rate of return on the capital expenditures: a general switching out of both cash and bonds; a rise in total assets (and sales); a rise in cash and bond holdings in response to the rise in assets (and sales); and increases in both the sales-to-cash ratio and market interest rates on bonds and debt-type financial instruments. Note, in contrast to the other alternative explanations, this one does not lead to the prospect of a significant decline in the ratio of cash to governments as market interest rates rise.

HYPOTHESES INVOLVING SALES (OR ASSET SIZE)

Earlier, introductory monetary analysis (Sec. 3.2) was shown to involve the notion of equal percentage changes in income (or wealth) and the demand for money. There was also the prospect of other wealth effects (Sec. 3.5) in which the stock of money varied more or less than in proportion to wealth (or income), and a review of empirical evidence supporting the notion of equal proportional changes, at least in broad outline and for over-all aggregative measures (Sec. 6.3). The previous chapter and the present chapter, however, have introduced additional sets of prospective changes in income (or receipts, sales, and wealth) and cash as these may be reflected in the nonfinancial business sector in particular. What follows then is a list of the various explanations for changes involving sales (or asset size) and equal, greater than, or less than proportional changes in the demand for cash by nonfinancial or manufacturing corporations primarily. Of the six explanations listed, some posit the same testable hypotheses, and consequently differ primarily in name only or possibly in terms of the explanation for the phenomena in question. The first two are more conventional, although the first has traditionally been advanced mainly on a priori grounds and the second is in part a result of investigation involving the traditional view and empirical study. The third explanation is the most unique, as far as the changes expected are concerned. The last three call for about the same set of changes, except the last calls for additional changes and applies only to firms beyond some minimum asset size. The testable hypothesis associated with Fisher is no different from the economies-of-size hypotheses as far as the testing of cross-section data is concerned, but it is listed because various investigators have cited it, and because it was apparently one of the first statements of the prospect of increases in the velocity of money in response to increases in wealth.

The hypotheses concerning the relationship between cash and sales (income, asset size or wealth) include the following:

1. *The simple quantity theory hypothesis.* As emphasized in portions of the present chapter and in earlier analysis (Sec. 3.2), the simple quantity theory implies changes in cash in equal proportion to changes in income. In traditional theory the additional cash balances have been called for mainly as a means of effecting the additional transactions. This view is mentioned by numerous writers, and Baumol cites statements by Alfred Marshall, J. M. Keynes, and A. C. Pigou that may be interpreted in support of this view.[24]

2. *The Meltzer hypothesis.* Meltzer does not posit any testable notion that differs from the quantity theory, insofar as he is concerned with the demand for money (M) in relation to sales (S). His empirical studies of the business sector[25] led him to the model $M = \gamma S^\beta$ or $\ln M = \ln \gamma + \beta \ln S$, where $\beta \approx 1$, and where, accordingly, percentage changes in sales call forth approximately equal proportionate change in the demand for money.

3. *The luxury-goods hypothesis.* Friedman and Schwartz apply the Friedman luxury-goods hypothesis (Secs. 3.5, and 6.2)

---

24 See Baumol, *op. cit.*, note 1, p. 550.
25 Meltzer, "A Cross-Section Study of Business Firms," *op. cit.*, pp. 407–408.

directly to the business sector.[26] They hypothesize a wealth or "luxury goods" effect, in the language of consumption theory, according to which the demand for money rises more than in proportion to income.

4. *The Fisher hypothesis.* Irving Fisher wrote of the presence of economies in the use of cash as wealth (or income) increased. We quote him from *The Purchasing Power of Money* (1922) as cited by Baumol:

"It seems to be a fact that, at a given price level, the greater a man's expenditures, the more rapid his turnover; that is, the rich have a higher rate of turnover than the poor. They spend money faster, not only absolutely but relative to the money they keep on hand."[27]

5. *The Baumol and Tobin economies-of-size hypothesis.* Although an economies-of-size hypothesis is questionably deduced from the analyses due to Baumol (Sec. 8.1) and Tobin (Sec. 8.2) in view of the evaluation of the analyses by Brunner and Meltzer, such a hypothesis has been loosely associated with their analyses by analysts such as Meltzer, Heston, and Whalen.[28] Their hypothesis, as stated by Heston, is simply "that cash held for transactions purposes will rise less than proportional to the volume of transactions."

6. *An alternative hypothesis.* An alternative to the above hypotheses involves liquidity and a form of the precautionary motive (Sec. 3.4) in addition to an economies-of-scale notion or a Friedman-type, asset-size ("luxury" goods) effect on overall liquidity. There is the requirement that cash and bank loans on the liabilities side of the balance sheet rise less and government securities more than in proportion to asset size (or sales),

---

[26] See Milton Friedman and Anna Jacobson Schwartz, *A Monetary History of the United States, 1867–1960* (Princeton, New Jersey: Princeton University Press for the National Bureau of Economic Research, 1963), p. 639, and note 12, p. 654. The latter note concerns work due to Richard Selden on sector velocities.

[27] See Baumol, *op. cit.*, note 1, p. 550; also Meltzer, "A Cross-Section Study of Business Firms," *op. cit.*, note 4, p. 410.

[28] See Meltzer, "A Cross-Section Study of Business Firms," *op. cit.*, pp. 409–418; Allan W. Heston, *op. cit.*, p. 120, note 1; and Whalen, *op. cit.*, pp. 423–443.

for firms with assets in excess of 10 million dollars.[29] These firms have been characterized as money-market firms in that they become increasingly interested in government securities as a means of effecting adjustments in the cash account as asset size increases. (The phenomenon in question works this way: (1) there is an asset-size effect on over-all liquidity; (2) the effect, as asset size increases, is less than proportional increases in bank loans and cash, and a greater than proportional increase in noncash liquid assets (such as government securities and similar types of liquid assets); and (3) via a form of the precautionary motive involving the need for cash to meet a subsequent liability, there is a release of cash to noncash liquid assets.

THE INTEREST RATE HYPOTHESES: STATISTICAL RESULTS

The results from the analyses of data are presented as a means of testing the various hypotheses listed above against one another. They are presented in two parts that correspond to the respective sets of hypotheses.

The first part involves results from analyses of quarterly data (seasonally adjusted, 1952–64) for firms with assets in excess of 10 million dollars in the case of the balance-sheet type of data, as reported earlier (Sec. 5.2). For the respective regressions of the ratio of sales to cash, the ratio of government securities to bank loans, and the ratio of cash to governments, all on the rate of interest on long-term, high-grade, corporate bonds, the results are as follows:[30]

Dependent variable	Regression Coefficient	Coefficient of Determination
Ratio of sales to cash	1.0	0.85
Ratio of governments to bank loans	−1.12	0.49
Ratio of cash to governments	0.04	0.01

[29] See William J. Frazer, Jr., "The Financial Structure of Manufacturing Corporations and the Demand for Money," *op. cit.*, pp. 176–183; Frazer, "Firms' Demands for Money," *op. cit.*; and Frazer and Yohe, *op. cit.*, pp. 354–359.

[30] Similar results may be shown for the Treasury-bill rate.

These results are consistent with the prospective relationship between the sales-to-cash ratio and the rate of interest—a percentage change in the latter variable roughly parallels an equal percentage in the former, as the regression coefficient indicates. The results for the regression of the last ratio on the rate of interest, however, are not consistent with the first three explanations in the first set above concerning a switching between cash and governments in response to a rise in the rate of interest, since the regression coefficient 0.04 reflects no significant decline in the ratio as interest rates rise. Neither are they consistent with the fourth explanation, but a bit more must be considered because Duesenberry's hypothesis applies primarily to the long run. The regression results for the ratio of governments to bank loans and the ratio of cash to governments, nevertheless, are consistent with the fifth explanation given above for the velocity–interest rate association. Apparently the first three explanations fail when tested against an alternative.

The Duesenberry explanation also fails the test against the alternatives, when additional data for a long period are considered. For example, over the post-World War II years, when manufacturing firms were active participants in the government-securities markets, the ratio of cash to governments did not decline, even while the yield on Treasury bills underwent a secular increase of over 100 per cent. In particular, from year-end 1952 to year-end 1964, the ratio of cash to bonds for manufacturing corporations actually rose nominally from 1.02 to 1.04, and over these same years the Treasury-bill rate mentioned by Duesenberry increased by over 100 per cent from an average in 1952 of 1.72 per cent to an average in 1964 of 3.54. The average market yield on Treasury bills for the three years preceding year-end 1952 was 1.48 per cent and the average for the three years preceding year-end 1964 was 3.54 per cent, an increase in the three-year average of over 100 per cent.

THE INCOME (OR WEALTH) EFFECT HYPOTHESES:
STATISTICAL RESULTS

Evaluating the statistical results involving the presence or absence of special income (receipts, sales, wealth, or asset size) effects on the velocity of money (or sales-to-cash ratio) are a bit more complicated than evaluating the results for the rate of interest and the ratio of cash to governments. For one thing, relevant cross-section data have been analyzed by several analysts, including Meltzer, Maddala and Vogel, and others, and the analysts named have relied heavily on analyses of data for firms by industry groups. For another thing, the cross-section data that have been analyzed are primarily from two sources—the U. S. Treasury's *Statistics of Income,* and the Federal Trade Commission and Securities and Exchange Commission, *Quarterly Financial Reports for Manufacturing Corporations.* Both sources report balance-sheet and income-statement data for industries and asset-size groups, but only the Treasury reports industry-group data for firms by asset size, and they report fewer size classes for large firms.[31]

To deal with the above complexities, data have been analyzed for both industry groups and for all manufacturing firms by asset size. The results indicate the following:[32] (1) that the relation between changes in cash balances and changes in sales is such that cash balances at first increase in greater proportion than sales or assets and after a point in lower proportion (i.e., the velocity of cash at first declines and then rises); (2) that [among those who have analyzed such data] Meltzer and Maddala and Vogel were led astray by analyzing data for some industry groups in which cash varied significantly more than in proportion to sales and for some

---

[31] The size classes in the Treasury's *Statistics of Income* include only one class for firms with assets over 250 million dollars. The FTC-SEC, on the other hand, reports data for asset-size classes including class 250 million to 1,000 million, and 1,000 million and over, and this additional breakdown of size classes becomes of possible importance in evaluating the results from the analysis of data in some instances. For example, at year-end 1962 the mean value for the asset-size variable in the Treasury's largest class for manufacturing firms was about 987 million, and that for the FTC-SEC largest class was about 2,554 million or over two and one-half times as large. This means, in the case of a tendency for cash to increase less than in proportion to asset size as firms increase in size, that the results from the analysis of the Treasury data are considerably more biased in reflecting asset-size effect than the results from the FTC-SEC data over the upper and major portion of the values the asset-size variable may take on.

[32] Frazer, "Firms' Demands for Money," *op. cit.*

in which cash varied significantly less than in proportion to sales; and (3) that differences in manufacturing industry's demands for cash can be explained by differences in firm sizes.

However, the upturn in velocity comes after the asset-size variable has increased over less than 1 per cent of the values it may take on. The results, therefore, would appear to favor "the alternative hypothesis" listed above, the Fisher hypothesis insofar as it applies to business firms, and the Baumol and Tobin hypothesis of economies of size, but results from additional data may be examined as a means of evaluating these hypotheses.

Representative results from regressing ln cash on ln sales, and ln cash on ln asset size, as well as the additional results from regressing the ratio of governments to bank loans on asset size, are shown in Table 8–1. These results provide evidence mainly in support of "the alternative hypothesis" calling for asset-size elasticity of less than one and a Friedman-type wealth effect on the ratio of government securities to bank loans. They are not, however, inconsistent with the Fisher hypothesis and the economies-of-size hypothesis sometimes identified with Baumol and Tobin. The Brunner-Meltzer analysis of economies of scale in transactions balances, nevertheless, would lead us to question the propriety of identifying an economies-of-size hypothesis with Baumol and Tobin, and of course Tobin denied any particular interest in such a hypothesis.

8.4. SUMMARY

Two somewhat related and commonly cited papers on the transactions demand for cash are by Baumol and Tobin, respectively. Two hypotheses have been identified with the analyses by the respective authors—one an interest-elasticity hypothesis of the demand for money, and another an economies-of-size hypothesis. Brunner and Meltzer question whether the latter hypotheses follow from the Baumol and Tobin analyses. Even so the various hypotheses may be dealt with empirically and tested against other hypotheses concerning interest rates, asset size, and the demand for money.

Apart from critical evaluations of the Baumol and Tobin analyses, both are subject to criticism over the segregation of balances into

Table 8–1. Cash with Respect to Sales, Cash with Respect to Asset Size, and the Ratio of Government Securities to Bank Loans with Respect to Asset Size: Results from Cross-Section Data for Firms by Asset Size

Year	Quarter	Cash with respect to sales for firms with assets of over 10 million dollars, after a ln transformation of the data		Cash (per firm) with respect to asset size for firms with assets over 5 million dollars, after a ln transformation of the data		Ratio (as a percentage) of government securities to bank loans with respect to asset size for firms with assets over 10 million dollars	
		Coefficients of		Coefficients of		Coefficients of	
		Regression (b)	Determination (r^2)	Regression (b)	Determination (r^2)	Regression (b)	Determination (r^2)
1959:	4th	0.83*	0.99	0.86*	1.00	0.31†	0.97
1960:	4th	0.83*	0.99	0.87*	1.00	0.19†	0.97
1961:	4th	0.81*	0.99	0.86*	1.00	0.14†	0.98
1962:	4th	0.84*	0.99	0.87*	1.00	0.17†	0.96
1963:	4th	0.84*	0.99	0.87*	1.00	0.17†	0.98
1964:‡							

* Significantly less than one at the 5 per cent level of significance.
† Significantly greater than zero at the 5 percent level of significance.
‡ Changes in accounting classification of time certificates of deposit resulted in a change in the method of reporting cash and government securities (and similar liquid assets) in 1964.

Notes: The size classes in the FTC-SEC's *Quarterly Financial Report* include, in millions of dollars, under 1, 1 to 5, 5 to 10, 10 to 25, 25 to 50, 50 to 100, 100 to 250,250 to 1,000, 1,000 and over.

Coefficients of determination of 1.00 are the results of rounding coefficients such as 0.99906565 for the fourth quarter 1963.

Source: William J. Frazer, Jr., "Firms' Demands for Money: The Evidence from the Cross-Section Data," *Staff Economic Studies*, No. 25 (Washington, D.C.: Board of Governors of the Federal Reserve System, 1967).

separate stocks for the various classes of balances, namely, transactions, precautionary, and speculative balances. There are questions about the need and desirability for such a separation, as
well as possible interrelationships between the several possible
demands for money.

Baumol's analysis of the transactions demand for money results
from an attempt to apply analysis from the literature on inventory
control to the demand for money. It involves the demand for cash
as dictated by rational behavior and as defined by a square-root
equation. Despite reservations, Baumol was inclined toward some
conclusions from the relationships implied between the variables
in his equation. According to one, the elasticity of the transactions
demand for money was less than unity, given the price level and
an implicit homogeneity of degree one for the demand for money
with respect to prices. According to another, the ratio of transactions to cash (i.e., the velocity of cash) increased in response
to increases in the rate of interest.

Both major and less major criticisms of the Baumol model are
made by Brunner and Meltzer. The major criticisms concern the
model as an incomplete statement of individual firm behavior, its
unsuitability for aggregation, and the portion of the values the
asset-size variable may take on for which cash increases less than
in proportion to asset size. A particularly strong criticism concerns
the length of the time period in the analysis over which the stock
of cash for a single individual or firm is given. The time period is
either very short or the prospect of receiving cash from sales (or
receivables) during the period increases. In dealing with the difficulties imposed by "given cash" and the increasing likelihood of
receiving cash during the period, Brunner and Meltzer view the
square-root equation as a special case and deny the possibility of
deriving an economies-of-size hypothesis for the transactions demand
for money from Baumol's analysis. Other Brunner-Meltzer criticisms deal with Baumol's statements about the use of cash to purchase securities as interest earnings exceed brokerage costs, the
existence of speculative balances, and probabilistic statements
implying precautionary aspects of the demand for money.

Tobin's principal concern is with the interest elasticity of the
demand for money. He says so, and Brunner and Meltzer recog-

nize such a concern. They do not question, moreover, the basis for the interest-elasticity hypothesis, except to question the applicability of the Tobin analysis to changes over time. Even so, according to Tobin, changes in the demand for money are supposed to result from the transfer of transactions-cash balances to transactions-securities balances, as interest rates rise above the cost of switching into and out of interest-bearing assets, given optimizing behavior. In other words, the share of transactions balances in cash varies inversely with the rate of interest and the share in bonds varies directly. There is also a minor basis in the Tobin analysis for the hypothesis whereby switching into bonds results from an increase in income (or asset size). This follows from Tobin's notion that the number of switching transactions for maximizing revenue from bonds increases as size increases and contributes to a rise in the average transactions balances held in the form of bonds. In this latter instance, however, Brunner and Meltzer question the suitability of the Tobin analysis for dealing with cross-section changes, the rate of interest being given. They introduce "jump points" at which economies of size might exist, and they note that jumps become negligible in response to increases in size beyond relatively small sizes. They find that the Tobin model suggests a simple quantity theory sort of hypothesis.

With respect to both the Baumol and Tobin analyses, Brunner and Meltzer find the suggestion of a simple quantity theory hypothesis—i.e., equal percentage changes in both cash and income. Meltzer's own hypothesis of the demand for money runs along this line.

Interest-elasticity hypotheses include, in addition to the one identified with Baumol and Tobin, the following: one from the traditional liquidity-preference analysis, one from a Duesenberry analysis, and an alternative. Only the alternative, however, meets the tests of the interest-elasticity hypotheses against one another. The others call for a significant decline in the ratio of cash to government securities as interest rates rise, either in the short or long run. The alternative hypothesis, on the other hand, involves switching between broader classes of assets—namely, those with fixed claims against future income such as cash and bonds, and those with a residual claim such as plant and equipment. As factors impinge upon the prospective stream of returns from additional capital outlays, the rate of return on these outlays increases. The latter gives rise to switching out of cash and bonds, and to an increase in velocity and the rate of interest as the various assets vary as proportions of the total. The increases in income (and asset size), however, give rise to further increases in cash and bonds.

Asset or sales-elasticity hypotheses include, in addition to the Baumol-Tobin type of economies-of-size hypothesis, the simple quantity theory hypothesis, the Meltzer hypothesis, the luxury-goods hypothesis, the Fisher hypothesis, and an alternative economies-of-size hypothesis with a Friedman-type "luxury" or wealth effect on the ratio of government securities to bank loans. The first three of this latter list of hypotheses call for percentage changes in cash that are equal to or greater than percentage changes in sales (or asset size). They are unsupported by results from analyses of cross-section data for business firms. Some results due to Meltzer, and Maddala and Vogel tend to support the simple quantity theory and Meltzer hypothesis, but the latter analysts are said to have been led astray by analyzing data for some industry groups in which cash varies significantly more than in proportion to sales and for some in which cash varies significantly less than in proportion to sales. The economies-of-size hypotheses fare better in the analyses of data for firms by asset size. They also fare better in the analyses of data for industry groups, when it is recognized that firm size determines industry groups' demands for money. The Fisher hypothesis and the economies-of-size hypothesis with the Friedman-type wealth effect on the ratio of government securities to bank loans are consistent with statistical results. In the latter instance, money balances increase less than in proportion to asset size (or sales), and the ratio of government securities to bank loans varies directly with asset size. These changes involve, as well, a release of cash to government securities as the wealth effect takes the form of reduction in bank loans relative to government securities. The relative decline in bank loans reduces the need for cash to meet liabilities, as size begins to make expert management and operations in government securities worthwhile.

Chapter 9

THE DEMAND FOR MONEY: THE HOUSEHOLD SECTOR

Some studies of the demand for money have dealt with consumers. These have attempted to analyze data for a behavioral group loosely designated as the consumer sector or, in some instances, the household sector. Usually the studies have described changes in the turnover of money balances held by consumers[1] or sought to test hypotheses concerning monetary analysis, frequently as applied to the economy as a whole. Usually, too, the studies have encountered special difficulties with respect to the availability of satisfactory data. They have relied upon data from foreign-country surveys[2] or upon domestic survey data,[3] and, at times, data from the Federal Reserve's flow-of-funds accounts.[4] As Selden has said,

---

[1] See Richard T. Selden, "The Postwar Rise in the Velocity of Money: A Sectoral Analysis," *Journal of Finance,* December 1961, pp. 483–534; and E. R. Wicker, "The Behavior of the Consumer Money Supply Since World War II," *Journal of Political Economy,* October 1961, pp. 437–446.

[2] H. F. Lydall, "Income, Assets and the Demand for Money," *Review of Economics and Statistics,* February 1958, pp. 1–14; and Boris P. Pesek "Determinants of the Demand for Money," *Review of Economics and Statistics,* November 1963, pp. 419–426.

[3] Tong Hun Lee, "Income, Wealth and the Demand for Money: Some Evidence from Cross-Section Data," *Journal of the American Statistical Association,* September 1964, pp. 746–762.

[4] Michael J. Hamburger, "The Demand for Money by Households, Money Substitutes and Monetary Policy," *Journal of ·Political Economy,* December 1966; Selden, *op. cit.,* and Wicker, *op. cit.* The flow-of-funds accounts have been widely publicized since their appearance in annual form in 1955 and quarterly form in 1959. They have from time to time been revised, but the accounts appear in the *Federal Reserve Bulletin,* and back data and revised versions of the accounts are available from the Research Department, Board of Governors of the Federal Reserve System.

257

"it is regrettable . . . that there are no data on cash behavior within consumer subgroups, such as exist for the corporate sector."[5] Hamburger says, "the data [i.e., flow-of-funds data] undoubtedly contain errors, however, it seems very unlikely that corrections for these errors would reverse any major conclusions. . . ."[6]

Households, nevertheless, account for a major portion of money demand—a portion only somewhat less volatile than that of business firms,[7]—and a variety of theories about the determinants of the demand for money apply to them. This chapter, therefore, deals with studies of the demand for money by households, with emphasis on those by Hamburger and Lee, respectively. The former has relied upon time-series data for households in the United States and the latter has relied upon cross-section data from 1957–58 surveys in the United States and upon other data.

---

[5] Selden, *op. cit.,* p. 523.

[6] Hamburger, *op. cit.* All the references to the Hamburger paper are to a pre-publication copy. Hamburger was helpful in discussing the latter copy with the present author and with John A. Doukas.

[7] Percentages of the total money balances held by the household sector and the ratios of personal income to the money balance held by that sector (i.e., measures of the velocity of money for the household sector) are as follows:

Year end	Household money balances as per cent of total	Velocity ratio	Year end	Household money balances as per cent of total	Velocity ratio
1952	47.4	4.45	1958	45.3	5.53
1953	47.4	4.66	1959	46.1	5.74
1954	47.1	4.58	1960	45.6	6.08
1955	46.2	4.87	1961	44.3	6.25
1956	46.4	5.09	1962	46.2	6.25
1957	45.9	5.52	1963	48.1	6.11

Source of data: Board of Governors of the Federal Reserve System and U.S. Department of Commerce.

Over the period 1952–63 the velocity of money for the household sector increased by 37 per cent or from 4.45 to 6.11. Over the same period the ratio of sales to cash for manufacturing corporations with assets over 10 million dollars increased by 50 per cent.

The following topics are dealt with: (1) the determinants of the household sector's demand function for money; (2) changes in the quantity of balances held by the household sector in response to changes in yields (as rates) on both equity and debt-type marketable securities; (3) the relevance of the Tobin notion where, to quote Hamburger, "financial assets are closer substitutes for one another than for other assets, e.g., equities"; (4) the lag pattern in relative first differences in time series for the household sector's real money stock, and for bond and equity yields; (5) the appropriate empirical definition for the money stock, as revealed by regression analyses for the household sector; (6) "the Gurley-Shaw hypothesis that a substantial volume of close substitutes for money created by non-bank financial intermediates has tended to reduce the demand for money,"[8] and (7) income and wealth elasticities of the demand for money as revealed by analyses of cross-section data from the 1957–58 reinterview Surveys of Consumer Finances.

Hamburger deals with the role of yields on bond and equity-type financial instruments, and possible lagged responses in the quantity of money—all as introduced in previous chapters. He concerns himself with the first six of the topics in the preceding list. Lee—dealing with survey data in the tradition of Lydall and Pesek—concerns himself with the last two of the topics in the preceding list,[9] at least, as his results pertain most directly to the demand for money. Hamburger refers to his results as applying in the short run, while Lee views his analyses as applying in the long run, since cross-section data are typically viewed as providing the basis for estimating long-run demand relations. The uses of the designation "short run," however, are varied. Sometimes, "short run" is used to imply an analysis of changes taking place in a relatively short period of time, such as a year, and at times it is used to imply that quarterly data are used rather than annual data. At other times, a long-run demand relation is estimated from quarterly data as in earlier analyses (Sec. 6.5) involving

---

8 See Lee, *op. cit.*, p. 746.
9 See Lydall, *op. cit.*; Pesek, *op. cit.*, and Lee, *op. cit.*

equilibrium or expected values. Hamburger's analyses are of the latter type.

9.1 SOME PRELIMINARY EVIDENCE FROM TIME SERIES

Some results from simple and multiple regression analyses are shown below, prior to the review of Hamburger's evidence from the time series (Sec. 9.2) and Lee's evidence from the survey data (Sec. 9.3). The analyses deal with such determinants of the demand for money by households as income (or some substitute measure) and the rate of interest. The results are presented as a means of providing household-sector results that correspond to others from aggregate data, and the results are interpreted briefly, in some instances, in anticipation of subsequent discussions. In particular, results are shown concerning the velocity–interest rate association and the Latané-Tobin explanation of that association. According to the latter, a rise in the rate of interest calls forth a rise in the velocity of money by encouraging a form of switching into noncash liquid assets and economy in the use of money balances relative to income.

Discussion of preliminary results anticipates some topics that are dealt with by Hamburger and Lee—namely, income (or income and wealth effects), and the definition of money. The income (or wealth) effect does not enter significantly into Hamburger's demand function which results from an analysis of relative first differences of time series, while Lee finds a unit income elasticity of the demand for money. The results, in the latter respect, are not necessarily inconsistent, even though they come from analyses of different kinds of household-sector data. But some review of results pertaining to econometric problems and time-series analyses may facilitate a reconciliation of otherwise apparently irreconcilable results.

The preliminary results are from analyses of data for the eighteen-year period ended in 1965. They are as follows:

$$(1.1) \qquad \ln \frac{Y}{M} = 0.6041 + 0.8108 \ln r \qquad\qquad r^2 = 0.9307$$
$$(0.0553) \qquad\qquad\qquad \text{D-W} = 0.8085$$

$$(1.2) \qquad \ln \frac{M}{A_1} = 0.0084 - 1.0054 \ln r \qquad\qquad r^2 = 0.9301$$
$$(0.0688) \qquad\qquad \text{D-W} = 1.1391$$

$$(1.3) \qquad \ln \frac{M}{A_2} = -0.2434 - 1.1650 \ln r \qquad\qquad r^2 = 0.8456$$
$$(0.0699) \qquad\qquad \text{D-W} = 1.4257$$

$$(1.4) \qquad \ln \frac{M}{S_A} = 1.5662 - 1.7422 \ln r \qquad\qquad r^2 = 0.9333$$
$$(0.1165) \qquad\qquad \text{D-W} = 1.2527$$

$$(1.5) \qquad \ln \frac{M}{C_{\mathrm{MKT}}} = -0.2811 - 0.1470 \ln r \qquad\qquad r^2 = 0.1852$$
$$(0.0771) \qquad\qquad \text{D-W} = 0.4919$$

$$(2.1) \qquad \ln M = 1.6282 + 0.4399 \ln Y \qquad\qquad r^2 = 0.8404$$
$$(0.0479) \qquad\qquad \text{D-W} = 0.3816$$

$$(2.2) \qquad \ln M = 0.1327 + 0.8207 \ln Y - 0.5688 \ln r$$
$$(0.1207) \qquad (0.1713) \quad R^2 = 0.9080$$
$$\text{D-W} = 0.6155$$

Partial Correlations: $r_{12.3} = 0.87$ $\qquad r_{13.2} = -0.65$

$$(2.3) \qquad \ln A_1 = -0.6743 + 1.0144 \ln Y + 0.1771 \ln r$$
$$(0.1733) \qquad (0.2460) \quad R^2 = 0.9672$$
$$\text{D-W} = 0.4547$$

Partial Correlations: $r_{12.3} = 0.83$ $\qquad r_{13.2} = 0.18$

$$(2.4) \qquad \ln A_2 = -0.18907 + 1.1291 \ln Y + 0.1792 \ln r$$
$$(0.1432) \qquad (0.2032) \quad R^2 = 0.9813$$
$$\text{D-W} = 0.6670$$

Partial Correlations: $r_{12.3} = 0.90$ $\qquad r_{13.2} = 0.22$

$$(2.5) \qquad \ln S_A = -4.5633 + 1.5824 \ln Y + 0.1460 \ln r$$
$$(0.1972) \qquad (0.2800) \quad R^2 = 0.9804$$
$$\text{D-W} = 0.6922$$

Partial Correlations: $r_{12.3} = 0.90$ $\qquad r_{13.2} = 0.13$

where Y is personal income, M is demand deposits and currency held by households, r is the yield (as a rate) on Aaa corporate bonds, A_1 is noncash liquid assets narrowly defined to include households' savings accounts and credit and market instruments, A_2 is noncash liquid assets narrowly defined plus life insurance and pension fund reserves, S_A is households' savings accounts at commercial banks and savings institutions, and C_{MKT} is credit market instruments.[10]

Equations (1.2) to (1.5), in contrast to some business sector developments (Sec. 7.3), reflect declines of varying degrees in the holdings of money balances in relation to various classifications of liquid assets, as the rate of interest has risen during most of the postwar years, 1948–65. On the surface, these latter changes would appear to be consistent with the Tobin-Latané type of explanation (Sec. 5.1) for switching between money balances and noncash liquid assets, except possibly in the case of marketable credit-market instruments. Hamburger, however, reports some additional evidence.

Equation (1.1) reflects a velocity–interest rate association for households with a high coefficient of determination, not significantly unequal percentage changes in the velocity of money and the rate of interest, and the prospect of almost equal percentage changes in the money stock and income, the rate of interest remaining constant over time—all as shown on other occasions for the economy as a whole (Secs. 2.2, and 5.1). The results in Eq. (1.1) and the related analysis, however, are inconsistent with the results in Eq. (2.2), due possibly to the presence of multicollinearity—i.e., due possibly to some correlation between income and the rate of interest and the dependence of any predicted value for the money stock on this intercorrelation. Even so, a strong relation apparently exists between the money stock and income as reflected in Eqs. (1.1) and (2.2), although this relation may not be reflected in regression analyses of the time-series variables in question. This is possible because of some relation between income and the rate of interest, and because of the inability of the regres-

---

[10] Credit-market instruments include all market instruments except equity-market instruments, and only debt-type assets are included under the definitions for noncash liquid assets.

The statistical results in the equations are from analyses of data from the following sources: *Survey of Current Business,* August 1965, Table 5; *Federal Reserve Bulletin;* and *Flows-of-Funds: Assets and Liabilities, 1945–65* (Washington D.C., Division of Research and Statistics, Board of Governors of the Federal Reserve System, May 1966).

sion technique to estimate values for the dependent variable separately from the presence of a relation between dependent variables. The point is important, because it helps us to deal with possible discrepancies between estimates from time-series and estimates from cross-section data. Techniques, of course, may be employed to remove some of the correlation in the data, but these may in effect net out underlying relationships.

The regression equation (1.4) and related results throw some light on the question of the statistical definition of money. Here, one may see quite clearly a sharp distinction in the behavior of money defined as demand deposits and currency and the behavior of savings accounts at commercial and savings institutions. The ratio of money balances to savings accounts has declined considerably in the postwar years, possibly in response to a rise in the rate of interest or other factors. This distinctive response would be consistent with Laidler's conclusion (Sec. 6.4.) "that a different theory from that which explains the demand for money does better in explaining the demand for such assets (i.e., time deposits)."

Equation (2.1) reflects the fact that the percentage increase in household money balances was less than half of the percentage increase in personal income in the eighteen-year, postwar period in question. Over-all, multiple regression Eqs. (2.2) through (2.5) reflect fairly strong associations between selected financial stocks and personal income when the rate of interest is in the computational sense held constant. The signs on the interest rates coefficients are consistent with the results reflected in Eqs. (1.1) through (1.4). However, as Laidler has noted (Sec. 6.4), "to include the rate of interest in a linear relationship (or even a loglinear one for that matter) suggests that its effect is merely additional to that of other variables, and that its importance as a determinant of the demand for money declines as the money stock increases." The same criticism, of course, does not apply to an equation such as (1.1), and the high coefficient suggested there between a change in the money stock and a change in the rate of interest need not be inconsistent with the results in Eq. (2.2), in view of a likely interdependence between the independent variables in Eq. (2.2).

9.2   HAMBURGER'S EVIDENCE FROM THE TIME SERIES

The evidence from regression analyses of time-series data pertaining to the demand for money by households consists primarily of that provided by Hamburger. His results are from analyses of quarterly data for the nine-year period, 1952-60. They are transformed into relative first differences, and this—along with the introduction of some special methods for dealing with lagged variables—increases the complexity of Hamburger's work relative to much of the other work on the demand for money. In proceeding, therefore, some special aspects of the method employed by Hamburger are dealt with. Some other methodological aspects of lagged variables were introduced earlier (Sec. 6.5). They are also dealt with in a subsequent chapter (Secs. 10.1 and 10.2).

SOME GENERAL EQUATIONS AND HAMBURGER'S
STATISTICAL PROCEDURE

Hamburger assumes that changes in the money stock of households are responses to market events with some distributed lag. He recognizes that the monetary authorities control the aggregate money stock but that the household sector (or individuals comprising the sector) can very readily adjust its liquid money balances to the "desired" level by effecting changes in the composition of the sector's assets. Consequently, Hamburger cites reasons for the lags:

> Many individuals may be deterred from attempting to take advantage of transitory fluctuations in the variables. The frequency with which it is worth-while to review and alter the portfolio will undoubtedly vary with the investor and depends on such reasons as: (1) the size of the portfolio; (2) his position with respect to the cost of obtaining information and engaging in transactions; and (3) the opportunity cost which he attaches to his time.[11]

It is possible, however, in contrast to the assumption of lagged adjustments, that the so-called lags in some observed series with respect to others reflect the results of adjustments in accordance

---

[11] Hamburger, *op. cit.*

with expectations, as in the business sector (Sec. 7.2), rather than a lagged response, although this prospect is possibly less likely in the case of households, as some of Hamburger's references indicate. Nevertheless, Hamburger proceeds with an equation of a form that is common to those used in dealing with adjustment processes in a variety of behavioral contexts, including those dealing with the demand for money (Secs. 6.4 and 10.1). In this case, the equation is stated as follows:

$$(3) \quad \log M_t^* = \log \gamma_0 + \gamma_B \log \rho_{Bt}^* + \gamma_E \log \rho_{Et}^* \\ + \gamma_y \log Y_t^* + \gamma_W \log W_t^*$$

where the γ's are elasticity coefficients, Y is income, W is wealth, ρ_B is the yield (as a rate) on bonds, and ρ_E is a yield (i.e., the dividend to share price ratio) on equities, M^* is the ratio M'/P'^*, prime symbols are used as superscripts to denote variables valued in nominal units, P' is the price level,[12] and the $*$'s are used as superscripts to denote some hypothetical long-run equilibrium or expected value. Such a long-run value (X^*) is, as commonly defined,

$$(4) \quad X_t^* = (1 - \theta_{Lx}) X_{t-1}^* + \theta_{Lx} X_{t-L}$$

where θ is the adjustment coefficient, the coefficient approaches zero (i.e., $\theta \to 0$) as the time required for the adjustment increases, the coefficient approaches one as the adjustment tends to be immediate, and the subscript L is one or zero (i.e., $L = 1$ or 0) depending on whether the lagged adjustment begins to take place immediately or after one period.

As it would appear, Eq. (4) is a first order difference equation. For a number of observations (i.e., X_t, t sufficiently large), Eq. (4) may be written to define "a weighted average of past and current values of X_t with the weights of all the observations except the first given by $\theta_{Lx}(1 - \theta_{Lx})^{t-i}$," i.e.,

$$X_t^* = (1 - \theta_{Lx})^t X_0 + \sum_{i=1}^{t} \theta_{Lx}(1 - \theta_{Lx})^{t-i} X_{i-L}, \quad t \geq 1.$$

As illustrated later (Sec. 10.1), an equation of this latter form can

---

[12] The only component of M_t^* that has a star superscript is P_t'. This is not true of Y_t^* and W_t^*.

be obtained by defining separate equilibrium or expected values for each period and then by a repetitive substitution of the values so defined for the t periods (t sufficiently large). From weighted averages of past and current values new time series are derived from original series and least-squares regression analysis is then applied to the new series in the form of weighted averages. Different values for the adjustment coefficient (i.e., θ) may be substituted, and these may alter the series in the form of weighted averages, but the set of θ-values for the respective series (or lagged variables) yielding the highest coefficient of determination in the least-squares regression analysis is the set selected as the estimates of adjustment to the respective market variables. In Hamburger's analysis, as implied, each market variable may have a different value for the adjustment coefficient. In the de Leeuw analysis considered in the next chapter (Sec. 10.1), all the independent variables are assigned the same adjustment coefficient. Still, all of the studies involving adjustment coefficients and difference equations, such as (4), suffer from the inability of the procedures to deal with changes in the time dimension of a given lag, such as may occur at upper and lower turning points of cyclical changes (Sec. 7.2).

In Hamburger's empirical analysis estimates are derived for the adjustment coefficients and for the parameters in an equation of the following form:

(5)
$$\bar{M}_t^* = \gamma_T + \gamma_B (\bar{\rho}_{Bt}^*) + \gamma_E (\bar{\rho}_{Et}^*) + \gamma_Y (\bar{Y}_t^*) + \gamma_W (\bar{W}_t^*) + u_t$$

where, in addition to the notation defined earlier, bars over the variables are used to indicate that the variables have been transformed into "relative first differences" or percentage changes. For example, $\bar{M}_t^* = \Delta M_t^* / M_{t-1}^*$, and so on. Hamburger chose relative first differences of the data for two reasons: to possibly reduce the correlation among the explanatory variables and to avoid suppressing the constant term in the regressions. He says, "The bias resulting from the omission of slowly moving variables (e.g., population) from a regression equation is reduced if the constant term is not suppressed."[13] These reasons, however, do not necessarily

---

[13] Hamburger, *op. cit.*

indicate why relative first differences were used rather than logarithmic transformations. Even so, some special features follow from the use of relative first differences: equations of the form of equation (5) are viewed as linear equations; and, at the same time, regression coefficients are viewed as elasticity coefficients, a demand elasticity being the ratio of the percentage change in the money stock to the percentage change in another variable, in a properly identified demand schedule.[14]

In the regression analyses concerning equations of the form of Eq. (5), the variety of independent variables shown in Eq. (5) is considered. In the end, the demand function yielding the most satisfactory results is

$$(6) \qquad \bar{M}^* = \gamma_T + \gamma_B(\bar{\rho}_B^*) + \gamma_E(\bar{\rho}_E^*) + u$$

Results pertaining to regressions in this form are reported as Hamburger considers the role of interest rates, speed of adjustment, and the definition of money. This same order is followed below in considering these topics. Since these topics deal with Hamburger's more satisfactory results, no further attention is given to other topics dealt with by him.

As Hamburger's conclusions and results reveal, the money demand function for the consumer sector for the period 1952–60 is of the form of Eq. (6). The earlier Eqs. (1.1) and (2.2), on the other hand, suggest that income is an important determinant in any demand function for the nominal money balances held by households. It is possible, then, that Eq. (6) does not represent an identified demand relation as usually considered. Possibly Hamburger's linear analysis of relative first differences was a bit too strenuous to reveal a demand relation of the type implicit in monetary theory. Possibly, too, there are some unusual effects resulting from including yields (as rates) on bonds and equities in a linear relation, since these tend to move inversely over time and since, as Laidler states, the inclusion of a rate of interest "as a determinant of the demand for money" in a linear relation

---

[14] In equation (5), the coefficient

$$\partial \bar{M}^* / \partial \bar{\rho}_B^* = \gamma_B$$

suggests some sort of higher order elasticity—a change in the percentage change. One should stop short of this use of partial differentiation.

suggests that "its importance as a determinant of the demand for money declines as the money stock increases." Even so, Hamburger's single-equation model simulates in a very interesting fashion the decline in real money balances held by the household sector over the period 1952–60, when percentage changes in bond and equity yields over the period are considered. It permits, too, an interesting conclusion about a form of switching between money balances and equities as distinct from money balances and bond-type assets.

THE ROLE OF YIELDS

With respect to yields (as rates), regression results are reported, such as the following:

$$(6.1) \quad \overline{M}^* = -0.001 - 0.160 \, \bar{\rho}_B^* - 0.128 \, \bar{\rho}_E^*, \qquad R^2 = 0.446$$
$$t\text{-values:} \qquad\qquad 2.33 \qquad\quad 3.39 \qquad\quad \text{D-}\overline{W} = 1.74$$

(twenty-nine degrees of freedom)

adjustment coefficient for prices[15] (θ_{LP}): 0.30_0
adjustment coefficient for bond yields (θ_{LB}): 0.35_1
adjustment coefficient for equity yields (θ_{LE}): 0.50_0

where, as operational definitions, the money-stock data are seasonally adjusted, M_1 is "the demand deposit and currency holding of the consumer and nonprofit organizations sector in the flow-of-funds accounts," the money stock is deflated by the GNP deflator, ρ_B is an average yield on Aaa rated corporate bonds, ρ_E is a yield on common stocks as indicated by Moody's dividend to price ratio for 125 industrial stocks,[16] and the subscripts on the adjustment

---

[15] An adjustment coefficient is reported for prices, since the series underlying regression Eq. (6.1) include the implicit deflator for Gross National Product, and since the adjustment coefficients appear in series consisting of weighted averages of the original time series.

[16] In addition to the dividend-to-price ratio, Hamburger mentions other measures that may have been included in his demand function for money. Two of these were "(1) the ratio of expected corporate earnings to the price of shares and (2) the dividend yield plus the expected rate of growth in corporate earnings." He notes problems with respect to the introduction of these variables, and then says, "the dividend yield is taken as a first approximation of the yield on equities." Continuing, he says, "the simple correlations

coefficients indicate whether the lagged effect begins initially or after one period with the response pattern thereafter being described by a simple decay function (with a parameter of 0.35 in the case of θ_{LB}). Viewing the above and some additional results, Hamburger notes that the regression coefficients have the expected negative signs, "their numerical values are very close (i.e., their sampling distributions overlap), and the probability that either could be zero is quite low."

Continuing he says, "The elasticity of the demand for money by households with respect to the yield on long-term corporate bonds is approximately −0.15 [actually −0.16 in Eq. (6.1)] while the elasticity with respect to the yield on equities is between −0.14 and −0.13 [i.e., the −0.128 coefficient in Eq. (6.1)]." He notes, further, "the two interest rates used here in conjunction with the level of prices explain nearly one-half of the variation in the relative quarterly first differences in real money balances [for the period 1952_{I}–1960_{IV}]."[17]

Hamburger views the above evidence as supporting the sensitivity of households to changes in the rate of interest. Secondly, and perhaps of most importance in his view, the yields for both debt and equity instruments enter the demand function with regression coefficients of about the same magnitude. He cites this as being inconsistent with the Tobin view that "financial assets are much closer substitutes for money than equities." "On the margin," Hamburger says, "similar changes in the yields on financial assets and equities will induce approximately equal shifts between money and bonds, and between money and equities." The yields on bonds and equities as defined, of course, tend to move inversely over cycles similar to the postwar ones. The above regression coefficients, consequently, suggest that households effect some form of switching from deflated money balances into equities during some periods and from the deflated balances into bonds during others,

---

between the relative first differences in the dividend yield and the two measures listed above (for the period 1952–60) both exceed 0.91. The correlations between their levels exceed 0.99." (See Hamburger, *op. cit.*, note 19.)

[17] See Hamburger, *op. cit.*

with allowance for lags and that the switching into equities would be at the time of relatively low stock prices (and, therefore, high dividend-to-price ratios), at least as far as the yield effects are concerned.

For Hamburger there may be other factors affecting actual bond and stock holdings, but the possible yield effects alone suggest a degree of sophistication that has rarely been attributed to households. However, yields on Aaa bonds rose from an annual average of 2.96 in 1952 to 4.41 in 1960 (a rise of about 49 per cent), and the yield on Moody's industrials declined from 5.55 to 3.48 (a decline of about 37 per cent). And, as a consequence of the net effect of the latter percentage changes, one may very well expect the observed decline in the household sector's real money balances of from 70.02 billion dollars in 1952 to 68.08 billion in 1960.

SPEED OF ADJUSTMENT

As a means of assessing the importance and meaning of the adjustment coefficients, such as those shown with Eq. (6.1), Hamburger presents a table of selected magnitudes for the adjustment coefficients and the approximate number of quarters it takes for certain portions of the adjustment to work themselves out. From this table and the adjustment coefficients shown above (i.e., $\theta_{LP} = 0.30_0$, $\theta_{LB} = 0.35_1$ and $\theta_{LE} = 0.50_0$), the following lagged adjustments are indicated: about 50 to 90 per cent of the adjustment in money balances to changes in prices takes place during the first two to six quarters; about 50 to 90 per cent of the adjustment in response to bond yields takes place during the first three to six quarters; and about 50 to 90 per cent of the adjustment in response to equity yields takes place during the first one to three quarters.

THE DEFINITION OF MONEY

Hamburger deals, as others have (Sec. 6.4) with the question of whether savings accounts should be included in the definition of money. To deal with this question, regression results are produced with different definitions of money and with bond and equity yields as independent variables, as in Eq. (6.1). As a test to determine whether the definition of money should be broadened, similarities or differences in the responses to changes in yields on bonds and equities are sought. In the particular tests undertaken, two definitions of "savings accounts" are employed—one for time and savings deposits at commercial banks (T) and another for savings accounts at all financial institutions (S_A). Adding the first of these components to the narrow definition of money (M_1), and then adding the second separately provides two additional definitions of money—$M_2 = M_1 + T$, and $M_3 = M_2 + S_A$.

Results concerning the question of the definition of money are of the following type:

(6.2)
$$\bar{T}^* = \text{const.} - 0.024\bar{\rho}_B^* - 0.014\bar{\rho}_E^*, \qquad R^2 = 0.199, \text{D-W} = 1.13$$

(6.3)
$$\bar{M}_2^* = \text{const.} - 0.091\bar{\rho}_B^* - 0.060\bar{\rho}_E^*, \qquad R^2 = 0.662, \text{D-W} = 1.37$$

(6.4)
$$\bar{S}_A^* = \text{const.} - 0.089\bar{\rho}_B^* - 0.011\bar{\rho}_E^*, \qquad R^2 = 0.552, \text{D-W} = 1.23$$

(6.5)
$$\bar{M}_3^* = \text{const.} - 0.104\bar{\rho}_B^* - 0.043\bar{\rho}_E^*, \qquad R^2 = 0.743, \text{D-W} = 1.44$$

(6.6)
$$\bar{M}_1^* = \text{const.} - 0.160\bar{\rho}_B^* - 0.128\bar{\rho}_E^*, \qquad R^2 = 0.726, \text{D-W} = 1.79$$

Noting regression coefficients, Hamburger points out that $\bar{S}_A^*$ and $\bar{M}_1^*$ appear to reflect about equal responses to bond yields but extremely different responses to equity yields. Over-all he finds no sufficient similarities in the regression results to warrant extending the definition of money to include either time and savings accounts at commercial banks or to include savings accounts at financial institutions generally. He concludes as follows:

> These results cast considerable doubt on the commonly held belief that the liabilities of financial intermediaries may be treated as if they were perfect substitutes for demand deposits and currency. They suggest that the latter assets, which possess a rather broad range of substitutes, may be viewed as active (or working) assets, whereas savings accounts, whose substitutes are limited primarily to other financial assets, may be viewed as inactive (or idle) assets.

Some Conclusions

Among the principle conclusions to be drawn from the preceding survey of some of Hamburger's results and related analyses are these:

(1) Changes in relative first differences in the yield on high-grade corporate bonds and a dividend-to-price ratio on common stocks explain nearly one-half of the variation in the relative first differences in the real money balances of the consumer and non-profit organization sector for the 1952–60 period, given adjustment coefficients.

(2) Adjustment coefficients indicate that changes in relative first differences in the household sector's real money balances lag behind changes in relative first differences in selected yields (as rates) and prices.

(3) The elasticity coefficients of the demand for real money balances with respect to the interest rate and a dividend-to-price ratio are about equal, as revealed by Hamburger's particular analyses of time series over the period 1952–60.

(4) "On the margin equal percentage increases in the yields on . . . [marketable financial assets] will set off similar shifts from money to bonds and from money to equities."

(5) On the basis of Hamburger's regression results, there is no apparent reason for broadening the empirical definition of money to include time and savings-type deposits.

Hamburger's single equation regression model simulates a decline in the household sector's real money balances during the 1952–60 period in response to an excess in the percentage increase in bond yields over the absolute value of the percentage decrease in equity yields. With respect to the first of the above conclusions, however, Hamburger's single equation model with only relative first differences in yields as independent variables is likely not a demand function for money of the type monetary analysis would lead one to seek. The income (or wealth) effect on the demand for money over the period in question may simply have been suppressed by the technique employed and by factors involving the relation between income and the rate of interest. In fact, results such as reflected in Eq. (1.1) would seem to suggest that something relevant to the demand relation gets suppressed when the variables for the money stock, yields, and income enter differently in alternative regression models. Hamburger goes on to conclude, furthermore, that his marginal analyses of the effects of yield changes "says nothing about the sequence which individual investors will follow in adding assets to their portfolios as their wealth increases."

The evidence—as revealed in the preceding conclusions—does not support the view that liquid assets such as savings accounts should be included in the definition of money and that a short-term interest rate should be used as the principal measure of the opportunity cost of holding money. Hamburger associates such a view with Gurley and Shaw, and other economists. He says, "To the extent that this view provides an accurate description of the substitute relationships among assets, the smaller will be the effects of any given monetary operation and the more we will have to know about the behavior of financial intermediaries."[18]

With respect to conclusions (2) through (4) above, the lagged relations in the series analyzed may reflect a slow speed of adjustment in the household sector's money holdings to selected market variables or they may reflect some pattern of switching on the part of consumers and changes in the composition of assets that give rise to certain yield changes, as would appear to be the case in the business sector. The evidence provided by Eq. (1.2) to (1.4) indicates declines in the household sector's money stock as a proportion of liquid assets (exclusive of equities) as interest rates rise, but Hamburger's evidence of some switching in response to changes in the yield on equities is relevant too. The lagged increase in the sector's stock of equities in response to rises in the dividend-to-price ratio (as in a recession) may be the consumer sector's counterpart to an increase in the flow of capital outlays in the corporate manufacturing sector. The consumer sector's tendency during the postwar years to acquire larger proportions of savings-type assets, nevertheless, distinguishes it from

---

[18] Hamburger, *op. cit.*

the corporate manufacturing sector. Hamburger's evidence on the responsiveness of households to changes in the yields on equities is interesting, too, in that it sheds some light on Tobin's notion about money substitutes—i.e., in Hamburger's analysis the notion that "financial assets are closer substitutes for one another than for other assets, e.g., equities."

Hamburger does not have many conclusions to draw from his analysis and results about monetary policy except the following: "Open market purchases by the monetary authorities, which temporarily lower the yield on bonds, will lead investors to shift out of bonds and into other assets, including physical capital. It is this increase in the demand for physical assets which will ultimately stimulate a temporary increase in economic activity."[19]

Such a conclusion about the effects of an open-market purchase seems to be a common one. It is more extensively dealt with in the next chapter. As viewed there, the conclusion suggests a very inoperative notion about monetary policy.

9.3 LEE'S EVIDENCE FROM CROSS-SECTION AND OTHER DATA

Evidence from cross-section data on the demand for money by households in the United States is provided primarily by Lee in two papers.[20] In his first paper he reports on analyses of data for 729 units consisting of persons living together and pooling their income. The units for which data were analyzed included those responding in early 1957 and a year later to the 1957–58 reinterview surveys[21] and those providing information on the relevant variables. Among the variables were total liquid assets (L)—including

---

[19] See Hamburger *op. cit.* Hamburger identifies this policy position with Brunner and Meltzer, but his over-all analysis supports it as one of his conclusions.

[20] See Lee, *op. cit;* and Tong Hun Lee, "Substitutability of Non-Bank Intermediary Liabilities for Money: The Empirical Evidence," *Journal of Finance,* September 1966, pp. 441–457.

[21] The data are from the Surveys of Consumer Finances. The surveys are conducted through the Survey Research Center, University of Michigan, with the cooperation of the Board of Governors of the Federal Reserve System.

checking deposits (C), savings deposits in banks (SD), savings and loan shares (SL), U. S. Savings Bonds (SB), and credit union and postal savings accounts $(CU + PS)$. Others included disposable income (Y) as measured by the total income of the spending units minus federal income taxes, initial total assets $(TA)_{-1}$ as approximated by summing the recorded assets of spending units at the beginning of 1957, and initial net worth $(NW)_{-1}$ as estimated by deducting liabilities from the recorded assets by spending units at the beginning of 1957. All the latter variables were in thousands of dollars.

Lee's concern with respect to the demand for money by households in the earlier paper is with some selected wealth, income and asset-size effects, as well as with the relevance of the Gurley-Shaw hypothesis, and the effects of some socio-demographic variables. Among the principal conclusions are those pertaining to income elasticity and the Gurley-Shaw hypothesis. In the first instance, he says, "income elasticities of the demand for money in the form of liquid assets as a whole, checking accounts, savings deposits, savings and loan shares, and credit and postal savings accounts, are approximately unity. . . ." With respect to the Gurley-Shaw hypothesis, Lee concludes as follows:

> The present study, though not aimed at a direct test of the Gurley-Shaw hypothesis, raises questions concerning the adequacy of the hypothesis that the rapid growth of non-bank financial intermediaries together with the large volume of their liabilities has had the effect of substituting non-bank intermediary liabilities for money and thereby reducing the demand for money. In particular, we argue that a relative increase of interest bearing liquid assets in household money holdings may be attributable to a rise in wealth and readily available liquid assets for the past decades rather than to the substitution between the liabilities of commercial banks and other non-bank financial intermediaries as Gurley and Shaw maintain.[22]

The regression equations in Lee's first study are nonlinear as a result of the addition of a squared income variable, e.g.,

---

[22] Lee, "Some Evidence from Cross-Section Data," *op. cit.*, p. 760.

$$
\begin{cases}
(1) \\
\quad L = -415.5 + 447.1Y - 19.6Y^2 + 1.69\,(NW)_{-1}, \qquad R^2 = 0.289 \\
(2) \\
\quad L = -232.2 + 290.1Y - 15.1Y^2 + 161.2(TA)_{-1}, \qquad R^2 = 0.261
\end{cases}
$$

where the variables are those defined earlier and all the regression and determination coefficients are significant at the 5 per cent level as indicated by a conventional F-test (see F-ratio, Sec. 2A.3) instead of the t-test. Apparently, the introduction of the squared income terms does not affect the conclusions greatly. Lee says it gives a better fit, as might the introduction of almost any remotely relevant variable. There apparently were no attempts at the use of logarithmic transformation. Elasticities, therefore, were estimated by the method of taking the product of the ratio of the mean values of two variables and the inverse of their corresponding regression coefficients.[23]

WEALTH (OR INCOME AND WEALTH) EFFECTS

In dealing with wealth (or income and wealth) effects, Lee proceeds via a stream of thought that evolves from Alfred Marshall, John Maynard Keynes, Alvin Hansen, and Milton Friedman. Ultimately he focuses on a variant of an earlier (Sec. 6.1) demand relation in which wealth enters as a determinant. In proceeding along these lines, Lee focuses on his own variation of an "income-wealth" effect that turns out to be essentially a wealth effect after allowance for human capital as well as a measure of total assets.

The Marshall-Keynes-Hansen-Friedman stream[24] of thought was outlined as follows:

> The influence of assets on the demand for money was originally indicated by Marshall . . . in his illustration of the "Real Balance" equation of money. As Marshall put it: ". . . suppose that the inhabitants of a country, taken one with another (and including therefore all varieties of character and of occupation) find it

---

[23] E.g., in the case of the income elasticity of liquid assets,

$$
\frac{\partial L}{\partial Y} \frac{(\text{mean } Y)}{(\text{mean } L)} = \frac{\partial L/(\text{mean } L)}{\partial Y/(\text{mean } Y)}
$$

[24] Lydall dealt with the pre-Friedman portion of this stream in his 1958 article. (See Lydall, *op. cit.*, pp. 1–3; and see also Sec. 3.5.)

just worth their while to keep by them on the average ready purchasing power to the extent of a tenth part of their annual income, together with a fiftieth part of their property. . . ." In this example, he stressed assets as well as income as determinants of money holdings but the asset effect was not introduced explicitly by Marshall (and forgotten wholly by his followers) in the formulation of the real balance equation. The strict version of the real balance equation of money which treats income as the only constraint on money balances has subsequently been subjected to considerable criticism by many economists. In the *General Theory*, Keynes . . . split the money demand function into two parts for his analytical convenience: the transactions demand for money as a function of income and the asset demand for money as a function of the rate of interest. Aside from a technical question of the feasibility of splitting the money demand function in an empirical sense, the aggregate money demand function was considered to include both income and the rate of interest as its determinants. From historical observation, however, the quantity of money demanded does not seem to hold a dependable relationship to national income even with a proper account of the movements of the rate of interest. Hansen . . . , apparently recognizing this instability as due to the omission of the wealth variable and noting Marshall's anticipation of the wealth effect, advanced the hypothesis that the total demand for money as money balances was a function of income, the rate of interest, and wealth. . . . Friedman . . . , on the other hand, restated the quantity theory as a theory of the demand for money, and his subsequent empirical study . . . introduced permanent income as the explicit constraint on the demand for money. Permanent income in Friedman's money demand function was defined as the net return on a stock of human and non-human wealth, thereby introducing conceptually a combination of the effect of income earned from human wealth and the effect of non-human wealth through its yields as the constraint on money balances.[25]

In the case of Friedman's per capita money balances (M_t), expressed as a function of per capita permanent income (Y_t^p), Lee writes in symbolic form:

(3) $$M_t = RY_t^p$$

He assumes, "since an estimate of permanent income is given by

---

[25] Lee, "Some Evidence from Cross-Section Data," *op. cit.*, pp. 746–747.

278   The Demand for Money

a weighted average of past incomes with exponentially declining weights for the more remote past," that

$$(4) \qquad Y_t^p = \alpha Y_t + \alpha\lambda Y_{t-1} + \alpha\lambda^2 Y_{t-2} + \alpha\lambda^3 Y_{t-3} + \ldots,$$
$$\alpha < 0, \qquad 0 < \lambda < 1$$

Using Koyck's scheme,[26] Eq. (4) is reduced by Lee to

$$(5) \qquad Y_t^p = Y_t + Y_{t-1}^p$$

After substituting the latter expression for per capita permanent income in Eq. (3),

$$(6) \qquad M_t = k\alpha Y_t + k\lambda Y_{t-1}^p$$

Lee, next, assumes that Y_{t-1}^p is an increasing linear function of nonhuman wealth (i.e., $Y_{t-1}^p = cW_{t-1}$). Eq. (6), thus, becomes

$$(7) \qquad M_t = KY_t + K'W_{t-1}, \qquad K = k\alpha > 0, \ K' = k\lambda c > 0$$

Lee, then, views Eq. (7) as a statement of an "income-wealth hypothesis that the demand for money is an increasing function of income as well as wealth."[27] This view would especially seem to be motivated by the above review of the antecedents to some aspects of contemporary monetary analysis.

There are complications, however, with respect to the analysis leading to an incorporation of both income and wealth variables in the money demand function. With the rate of interest constant (i.e., r = constant), the discounted income (i.e., Y_t/r) is likely little more than the value of human capital in Friedman's scheme. Consequently, in Eq. (7) Lee is mainly expressing per capita money balances as a function of wealth, with total wealth denoted separately as human and nonhuman wealth.

Perhaps no more is gained by the preceding exercise than some insight into antecedents to contemporary expressions of the demand for money as a function of wealth, the rate of interest constant. Lee, nevertheless, cites income and net worth regression coefficients, of the type shown in Eqs. (1) and (2), for total liquid

---

[26] Lee cites L. M. Koyck, *Distributed Lags and Investment Analysis* (Amsterdam: North-Holland Publishing Company, 1954).

[27] Lee, "Some Evidence from Cross-Section Data," *op. cit.*, p. 756.

assets and the components comprising the total. He finds them to be positive and highly significant, and to confirm the need to include both income and wealth in the demand function for money. No evidence is given on the likely correlation between the net worth and income variables[28] and the possible redundancy resulting from including both in the demand function. The estimates of the current income elasticity of the demand for money, however, are consistent with basic monetary analysis (Sec. 3.2); "the current income elasticities, evaluated at mean values for liquid assets as a whole and also for each component of liquid assets with the exception of U. S. savings bonds, are significantly greater than zero but are not different from unity."[29]

The Gurley-Shaw Hypothesis

In his first paper Lee reviews some analysis due to Gurley and Shaw from which a testable hypothesis follows. The review, also, anticipates a test he wishes to apply in dealing with the hypothesis. In particular, regression results are reviewed for a given set of determinants of the demand for money narrowly defined to include only commercial bank liabilities. These are then compared with those resulting from regressing other liquid

---

[28] Results from regressing sales per firm (S_A) on assets per firm (A_A), and from regressing stockholder's equity per firm (E_{SH}) on assets per firm, suggest that asset size, income, and net worth (or owners' equity) are all highly correlated, especially for manufacturing firms. Typical results are as follows:

Period

4th qtr. 1959	$\ln E_{SH} = -0.41 + 1.00 \ln A_A,$	$r^2 = 1.00$
	(0.01)	
4th qtr. 1963	$\ln E_{SH} = -0.49 + 1.01 \ln A_A,$	$r^2 = 1.00$
	(0.01)	
4th qtr. 1959	$\ln S_A \quad = \quad 0.74 + 0.91 \ln A_A,$	$r^2 = 1.00$
	(0.01)	
4th qtr. 1963	$\ln S_A \quad = \quad 0.67 + 0.93 \ln A_A,$	$r^2 = 1.00$
	(0.01)	

The data are of the type for which results are shown in Chapter 7 for firms with assets over 5 million dollars.

Source of data: U. S. Federal Trade Commission and Securities and Exchange Commission.

[29] Lee, "Some Evidence from Cross-Section Data," *op. cit.*, p. 756.

assets on the same set of determinants to see whether the determinants explain the variability of money to any greater extent than the variability of other assets. With respect to the Gurley-Shaw analysis and the test, Lee says:

> In recent years, there has been increasing concern over the rapid growth of non-bank financial intermediaries which have provided a substantial volume of liquid assets closely substitutable for money. Gurley and Shaw . . . in particular argue that the presence of a large volume of non-bank financial liabilities has had the effect of reducing the demand for money provided by the banking system, thereby curtailing the effectiveness of monetary policy that operates primarily through the commercial banking system. One implication of their assertion is that the determinants of the money demand equation would explain the variability of the demand for liquid assets more fully than that of the demand for money defined narrowly to include only the commercial bank liabilities.[30]

The results from the test of the Gurley-Shaw hypothesis that consist of a comparison of coefficients of multiple determination are described as follows:

> The R^2 of the liquid asset equation . . . is smaller than that of checking deposits. Furthermore, a direct comparison between checking deposit functions and other deposit functions indicates that the determinants of the demand for money explain much more of the variations in checking deposits than the variations in other liquid asset components. These all suggest that the reductions of the demand for money that are attributable to the growth of non-bank financial intermediaries are not likely to be very significant, and that the predictability of the demand for money is not to be improved significantly by introducing the liabilities of non-bank financial intermediaries in the definition of money. Since Gurley and Shaw also refer to the possibility that

---

[30] *Ibid.*, p. 748. He cites the following four works due to Gurley and Shaw: Gurley, John G., and Shaw, E. S., "Financial Aspects of Economic Development," *American Economic Review*, September 1955, 515–538; "Financial Intermediaries and the Saving-Investment Process," *Journal of Finance*, March 1956, 257–276; *Money in a Theory of Finance.* Washington, D.C.: Brookings Institution, 1960; and "The Growth of Debt and Money in the United States, 1800–1950: A Suggested Interpretation," *Review of Economics and Statistics*, August 1957, 250–262.

the growth of financial intermediaries may have brought about qualitative changes in the liabilities of financial intermediaries, one might wonder whether a consumer preference for liquid asset components provided by non-bank intermediaries may be greater than for checking deposits with respect to income. Although the numerical income elasticity for savings and loan shares appears larger than that for checking deposits, its variance is much larger than that of checking deposits, and the null hypothesis of unitary income elasticity can not be rejected statistically for both checking deposits and savings and loan shares. Furthermore, income elasticity for checking deposits is greater than that for the rest of the liquid asset components and the liquid assets as a whole.[31]

LEE'S LATER EVIDENCE

In Lee's second paper, as cited above, his position with respect to the Gurley-Shaw hypothesis is reversed, although no explanation is given for the change, except possibly that implicit in the introduction of rates of interest. On this latter occasion evidence is reported from multiple regression analyses of time-series data (after a logarithmic transformation) and from additional survey data. The time-series data are annual for the years 1934–64 (excluding 1942–45) and the cross-section data are from the 1956–59 Surveys of Consumer Finances.[32] On this second occasion—after introducing regional interest rates in the analyses of cross-section data—Lee concludes, among other things, that "the empirical evidence from the various data investigated in this paper unequivocally substantiates the substitution hypothesis of Gurley and Shaw." Continuing, he says, "The demand for money is negatively related to changes in yields on non-bank intermediary liabilities, and it has in fact been reduced by quality changes in non-bank intermediary liabilities as Gurley and Shaw argue."

9.4 SUMMARY

Studies of the demand for money by the household sector have encountered difficulties in obtaining satisfactory data. Selden, for

---

[31] Lee, "Some Evidence from Cross-Section Data," *op. cit.*, p. 759.

[32] For a discussion of 1963–64 survey results and "Consumer Preferences for Holding Different Assets," see Dorothy S. Projector and Gertrude S. March 1956, 257–276; *Money in a Theory of Finance*, Washington, D.C.: Board of Governors of the Federal Reserve System, 1966).

example, has spoken of the lack of "data on cash behavior within consumer sub-groups," and Hamburger speaks of flow-of-funds data as "undoubtedly containing errors." The sector accounts for a major portion of the aggregate money stock, however, and the quality of the available data has not thwarted some analysts. Results from regression analyses of data for households in the United States, in fact, have been provided by Hamburger and Lee. Hamburger's results are from analysis of postwar, quarterly, flow-of-funds data, after transforming the data into relative first differences. He introduces lagged variables. Lee's results, on the other hand, are from analyses of cross-section data obtained from a 1957–58 reinterview survey and from other data. In one instance, he analyzes data for 729 units consisting of persons living together and pooling their income. These analyses of survey data are in the tradition of analyses of data for foreign countries by Lydall and Pesek.

The statistical results and related analysis—along with other preliminary results—provide the basis for some conclusions with respect to the demand for money by households and with respect to monetary analysis. After relative first differencing and the introduction of lagged variables, a demand relation is provided with bond and equity yields as the main determinants of the demand for money. The bond-yield elasticity and the equity-yield elasticity coefficients are found to be of about the same magnitude, and these in turn suggest forms of switching between money balances and bonds as well as between money balances and equities. This is in contrast to the views of some analysts that debt-type assets are better substitutes for money than other assets such as equities. There is, moreover, no evidence in support of broadening the definition of money, such as may be obtained from regressing money balances (narrowly defined) and broader classes of assets on a given set of independent variables so as to determine the possible presence of different responses to the independent variables.

The inclusion of only yields in a demand function for money seems unusual. Even so, a single equation model including these yields simulates some unusual changes over the 1952–60 period. In that period average Aaa bond yields rose 49 per cent, and an average of yields on Moody's industrials declined 37 per cent, so as to call for a decline in real money balances, which did in fact occur. The exclusion of wealth (or income) effects from the demand function is unusual, too, but it can possibly be explained by the changes during the period and the strenuousness of the regression technique for dealing with them. Indeed, preliminary results from analysis of logarithmically transformed data reflect a velocity–interest rate association—all in such a way as not to violate too strongly the notion of income-elasticity and interest-elasticity coefficients of the demand for money of unity. Also, an income elasticity of the demand for money of unity is found as a result of analysis of cross-section data.

The velocity–interest rate association appears to be consistent with the Latané-Tobin type of explanation whereby a rise in bond yields calls forth switching from money balances to bond-type assets, all in relation to income. This is the case with respect to households, because many classes of liquid assets increased in relation to money balances over the period in question. There is no conclusive evidence on the switching between cash and equities. In this case, the equity yields declined and the switching favored money balances. There are possible fundamental differences in the sort of switching phenomena actually exhibited by households and business firms over a period such as the postwar one.

Hamburger reports lagged relations between the money stock and other variables for which data were analyzed. These may reflect lags in adjustments of money stocks to changes in the independent variables or they may reflect a form of switching whereby the changes in the asset structure give rise to yield and other changes rather than the reverse. Even so, there are likely differences between the business and household sectors as comparative results reveal.

Hamburger's results with respect to switching between money balances and equity-type assets as well as debt-type assets shed some light on the Gurley-Shaw hypothesis, and Lee's results from cross-section data also concern this hypothesis. Lee, in one instance, raises questions about whether the rapid growth of the liabilities of nonbank financial intermediaries has had the effect of substituting nonbank intermediary liabilities for money and thereby reducing the demand for money. He finds that income elasticities of the demand for money and other debt-type assets are about unity and this provides him with an indirect means of rejecting the hypothesis. But, in another instance, he supports the hypothesis. Hamburger criticizes the hypothesis because his debt and equity yield elasticities are approximately the same, and he finds no basis for viewing the liabilities of nonbank financial intermediaries as unique money substitutes.

Lee introduces into his earlier analysis an "income-wealth" effect. He traces the evolution of the notion via Marshall, Keynes, Hansen, and Friedman. He then indicates support for the hypothesis after presenting some analysis and finding significant regression coefficients for both net worth (as a substitute variable for wealth) and income. However, there are complications. In the hypothesis, Lee is mainly expressing money balances as a function of wealth, with total wealth denoted separately as human and nonhuman wealth.

Chapter 10

SOME STATISTICAL RESULTS, POSSIBLE ADJUSTMENT LAGS, AND MONETARY POLICY

Studies of the demand for money have been conducted for a variety of reasons—as a possible means of discovering stable demand relations and advancing economics as an empirical science, of discovering empirical truths or laws for establishing rules or guides for the conduct of monetary policy, and of shedding light upon the effects of monetary policy. Indeed, many such studies have been mentioned in earlier chapters. In this chapter, however, some additional studies are introduced that have emphasized the demand for money and monetary policy, and/or the speed of adjustment in the quantity of money demanded in response to changes in the interest rate and other variables.[1]

The causal sequences suggested by the studies in question and the speed of adjustment notion are particularly relevant to questions concerning monetary policy, as is the particular measure adopted to indicate changes in monetary policy. The presence or absence of causal sequences is important because of the prospect of influencing the demand for and velocity of money with the view to influencing the levels of expenditures, employment, and so on. The presence or absence of lags in the effects of policy

---

[1] See, e.g., Frank de Leeuw, "The Demand For Money—Speed of Adjustment, Interest Rates, and Wealth," *Staff Economic Studies* (Washington, D.C:. Board of Governors of the Federal Reserve System, 1965), also republished in George Horwich, ed., *Monetary Process and Policy: A Symposium* (Homewood, Illinois: Richard D. Irwin, Inc., 1967); Patric H. Hendershott, "The Demand for Money: Speed of Adjustment, Interest Rates, and Wealth—A Sequel," *Staff Economic Studies* (Washington, D.C.: Board of Governors of the Federal Reserve System, 1965).

changes is related to questions concerning the adequacy of monetary policy as a control device—a long lag suggesting shortcomings in the control device.[2] With respect to responsiveness to interest-rate changes, Daniel Brill—Senior Adviser to the Board and Director of Research, Board of Governors of the Federal Reserve System—may be quoted as follows:[3]

> Friedman's model predicts poorly in the postwar period largely, I think, because it grossly underestimates the role of interest rates as a factor *influencing* [italics supplied] the demand for money. An impressive number of empirical studies undertaken during recent years—including those of Brunner and Meltzer, de Leeuw and Teigen, to name a few—have found that interest rates on money substitutes play a prominent role in the public's money demand function.

_____

> Velocity depends, as does money demand, on rates of interest.

_____

> There is a way out of this difficulty [i.e., the difficulty of satisfying the "crude empiricists" of Washington], but it involves getting down to the serious business of estimating expenditure responses—category by category—to changes in interest rates and other financial variables.

_____

> There seems little doubt that interest rates are empirically important in the demand function [for money], and we seem to agree that a wealth or permanent income variable helps to explain money holdings. But there remains some question about the appropriate interest rate or rates to include, and the role of cur-

_____

[2] On monetary policy and time-lag problems, see William J. Frazer, Jr., and William P. Yohe, *Introduction to the Analytics and Institutions of Money and Banking* (Princeton, New Jersey: D. Van Nostrand Company, Inc., 1966), Chapter 26. Note the works cited in the latter text, and see also Milton Friedman, "The Lag in Effect of Monetary Policy," *Journal of Political Economy*, October, 1961, pp. 447–466; and Karl Brunner and Allan H. Meltzer, *The Federal Reserve Attachment to the Free Reserve Concept* (Washington, D.C.: U. S. Government Printing Office, 1964), pp. 31–50.

[3] The quotes are from Daniel H. Brill, "Criteria for Conduct of Monetary Policy: Implications of Recent Research," *Staff Economic Studies* (Washington, D.C.: Board of Governors of the Federal Reserve System, 1965), pp. 9–10, p. 17, p. 18, and p. 20, respectively. This study is also republished in Horwich, *op. cit.*

rent income, along with wealth or permanent income as an argument in the function.

An equation system condensed from the larger financial sector model incorporated in the Brookings Quarterly Economic Model of the United States also has been used to deal with the effects of an interest-rate variable on the demand for money and the level of income.[4] Gary Fromm, in particular, used the condensed system to illustrate the potential usefulness of the larger, multiequation model in its "preliminary form." Using parameters in the model for the 1961–62 period and inserting values for the variables for government expenditures, population, and so on, Fromm introduces late 1965 Federal Reserve actions with respect to increases in "the Federal Reserve Banks' discount rates and the maximum allowable rate payable on time deposits" as a means of simulating effects on real GNP and other variables. He concludes from the simulation "that the Federal Reserve Board's policy moves are *restrictive*, whether taken alone, or in combination with the increase in the maximum allowable rate payable on time deposits."

The particular measure adopted to indicate policy changes is important and relevant to the present literature in several respects. For one, a money demand function incorporating interest-rate and income arguments and a method revealing a lagged response to interest-rate changes may simply reflect a velocity–interest rate association and a change in monetary policy or a tendency for changes in the stock of money to vary less than in proportion to income, at times of cyclical and/or secular expansion in economic activity. For example, de Leeuw observes fluctuations in long-term rates that lead inverse fluctuations in real per capita demand deposits.[5] He says, "To the naked eye, then, there seems to be some simple evidence of a lagged reaction of money holdings to

---

[4] See Gary Fromm, "Recent Monetary Policy: An Econometric View," *National Banking Review*, March 1966, pp. 299–306. For the larger model, see Frank de Leeuw, "A Model of Financial Behavior," *The Brookings Quarterly Econometric Model of the United States*, James S. Duesenberry, Gary Fromm, Lawrence R. Klein, and Edwin Kuh, eds. (Chicago and Amsterdam: Rand McNally and Company, and North-Holland Publishing Company, respectively), pp. 465–530.

[5] See de Leeuw, "Demand for Money," *op. cit.*

interest rates." Yet, these changes could simply be the result of parallel and equal percentage changes in the income velocity of money and interest rates and a tendency for the monetary officials to vary the money stock less than in proportion to income at times and more than in proportion at other times. The stock of money per capita may simply appear to be lagging independently of any adjustment lag in the demand for money in response to interest-rate changes.

In another instance, the measure adopted to indicate policy changes may imply an absence of any lag in the implementation of a monetary policy. For example, if either changes in the rate of interest or the velocity of money are adopted as indicators of changes in monetary policy (Sec. 2.1), then there is no lag in the implementation of a change in policy, since the change in question is simply one of definition. Further, if money is viewed as being highly liquid and readily adjustable with respect to the portion of balances held in relation to nominal income (or assets), then an absence of a lag in the adjustment of the desired quantity is implied (Sec. 9.2), and the identification of the demand function for money is facilitated, in a rather crude way, at least (Secs. 2.2 and 2A.2). On previous occasions (e.g., Secs. 2.2 and 3.2), economic agents have been said to be in a position to adjust their money holdings towards desired levels by spending more or less. The discrepancy between "actual" and desired balances has been assumed to be relatively small.

With respect to the use of empirical demand functions for forecasting, Brill notes one such instance in which a least-squares regression line was "described as fitting 'reasonably well' " but in fact missed "the only recession in the period covered" and achieved "errors of up to 22 billion in annual forecast." Prediction is of course important, but a more fundamental matter with which many of the monetary analyses surrounding regression results deal is that of "explanation" in the operational sense as distinct from the least-squares computational sense. This is the sort of analysis being dealt with where the interest rate is said to "influence" the quantity of money demanded and play a "prominent role" in the public's money-demand function.

Against the above background, analysis, statistical results, and conclusions are dealt with as they concern two studies involving lags in the adjustment of desired currency and demand-deposit holdings in response to changes in other selected variables. An alternative explanation for the behavior of time series for interest rates and the money stock in relation to an income (or wealth) constraint was introduced earlier (Secs. 7.2 and 7.3). It reappears in the next chapter. There the explanation will also be shown to involve the problem of the identification of a money-demand function and a broader definition of monetary policy than that suggested by the use of tools, such as open-market operations, alone.

One of the studies in question is by de Leeuw and the other is a sequel to the de Leeuw study by Hendershott.[6] De Leeuw, in his study, uses two slightly different techniques. The first technique is regarded by de Leeuw as providing an "adequate first approximation to any plausible lag distribution." The second is regarded by Hendershott as de Leeuw's most promising technique. The latter technique is dealt with by Hendershott. He also employs an additional technique. The techniques are introduced in the subsequent sections in their preceding order.

10.1 DE LEEUW'S ANALYSIS AND INITIAL RESULTS

De Leeuw in effect proceeds, as in an earlier section (Sec. 6.5), with the assumption of an equilibrium demand function and the assumption of a lag in the adjustment of actual money holdings to equilibrium holdings:

(1) $$M_t^* = \alpha_0 + \alpha_1 r_t + \alpha_2 Y_t$$

where M_t^* is the estimated equilibrium money stock, Y_t is the relevant income or wealth variable, and r_t is the rate of interest; and

(2) $$M_t - M_{t-1} = (1 - k)(M_t^* - M_{t-1})$$

where $M_t - M_{t-1}$ is the change in the money stock, $(1 - k)$ is a constant fraction of the discrepancy between the long-run desired holdings, M_t^*, and the observed stock of the previous period, M_{t-1}. Substituting the right-hand member of Eq. (1) into Eq. (2),

---

[6] See the references cited in note 1 on page 285.

(3) $M_t = kM_{t-1} + (1-k)\alpha_0 + (1-k)\alpha_1 r_t + (1-k)\alpha_2 Y_t$

or in general form, using vector notation,

(3.1) $M_t = kM_{t-1} + (1-k)(b_1 \dots b_n) \begin{pmatrix} x_1 \\ x_2 \\ \cdot \\ \cdot \\ \cdot \\ x_n \end{pmatrix} + u_t$

which is the common form of an equation with one lagged variable
for generating a distribution over time, where the coefficient of the
lagged variable is an indicator of the speed of adjustment, and
where $(b_1 \dots b_n)$ is a vector of n coefficients (also denoted **b**),
$(x_1 \dots x_n)^T$ is a vector of n variables (also denoted **x**), and u is
the unexplained residual. As the lag coefficient approaches zero
(i.e., $k \to 0$), the adjustment tends to be immediate, and as the
coefficient approaches one, the adjustment tends to be slow.

De Leeuw deals with matters other than the speed of adjustment, but he concludes that "probably the strongest evidence . . .
is on the matter of speeds of adjustment." As de Leeuw notes,
and as Hendershott emphasizes, "Knowledge of the length of the
lag is important to monetary policy-makers because the timing
of the impact of open market operations on interest rates depends
on the lag." Continuing, Hendershott says,

> If the response of money holders to interest rate changes is
> virtually immediate, an open market purchase will shift interest
> rates to a lower level (until the effect of the lower rates on the
> supply of new securities feeds back on the interest rates). But
> if there is a considerable lag in response, a purchase will produce
> a fluctuation in interest rates—a downward movement will be fol-
> lowed by a return toward the prepurchase interest rate level.[7]

Apparently, the rationale in the case of an open-market purchase is
this: as the money stock increases in response to open-market
operations, holders of balances in excess of "desired" balances will
buy bonds and lower the rate of interest and the latter will
continue low until new issues of securities reach the market. This
latter example, of course, is quite unrealistic in terms of the way

---

[7] See Hendershott, *op. cit.*, pp. 1–2.

policy-makers have historically issued directives concerning open-market operations and credit and monetary conditions, and in terms of the historical use of open-market operations as an instrument of general credit control. Historically, some form of directive has been issued to the manager of the open-market account in such terms as added "ease" or "tightness" of credit, and, indeed, given certain market conditions, a purchase of securities may even be effected in the process of effecting a policy of additional tightness. One cannot tell from the use of credit control tools alone what sort of credit or monetary policy is being carried out (Sec. 11.2).

De Leeuw reports results concerning a regression equation of the form of Eq. (3.1), after an ordinary least-squares regression analysis and after the use of three-pass least squares. He analyzes quarterly data[8] (seasonally adjusted) for the 1949–63 period, where interest rates are in percentages (e.g., four per cent is 4) and the dollar magnitudes are expressed in real, per capita form—i.e., "they are deflated by population and by a measure of the general price level (the GNP deflator)." The deflation by population, despite its role as a poor predictor of money demand (Secs. 6.2 and 6.4), is motivated by de Leeuw's desire to reconcile the data with theories dealing with the determinants of the quantity of money demanded by single economic units such as households and business firms as in earlier analyses of the transactions demand for money (Chapter 8).

---

[8] De Leeuw describes the data as follows: "The data consist of quarterly averages of currency in circulation, demand deposits, and time and savings deposits at commercial banks, all seasonally adjusted; yields on long-term U. S. securities, Treasury bills, and time deposits; national income seasonally adjusted at annual rates; and "wealth" defined as stocks of tangible goods (except those owned by the Federal government) plus net claims by the public on the rest of the world plus net claims by the public on the Federal Reserve System and the Federal government. For the time deposit yield and the wealth series quarterly levels were interpolated from annual figures—annual ratios of interest payments to deposit levels for the yield, and the Goldsmith estimates for wealth. Interpolations were based on regression relationships between annual averages of relevant quarterly series and the annual benchmarks. The interpolations were also used to extend the wealth series past Goldsmith's most recent published estimates for 1958. The wealth estimates even more than the other figures may therefore contain significant measurement errors. (See de Leeuw, "Demand for Money," *op. cit.*)

The ordinary least-squares regression is thought to yield an excessive estimate of the adjustment coefficient k in Eq. (3.1), "if the unexplained portion of M displays high serial correlation" (Sec. 2A.4). Three-pass least squares, on the other hand, is viewed as a means of reducing the serial correlation. It permits an application of ordinary regression analysis to an equation of the form

(4)

$$M_t = kM_{t-1} + (1 - k)(b_1 \ldots b_n) \begin{pmatrix} x_1 \\ x_2 \\ \cdot \\ \cdot \\ \cdot \\ x_n \end{pmatrix} + pu_{t-1} + e_t$$

which is the result of substituting the right-hand member of a relation of the form $u_t = pu_{t-1} + e$ into Eq. 3.1), where u_t and u_{t-1} are successive residual error terms, and e_t is not serially correlated. "Unexpectedly," according to de Leeuw, "the method of three-pass least squares yielded even slower estimates of average speed of adjustment (that is, estimates of k closer to one) than ordinary least squares."[9] The three-pass least squares did, however, improve the Durbin-Watson statistics.

Results of the type de Leeuw presents in dealing with relations such as the above are shown in Table 10–1. As shown there, currency and demand deposits, respectively, are treated as dependent variables. The independent variables involve the lagged money stock, real per capita wealth, a weighted average of real per capita income, deviations from average real per capita income, and the rate of interest, though all of these variables are not treated in every instance. As shown in the table, the use of three-pass least squares improves the results, as far as autocorrelation and the Durbin-Watson statistic (Sec. 2A.4) are concerned.

----

[9] De Leeuw, "Demand for Money," *op. cit.* De Leeuw apparently did not expect the higher value of k, because the presence of serial correlation in the results involving ordinary least squares was supposed to bias k upward. He cites Griliches (see Zvi Griliches, "A Note on Serial Correlation Bias in Estimates of Distributed Lags," *Econometrica*, January 1961). After the removal of some serial correlation, as indicated by the Durbin-Watson statistic, however, de Leeuw found higher values of k.

Commenting on results of the type shown, de Leeuw notes the following points:

(1) "The two income variables add up to current income," since one measure is simply a weighted average of current and past levels of national income and the deviations from the average are simply income minus the weighted average income variable.

(2) "The coefficients of interest rates and income are estimates of $(1 - k)b$; that is, they are single quarterly rather than long-run responses." He also notes "that the lagged stock variables have been divided by current population and prices, not by lagged population and prices." Continuing, he says, "Money holders . . . are viewed as evaluating their existing stocks at current purchasing power for comparison with desired stocks." De Leeuw concludes, from observing the high coefficients (i.e., k's $\to 1$) for the lagged stock and other results, that the "results provide support for the long-lag hypothesis."

10.2 RESULTS INVOLVING AN ALTERNATIVE TECHNIQUE

In view of the importance attached to possible lags in the adjustment process, de Leeuw tries an alternative technique—but one that still involves least-squares regression analysis. It involves rewriting Eq. (3.1) once for each time period, deriving a new equation involving weighted sums, and using the weighted time series instead of the series corresponding to x_1, x_2, and so on, in the vector in Eq. (3.1). Rewriting Eq. (3.1) for different time periods,

Period (1): $M_t = kM_{t-1} + (1 - k) \, \mathbf{b} \, \mathbf{x}_t + u_t$

Period (2): $M_{t-1} = kM_{t-2} + (1 - k) \, \mathbf{b} \, \mathbf{x}_{t-1} + u_{t-1}$

Period (3): $M_{t-2} = kM_{t-3} + (1 - k) \, \mathbf{b} \, \mathbf{x}_{t-2} + u_{t-2}$

Period (n): $M_{t-n} = kM_{t-(n+1)} + (1 - k) \, \mathbf{b} \, \mathbf{x}_{t-n} + u_{t-n}$

Now, the right-hand member of the equation for period (2) is substituted for M_{t-1} in the equation for period (1); e.g.,

Table 10–1. Demand Equations Relating Some Real Per Capita Asset Holdings to Interest Rates, Income, Wealth, and Lagged Stocks

Asset holding	Lagged stock	Real per capita wealth	Real per capita income		Interest rate on long-term gov't. securities	Constant term	R^2	Durbin-Watson ratio
			(Weighted average)	(Deviations from average)				
Currency								
Excluding lagged stock								
OLS*		−0.054 (0.004)	0.070 (0.015)	0.006 (0.008)	0.783 (1.803)	512.7	0.975	0.32
Including lagged stock								
OLS* (1)	0.978 (0.015)		0.002 (0.002)	0.012 (0.002)	−0.491 (0.368)	1.0	0.999	0.94
(2)	0.971 (0.025)	0.000 (0.001)		0.012 (0.002)	−0.405 (0.400)	5.1	0.999	0.91
3 PLS† (1)	1.007 (0.015)		0.002 (0.002)	0.011 (0.001)	−0.622 (0.328)	3.8	0.999	1.81
(2)	0.999 (0.022)	(0.001) (0.001)		0.011 (0.001)	−0.479 (0.344)	15.9	0.999	1.84

294

Demand Deposits

	lagged stock						
Excluding lagged stock							
OLS		−0.104 (0.015)	0.230 (0.054)	0.118 (0.028)	−27.743 (6.511)	1189.7	0.943	0.33
Including lagged stock							
OLS (1)	0.887 (0.027)	−0.003 (0.009)	0.033 (0.008)	−8.886 (2.042)	102.1	0.995	0.85
(2)	0.910 (0.032)		0.031 (0.008)	−10.253 (2.034)	57.5	0.995	0.90
3 PLS (1)	0.895 (0.021)	−0.002 (0.007)	0.025 (0.006)	−11.289 (1.712)	128.5	0.997	1.94
(2)	0.907 (0.026)		0.024 (0.007)	−11.987 (1.756)	96.4	0.997	1.91

* The symbol "OLS" refers to ordinary least squares.
† The symbol "3 PLS" refers to three-pass least squares.
Source of regression results: Frank de Leeuw, "The Demand for Money: Speed of Adjustment, Interest Rates, and Wealth," *Monetary Process and Policy: A Symposium,* George Horwich, ed. (Homewood, Illinois: Richard D. Irwin, Inc. 1967), Table 1.

(5)

$$M_t = k[kM_{t-2} + (1 - k) \mathbf{b} \, \mathbf{x}_{t-1} + u_{t-1}] + (1 - k) \mathbf{b} \, \mathbf{x}_t + u_t$$
$$= k^2 M_{t-2} + k(1 - k) \mathbf{b} \, \mathbf{x}_{t-1} + (1 - k) \mathbf{b} \, \mathbf{x}_t + u_t$$

and so on for each succeeding period,[10] until for the *n*th period
(*n* a large number),[11]

$$(6) \qquad M_t = \mathbf{b} \left[(1 - k) \sum_{i=0}^{n} k^i \mathbf{x}_{t-i} \right] + \sum_{i=0}^{n} k^i u_{t-i}$$

De Leeuw then proceeds to choose alternative values of k
between zero and one, and to compare regression results involving
Eq. (6). For each selected value of k, weighted sums of past x's
are implied, the infinite sum is approximated by one for twenty
quarters, and M is regressed on the alternative weighted sums.[12]

---

[10] The substitution of the type illustrated in Eq. (5) continues for the n
periods. For each substitution, the money stock is lagged one period further
back. Note, for example, that M_{t-1} drops out in equation (5). Also, note
the k is raised to a higher power in each substitution, so that eventually the
term with k to a high power drops out, for values of k between zero and
one i.e., ($k^n \to 0$, as $n \to \infty$, $0 \leq k < 1$).

[11] Equation (6), in the case of an interest rate (r) and an income variable (Y) may be written

$$M_t = \alpha (1 - k) \sum_{i=0}^{n} k^i r_{t-i} + \beta (1 - k) \sum_{i=0}^{n} k^i Y_{t-i} + \sum_{i=0}^{n} k^i u_{t-i} + k^n M_{t-n}$$

where $\mathbf{b} = (\alpha \; \beta)$, and $\mathbf{x} = (r \; Y)^T$. As $n \to \infty$, the last terms drop out, and
the equation suggests a function with $2(n+1)$ variables:

$$M_t = f(r_t, r_{t-1} \ldots, r_{t-n}; \; Y_t, Y_{t-1}, \ldots, Y_{t-n})$$

[12] In Eq. (6), we have vectors $\mathbf{b}$ and $\mathbf{x}_{t-i}$, but thinking of only two independent variables, such as r_{t-i} and Y_{t-i}, the factor $\sum_{i=0}^{n} k^i \mathbf{x}_{t-i}$ becomes

$$\sum_{i=0}^{n} k^i r_{t-i}, \; \sum_{i=0}^{n} k^i Y_{t-i}$$

With respect to the first of the latter two factors,

Period (1):	r
Period (2):	kr
Period (3):	$k^2 r$
. . . .	
Period (*n*)	$k^n r$

In this way, new time series are obtained and these are used as data in the
regression analysis.

Typical results of the type due to de Leeuw for an equation relating demand deposits to wealth, income deviations, and the rate on long-term Government securities are as follows:

	Coefficient of wealth	Coefficient of income deviations	Coefficient of interest rate	R^2
$k = 0.1$	−0.05	0.09	−33.14	0.92
	(0.01)	(0.03)	(7.34)	
$k = 0.5$	−0.04	0.06	−43.59	0.94
	(0.01)	(0.03)	(7.49)	
$k = 0.9$	−0.02	0.09	−57.20	0.96
	(0.01)	(0.05)	(9.97)	

With respect to these results, de Leeuw concludes that "the over-all goodness of fit improves" and the significance of the coefficient for wealth with the "wrong" sign declines, as the value of k increases. However, de Leeuw says: "the differences are not striking; and serial correlation in this group of regressions is very high as the final terms in equation (6) might lead us to expect." He then proceeds to introduce first differences to deal with the serial correlation problem. Once more the results are said to favor a slow speed of adjustment.[13]

10.3 ANOTHER TECHNIQUE: "A LESS RESTRICTIVE ESTIMATE OF THE REGRESSION PATTERN"

Hendershott introduces an alternative means of dealing with a relation of a form implied by de Leeuw's equation (6):

$$(7) \qquad M_t = (r_t, r_{t-1}, \ldots, r_{t-m}; Y_t, Y_{t-1}, \ldots, Y_{t-n}),$$

where M_t is a function of current and lagged variables, and where the number of lagged variables for r and Y, respectively, need not be the same (i.e., $m \gtreqless n$). He seeks less-restricted estimates of the response pattern, after referring to Eq. (6) above and noting two restrictions effected by de Leeuw—namely, "he [de Leeuw] as-

---

[13] See de Leeuw, "Demand for Money," *op. cit.*

sumed that the relative influence of current and successive past values of each explanatory variable on current money demand could be approximated by geometrically declining weights," and "the rate at which the weights declined was assumed to be the same for all explanatory variables."[14] Continuing, Hendershott says, "These restrictions were placed on the variables to conserve degrees of freedom and avoid problems of collinearity, but either or both of them might be responsible for the long lag that de Leeuw uncovered."

In Hendershott's study, further degrees of freedom and a possible reduction of collinearity in the independent variables are sought—first, by introducing averages of quarterly data to reduce the number of lagged variables and, second, by introducing first differences. "Each group of four successive [quarterly] observations of each independent variable is replaced," according to Hendershott, "by the means of the four observations." In this way annual averages replace quarterly data, and Hendershott proceeds to introduce no more than two lagged values for each first-year variable.[15]

---

[14] Hendershott, *op. cit.*, pp. 6–7. However, Hendershott notes the following: "These assumptions are not unusual. In fact, the interpretation of equations estimated using the lagged stock of the dependent variable as one of the regressors generally relies quite heavily on them."

[15] What he does is, in part, reflected in a regression of the following form:

$$\Delta M_t = \alpha_1 \left(\frac{\sum_{i=0}^{3} r_{t-i}}{4} - \frac{\sum_{i=4}^{7} r_{t-i}}{4} \right) + \alpha_2 \left(\frac{\sum_{i=4}^{7} r_{t-i}}{4} - \frac{\sum_{i=8}^{11} r_{t-i}}{4} \right)$$

$$+ \alpha_3 \left(\frac{\sum_{i=8}^{11} r_{t-i}}{4} - \frac{\sum_{i=12}^{15} r_{t-i}}{4} \right) + \beta_1 \left(\frac{\sum_{i=0}^{3} Y_{t-i}}{4} - \frac{\sum_{i=4}^{7} Y_{t-i}}{4} \right)$$

$$+ \beta_2 \left(\frac{\sum_{i=4}^{7} Y_{t-i}}{4} - \frac{\sum_{i=8}^{11} Y_{t-i}}{4} \right) + \beta_3 \left(\frac{\sum_{i=8}^{11} Y_{t-i}}{4} - \frac{\sum_{i=12}^{15} Y_{t-i}}{4} \right) + u$$

where the factors in parentheses are first differences of annual averages of quarterly data, the first differences in the second and fifth terms of the right-hand member of the equation are values lagged by one year, and the first differences in the third and sixth terms are values lagged by two

Some of Hendershott's results are as follows:

(8)
$$\Delta C = \underset{(0.0052)}{0.0122\Delta Y^P} + \underset{(0.0058)}{0.0184\Delta Y^P_{-1}} + \underset{(0.0024)}{0.0062\Delta Y^T} + \underset{(0.0020)}{0.0054\Delta Y^T_{-1}}$$
$$+ \underset{(0.0013)}{0.0014\Delta Y^T_{-2}} - \underset{(0.141)}{0.108\Delta r_b} - \underset{(0.150)}{0.427\Delta r_{b_{-1}}}, \quad \begin{array}{l} R^2 = 0.574 \\ \text{D-W} = 1.03 \end{array}$$

(9)
$$\Delta C = \underset{(0.0069)}{0.0047\Delta Y^T} + \underset{(0.0053)}{0.0123\Delta Y^P_{-1}} + \underset{(0.0024)}{0.0066\Delta Y} + \underset{(0.0022)}{0.0060\Delta Y_{-1}}$$
$$+ \underset{(0.0015)}{0.0015\Delta Y_{-2}} - \underset{(0.141)}{0.112\Delta r_b} - \underset{(0.151)}{0.422\Delta r_{b_{-1}}}, \quad R^2 = 0.571$$

(10)
$$\Delta DD = \underset{(0.0079)}{0.0050\Delta W} + \underset{(0.0055)}{0.0240\Delta W_{-1}} + \underset{(0.0035)}{0.0049\Delta W_{-2}} + \underset{(0.0095)}{0.0292\Delta Y}$$
$$+ \underset{(0.0080)}{0.0115\Delta Y_{-1}} + \underset{(0.0075)}{0.0125\Delta Y_{-2}} - \underset{(0.67)}{3.75\Delta r_b} - \underset{(0.85)}{2.70\Delta r_{b_{-1}}}$$
$$- \underset{(0.87)}{0.85\Delta r_{b_{-2}}} - \underset{(2.66)}{5.40\Delta r_{TD}}, \quad R^2 = 0.467 \quad \text{D-W} = 1.24$$

where dollar magnitudes are seasonally adjusted and deflated by population and the price level (i.e., the GNP deflator), ΔC is change in currency, Y^P is permanent income, Y^T is transitory income, ΔDD is the change in demand deposits, and Δr_b is the change in the bill rate, and Δr_{TD} is the change in the rate on time deposits. The data Hendershott uses are the same as de Leeuw's, except for time deposits and total income (Y).[16] Also, de Leeuw's results were shown for the yield on government bonds.

As regression equations (8), (9), and (10) reveal, lagged values for two years do not appear in some instances. This is because lagged values were dropped as soon as coefficients appeared with unexpected signs. When the absolute values of coefficients drop

---

years. As the equation indicates, the constant terms in Hendershott's regressions are constrained to zero. (The rationale of restricting the constant term to zero in regressions involving first differences is dealt with in note 38, Sec. 6.4).

[16] See Hendershott, *op. cit.*, p. 9.

off sharply, as for example between a second-year coefficient and a third-year coefficient, then Hendershott views this as a likely completion of the response. In other instances, the absolute values for the coefficients may rise, as from the first-year coefficient to the second, and indicate an increase in the lagged response pattern rather than a decline. Further, when the absolute value of a coefficient is much larger for a given variable in one equation than in another, Hendershott interprets this to mean a greater response on the part of the dependent variable in the equation with the larger coefficient. For example, the absolute value of the first-year, bill-rate coefficient in Eq. (10) is much greater than the absolute value of the comparable coefficient in equation (9)—i.e., 3.75 > 0.112—and Hendershott concludes that demand deposits are more responsive than currency to bill-rate changes.

After describing lag patterns implied by Eqs. (8), (9) and (10), Hendershott interprets the patterns. Some of his interpretations follow:[17]

> The response of currency demand to changes in the bill rate and permanent income are quite similar. The response builds up to a peak in the second year . . . and is negligible in the third year.

> The influence of a change in total national income (or transitory income) on currency demand over time is similar to that assumed by de Leeuw. Nevertheless the large difference between the second year coefficient and the third year coefficient compared with the small difference between the first and second year coefficients suggests that the response is probably completed within three years. . . .

> Interpolating a quarterly lag structure for the variable influencing demand deposit holders from the annual coefficients is not as easy as it was for the variables influencing currency demand. The response of demand deposits to wealth changes (a bell-shape response similar to the response of currency demand to bill rate changes) and to bill rate changes (a declining response similar to that of currency to transitory income) are quite unambiguous . . . but the response to national income is not. The coefficients of

---

[17] *Ibid.*, pp. 10–13.

the income variable rise from the second to the third year. This seems to imply that a significant part of the impact of current income changes on demand deposit demand occurs after three years and that the impact has been captured by the third year coefficient.

In a summary of his study in the *Federal Reserve Bulletin,* Hendershott made the following conclusions:[18]

Although lags in the adjustment of money holdings are substantial, they do not seem to be as long as de Leeuw's study suggested.

These dissimilarities in the response of money demand to changes in income, wealth, and interest rates emphasize the difficulties of interpreting empirical results of studies employing the typical lagged-stock formulation. The coefficient of the lagged-stock variable may provide an estimate of the average speed of adjustment to discrepancies between desired and actual holdings, but it very likely does not provide an accurate measure of the response pattern to changes in each particular determinant of desired holdings.

The behavior of time series involved in de Leeuw's and Hendershott's analyses and results may be explained on grounds other than those pertaining to the hypothesis of a relatively long lag in the speed of adjustment of desired money balances in response to selected economic variables. Such a prospect was suggested at the outset. As one analyst has pointed out, however—perhaps with the realization of the inadequacy of introspection as a source of evidence and perhaps with the view that common sense should serve as evidence—no economic unit should ever have any difficulty in effecting a rapid adjustment in currency holdings to the desired level, subject to an income (or wealth) constraint. Currency holdings may too easily be deposited at a bank, or run down in relation to income (or assets) through their use in purchases, in the repayment of debt or the acquisition of other assets of varying degrees of liquidity.

---

[18] See, *Federal Reserve Bulletin,* March 1966.

10.4   SUMMARY

De Leeuw observes fluctuations in long-term rates of interest that lead inverse fluctuations in real per capita demand deposits. He views these changes as suggesting some simple evidence of a lagged reaction of money holdings to interest rates. He then proceeds to present relations involving various sorts of lagged variables and to present results from regression analyses of time-series data. His analyses involve the assumption of an identified, long-run, equilibrium demand function for desired money balances, and his results involve the common econometric problems of serial correlation in the error term and multicollinearity. De Leeuw deals with the serial correlation problem by the use of three-pass least squares, but this alters his estimates of the speed of adjustment very little. He then introduces an additional technique relying upon weighted time series. In the latter instance the adjustment lag coefficient k that yields the best goodness of fit, is most consistent with the long-lag hypothesis. De Leeuw views his results as supporting the long-lag hypothesis.

Hendershott, too, attempts to deal with the prospect of a lagged adjustment in desired money holdings—i.e., currency and demand-deposit holdings. He views de Leeuw's estimates of the response pattern as somewhat restrictive, and seeks to achieve additional degrees of freedom and a possible reduction of correlation between the independent variables. In the latter instance, he introduces averages of quarterly data, reduces the number of lagged variables in the analyses, and uses first differences. His conclusions still reflect support for relatively long lags in adjustments, but the dissimilarities in response patterns for different independent variables introduce difficulties into the interpretation of the results.

Both de Leeuw and Hendershott imply rather orthodox notions about the relation between money demand and interest rates. They refer to theories about transactions demand that attempt to explain a rise in the velocity of money in terms of a form of switching from money balances in relation to income into liquid security holdings in relation to income. Statements due to Daniel Brill, the Board's director of research, also proceed along this line, as does Fromm's analysis of responses to discount rate changes. In Fromm's analysis an equation system involving de Leeuw's financial sector model for the U. S. economy is used.

De Leeuw and Hendershott view knowledge of the lagged response of desired money balances to interest-rate changes as relevant to a better understanding of the effects of monetary policy, narrowly defined to suggest an open-market purchase or sale. Apparently, as the money stock increases, for example, through an open-market purchase, holders of balances in excess of desired balances will buy bonds and lower the rate of interest and the latter will continue low until new issues of securities reach the market. This latter example of the relevance of the long-lag hypothesis may be viewed as somewhat naïve, however, in view of the historical practices surrounding the issuance of directives to the manager of the open-market account and in view of the historical use of open-market operations as an instrument of general credit control.

Observed behavior of time series whereby interest-rate changes lead changes in real per capita demand deposits may be explained in terms other than those of a long lag in the responsiveness of money holdings to interest-rate changes and so on. Furthermore, the notion of a long lag in the adjustment of desired currency holdings seems excessively in contrast to notions about the ease with which currency holdings may be adjusted in relation to income (or assets). Monetary policy, too, may be more operationally defined than is suggested by the notion of an open-market purchase as a monetary policy. The latter and other matters are dealt with in the next chapter.

Chapter 11

STATISTICAL RESULTS,
MONETARY ANALYSIS,
AND MONETARY POLICY

A major portion of the statistical results appearing in the demand-for-money literature concerns a velocity–interest rate association, of one kind or another, and regression equations with a logarithmically transformed money stock as a dependent variable and logarithmically transformed income (or wealth) and interest-rate variables as the so-called independent or "explanatory" variables. In many instances, the accompanying analysis and/or treatment given the results suggest(s) the prospect of exercising control over the stock of money demanded (and, therefore, expenditures and other variables) via some control over the rate of interest, or vice versa, but, in other instances, these prospects are questioned. There are questions in these instances about the role of the interest rate and, in some, about the possible role and effects of monetary policy. This chapter deals with these questions, the statistical findings, and the related bits of analysis: the first section reviews, in broad outline, the findings and the various notions about the possible effects and role of monetary policy; the next section deals with possible indicators of change in monetary policy, with some emphasis on the velocity of money as an indicator; and the third section deals with the implications of the definitions and analysis of the preceding sections for the conduct of monetary policy and the role of the monetary officials.

11.1   A SUMMARY OF FINDINGS AND VARIOUS NOTIONS:
THE POSSIBLE EFFECTS AND ROLE OF
MONETARY POLICY

A fundamental and frequently recurring result has been the association between the velocity of money and the rate of interest.

Latané succinctly dealt with the association in two papers—one in 1954 and another in 1960 (Sec. 5.1)—and Carl Christ dramatized it (Sec. 5.1). "As the years went by," Christ said, "I plotted the new data on Latané's graph, and something happened that is very remarkable in the brief history of econometric equations: the new points were closer to the regression line than the points of the sample period!" Indeed, the correlation between the velocity and interest-rate variables, after a logarithmic transformation of the data, is high, and equal percentage changes in one variable parallel almost equal percentage changes in the other. The relationship exhibits itself in a number of instances: over long periods when annual data are used (Secs. 4.1 and 5.1); and over the post-World War II years when quarterly data are used—either for the aggregates (Sec. 2.2), for the business sector (Sec. 7.3), or for the household sector (Sec. 9.1).

The relation between velocity and the rate of interest follows from liquidity-preference analysis, in one form or another (Secs. 2.2, 3.3, and 4.1). And, in fact, the liquidity-preference model has frequently provided the basis for the single equation regression models with money stock, interest rate and income (or wealth) variables, although much of the emphasis on a wealth component is due to the influence of Milton Friedman (Sec. 6.1). For the most part, high coefficients of single or multiple determination have resulted from the regressions—although the multiple regression coefficients have at times exhibited some instability, due possibly to differences in the characteristics of the different periods, and although the presence of multicollinearity and the nature of regression analysis must be allowed for in dealing with the possible inconsistency between the multiple regression results and the velocity–interest rate association (Sec. 9.1).

The explanations for the velocity–interest rate association, or for the negative regression coefficient for the rate of interest in multiple regression equations, have been associated with liquidity-preference analysis (Sec. 4.1), Tobin's and Baumol's analyses of the transactions demand for money (Secs. 8.1 and 8.2), and with Latané (Sec. 5.1). In one way or another, in most of these monetary analyses—sometimes after abstracting from the motives, whether speculative or transactions—the explanation for a rise in velocity commonly involves a form of switching from cash to bond-type assets and a rise in the rate of interest as the inducement for the switching, although there is the additional prospect that the switching gives rise to the observed interest-rate changes.

Some have analyzed data and found lagged relations between variables, such as the money stock, income, and the rate of interest. Some have attributed the lagged relations to lags in the adjustment of actual to desired balances (Secs. 6.5, 10.1 and 10.2), but in Hamburger's results the lagged responses of changes in the money stock are for other reasons and money balances are shown to be as closely related to equity yields as to bond yields (Sec. 9.2). In another instance, switching phenomena have been dealt with in such a way as to imply lagged relations, and there has been the indication that the switching gave rise to velocity and interest-rate changes, particularly with respect to the business sector's holdings of broad classes of fixed and residual claim assets (Sec. 7.2). Milton Friedman (Sec. 6A.2), moreover, is said to have emphasized the rate of change in prices, as an indicator of expectations, and greater certainty about the future as determinants of the demand for money. He has—apparently as a consequence, as we show later (Sec. 11.3)—de-emphasized the rate of interest as a determinant, in view of its relation to changes in expectations about the future. There is the prospect that the business and household sectors exhibit some differences in their switching patterns involving the various classes of assets, but, even in the event of this prospect, the regression results concerning the demand for money have frequently, and possibly incorrectly, been evaluated along conventional liquidity-preference lines, at least as far as the assessments of the effects of monetary policy are concerned.

Reviewing results from the demand studies, Brill says (Chapter 10) that "velocity *depends*, as does money demand, on rates of interest [italics added]." And Christ suggests the prospect of the monetary authorities effecting a rise in expenditures (i.e., the velocity of money) by raising the rate of interest. Others take what would appear to be an extremely short-run liquidity-preference point of view, and at the same time do little to define monetary policy. De Leeuw and Hendershott (Secs. 10.1 and 10.2), for example, refer to an open-market purchase as shifting interest rates to a lower level, via an increase in the money stock, because holders of money will immediately buy bonds. Hamburger, with an eye on investment demand, but still with emphasis on lower rates, speaks of (Sec. 9.2) "open market purchases by the monetary authorities, which temporarily lower the yield on bonds" and lead "investors to attempt to shift out of bonds and into other assets, including physical capital." They—de Leeuw, Hendershott, Hamburger, and others—would apparently increase the money supply in order to lower interest rates, whereas the reverse effect may be the case, as when an increase in the rate of change in the money supply contributes to the prospect of inflation, a rise in the rate of interest (Sec. 11.3) and a further imbalance between desired and actual money balances.

11.2 INDICATORS AND SOME ANALYSIS OF CHANGES IN CREDIT (MONETARY) POLICY

From time to time there have been references to "monetary policy," including references to the use of changes in the rate of interest (or the velocity of money) as an indicator of changes in credit (monetary) policy, references to the uses of tools of credit control, and references to the role of the rate of interest (or velocity) in facilitating the identification of the demand function for money (Secs. 2.2 and 2A.2). This section, in particular, enlarges upon these previous references to monetary policy and seeks to pin down the notion of "credit" or "monetary policy." In the process of enlarging upon the earlier references, interest rates and the income velocity of money are cited as possible indicators of changes in credit conditions ("policy") and, in a sense, monetary conditions. Portions of the analysis supporting the view of interest rates and velocity as indicators are then elaborated upon as a means of shedding some light on the "denigration of the influence of interest rate movements and the denial of an important role to interest rates in the demand for money function" in some monetary literature (Sec. 6A.2).

THE INDICATORS

The terms "credit policy" and "monetary policy," to begin with, may be used with reference to the Federal Reserve's objectives with respect to credit conditions and changes in the money stock in relation to income. In a fractional reserve banking system, as in the United States, changes in credit conditions with respect to the ease or tightness of credit are likely to parallel discrepancies between the rate of change in the money stock and the rate of change in some variable such as income, after allowances for some other factors such as currency and time-deposit drains.[1] In any event, we may cite indicators and the changes in question are closely related.

The previously widely accepted indicators of credit conditions have included selected short-term interest rates[2] and "free reserves" or "net borrowed reserves" (i.e., the reserves of the commercial banks less legally required reserves and reserves borrowed from the Federal Reserve Banks). The rates, of course, are independent of equal proportional changes in the supply and demand quantities of the instruments being traded, and, similarly, free reserves should most meaningfully be viewed in relation to the size of commercial-banking operations. The Federal Reserve's use of the free-reserves indicator, however, has invoked some criticism —notably, that bankers have a preference for reserves that may at times shift.[3] Meltzer notes, e.g.—somewhat along the lines of a liquidity-preference model for bankers and bank reserves—that at times "reductions in interest rates raised the banks' desired short-run reserve position" and that "substantial increase in the discount rate in 1920 and again in 1931 is described in terms of its effect on market interest rates and banks' desired reserve positions."[4] Even so, these are rather major events, of a type unlikely to have

---

[1] In the first instance, an increase in the currency to demand-deposit ratio affects the level of bank reserves, and, in the second, an increase in the ratio of time to demand deposits affects the money stock differently from commercial bank reserves. See William J. Frazer, Jr., and William P. Yohe, *Introduction to the Analytics and Institutions of Money and Banking* (Princeton, New Jersey: D. Van Nostrand Company, Inc., 1966), pp. 39–48.

[2] The rates usually cited are those on Treasury bills, commercial paper, and Federal funds (i.e., the rate on trading among commercial banks of reserves on deposit at the Federal Reserve).

[3] See, e.g., Frazer and Yohe, *op. cit.*, pp. 567–568; and the references cited in the latter work. See, also, George R. Morrison, *Liquidity Preference of Commercial Banks* (Chicago: University of Chicago Press, 1966).

[4] See Allan H. Meltzer, "Monetary Theory and Monetary History," *Schweizerische Zeitschrift für Volkswirtschaft und Statistik*, December 1965, p. 409. For a liquidity-preference model of the type suggested for bankers and bank reserves, see Frazer and Yohe, *op. cit.*, pp. 568–571.

occurred in the post-World War II United States and, in any event, the reserve positions of banks and the bankers' attitudes toward them get reflected in the rates of interest prevailing in the financial markets of the type functioning in the United States since 1951, the end of the era of pegged interest rates.[5]

Thus, there is apparently no compelling reason for not using "the interest rate" as an indicator of credit conditions, under the sorts of conditions that have come to prevail. In the analysis of changes in "the rate," however, one may think of an upward and downward moving structure of rates or a vector of all interest rates (Sec. 4.1). In this case, short-run changes in the so-called indicators of money-market conditions get reflected in changes in the structure of rates, following some switching and arbitrage transactions. For changes in credit conditions, then, the rate of interest is cited—a rise in the rate reflecting a tightness of credit and a decline reflecting ease.

On the stock of money side, changes in the reserve position and the rate of interest get reflected in percentage changes in the money stock in relation to percentage changes in income (i.e., they get reflected in changes in the velocity of money). Credit and, in a sense, monetary tightness, neutrality, and ease, in such a case, are respectively represented by rising, constant, and declining income velocity of money. For example, in the case of an earlier [Sec. 3.3, Eq. (4.1)] definition of the rate of interest— namely, $r = (bY)/(\gamma - cY)$—equal percentage changes in the money stock (γ) and income (Y) reflect no change in income velocity, no change in the rate of interest, and, therefore, no change in credit conditions, and a rise in the rate of interest gets reflected in a rise in velocity, and so on.

Now, the vast amount of empirical results reflecting the velocity–interest rate association support the use of the velocity of money as a substitute variable for the rate of interest as an indicator of credit conditions in the preceding framework. And, in a sense,

---

[5] The events and developments of the post-World War II years in the United States are recorded in Frazer and Yohe, *op. cit.*, Chapter 24. On the prospect of an upward shift in "desired" free reserves and rising interest rates during the second half of 1959, see Jack M. Guttentag, "The Strategy of Open Market Operations," *Quarterly Journal of Economics*, February 1966, pp. 14–15.

the two are indicators of monetary conditions, but the use of the words "tight" and "easy" may not reflect the same meaning in the case of credit when contrasted with the case of money. When credit is tight, for example, it is hard to get in relation to income, and if credit is expanding less rapidly than income, velocity and interest rates are rising. Rising velocity, however, has been associated with a weakening of the demand for money balances relative to income or total assets. Money balances, in such instances, are being disposed of or turned over faster; credit is tight in that it is hard to get in relation to the quantity sought, but it is sought as a liability and as a means of obtaining money balances for disposition in exchange for other assets.

The analysis and results thus far indicate that velocity and the rate of interest are reasonably good substitute variables, indicators of credit conditions, and, in a sense, monetary conditions. On the other hand, there are, at times, suggestions that changes in the credit and monetary policies of the central bankers are reflected in their uses of the instruments for controlling bank credit generally (Secs. 9.2, 10.1, and 10.2). In the United States these instruments include the discount rate, legal reserve requirements, and open-market operations, but the suggestions of viewing the uses of the instruments as indicators of changes in credit policy generally need not bother us, since the instruments are used in such a way as to render impossible their use as indicators of general credit policies.[6] For example: open-market purchases of securities may be made as a means of increasing bank reserves, at a time when legal reserve requirements are being raised to constrain the expansion of credit; the discount rates at the respective reserve banks may be changed, simply to bring them in line with market rates of interest; and, in any event, substantial changes may be brought about in credit conditions simply by inaction of monetary officials in the event of such occurrences as gold flowing out of the country or withdrawals of currency by the public, either of which reduces bank reserves.[7]

---

[6] For a review of the uses of general credit controls in the United States, see Frazer and Yohe, *op. cit.*, Chapter 8.

[7] For a review of the bank reserve equation and the prospect of changes in credit conditions coming about without action on the part of monetary officials, see Frazer and Yohe, *op. cit.*, Chapter 10.

SOME ANALYSIS

The analysis underlying the possible use of the rate of interest and the velocity of money as substitute variables (or indicators) has been facilitated by a form of the liquidity-preference model, and references to switching phenomena involving broad classes of assets. At times (Secs. 3.3 and 7.2), these have been so broad as to include assets with a fixed claim against future income, such as cash and bonds, and those with a residual claim, such as instrumental capital, and as long as credit policy is neutral (i.e., $r =$ constant) in such a context the following changes occur: broad classes of assets expand in equal proportion; the stock of money demanded increases in equal proportion to income (Y); and money balances increase in equal proportion to wealth (W) or total assets, since $W = Y/r$ (Sec. 6.1). Under these conditions the rates of return for relating the prospective streams of returns to given additions to the various classes of assets are equal, after allowance for risk factors and liquidity elements. Factors affecting the prospective returns disproportionately, however, give rise to switching with the view to avoiding losses and realizing gains. A prospective price increase, for example, affects adversely the returns from fixed-claim assets and favorably the returns from real capital goods, and greater certainty about the future affects the flow of returns (or utility) from holding money balances. These factors impinging on prospective returns may result in a change in monetary policy and switching. In the latter examples, the switching would likely be out of the fixed-claim type of assets—both cash balances and bonds. The switching, in these examples, gives rise to increased expenditures, and possibly output, employment and prices. Other factors may be cited, tax credits and so on, and the reverse sets of changes may be illustrated, but of special importance in the latter examples, velocity and the rate of interest are responding to the same changes in the setting. Also, as the switching proceeds from fixed-claim assets to residual-claim assets, as in a period of greater than average economic growth, all the absolute amounts for the various categories of assets increase, but those for the fixed-claim type increase less than in proportion to the residual-claim type of assets.

As mentioned on other occasions, when the switching of assets involves a reduction in cash in relation to assets or income (and therefore, a rise in velocity), there is said to be a tendency for "actual" balances to exceed "desired" balances. Conversely, when the switching involves an increase in cash in relation to assets or income (and, therefore, a decline in velocity), there is said to be a tendency for "desired" balances to exceed "actual" balances. The discrepancies are said to be small or the lags in the adjustment of desired to actual balances of little or no consequence, because economic agents are in a position to adjust their money holdings towards desired levels by spending more or less.

Now, the preceding analysis and examples should help further in explaining why Friedman and Schwartz de-emphasize the rate of interest as a determinant of velocity and resort to such factors as greater certainty about the future.[8] In referring to the effect of expected price changes on the value of real capital goods and suggesting a rise in velocity in response to a form of switching from money to real assets, Friedman and Schwartz note that changes in the interest rate and changes in price expectations are not additive, since "the postwar change in interest rates reflects the change in price expectations." Referring to their view, Meltzer notes, that "of principal interest in the light of recent studies is the authors' [Friedman and Schwartz] rejection of interest rates as an important influence in the explanation of the movement of velocity."[9]

11.3   MONETARY POLICY AND THE ROLE OF THE MONETARY OFFICIALS

The velocity–interest rate association, the definitions and the analysis of the preceding section hold certain implications for the conduct of monetary policy and the role of the monetary officials. These implications concern the following: a stable, constant-employment growth in income; the route by which the monetary authorities exercise major effects on the changes in the flow of

---

[8] Milton Friedman and Anna Jacobson Schwartz, *A Monetary History of the United States, 1867–1960* (Princeton, New Jersey: Princeton University Press, 1963), p. 645.

[9] See Meltzer, "Monetary Theory and Monetary History," *op. cit.*, p. 410.

income and output; and the functions of a governing body of monetary officials.

A STABLE, CONSTANT-EMPLOYMENT GROWTH IN INCOME

The analysis and the velocity–interest rate association in the previous section imply that the product of the average of prices and output (i.e., $Y = PQ$) is what the monetary officials make it. In that analysis, they simply effect a change in credit policy and, by definition, parallel movements occur in the rate of interest and income velocity (i.e., the ratio of the product of the average of prices and output to the money stock). Also, assuming a market economy with average wage and profit changes equal to a constant growth in productivity, there are further implications—notably, that equal proportional changes in the money stock and income, measured in constant prices, will result in stable prices; and that there is a built-in dynamic—a tendency for output to grow in an economy with a constant level of employment, given a neutral money policy. In the latter instance, technological change may displace some workers, but they get re-employed, and this is in effect the source of growth in output under a neutral monetary policy.

But what about the effects of changes in policy—i.e., changes in income velocity and the rate of interest? In terms of the definitions and the assumptions, there are none in the positive sense or in the sense of a causal sequence as from the rate of interest to velocity. The policy is set and changes simply take place. It can contribute to the assurance of stable prices and permit changes to take place that would ordinarily take place. Or it may contribute to price changes, given productivity and the level of employment, and these price changes may in turn exercise some effect. But here the policy as defined is having effect indirectly, or via some intermediate variable such as the rate of change in prices or expected price changes. This is in contrast to the role of the rate of interest in the money-demand functions in which the interest-rate change itself implicitly causes or "explains" changes in holdings of money balances in an operational sense. It is contrary, too, to the idea of any formal "linkages" or causal sequences of a type commonly mentioned by Federal Reserve and other economists in the mid-1960's. For example, there have been views such as the following: changes in credit conditions cause changes in economic activity (i.e., changes in the growth rate for the output of goods and services); fixed investment responds to changes in the long-term bond rate and to the availability of commercial loans; and inventory investment responds to loan-market conditions. A difficulty with such views, from the point of view of the present analysis, is that changes in economic activity and the switching phenomena giving rise to it contribute to changes in credit conditions, and changes in the flow of capital expenditures contribute to changes in velocity, the long-term bond rate, and loan-market conditions.

THE FRIEDMAN MONETARY RULE

In view of one preceding implication—notably, that of setting a policy of a constant growth rate in the money stock and achieving a constant level of economic activity—and in view of the national economic goal of stable prices, one may ask: Why not Friedman's monetary rule? Friedman, it will be recalled, suggests a 3 to 4 or more per cent growth rate for the money stock, depending on the growth in real income, with possible seasonal deviations from the constant rate.[10] He sees this as a better alternative than relying upon changes in monetary policy as effected in the past by monetary officials. As Meltzer says, in his review of the Friedman-Schwartz monetary history, Friedman will not be unhappy, "if the reader of *A Monetary History* concludes that errors in policy at crucial episodes in history suggest that rules would have done better than judgment."[11]

A possible reason for not adopting the Friedman rule is the

---

[10] See Milton Friedman, *Capitalism and Freedom* (Chicago: University of Chicago Press, 1962), pp. 54–55. See also Milton Friedman, *A Program for Monetary Stability* (New York: Fordham University Press, 1959), pp. 91–99; and for a review of the rules-discretion debate, see Richard T. Selden, "Stable Monetary Growth," Leland Yeager, ed., *In Search of a Monetary Constitution* (Cambridge: Harvard University Press, 1962), pp. 322–355. The latter item is also reprinted in Richard A. Ward, ed., *Monetary Theory and Policy* (Scranton, Pennsylvania: International Textbook Company, Inc., 1966), pp. 321–344.

[11] Meltzer, "Monetary Theory and Monetary History," *op. cit.*, p. 418.

following: the actions, antics, and inactions of the monetary officials may have desirable effects beyond those implied by the definition of monetary policy—mainly, they can affect the degree of certainty about the future. A greater degree of certainty about the future would, of course, increase velocity. It would, therefore, be a change in policy, but if the money stock were expanded to offset the rise in velocity, the change in the money stock may be inflationary and destabilizing, depending on the level of employment, and other factors. The expanded money stock may lead to the prospect of future price rises, and, therefore, a further rise in velocity and interest rates. When credit is tightening—in the sense that rates are rising—increasing the rate of change in the money stock does not reduce rates as numerous analysts have posited (Secs. 9.2, 10.1, and 10.2), and, at the same time, interest-rate changes emanating from such changes in the money stock are not on balance restrictive upon expenditures. Credit is, in these instances, simply tight in relation to the amounts sought by borrowers,[12] and the demand for balances as a proportion of income

---

[12] The question of the differential effects of the volume of credit available at banks on certain types of businesses—as distinct from the effects of rising interest rates in general on spenders and those units with access to funds from the wide range of financial markets—is an interesting one. However, it has not been formally dealt with as a separate question with respect to the effects of monetary policy under the conditions of unpegged interest rates (see Sec. 5.3).

The mechanics of placing new money balances in the hands of spenders via the banks is, of course, related to explanations of how velocity can rise, but there are a number of ways in which an increase in expenditures may come about via an increase in the turnover of balances. Analysis by Ettin provides the basis for one such list. (See Edward C. Ettin, "A Quantitative Analysis of the Relationships Between Money and Income," *Weltwirtschaftliches Archiv,* March 1966, pp. 122–123.) His list would include the following:

(1) Individual spenders can reduce money holdings or "use liquid assets from their portfolios, thus reducing the money holdings of some other household or firm."

(2) "Spenders can . . . finance their expenditures by issuing debt or equity securities. . . ."

(3) The banking system may sell a security in exchange for a relatively inactive balance and then grant a loan to a big spender.

(4) A "spender" may receive trade credit from the seller of goods, al-

or assets is declining. Money is, in the latter sense, readily available under the condition of rising interest rates in that "desired" balances are, in effect, less than "actual balances." When interest rates and velocity are rising and when there is a tendency for "actual" balances to exceed "desired" balances, an increase in the rate of change in the money stock simply, in effect, contributes to a greater discrepancy between "actual" and "desired" balances, and to further increases in velocity and the rate of interest.

Another question, then, is why might the officials effect counter-cyclical or stabilizing changes in monetary policy, as possibly implied by a combination of the definition of monetary policy and the data for income velocity of money (e.g., Tables 2.1 and 2A.1)? A possible answer, in view of the analysis, is that the changes in policy reduce the changes in expectations, either with respect to excessive buoyancy or inadequate buoyancy. Monetary policy has its major effects on the levels of income, output, and employment, via its effect on the degree of buoyancy in expectations.

MONETARY POLICY EFFECTS BEYOND THOSE RESULTING FROM ADHERENCE TO RULES

One may note that the smooth extrapolated growth curve for real output is itself a form of rule. He may even inquire further into the possibility of the effects of changes in monetary policy beyond those due to countering of buoyancy by varying the stock of money at a more or less rapid rate than income. But there are no such effects, as monetary policy has been defined. The chairman

---

though this credit must ultimately be repaid via the use of money balances.

And to the list, we may add the following:
(5) Individuals and other spending units may simultaneously start to increase expenditures and thus increase velocity (and income) and the balances they receive so that actual reductions in the effective holdings of balances are less characteristic (except in relation to income) than some analyses lead us to believe.

Ettin operates within a rather restrictive ex post, ex ante framework and makes an unnecessary and arbitrary distinction between "active" and "idle" balances. Nevertheless, the various routes via which increases may occur may be thought of as if they were independent of his framework.

of the Board of Governors or a similarly highly placed official in the monetary system may exert independent and hopefully stabilizing effects via individual pronouncements, especially if responding to possibly unstabilizing pronouncements from other quarters— such as the executive or legislative branches of government in the United States.

WHY A BOARD OF GOVERNORS

Why, in view of the apparently rather limited effects of monetary policy, do we have a Board of Governors? Do they exist just to oversee research and administer the Reserve System? The earlier analysis would suggest that their main function is deciding on the timing of the changes in monetary policy and the extent of the changes, consciously or unconsciously, with the view to varying the degree of buoyancy in expectations and achieving a growth rate consistent with other national economic goals.

11.4 SUMMARY

Results from simple regression analyses of time-series data reflect a high degree of correlation between percentage changes in the velocity of money and the rate of interest. They also reflect almost equal percentage changes in these variables over time. Results from the regression of the money stock on income (or wealth) and the rate of interest, following logarithmic transformations of the data, too, indicate that almost all of the variation in the quantity of money can be explained by the independent variables. In some of the contexts in which these results appear, moreover, there is the suggestion that the velocity of money or the quantity demanded can be controlled via changes in the rate of interest with a rise in the rate resulting in a reduction in the money stock in relation to income (wealth or total assets).

To explain the relations, in an operational sense, various analytical notions have been invoked, such as the conventional liquidity-preference analysis, and analyses due to Tobin, and others. Changes in the rate of interest, in these contexts, have been viewed as calling forth a sort of switching phenomena between money balances and bonds, and here again are suggestions of causal se-

quences. On some other occasions, expectations have been introduced such that switching proceeds between broader classes of
assets including assets with fixed and residual claims against
future income and gives rise to velocity and interest-rate changes.
Factors impinging upon degrees of certainty about the future and
expectations in general—such as tax credits and rates of changes in
prices—have been invoked on these occasions as a means of
explaining the switching phenomena—i.e., the phenomena giving
rise to interest-rate changes and changes in the stock of money
in relation to income (or total assets). In these latter instances
the causal sequence is quite different from that suggested by the
use of the rate of interest as an "explanatory" variable in the
operational sense. The degrees of certainty about the future and
role of factors such as the rate of change in prices, moreover,
suggest redundancy in the inclusion of such factors with interest
rates as determinants of the demand for money.

The latter sort of analysis suggests that the velocity of money
and the rate of interest are themselves responding to common
influences. Such analysis and the regression results, therefore,
suggest the use of the velocity of money and the rate of interest
as substitute variables. Indeed, the rate of interest is an indicator of
credit policy, and it is further suggested that the velocity of money
could serve as such an indicator as well. The notion of changes
in policy that consist of differences between the rate of change in
income and the rate of change in the stock of money, however,
has some unusual implications for the nature of a policy of credit
tightness and for the role of the monetary officials.

Credit in the preceding context is tight when interest rates are
rising. It is tight in the sense that relative to the changes in
income (or total assets) it is less available at the banks and
available only at higher rates in other sectors of the financial
markets. The money stock, on the other hand, may be expanding
at a less rapid rate than income, and an increase in the rate of
expansion for the money stock may contribute to a further rise
in interest rates via, say, the price expectations effect. In fact,
money balances are actually being disposed of in relation to assets
(or income) so as to indicate an abundance of money when
velocity is rising. The prospect, too, that an increase in the rate

of expansion of the money stock may contribute to higher interest rates is in contrast to some rather common notions about the effects of monetary policy—notably, those implicitly employing a definition of monetary policy that equates uses of the tools of general credit control with changes in monetary policy, and those implying a direct causal link between changes in the money stock and changes in the rate of interest. An open-market purchase, for example, has been treated by some analysts as a monetary policy in which an increase in the money stock caused lower rates via the exchange of an excess of desired money balances for bonds. An inconsistency, then, is revealed between the presence of parallel changes in the rate of interest and velocity, and two conventional notions—that of a direct causal sequence from money supply to interest-rate changes; and that whereby monetary policy exerts its effect via changes in the rate of interest.

The apparent response of interest rates and velocity to similar factors and the prospect of both serving as indicators of changes in monetary policy hold certain implications for the route via which monetary policy exerts its effect and for the role of the monetary officials. In such a context, monetary policy exerts its major effects on the levels of income, output, and employment, via buoyancy in expectations—i.e., on the flows of returns from the various classes of assets after allowing for risk and liquidity elements. In the above context, furthermore the main function of the monetary officials is to decide on the timing and the extent of changes in monetary policy, consciously or unconsciously, with the view to affecting the degree of certainty about the future, varying the degree of buoyancy in expectations, and achieving a growth rate consistent with other national economic goals.

Chapter 12

SOME CONCLUSIONS: A SUMMARY

This chapter consists of a restatement of some selected conclusions—notably, those pertaining most directly to the questions posed toward the end of Chapter 1. In broad outline they tend to concern the following: changes implicit in responses to manipulations of variables in monetary analysis; the velocity–interest rate association or somewhat related material on the liquidity trap; the stability of the demand function for money narrowly or broadly defined and the somewhat related question of the appropriate empirical definition of money; the wealth or "luxury" goods hypothesis; evidence from sector studies about the demand for money; the prospect of lags in the adjustment of "desired" balances to interest-rate changes, and so on; definitions of monetary policy and some effects of changes in monetary policy; and the support for the underlying foundations of monetary analysis.

To begin with, changing the scale of operations in the framework of monetary economics calls for equal proportional changes in the stock of money, total assets (or wealth), and the flow of income, and such changes and the unit elasticities they imply are reflected in the various analyses of data over long periods of time. The rate of interest does not change in response to the scale changes, but, a change in the rate of return on additions to real capital in response to various factors will apparently give rise to changes in income and assets such that parallel movements in the velocity of money and the interest rate occur when the stock of money increases less than in proportion to income. Next, working with a form of the velocity–interest rate association, Meltzer indicates that empirical evidence of the United States fails to support the liquidity-trap hypothesis. His approach implied that changes in the speculative demand for balances relative to the over-all demand were varying inversely with the rate of interest, and using a special definition (the inverse of permanent velocity) he found the inverse to have an elasticity of about one with respect to the rate of interest. His results and analysis supported the notion of a constant elasticity. His scatter diagram for inverse velocity and the rate of interest, using arithmetic scales, suggests a hyperbolic curve of the type characterizing the liquidity-preference function in the common two-dimensional sketches.

The velocity–interest rate association may be cited as simply a covariation in the respective variables, independent of any causal relationship between the variables. Latané did this in his earlier work. On some other occasions, however, explanations are given for the velocity–interest rate association that imply causal relationships. Usually, these explanations have some relevance to questions concerning the effect of changes in the rate of interest (possibly by the monetary officials) on velocity. On some other occasions, on the other hand, expectations have been introduced such that switching proceeded between broader classes of assets—including assets with fixed and residual claims against future income. Factors impinging upon degrees of certainty about the future and expectations in general—such as tax credits and rates of changes in prices—have been invoked on these occasions as a means of explaining the switching phenomena which, in turn, would give rise to interest-rate changes and changes in the stock of money in relation to income (or total assets). In these latter instances the causal sequence is quite different from that suggested by the use of the rate of interest as an "explanatory" variable in the operational sense. The empirical evidence, furthermore, does not support the notion of a ceiling on velocity, in part because the evidence does not support the notion of a rise in interest rates causing an activation of idle balances, and, in part because the interest elasticity of proportionate cash balances seems to be sufficiently unchanged by changes in the rate of interest. According to the notion of a ceiling on the velocity of money, increases in the rate of interest are supposed to activate idle balances; but at some rate idle balances become depleted and velocity reaches a ceiling. In the context of this explanation of a rise in velocity and a ceiling, some maintain that the evolution of institutional changes will cause the ceiling to gradually move. Such notions arose in connection with the availability of credit doctrine, whereby increases in the rate of interest were supposed to meet a ceiling on velocity and, via a "pinning-in" effect on credit granting institutions, constrain further increases in expenditures and reduce the availability of credit.

A good bit of evidence supports the prospect of interest-rate changes paralleling some form of switching phenomena, independent of any direct causal relationship. The case for switching from cash to time deposits in response to interest-rate changes, however, seems rather strong, and the prospect of differential responses, too, suggests some basis for excluding time deposits from the definition of money. In the case of switching into time deposits, Meltzer finds that broadening the money stock to include time deposits weakens the velocity–interest rate association, and Christ, also, has mentioned the tendency for the rate of interest to explain less of the variation in inverse velocity when including time deposits as a part of the money stock in the velocity ratio. Meltzer's results involving the regression of different empirical definitions of money on income and the rate of interest indicate, moreover, that the demand function for the stock of money balances narrowly defined is at least as stable as the stock for balances broadly defined to include time deposits.

According to Laidler's results, the inclusion of time deposits in the empirical definition of money yields stable coefficients for a number of periods for permanent income in linear regression analyses of first differences. The particular analyses in question, however, indicate the presence of a role for time deposits as a nonmonetary asset, and they indicate, as well, an element of arbitrariness in the statistical definition of money. Hamburger's and Lee's results from analyses of data for the household sector also fail to provide any support for broadening the definition of money.

Some analysis indicates that Milton Friedman's support for the wealth hypothesis is apparently a result of his use of a money stock that includes time deposits. In any event, the wealth or "luxury" goods hypothesis, as it applies to money, fails to predict the direction of the post-World War II trend in the velocity of money. In addition, estimates from survey data for the household sector indicate a unit income elasticity, and the evidence from a variety of other analyses supports the unitary hypothesis. The evidence in the case of cross-section data for manufacturing corporations, moreover, supports the less than unitary asset size (or sales) elasticity hypothesis.

The evidence from the time-series data for manufacturing corporations for the period 1952–64 reflects the recurring association between velocity and the rate of interest, but there is no negative association between the ratio of cash to governments and the rate of interest. In fact, the standard hypothesis calling for switching between cash and governments is unsupported by the data. It fails the test against the alternative too, in so far as manufacturing corporations are concerned. Apparently, the form of switching that is paralleling changes in the rate of interest involves switching between broader classes of assets. The ratio of households' cash balances to various classes of noncash liquid assets, on the other hand, declines in the post-World War II years when interest rates are rising, but the statistical evidence concerning the cause is inconclusive. There are possible differences in the sort of switching phenomena exhibited by the manufacturing and household sectors.

The increases in the over-all liquidity structure of manufacturing firms occur in response to increases in size as measured by sales or assets. The process involves a reduction in bank loans relative to total assets as size increases, a decline in the need for cash in relation to assets as bank loans decline in relation to assets, and a release of cash to government securities. The latter changes in the sources of liquidity involve, in a sense, a reduction in the demand for money, but the liquidity of firms has declined as velocity has increased over the postwar years. For the household sector, moreover, Lee estimates income elasticities of the demand for money and other debt-type assets of about unity, and provides, in doing so, a basis for rejecting the Gurley-Shaw hypothesis. In a second paper, however, Lee reverses his position on the Gurley-Shaw hypothesis.

Apparently, differences in manufacturing industries' demands for cash can be explained by differences in firm sizes; industry groups populated by relatively small firms have greater than unitary sales elasticity coefficients, and other groups have other elasticities. What happens is that the velocity of cash at first declines and then rises, as firms increase in asset size. But the decline in velocity occurs only over a small fraction of the lower portion of the values the asset-size variable may take on. As firms increase beyond 10 million dollars in asset size, cash holdings increase less than in proportion to sales and continue to increase less than in proportion to asset size. This asset size of 10 million occurs before the asset-size variable takes on one per cent of its values, as size increases.

The structural and interest-rate changes of the type outlined imply lagged relations between selected time series, but some analysts have tended to deal with these as evidence of an adjustment lag in the level of "desired" money balances. De Leeuw, for example, observes fluctuations in long-term rates of interest that lead inverse fluctuations in real per capita demand deposits, and views these changes as suggesting some simple evidence of a lagged reaction of money holdings to interest rates. Both he and Hendershott present results in support of the presence of relatively long lags in the adjustment of "desired" balances to changes in the rate of interest and so on. These authors imply rather orthodox notions about the relation between money demand and interest rates, but observed behavior of time series whereby interest-rate changes lead changes in real per capita demand deposits may be explained in terms other than those of a long lag in the responsiveness of money holdings to interest-rate changes and so on. The notion of a long lag in the adjustment of desired currency holdings, moreover, seems excessively in contrast to notions about the ease with which currency holdings may be adjusted in relation to income (or assets). Hamburger, in fact, recognizes the ease with which households can adjust the level of their balances in relation to other variables, and he cites other factors than an adjustment lag in dealing with lagged relations. Allais, in a restatement of the quantity theory says, "The discrepancy between the actual and the desired value of money holdings is always relatively small."

De Leeuw, Hendershott, Hamburger, and others have attempted to deal with some questions about the effectiveness of monetary policy, in the context of perhaps excessively conventional notions about the relation between money demand and interest rates. They deal, for instance, with the unqualified notion that an open-market purchase increases the money supply and reduces interest rates. When interest rates and velocity are rising, however, money balances are being drawn down in relation to income (or assets) so as to suggest both tight credit and an excess of "desired" money balances, and increasing the money stock at a faster rate under such conditions contributes to further tightness of credit relative to its demand and a further rise in the rate of interest and velocity via, say, the price expectations effect of the policy of increasing the money stock at a faster rate. This prospect, of course, is contrary to the unqualified notion that an increase in the money stock causes lower rates via the exchange of an excess of desired balances for bonds.

Apparently an inconsistency exists between these two notions: the one where increases in the growth of the money stock contribute to higher interest rates and velocity at times of rising velocity; and the unqualified notion that an increase in the money stock causes lower interest rates via the exchange of an excess of desired money balances for bonds. The inconsistency results from the failure to allow for the presence of effects that are intermediate to the change in the money stock and the change in the rate of interest such as the price expectations effect. The causal sequence between money-stock changes and interest-rate changes is not a direct one, as numerous bits of analysis and accompanying demand functions with an interest-rate determinant suggest. The role of factors such as the rate of change in prices as determinants of both interest rates and the demand for money suggests, furthermore, redundancy in the inclusion of such factors along with interest rates as determinants of the demand for money.

Over-all, results from regression analyses of aggregate and much of the sector data appear to support, in a very general way, the underlying foundations of monetary analysis as it would apply to changes over several-year spans and even longer periods. As a first approximation and in broad outline the foundations may be viewed as calling for the following changes: equal percentage changes in the money stock and income (wealth or total assets), equal percentage changes in the money stock and prices (or income)—all in response to changes in the scale of operations; and parallel and almost equal percentage changes in the income velocity of money and the rate of interest, when disproportionate changes occur in the stock and flow variables. There are apparent differences in income or asset-size elasticities that are readily evident or implicit in several sets of regression results, after logarithmic transformations of the data—namely, those involving cross-section data and the regression of corporate cash on asset size (or sales); those involving the regression of the velocity of money on the rate of interest; and those involving the regression of the money stock on income and the rate of interest. However, these differences may be explained by allowing for the following: differences in the relevant time dimensions; difficulties imposed upon the interpretation of the meaning of the respective multiple regression coefficients in the presence of multicollinearity; and the relevance of certain results to the various constructs of monetary theory after the use of strenuous methods or techniques in attempts to remove or reduce the multicollinearity and/or, in some instances, autocorrelation in the error terms.

GLOSSARY OF STATISTICAL TERMS
AND CRITERIA*

A glossary of statistical terms and criteria commonly appearing in, or related to, the literature on the demand for money appears below.[1] Critical comments and/or elaborations of definitions and criteria are at times included with a view to suggesting—at the intuitive level—their more formal meanings. In many instances

---

* This glossary was prepared with the collaboration of Montgomery D. Anderson, Professor of Economics and Statistics, University of Florida.

[1] Dictionaries of statistical terms are available, but they tend to be inadequate with respect to some of the usages involved in the literature in question. For a possibly useful dictionary, see, e.g., Maurice G. Kendall and William R. Buckland, *A Dictionary of Statistical Terms*, Second Edition, (New York: Hafner Publishing Company, 1960).

For the most part, the statistical terms and criteria concern regression analysis. Readily available works setting forth the general linear-regression model include Arthur S. Goldberger, *Econometric Theory* (New York: John Wiley and Sons, Inc., 1964); and J. Johnston, *Econometric Methods* (New York: McGraw-Hill Book Company, Inc., 1963).

For a possibly helpful introduction to research methods in general, see Robert Ferber and P. J. Verdoorn, *Research Methods in Economics and Business* (New York: The Macmillan Company, 1965). For an introductory review of econometric problems, see Richard C. Clelland, John S. deCani, Francis E. Brown, J. Parker Bursk, and Donald S. Murray, *Basic Statistics with Business Applications* (New York: John Wiley & Sons, Inc., 1966), pp. 522–552.

For a treatment of some statistical methods and distributed lags in demand relations, see Marc Nerlove, *Distributed Lags and Demand Analysis for Agricultural and Other Commodities* (Washington, D.C.: U. S. Government Printing Office, 1958). Distributed lag distributions are involved in some of the demand for money papers cited in Chapters 6, 9 and 10. For a forthcoming survey article, see Zvi Griliches, "Distributed Lags: A Survey," *Econometrica*.

readily available and/or classical sources are cited that deal at greater length with the statistical methods involved. The glossary is provided for the nonspecialist as a ready reference to technical terms and criteria. The various entries appear in alphabetical order, but cross references are made on occasion to related or more elementary terms. There are also some references to the Appendix to Chapter 2, since the glossary is in some respects an extension of the appendix.

ANALYSIS OF VARIANCE.   (*See* Sec. 2A.3 of Appendix to Chapter 2.)

ARGUMENT.   The term "argument" sometimes refers to an independent variable in a mathematical function, and sometimes it refers to an independent variable in a regression analysis or in an empirically derived demand function.

(*See also* Independent variable; Dependent variable.)

AUTOCORRELATION.   (*See* Sec. 2A.4 of Appendix to Chapter 2.)

BEHAVIORAL EQUATION.   (*See* Definitional equation.)

BEHAVIORAL RELATIONSHIP.   (*See* Definitional equation.)

"CAUSATION" AND REGRESSION ANALYSES.   Regression analyses impute functional relationships and, at times, suggest that there is a causational nexus between the dependent variable and the independent variable or variables. A case in point is our regression analysis concerning the relationship between velocity and the rate of interest. Christ presents similar regression results and suggests that "changes in the velocity of money in response to interest-rate fluctuations may be substantial enough to be of concern to monetary authorities in their attempts to stabilize the economy."[2] The direction of causation in the area in question, however, is not determined by regression analysis. This question is primarily a matter to be dealt with by a priori considerations in monetary analysis (theory), with the support of results from analyses of empirical data.

CHOW TEST.   (*See* Analysis of variance.)

---

[2] See Carl F. Christ, "Interest Rates and 'Portfolio Selection' among Liquid Assets in the U.S.," *Measurement in Economics* (Stanford, California: Stanford University Press, 1963), p. 204.

COEFFICIENT OF CORRELATION (r). (*See* Coefficient of determination.)

COEFFICIENT OF DETERMINATION (r^2). According to the classical theory of regression the coefficient of determination tells the proportion of variation in the dependent variable (y) that is "accounted for" by variations in the independent variable (x)—i.e.,

$$r^2 = \frac{\text{Variance in } y \text{ "explained" by variance in } x}{\text{Total variance in } y}$$

As the formula suggests, r^2 may vary between zero and one, and $r^2 = 1$ when all the variation in the dependent variable of a linear relationship is accounted for by the variation in the independent variable. Further, r is the coefficient of correlation; a perfect correlation in indicated by one; a total absence of correlation by zero, and so on ($1 \geqq r \geqq 0$); and a plus or minus sign may be attached, depending on the presence of a positive or negative relationship between x and y. These coefficients reveal the goodness of fit of a linear regression line to observations involving two variables, even when they do not mean anything else, because by definition $r^2 \equiv$ (variance of classical line of regression of y and x)/(total variance of y).

(*See also* Standard error of estimate; Analysis of variance; Least-squares regression line.)

COEFFICIENT OF MULTIPLE DETERMINATION (R^2). The coefficient of multiple determination is the proportion of the variance in the dependent variable which can be estimated by changes in the independent variables in a linear multiple regression analysis. (It is usually denoted by R^2, and its square root is the coefficient of multiple correlation.) The formula for computing R^2 directly is rather complicated, but one way of getting around the complexity and, at the same time, at the intuitive meaning of the coefficient, is to resort to the fundamental definition of the coefficient of multiple determination itself. Thus, if we have a measure for the variance (denoted s_y^2) in the observed values and a multiple regression equation to provide estimates of the dependent variable (denoted $\hat{y}$), then we may do several things: compute the differences in the observed values and the estimated values (e.g.,

$y_t - \hat{y}_t$, $t = 1, 2, \ldots, n$); take the ratio of the variance in the latter differences (denoted $s^2_{y-\hat{y}}$) to the variance in the observed values to get the proportion of "unexplained" variance in the dependent variable (i.e., $s^2_{y-\hat{y}}/s^2_y$); and compute R^2 by the expression $R^2 = 1 - (s^2_{y-\hat{y}}/s^2_y)$ by analogy with the process dealt with above in the discussion of r^2. The ratio in the right-hand member of the latter expression vanishes when all the variability in the dependent variable is "explained" (i.e., $s^2_{y-\hat{y}} \to 0$), and $R^2 = 1$.

The above result may be interpreted in terms of the following equation from Sec. 2A.5 of the text:

$$\ln (M/P) = \ln a - 0.674 \ln i + 0.971 \ln Y/P, \qquad R^2 = 0.98$$

Here we note that ninety-eight per cent of the variability of the variable $\ln (M/P)$ may be computed from the equation. The remaining two per cent is the variance of the error made by the computed equation.

(*See also* Coefficient of multiple determination, adjusted for degrees of freedom; Least-squares regression line analysis; Coefficient of determination; Variance; Analysis of variance.)

COEFFICIENT OF MULTIPLE DETERMINATION, ADJUSTED FOR DEGREES OF FREEDOM. The coefficient of multiple determination (R^2) is an approximation to the coefficient of multiple determination after correction for the number of constants (m) in the regression equation. The approximation improves and the need for the adjustment diminishes as the number of observations (n) increases, given m. The adjusted coefficient is denoted $\bar{R}^2$,

$$\bar{R}^2 = 1 - \left[(1 - R^2) \frac{n - 1}{n - m} \right]$$

where n and m are the number of observations and the number of stants, respectively.[3]

(*See also* Coefficient of multiple determination; Degrees of freedom.)

---

[3] See Frederick C. Mills, *Statistical Methods*, 3rd edition (New York: Henry Holt and Company, 1955), p. 626.

COEFFICIENT OF TOTAL DETERMINATION (R^2). (*See* Coefficient of multiple determination.)

CONFIDENCE INTERVALS. (*See* t-Tests and confidence intervals.)

DEFINITIONAL EQUATION. Definitional equations are identities that hold under all circumstances by the definition of the terms. An example of a definitional equation is $V_y \equiv Y/M$, where V_y is the income velocity of money. Y is income, and M is the money stock. A behavioral equation, in contrast, defines some relationship between variables concerning some form of behavior by groups or individuals, firms, or households.

Examples of behavioral equations are $\ln r = 0.02 + 1.09 \ln V_y$, and $\ln V_y = 0.11 + 0.81 \ln r$, where r is the rate of interest.

DEGREES OF FREEDOM. In regression analysis, as a rule of thumb, the number of degrees of freedom is equal to the number of observations involved in estimating a regression equation minus the number of parameters in the regression equation in question. The number of parameters represents the degrees of freedom "given up" and used to fix points from which deviations are measured. The number of degrees of freedom is the number appropriate when Student's t-distribution is used to draw inferences in regression analysis. In general, the degrees of freedom are the observations not used up in the estimating or statistical procedure involved in a given computation. They are, in other words, the number of observations in excess of the number which would prohibit any imperfection of a statistical inference made without regard to degrees of freedom.

If we should fit a straight line to two observations on two variables, the fit would have to be perfect in all such cases. The inference drawn (without regard to the degrees of freedom, in such a case) would be that the relationship between the variables is linear. But if we fit a straight line to a sample of three observations, there would be one degree of freedom—i.e., one more observation than the number compelling perfection in the sample, regardless of the situation in the population.

(*See also* t-Tests and confidence intervals.)

DEPENDENT VARIABLE. The term "dependent variable" in a regression analysis usually refers to the value of the variable being estimated. For example, given the equation $\ln V_y = 0.11 + 0.81 \ln r$, a value for $\ln V_y$ is estimated when a value is assigned to the variable $\ln r$. "Dependent" in ordinary statistical parlance should not be confused with the definition of dependency as given by pure mathematics.

(*See also* Independent variable.)

DETERMINANTS OF THE DEMAND FOR MONEY. Mathematically speaking, a determinant is a square array of quantities called "elements," and it is a number—the number being symbolized by the sum of certain products of the elements. In statistical analyses, however, we speak of the determinants of a demand function (such as that for money) to mean the independent variables in an estimatin~ equation. In these analyses, the dependent or predicted variable is determined by the value of the independent variable(s). In re gression equations, furthermore, the error terms are usually random variables, since their values are not determinable by any systematic relationship.

(*See also* Independent variable; Random variable.)

ENDOGENOUS VARIABLE. An endogenous variable is one that is explained or determined by the model in which it appears. It contributes to the determination of other variables in the model, and it is in turn determined by the other variables.

(*See also* Exogenous variable.)

EQUATION SYSTEM. (*See* Nonstochastic equation system.)

EXOGENOUS VARIABLE. An exogenous variable is determined by forces outside of the model. It is a parameter or constant (and possibly a variable parameter or constant) of the model. Exogenous variables determine the endogenous variables, and they are independent of the endogenous variables. In the case of the liquidity-preference model (Sec. 4.2), the rate of interest (r) is determined by the parameters, given income, (Y), in the following manner:

$$r = \frac{b}{(c/Y) - a}.$$

F-RATIO. (*See* Analysis of variance, Sec. 2A.3 of Appendix to Chapter 2.)

GOODNESS OF FIT. (*See* Standard error of estimate; Coefficient of determination.)

IDENTIFICATION PROBLEM.   Identification is one of the problems encountered in regression analyses of time-series data concerning
supply and demand schedules.[4] It is mentioned under simultaneous-
equations bias, Sec. 2A.2 of Appendix to Chapter 2.

INDEPENDENT VARIABLE(S).   Independent variables are loosely defined as the variables upon which the computations of a dependent
variable depend. The independent variables are simply taken as
observed, and they are sometimes called predictors or regressors.
There is one independent variable in a simple regression analysis
and two or more in a multiple regression analysis. So-called independent variables, as the term "independent" may suggest, are not
necessarily independent of the dependent variable in any real-
world phenomena under consideration, nor are they necessarily
independent of each other.

(*See also* Dependent variable; Multicollinearity.)

LEAST-SQUARES REGRESSION LINE.   The least-squares regression line
is the regression line resulting from an application of ordinary
least-squares regression analysis. It is usually thought of as the
line fitted to a set of observations such that the sum of the square
of the vertical distances between the line and the observed points
is a minimum. Minimizing the square of the vertical distances,
moreover, implies a minimum absolute value of the average error
term. (*See* Random variable.) For example, if we write the
empirical equation $\ln \widehat{V}_y = \widehat{\alpha} + \widehat{\beta} \ln r + u$, where $\widehat{\alpha}$ and $\widehat{\beta}$ are
estimated parameters, and $\ln \widehat{V}_y$ is the predicted value of the de-
pendent variable, we may then write for each of the 72 actual or
observed values of $\ln V_y$ in Table 2A–1,

$$(\ln V_y)_1 - (\ln \widehat{V}_y)_1 = u_1 = (\ln V_y)_1 - \widehat{\alpha} - \widehat{\beta}(\ln r)_1$$
$$(\ln V_y)_2 - (\ln \widehat{V}_y)_2 = u_2 = (\ln V_y)_2 - \widehat{\alpha} - \widehat{\beta}(\ln r)_2$$

$$\cdots$$

$$(\ln V_y)_{72} - (\ln \widehat{V}_y)_{72} = u_{72} = (\ln V_y)_{72} - \widehat{\alpha} - \widehat{\beta}(\ln r)_{72}$$

This is written with the condition that the mean value for the

---

[4] For introductory discussions of the problems, see Clelland, *et al., op. cit.,*
pp. 530–538; Ferber and Verdoorn, *op. cit.,* pp. 411–413; Goldberger, *op.
cit.,* pp. 306–318; and Johnston, *op. cit.,* pp. 240–252.

seventy-two u's is zero. Indeed, the latter condition is implied in the use of the ordinary least-squares, as well as the assumption that the errors $u_1, u_2, \ldots, u_{72}$ are random and independently distributed, i.e., independently distributed in the sense that the distribution of the error term is independent of the value of $\ln r$. We need not assume that the distributions for the random error terms are normal.

MULTICOLLINEARITY.   (*See* Sec. 2A.5 of Appendix to Chapter 2.)

MULTIPLE REGRESSION ANALYSIS.   (*See* Regression analysis.)

NONSTOCHASTIC EQUATION SYSTEM.   An equation system such as that constituting the liquidity-preference model (Sec. 3.3) is said to be nonstochastic. This is because it contains no allowance for possible errors in measurement or discrepancies in empirically estimated values and actual values.

(*See also* Random variable.)

ONE-TAIL TEST.   (*See* Two-tail test; t-Tests and confidence intervals.)

PARTIAL CORRELATION.   A partial correlation coefficient is, according to the classical theory of regression analysis, a measure of the degree of association between a dependent variable and a given "independent" variable. In essence, it is the simple linear correlation between a dependent variable and a given independent variable, the effect of any additional independent variables being "held constant." If we think of X_1, X_2, and X_3 as representing the three variables in the three-variable case, then partial correlation coefficients may be denoted as $r_{12.3}$, $r_{13.2}$, and $r_{23.1}$, where

$r_{12.3}$ is the value of the correlation coefficient resulting from the correlation of the first and second variable, the third variable being held constant,

$r_{13.2}$ is the value of the correlation coefficient resulting from the correlation of the first and third variable the second being held constant, and

$r_{23.1}$ is the value of the correlation coefficient resulting from the correlation of the second and third variable, the first being held constant.

In each instance—$r_{12.3}$, $r_{13.2}$, and $r_{23.1}$—the variable being held constant is constant only in a computational sense (i.e., being held constant as in the case of *ceteris paribus* in economics) as distinct from the operational sense.

To illuminate partial correlation coefficients further, first recall the definitions for the coefficient of multiple determination and its square root, the coefficient of multiple correlation—namely

$$R^2_{1.23} \equiv 1 - \frac{s^2_{1.23}}{s^2_1}$$

where the first figure in the subscripts indicates the variable on the left hand side of the regression equation, and where the figures after the point indicate other variables taken account of by the analysis. One way of deriving the partial correlation coefficient (i.e., $r_{13.2}$) is to take the square root of the coefficient of partial determination (i.e., $r_{13.2} = \sqrt{r^2_{13.2}}$), where[5]

$$r^2_{13.2} \equiv \frac{R^2_{1.23} - r^2_{12}}{1 - r^2_{12}}$$

Here one is, in effect, attempting to measure the influence of the third variable on the dependent variable with the second variable "kept constant." An alternative computational form is

$$r^2_{12.3} = \frac{(r_{12} - r_{13}r_{23})^2}{(1 - r^2_{13})(1 - r^2_{23})}$$

where $r_{12.3}$ is the partial correlation coefficient and variables one and two are being correlated, the third variable held constant. Coefficients r_{12}, r_{13}, and r_{23} are simple correlation coefficients for the correlation between the variables designated by the subscripts.

Recalling one of Meltzer's equations,

$$\ln M = -1.65 - 0.781 \ln r + 1.01 \ln W + u$$

Partial Correlations: $r_{12.3} = -0.88$ $r_{13.2} = 0.99$

where M is the money stock, r is the rate of interest, and W is nonhuman wealth, and where -0.88 is the partial correlation co-

---

[5] For this and some other formulas concerning the partial correlation coefficient in three space, see Johnston, *op. cit.*, pp. 54–61.

efficient for $\ln M$ and $\ln r$ when one attempts to remove the influence of $\ln W$ from $\ln M$ and $\ln r$, and so on.

(*See also* Partial regression coefficient.)

PARTIAL REGRESSION COEFFICIENT(s). In a multiple regression equation of the type represented in Table 2A–3,

$$\ln (M_1/P) = \ln a -1.001 \ln i + 1.150 \ln (W/P),$$

the multiple regression coefficients are sometimes called partial regression coefficients. They follow from the partial differentiation of the equation—e.g.,

$$\frac{\partial \ln (M_1/P)}{\partial \ln i} = -1.001 \quad \text{and} \quad \frac{\partial \ln (M_1/P)}{\partial \ln (W/P)} = 1.150$$

and they show how much the variables $\ln i$ and $\ln (W/P)$, respectively, contribute to the estimation of the value of the variable $\ln (M_1/P)$. This contribution may, for example, be viewed as the effect of one unit of increase in one "independent" variable on the "dependent" variable, on the average in the plane of best fit, the other independent variable constant. The "influence," in a computational sense, however, does not necessarily signify an equivalent operational influence, due to the difficulties of multicollinearity and other implied restraints in the statistical method.

(*See also* Regression coefficient.)

POPULATION. The population is the parent set from which a sample set may be observed or delineated, usually with the view to investigating the properties of the parent set. The population may be a finite or infinitely large set of observations, units, balls, and so on. The method of ordinary least-squares regression analysis is said to provide, as estimates of unknown population values, those sample values that minimize the sum of the squares of the deviations of the sample observations from the sample values or estimates.

RANDOM VARIABLE. A random variable is distinct from an ordinary mathematical variable that may be specified merely by a portion of a numbered line. It is, in fact, a variable to whose values or intervals only probabilities can be assigned. If the functions $f(x)$ and $f(x,y)$ in the one and two variable cases, respectively, are probability distributions, then x and y, respectively, are random variables. Indeed, by the introduction of a random variable, a model, such as $\ln V_y = \alpha + \beta \ln r$, is prepared for statistical analysis—that is, a random error term may be introduced to deal with the inexact relation between the variables $\ln V_y$ and $\ln r$. Thus the model becomes

(1) $$\ln V_y = \alpha + \beta \ln r + u$$

where u is the random error term. The value $\ln V_y$, however, depends on the random error term and, consequently, $\ln V_y$ must be regarded as a random variable in the above context.

Any disturbance in $\ln V_y$ not explained by $\ln r$ is usually assumed to be explained by additional variables or to be random. If we assume that $\ln r$ is the only explanatory variable for $\ln V_y$ then the unexplained disturbance in $\ln V_y$ may be due to random errors. On the other hand, rearranging the terms of relation (1), one obtains

(2) $$\ln r = -\alpha\beta^{-1} + \beta^{-1} \ln V_y - \beta^{-1}u$$

or

(2.1) $$\ln r = \gamma + \partial \ln V_y + \epsilon$$

where $\gamma = -\alpha\beta^{-1}$, $\partial = \beta^{-1}$, and $\epsilon = -\beta^{-1}u$. Hence, we see that u may be a random error in either $\ln r$ or in $\ln V_y$. The point is that the relationship between $\ln V_y$ and $\ln r$ is a probability structure in which either variable may be regarded as a probability function of the other. But u cannot be independent of both $\ln r$ and $\ln V_y$.

REGRESSION ANALYSIS. Ordinary least-squares regression analysis is a statistical method for dealing with imperfect relationships between variables. The terms "regression analysis" and "correlation analysis" are terms which once pertained to the nature of the relationship and the degree of the relationship, respectively, but the original distinction has tended to fade. The analysis is called simple regression analysis when the relation involves only one "independent" variable and an error factor. It is a multiple regression analysis when two or more variables are used to "explain" the behavior of the so-called dependent variable.

Ordinary least-squares regression analysis is widely used when dealing with single equation models because, as Ferber and Verdoorn note, "of the convenient properties of the estimates." This widespread use occurs despite the prospect of bias in the probable errors of estimates due to the presence of autocorrelation, and in spite of such problems as multicollinearity. Continuing, Ferber and Verdoorn say, "the fact that alternative criteria can be used for estimating parameters of single equations is hardly ever considered."[6] But this statement is less generally true now than formerly.

(*See also* Autocorrelation; Multicollinearity.)

REGRESSION COEFFICIENT. A regression coefficient is defined by the equation for β in our discussion of the least-squares regression line. It is a measure of the expected response of the predicted value of the dependent variable to changes in the independent variable. In the case of linear regressions involving logarithmically transformed data (Sec. 3.3) it is a measure of the elasticity of the response or the percentage change in the dependent variable associated with a unit percentage change in the independent variable. A serious understatement of the probable error of estimate of a regression coefficient is said to arise when the error terms in a regression analysis are autocorrelated. The errors of estimate are simply the deviations of the actual values of the dependent variable from the expected values.

(*See also* Autocorrelation; Partial regression coefficient; Standard error of the regression coefficient.)

REGRESSION CURVE (SURFACE). A regression curve is a set of points consisting of ordered pairs $(x_i, \hat{y}_i)$, $i = 1, 2, \ldots, n$, where the x's are the observed values of the independent variable and the $\hat{y}$'s are the corresponding expected values for the dependent variable, and where the locus of points is a curved line rather than a straight line. For cases with more than two independent variables the coordinates define a curvilinear surface.

REGRESSION LINE. (*See* Sec. 2A.1 of Appendix to Chapter 2.)

SAMPLE. A subset from a set of units referred to as the population, parent population, or set. The sample may consist of a set of

---

[6] See Ferber and Verdoorn, *op. cit.*, p. 413.

observations selected with a view to investigating the properties of a large set of possible observations of the same type.

SCATTER DIAGRAM. A scatter diagram is a diagram showing a set of observations concerning a simple regression analysis. The observations are points specified by the coordinates consisting of the raw data being analyzed. Figure 2A–1 contains examples of such diagrams. The coordinates for the respective points shown in the figure are from Table 2A–1.

SIMPLE REGRESSION ANALYSIS. (*See* Regression analysis.)

SIMULTANEOUS-EQUATIONS BIAS. (*See* Sec. 2A.2 of Appendix to Chapter 2.)

STANDARD ERROR OF ESTIMATE. The standard error of estimate is an absolute measure of dispersion or scatter about the line of regression, usually measured along the axis of the dependent or predicted variable. It is a form of average of deviations about the regression line, and one standard error of estimate measured off plus and minus about the regression line will include 68 per cent of the observations scattered about the regression line if the scatter is normally distributed and independent of the regression line. In this respect, the standard error of estimate is similar to the standard deviation, except the *standard deviation* measures the scatter about the arithmetic mean of the dependent variable. In case the conditions of the classical theory of regression obtain, the standard error of estimate is, further, the square root of the "unexplained" variance in a dependent variable:

$$\sigma_u = \sqrt{\frac{\Sigma(y - \hat{y})^2}{n}}$$

where n is the number of observations in the sample, and $\Sigma(y - \hat{y})^2$ is the sum of the square of the vertical differences between the observed and estimated values of the dependent variable.

As an absolute measure in the form of an average, the standard error of estimate is expressed in terms of original units of the dependent variable. In Sec. 2.2, for example, results from regressing the money stock and the time deposits on time for the 76 quarters (i.e., $t = 1, 2, \ldots, 76$) 1947–65, included standard errors of approximately 2.8 and 12.2 billion dollars respectively. In comparing such results, however, the scale as well as the size of the estimated values are relevant. In the present instance, the difference between the standard errors for the money stock and time deposits is really more than the absolute figures suggest, before allowance is made for the difference in the average size of the money stock and the time deposits. This "allowance" can be made by dividing each standard error by the arithmetic mean of the respective series.

(*See also* Variance; Analysis of variance.)

STANDARD ERROR OF THE REGRESSION COEFFICIENT.   The values for the parameters in the regression equation (e.g., α and β, under "least squares regression line") are of the nature of averages, and it is often necessary or important to measure the amount of sampling error in these sample averages. This necessity may lead to the use of the standard error of the regression coefficient (denoted s_β) in computing t-values for use in t-tests of significance. (*See t-Tests* and confidence intervals.) Coefficients in logarithmically linear relations, furthermore, are widely used in the literature on the demand for money as measures of elasticity and, in these instances, the standard errors of the regression coefficients may give some idea of the upper and lower limits of the elasticities. In any case, the standard errors may be seriously understated in the presence of autocorrelation, if they are evaluated by the classical formula for $s_{\hat{\beta}}$.

Usually, in econometric literature, the standard error appears in parentheses below the regression (or elasticity) coefficient to which it applies. For instance, in the case of the regression equations based on the data in Table 2A–1, we have:

$$\ln r = 0.02 + 1.09 \ln V_y, \qquad r^2 = 0.89$$
$$(0.047)$$

$$\ln V_y = 0.11 + 0.81 \ln r, \qquad r^2 = 0.89$$
$$(0.035)$$

STOCHASTIC VARIABLE.   (*See* Random variable.)

SYSTEMATIC VARIABLE.   One relation with which we work is that between the income velocity of money (V_y) and the rate of interest (r). It may be defined, after a logarithmic transformation of the variables, as follows:

$$\ln V_y = \alpha + \beta \ln r + u$$

where α and β are parameters, and u is a "stochastic" or random error term. If $u = 0$, then the relationship is exact. In any case, the variables $\ln V_y$ and $\ln r$ may be said to be systematic in the sense that definite values can be assigned to r and other definite values predicted for V_y with greater accuracy than if there was no systematic relationship between them.

In practice, the variable u is added or implied in equations of the preceding type to indicate an inexact relationship. This is to indicate that the estimates of V_y from the equation can be expected to deviate from the corresponding actual values because of the effect of errors of measurement or of other factors than r, even though these other factors may not be entirely independent of r. As the coefficient of determination $\rightarrow 1$, then $u \rightarrow 0$.

(*See also* Random variable; Coefficient of determination.)

t-TESTS AND CONFIDENCE INTERVALS. Given the standard error of the slope parameter ($s_{\hat{\beta}}$), the estimated regression coefficient ($\hat{\beta}$, and some hypothetical slope being considered (such as $\beta = 0$, or $\beta = 1$), a t-value may be computed—namely, $t = (\hat{\beta} - \beta)/s_{\hat{\beta}}$. The t-values generated by an application of this formula, then, may be used in conjunction with selected t-values from Student's t-distribution,[7] in the process of testing hypotheses concerning slopes of regression coefficients. The t-values are useful in conducting tests of statistical significance and in estimating confidence intervals, as defined below, if the population of the residual errors $u_1, u_2, \ldots, u_n$ for the n observations ($n = 15$, in the present illustrations) are normally distributed, as well as random and independent. Under the stated assumptions, the quantity t follows Student's distribution. The t-test, moreover, continues to be useful

---

[7] Tables for Student's t-distribution are available in several sources. For a relatively complete table, see J. F. Kenney and E. S. Keeping, *Mathematics of Statistics* (Part I), third edition (Princeton, New Jersey: D. Van Nostrand Company, Inc., 1954) pp. 322–323.

even when the sample size is relatively small and when the assumption of a normal distribution of the sample standard errors would not apply, since adjustments are made by the t-distribution for the abnormal kurtosis or difference in the degree of "peakedness" of sample distributions of $\hat{\beta}$.

To illustrate the t-test the following regression results are used:

$$\ln C = -1.75 + 0.9101 \ln A, \quad r^2 = 0.9995$$
$$(0.0058)$$
$$s_{\hat{\beta}} = 0.0058$$

empirical t-value for $\beta = 1$: $t = 15.45$

where C is cash per firm, and A is assets per firm. The results are from an analysis of cross-section data at year-end 1960 for fifteen asset-size classes (i.e., $n = 15$) of manufacturing corporations as reported by two combined sources—*Statistics of Income* and *Quarterly Financial Report for Manufacturing Corporations* (Sec. 7.3). In this illustration, cross-section data are used to avoid the obvious presence of autocorrelation in the error terms for the equations involved in the analysis of data from Table 2A.1 (*See* Autocorrelation, Sec. 2A.4). This is important because the t-test assumes no autocorrelation (as distinct, e.g., from randomness and independence), and because autocorrelated error terms result in an understatement of the sampling variance ($s_{\hat{\beta}}$) and, therefore, an overstatement of the empirical t.

In the case of the t-test of the significance of a given empirical coefficient $\hat{\beta}$, the objective is to test whether the empirical coefficient is significantly less than, greater than, or different from some hypothesized coefficient (e.g., $\beta = 1$), at a given level of significance. To carry out this test, the theoretical t is compared with $t = (\hat{\beta} - \beta)/s_{\hat{\beta}}$. Testing for an empirical t that is significantly less than one, in the present illustration,

$$t = (\hat{\beta} - \beta)/s_{\hat{\beta}} = 15.45 > t = 2.650$$

where the latter t-value is the one-tail t from the t-table for the 1 per cent level of significance for 13 degrees of freedom. In this instance, the hypothesis of an empirical t of less than unity is accepted, and apparently firms' demands for money increase less than in proportion to asset size. Had we tested for an empirical *t* simply different from one (i.e., significantly greater than or less than), a two-tail test would be implied. The concern in the one-tail test was only with the possibility of rejecting correct estimates less than one, since the hypothesis $\beta = 1$ was being tested as a means of dealing with the possibility of a less than unitary asset-size elasticity of the demand for cash. The concern in a two-tail test would be with the possibility of rejecting a correct estimate either greater than or less than one.

To say that the *t*-test is applied at the given per cent level of significance is to say that there is a given chance (expressed as the given percentage) of committing the error of excluding a correct value of a population parameter. The use of a given level of significance, too, amounts to the error of excluding a correct value of the population parameter from a "confidence interval." In fact, testing a hypothesis concerning a slope parameter at a given level of significance is equivalent to computing a confidence interval for the population parameter and accepting the hypothetical value of the parameter if it is enclosed by the confidence interval. To establish 99 per cent confidence intervals for the regression coefficient in the regression equation above, rewrite the formula for the empirical *t* with the β value unassigned, i.e., $t = (0.91 - \beta)/0.0058$; substitute the appropriate *t*-value from the *t*-table (i.e., $t = \pm 2.650$) for the empirical *t*; and solve for β, i.e.,

$$\beta = 0.91 \pm 2.650 \, (0.0058)$$
$$\beta = 0.93 \qquad \beta = 0.89$$
$$\text{upper limit} \qquad \text{lower limit}$$

The confidence limits, then, that enclose the true population coefficient at the 99 per cent confidence level are 0.93 and 0.89. Such limits computed for many samples drawn from the parent population are said to enclose the true population parameter in 99 out of 100 cases. The remaining 1 per cent of such limits would not enclose the true population parameter. In general, 99 per cent confidence limits imply a significance level of 0.5 per cent in each direction (i.e., a two-tail significance level of 1 per cent). A one-tail significance level of 1 per cent would in general be the obverse of 98 per cent confidence limits.

Applying the t-test to the results from analyses of time-series data in Table 2A–1, despite the presence of autocorrelated error terms, we have

(1) $\ln r = 0.02 + 1.09\,\ln V_y,$ $r^2 = 0.89$

           t-value for hypothesis $\beta = 1$: $t = 2.02$

           t-value for hypothesis $\beta = 0$: $t = 23.27$

                 $s_{\hat{\beta}} = 0.047$

(2) $\ln V_y = 0.11 + 0.81\,\ln r,$ $r^2 = 0.89$

           t-value for hypothesis $\beta = 1$: $t = 5.47$

           t-value for hypothesis $\beta = 0$: $t = 23.27$

                 $s_{\hat{\beta}} = 0.035$

where Eqs. (1) and (2) are the same as those in Figure 2A–1. In this illustration,

$$\hat{t} = (\hat{\beta} - \beta)/s_{\hat{\beta}} = 2.02 < t = 2.576,$$

where the latter t is from the t-table for the two-tailed 1 per cent level of significance for a large number of degrees of freedom. In this instance, the hypothesis $\beta = 1$ is accepted. In the case of Eq. (2) above, where $\hat{\beta} = 0.81$, the hypothesis $\beta = 1$ would be rejected at the 1 per cent level of significance. These latter tests, however, are tests of rather strong hypotheses. A satisfactory, and yet weaker, set of hypotheses may concern the simple prospect of some logarithmically linear relation between the variables in question. In this instance, the respective hypotheses $\beta = 0$ and $\beta = 0$ would readily be rejected in favor of prospective logarithmically linear relations as first approximations, since the t-values (i.e., $t = 23.27$ and $t = 23.27$) are significantly larger than the values for t from Student's t-distribution of 2.326, at the one-tailed 1 per cent level, and of 1.645, at the 5 per cent level of significance. Values of t from the table are those values that could be the result of a difference between zero and the empirical $\hat{\beta}$ due to chance or sampling error, but the larger t-values ($t = 23.27$ and $t = 23.27$) could not be accounted for by chance alone. In the latter instances, we may say that the estimated slope parameters are significantly different from zero at the 1 or 5 per cent levels of significance.

Though it was not crucial in the illustration involving Eqs. (1) and (2), the two-tail t-test was used in the set of hypotheses for

β's $= 1$ and the one-tailed t-test was used in the set for β's $= 0$. This is because the concern, in the first set, was with the possibility of rejecting correct estimates greater than or less than one. The concern, in the second set, was only with the possibility of rejecting correct estimates greater than zero, since hypotheses $\beta = 0$ were actually being tested as a means of dealing with the possibility of a positive, logarithmically linear relation. Whether one-tail or two-tail tests are used affects the selection of the t-values from the t-tables.

To establish 99 per cent confidence intervals for the regression equation (1), $t = (1.09 - \beta)/0.047$, and substituting the appropriate t-value from the t-table (i.e., $t = \pm 2.576$) for the empirical t,

$$\beta = 1.09 \pm 2.576 \,(0.047)$$

$\beta = 1.22$	$\beta = 0.96$
upper limit	lower limit

(*See also* Autocorrelation; Standard error of the regression coefficient; t-Tests for the statistical significance of multiple regression coefficients; Two-tail test.)

t-TESTS FOR THE STATISTICAL SIGNIFICANCE OF MULTIPLE REGRESSION COEFFICIENTS. The general notions of the t-test for the statistical significance of multiple regression coefficients are basically the same as those for simple regression coefficients (*See* t-Tests and confidence intervals). Recalling the formula for the t-value in the simple regression analysis (i.e., $t = [\hat{\beta} - \beta]/s_{\hat{\beta}}$), however, we may point out that the difference and additional complexity lies in the computation of the standard error of the multiple regression coefficient. Apart from this difference, the same test and tables can be used that were used in the simple case, and each of the regression coefficients may be tested separately for its statistical significance. The formula for the empirical t-values in the multiple regression case is as follows:

$$t = \frac{\hat{\beta}_i - \beta_i}{s\sqrt{a_{ii}}}$$

where $\hat{\beta}_i$, $i = 2, 3, \ldots, k$, are the $k - 1$ slope parameters in a linear regression analysis,

k is the number of constants in the estimating equation,

s is the standard deviation of the dependent variable,

s^2 is the sum of the squares of the n differences between the observed and estimated values for the dependent variable, all divided by the degrees of freedom (i.e., $n - k$), and

a_{ii} is the ith diagonal element of the inverse matrix concerning the normal equations used in deriving formulas for estimating the respective constants in the regression equation.[8]

The t-test has been discussed mainly with respect to the statistical significance of slope parameters. However, a similar test is provided for the intercept parameter.[9]

THREE-PASS LEAST SQUARES.   In effecting ordinary least-squares estimates of regression coefficients, multiple coefficients are likely to be inconsistent if the error term displays high serial correlation. Moreover, two-stage least squares does not deal with this difficulty. So-called three-pass least squares, however, has been proposed as a technique for eliminating the effect of serial correlation in models with a lagged dependent variable.[10] This technique has been summarized and applied by de Leeuw[11] (Sec. 10.1) in a study dealing with an equation of the form

$$(1) \qquad m_t = km_{t-1} + (1 - k)b_1 w_t + (1 - k)b_2 r_t + u_t$$

where m is real per capita money holdings, w_t is some measure of real per capita wealth, r_t is the rate of interest on long-term government securities, k is a parameter for the measure of the speed of adjustment in the money holdings in response to wealth and interest rate effects (if $k \to 0$, then adjustment is in the current quarter), b_1 and b_2 are additional parameters, and u is the residual

---

[8] For the formula for the empirical t-values, and for references to the ith diagonal element of the inverse matrix, see Johnston, *op. cit.* pp. 115–118. Also see Gerhard Tintner, *Econometrics* (New York: John Wiley & Sons, Inc., 1952), pp. 83–89.

[9] See Tintner, *op. cit.* p. 89.

[10] See Lester Taylor and Thomas Wilson, "Three-Pass Least Squares: A Method for Estimating Models with a Lagged Dependent Variable," *Review of Economics and Statistics*, November 1964, pp. 329–346.

[11] See Frank de Leeuw, "The Demand for Money: Speed of Adjustment, Interest Rates, and Wealth." *Monetary Process and Policy: A Symposium*, George Horwich, ed. (Homewood, Illinois: Richard D. Irwin, Inc. 1967).

error term. The technique as emphasized by de Leeuw, "assumes a relation between successive residuals of the form $u_t = pu_{t-1} + e_t$ where e_t (an error term) is not serially correlated." Upon substituting the latter expression for u_t in Eq. (1),

(2)
$$m_t = km_{t-1} + (1-k)b_1w_t + (1-k)b_2r_t + pu_{t-1} + e_t$$

and, again as pointed out by de Leeuw, ordinary least squares could be applied in the case of Eq. (2), if values u_{t-1} were available. Since they are not available, "the method of three-pass least squares consists of developing, by successive approximations, estimated values of u_{t-1} and then applying ordinary least squares."

TWO-TAIL TEST. In testing a hypothesis about the true value of a population, half of the probability of rejecting a true value may be allocated to either one of two extremes, in the case of a symmetrical test. The two-tail test then is one where areas of rejection lie at both extremes, as in a normal probability distribution. A one-tail test, on the other hand, is one in which the region of rejection is at only one end of the distribution.

(*See also t*-Tests and confidence intervals.)

TWO-STAGE LEAST SQUARES. Two-stage least squares is a procedure for estimating coefficients when some of the assumptions of ordinary regression analysis are not met—notably when the random disturbance term is correlated with one or more independent variables or when two or more "independent" variables are jointly dependent. In the first part of the two-part procedure, a linear equation may be fitted for each of the interdependent variables in the right-hand member of the original equation. This is done by regressing the variable or variables in question on all of the exogenous variables implied by the larger system of equations needed to explain the interdependence. Then, as a second part of the procedure following the substitution of the variables estimated in the first stage into the original equation,[12] least-squares regression analysis may be applied to the original equation.

---

[12] The outline of the procedure by Ferber and Verdoorn is somewhat different from that by Clelland, *et. al.* See Ferber and Verdoorn, *op. cit.*, pp. 417–418; and Clelland, *et al.*, *op. cit.*, pp. 549–552.

After using two-stage least squares in analyses of some demand-for-money relationships, de Leeuw has noted that "ordinary least squares and two-stage least squares often seem to give similar results for these relationships."[13]

VARIABLE. (*See* Systematic variable; Random variable; Independent variable; Dependent variable; Endogenous variable; Exogenous variable.)

VARIANCE. The variance is the second moment about the mean (μ) of the population. For the random variable x, the first moment is the sample mean (μ') or expected value $[E(x)]$, and the second moment (μ'_2) is $E[(x - \mu)^2] = $ var. (x). The second moment is a measure of dispersion, and the x's are not widely scattered about the population mean (μ), if dispersion is small. The *standard deviation* of the random variable x is denoted $\sqrt{\mu_2}$ or σ.

In the case of quarterly averages of daily Aaa bond yields and Treasury bill yields for the period 1952–65, we get the following results:

(seasonally unadjusted data)

mean of Aaa bond yields	3.83
variance of Aaa bond yields	0.37
mean of Treasury bill yields	2.56
variance of Treasury bill yields	0.79

(seasonally adjusted data)

mean of Aaa bond yields	3.87
variance of Aaa bond yields	0.44
mean of Treasury bill yields	2.59
variance of Treasury bill yields	0.87

In these instances, variance is higher for Treasury bill yields than for Aaa bond yields—almost twice as high, in fact. This reveals that the Treasury bill yields fluctuate more widely about their mean in the present sample.

(*See also* Standard error of estimate.)

---

[13] See de Leeuw, *op. cit.*, p. 9.